THE TWO OF US

THE TWO OF US

Tony Martin
&
Cyd Charisse

AS TOLD TO DICK KLEINER

MASON / CHARTER

NEW YORK 1976

1 2 3 4 5 6 7 8 9 10

Library of Congress Cataloging in Publication Data

Martin, Tony.
  The two of us.

1. Martin, Tony. 2. Charisse, Cyd.
3. Musicians—Correspondence, reminiscences, etc.
I. Charisse, Cyd, joint author. II. Title.
ML420.M3325A3   784'.092'4 [B]   76–20713
ISBN 0–88405–363–6

I dedicate this book to my husband for all the
   joy he has put into my life.

   Cyd Charisse

I dedicate this book to Cyd because without her
   I would never have known how wonderful
   the world could be.

   Tony Martin

BOYHOOD AND
BEGINNINGS

I was a Christmas present in a family that didn't believe in Christmas. The name they gave me, when I was born on Christmas Day, 1913, was Alvin Morris. Tony Martin wasn't born for a long time after that.

My father was Edward Clarence Morris. I never knew him. He and my mother were divorced when I was an infant and, when I was four or five, my father killed himself. I don't know why. I don't particularly care to know why. As far as I'm concerned, Mike Myers was my dad. He was my stepfather, really, but he was a real, genuine father to me. I know no other father. Edward Morris is just a name to me, but Mike Myers was real.

My mother was real, too. Her name was Hattie Smith. Maybe that sounds like a funny name for a Jewish lady, and I guess it is. So let me tell you the story of how she came to be a Smith. In the 1850s, so the story goes, the United States needed trappers and worked a deal with Russia to import some. My grandfather was one of those trappers brought over. His name was something like "Radomsky," although I'm not sure exactly.

My grandfather traveled for thirty-eight days on the ship from Russia, along with a lot of other immigrants from other countries. En route, he made friends with some of these immigrants. They shared what they had. There was a Frenchman with a lot of wine, an Italian with some salami and cheese, and an Irishman with bottles of whiskey and a hunk of ham. My grandfather had some loaves of Russian bread. They couldn't speak each other's languages, but they knew how to make signs for thirst and hunger and they all had a peasant's knowledge of trading. So they ate and drank and made friends, and eventually reached Ellis Island. The Irishman was the only one who could speak English, of course. The inspectors asked him his name.

"Smith," he said.

Radomsky was next in line. He heard his Irish friend say "Smith," and he thought that was what he was supposed to say. So when the inspector asked him a question he couldn't understand, he said "Smith," too. They had asked him his name. He was duly entered as Smith.

So Yonkel Smith went to Astoria, Oregon, and worked as a trapper in the northwestern woods. Eventually, his twin brother came over, too, and settled in Massachusetts. They kept in touch and decided they should get married, so they sent back home to Russia for a pair of picture brides, who were also twins. I think I still have relatives in Massachusetts, descendants of my grandfather's brother. My grandmother came over and they were married. He quit trapping, bought a horse and wagon and peddled fruit. He and his wife drifted down the Pacific Coast, eventually settling in Oakland, California, which is where I came into the picture.

My grandfather was still living when I was born. In fact, we lived with my grandparents when I was a kid, because of the divorce. My grandfather was a character. By the time I was born, he had a little store but he was also a professional mourner. A funeral came along and he would be there, in his best black suit, sobbing up a storm. It helped pay the rent.

If my grandfather was a character, my grandmother was the typical matriarch. There was no question about it; she ran the family. Whenever there was a problem, I knew that if I went to my mother or father or grandfather, they would always say, "Ask Grandma."

She was an Orthodox woman, of course. Saturday, the Sabbath, was holy to her. The Orthodox ladies couldn't even turn on the stove on Saturdays. And that's how I made my first money—I'd light the stoves for the very Orthodox housewives in the neighborhood. The going rate was a nickel a stove. Not in my house, of course. I couldn't profiteer from my own family's religiosity. One day my grandmother found me with a fortune—$1.80—in my pocket. She wanted to know where I'd gotten all that money. I couldn't tell her the truth so I said I won it gambling. That was by far the lesser of the two evils; gambling wasn't as nearly as big a sin as lighting stoves on the Sabbath. I don't think my grandmother believed my story, but she couldn't disprove it, so she let it go.

Nobody worked or ate on Saturdays. They came home once and found I had cut some cheese with a meat knife, which was against the dietary laws. There was hell to pay. A big scene. They took that knife and washed it, then buried it in the ground and said a prayer over it. So much for the knife. Then they gave me a bad beating.

My grandfather couldn't read or write. Neither could my grandmother. Every Friday, I'd get a nickel. A legitimate nickel, unlike my stove-lighting nickels. That was my salary for reading the news to my grandmother. The *Daily Forward* came from New York—it was eight days old by the time it reached Oakland—and I'd read it to my grandmother in the evenings, and get a nickel every Friday for the chore.

Because he couldn't read, my grandfather took me along when he went to the silent movies so I could read him the captions. He loved Westerns, particularly. It embarrassed me as a boy, because I'd have to go with him to the movies and read the captions and the people around us would be unhappy.

"Shut up," they would say.

"Shut up, yourself," my grandfather would say. "This is my grandson. He's telling me the picture."

It was a full house, at the Smiths'. My mother, Hattie, me, my brother, and my uncles George and Willie. George died young; I think he was hurt in World War I and his wounds killed him soon after. But Willie was always there, and he was my boyhood idol until my mother remarried. Willie worked in the commission markets in San Francisco, and he was big and strong, a bull of a man, and a real tough guy. But, eventually, he died, too. What happened was that one day some of his pals bet him he couldn't carry ten tires along Madison Street from Fourth to Fifth Street. He said he could. I forget what the bet was, but it was a big event. People came from miles to see if Willie Smith could carry those ten tires for a block. He did it, but he got a double hernia and died.

My real father had been well off and, I'm told, was something of an intellectual. He had graduated from Stanford and was a Mason and a Shriner and he owned a lot of property. He was a tombstone maker by trade, and owned a big cemetery in Oakland. The family gossip says his infatuation with a nurse led to the breakup of the marriage. Nobody talked about it when I was a kid. It was one of those hush-hush subjects. Then came his suicide. They whispered about that. But it didn't mean anything to me. I never shed a tear. Why should I? I wouldn't have known the man if I stumbled over him.

My real father's sister, my Aunt Pauline, married a man named Peter Luttrell, who was a doctor on the staff at Stanford. Their daughter, my cousin Ramona, keeps in touch with me. She's a Catholic. I didn't meet her until I was nineteen or so, when she came into a café where I was singing and said, "Hi, I'm your cousin, Ramona Luttrell."

The Morris side of my heritage was a lot different from the Smith side. The Morrises were German Jews, from Hamburg, who had come over

3

several generations before. I think that it was my great-great-grandfather who was the first Morris to come to the United States. He had settled in Virginia. They were Reformed, not Orthodox. They were in with the elite of American Judaism, mingling with the Baruchs and "Our Crowd." But none of that rubbed off on me. Maybe it was my heritage, but my environment was different. There was nothing upper-crust about my environment. It was pretty heavy going for us, even after my mother remarried. My mother was actually a very bright lady, well-read and well-educated. I don't know how they managed it, but they did. She had taught elocution before her first marriage, giving lessons at the University of California and Mills College.

When I was five or six, my mother met and pretty quickly married Meyer Myers. He was as different from Edward Clarence Morris as night and day. Morris was a Stanford graduate; Myers couldn't read or write English. I don't know what the attraction was between my mother and Mike, except that they loved each other, and were good to each other. I guess that's enough.

Myers had left his native Poland when he was fifteen and gone to London and then, some years later, had come to the United States. He worked in the garment trades in New York. He used to tell me about that, about how he worked twenty hours a day for six dollars a week. He said that six dollars went as follows: two dollars for a room, two dollars for food, fifty cents for tobacco and one dollar to play poker.

"But that leaves fifty cents," I said to him. "What did you do with the other fifty cents?"

He winked at me. "Once in a while, I'd see a girl I liked."

When they married, Myers was a buttonhole maker. But when I was about nine, he opened a tailor shop in Oakland. He was Meyer Myers then. But the man in the next store, a German named Tarr, said that wasn't a good name.

"Myers," Mr. Tarr said, "you won't get any business unless you have an intimate name."

So Myers said that sounded sensible, and he began calling himself Mike. It was Mike Myers' Tailor Shop. It didn't help much, having that "intimate name." His business was always a struggle.

Mike had been married before, and had a couple of sons. I think they were twins. Their mother had custody of them. I never met them, as a boy, but one night when I was playing in Las Vegas, the headwaiter came up to me and said, "Your brother wants a good table."

"My brother? What's his name?"

"Sid Myers."

So I went out and met this man and he said, "Mike Myers was my father, too."

I do have a real brother. Harold, or Hal, Morris is a few years older than me. When the divorce came, Harold stayed with my father and I went with my mother. When my real father died, he left a lot of money. But there wasn't a cent for my mother, not even any child support. The will named a man named Harry K. Wolff as Harold's guardian. It gave Harold $500,000 and me five dollars, which was the minimum acceptable in California law. My mother spent her last savings, $1,200 or so, fighting the will, but she lost. All through my childhood years, when I had to scrounge for a nickel, my brother was going to the best schools, Mt. Tamalpais Military Academy, and wearing the finest clothes and riding his own horses. He had the best of everything, materially, and I had nothing. But I think I was happier than he was.

Harold ran away to the Merchant Marine when he was only fifteen. My mother, who loved him, I think, more than she loved me, went through a big hassle to get him out. When he was seventeen, he came knocking at our door one day and begged to be allowed to live with us. My mother took him in, naturally. And he lived with us until he was twenty-five. He inherited his money when he was twenty-one, but didn't share it with either my mother or me. He gambled away most of it.

I think I was always secure, so my mother worried more about Hal than she did about me. Besides, he was her first-born and I guess a woman always has a special place in her heart for her first-born. Maybe if there hadn't been that divorce, Hal would have been close to me. But the divorce broke the bond between us and it was never again knit tight. It may not be right, but it happened.

Mike Myers was, to all intents and purposes, my father. He was the only father figure I had, and I loved him and I think he loved me. He was the dearest man I ever knew. When I was a teen-ager, I said I wanted to take his name, and become Al Myers. He said I shouldn't bother, that it was OK, that he knew no matter what my name was, I was his son. I was happy, when I became successful, to repay some of his kindness. He lived to be eighty-four and my mother was ninety when she died, and for many years I was happy and proud to be able to provide for them.

Actually, I think a stepfather can be more than a real father. He accepted me because he loved my mother, and he became my best friend. Many of my ideas come from Mike Myers. My ideas of a good marriage, for example. Mike and Hattie had one. He waited on her, made her breakfast every morning. But they had their arguments. Even when they were in their seventies, they had a big fight over a gin game. I had to run over and settle the fight.

Mike never had anything. No luxuries, few pleasures. His life was hard work, day in and day out. Maybe I learned something from that, too. I didn't want his kind of life. I loved the man and respected him, but never would I lead the existence he led. Something stirred in me when I was a kid, something that said, "There is something more than that." When Mike was an old man, I was able to treat him well. He lived like a king in his last years. He wore the finest clothes, ate the best food, had money in his pocket. I think it made him feel good. I sure know it made me feel good.

I'm not certain about this, but I think my mother and my stepfather may have had a child together, a year or so after they got married. If they did, it died, got lost on the wind. When you're seven or eight, they don't tell you about things like that. And I never asked them, but, somehow, I've always had the feeling that that's what happened.

We never had much money when I was a boy. I remember my mother would send me to the butcher, to buy a chicken, and I was supposed to ask the butcher to throw in extras. That was the way it worked in those days. You bought a chicken for seventy cents and the butcher tossed in a marrow bone and a piece of soup meat free. Today, at the big, impersonal supermarket, you're lucky to get out with your shirt still on your back, but in those days the neighborhood shopkeepers knew you and did right by you.

"So, Alvin," the butcher would say, "here's your chicken and I'll just toss in this marrow bone, too, OK?"

That chicken and the other things would last us through the week. My mother knew how to stretch a chicken! There was roast chicken on Sunday, leftover chicken on Monday, chicken hash on Tuesday, chicken soup on Wednesday. Once in a while some lamb chops or a piece of fish. Never beef. I didn't have a steak until I was sixteen. For dessert, Jell-O, lots of Jell-O. And always bread and peanut butter. My mother was a great baker, and there was always lots of fresh bread around the house.

When you're brought up in poverty and things go your way later, there is a tendency to make up for lost meals. When I started making pretty good money, I ate everything in sight for a few years. Mario Lanza was the same way. He once told me he dieted so he'd be thin in films, then he'd go right out and eat seventy pounds' worth as quick as he could. He was even poorer, as a kid, than I was. So, later, he would eat, leave the room, regurgitate, then come back in and eat some more. He could never eat his fill. His appetite finally killed him; it was some nutritional problem that ended his life.

6

I was never that bad. Maybe that was because I was never that poor. There was always something to eat—leftover-leftover chicken, maybe, but something. And always clothes to wear that my dad would mend and re-mend and let out as I grew bigger. He worked hard, but it didn't seem to lead to success. A big week for him was thirty dollars to bring home.

We didn't have Christmas, of course. I had my birthday on December 25, and I made believe the present I got—usually a handkerchief or some underwear—was a Christmas present.

Religion was always present in our house, because it was my grandparents' house, and they were very Orthodox. But my mother wasn't a religious woman. I don't remember ever seeing her go to synagogue. I had to go to Sunday school, out of respect to my grandparents, but it never hooked me. I have never been a religious person in my life. Of course, when I reached my thirteenth birthday, I was *bar mitzvahed*. But I got paid to be *bar mitzvahed*—I said I didn't want it, but my grandparents said they'd like it, and they gave me a dollar, I think, if I'd go through with it. So I did. I'm ashamed of that now, but then I was just a kid and what did I know about repaying kindnesses? It was funny, many years later, how my stepson, Nicky Charisse, came to me when he was thirteen and said he'd like to be *bar mitzvahed*. I thought for a few minutes that I had a real religious kid on my hands. But when I asked him why he wanted to be *bar matzvahed*, he said, "My friend, Joey, was *bar mitzvahed* and he got lots of presents."

The *bar mitzvah* service wasn't the first one I memorized. A few years before that, when I was, maybe, ten, my grandmother said if I would go to Hebrew religious school, known as *cheder*, she'd give me anything I wanted—"within reason, of course." I said how about a saxophone? She said she'd see. So I went to *cheder* and she went down to Sherman Clay, a big music store, and bought me a little soprano sax. I began tootling that thing around the house. It was the start of my musical career.

Until I learned what I was doing with that sax, I really disturbed the household. I guess there's no sound quite as screechy as an off-key soprano sax. My poor dad would come home, dead tired, and all he'd want was some peace and quiet. He'd lie down and listen to "Amos 'n' Andy" on his crystal radio set, and almost fall asleep halfway through. After dinner, he and my mother would play a little two-handed whist. That was the every evening ritual. But then I'd start blasting away on my little sax and shatter the calm. They didn't say anything. They figured I could only get better.

The big event in my day, during those childhood years, was meeting my father. He'd come home on the train from his tailor shop, and get off at Forty-first and Broadway. I can remember the time even now—5:55 sharp. He'd come trudging off the train, bowed down by his worries and fears and responsibilities, and I'd come charging along and leap into his arms. Then his worn-out eyes would light up and he'd give me a big hug and sometimes piggyback me home. He was very good to me but he had his temper, too. I knew just how far I could go with him and stayed inside that line most of the time. Once, however, I went too far. It was when I was taking a typing course, so I guess I was in high school. Anyhow, I had to be there at seven P.M., and this one night I sat in my father's chair before I left to go to take my typing course. I don't remember why. But he came home and he saw me in his chair—shades of Archie Bunker!—and he gave me one of his hard looks.

"What's the matter, I'm dead already?" he said.

I don't think I ever sat in his chair again.

They didn't mingle much, my grandparents and my parents. They had very few friends, never entertained, never went out. In those days, people didn't. I was raised not even to know the neighbors. My mother actually said she didn't believe in knowing your neighbors. So we maybe nodded and said hello, but that was it.

There were a lot of Orientals—Japanese as well as Chinese—in our neighborhood. Right around the corner there was a Japanese temple, and I'd go there often with my Japanese friends. Every Saturday and Sunday, at five o'clock, they'd hand out free candy and ice cream. That was a lot more than I ever got in a synagogue, so I figured they had it made, those Japanese. There was one Japanese girl, Fumi Fikuda, who was always nice to me. We'd go to the Japanese temple together. During the week, we'd bum ice from the ice man. If we had a dime, we'd buy a slab of watermelon and have a treat. That was the excitement in my life in those days.

At home, life was more severe. I didn't get punished too often, but there wasn't much joy around the house, either. I had found friends outside, particularly friends of other religions—Catholic, Protestant, the Japanese. That was frowned on at home. They'd keep hammering at me, *shikseh, goy,* making me think it was terribly wrong to talk to anybody but a Jew. And, God forbid, a gentile girl! As I grew older, and began to think for myself, that constant hammering got to me. One night I had enough.

"Stop it!" I said. "All this talk about *goys* and *shiksehs!* I can't eat here any more."

"Are you ashamed of what you are?" my grandfather asked me.

"No, I'm ashamed of what you are."

All that seemed to matter to them, all that seemed of importance, was summed up in three words: Buick, *shikseh,* Shriner. Buick and Shriner. Those were the badges of success. Anybody who owned a Buick or belonged to the Shriners was OK in their book. And *shikseh,* a non-Jewish girl, that was the most terrible thing in the world. At all costs, I was to avoid getting involved with a *shikseh*.

But, as it turned out, I had little choice. There were two boys who played a big part in my growing-up process. One was Jewish, one wasn't. Both became my best friends in my youth. The non-Jew was named Octave Guiradeaux. When I first met him, I was kind of overweight. He was slim and trim. So, naturally, Octave picked on me. He called me a fat Jew boy. I was so mad I wanted to hit him, but I didn't. Why? Because I wasn't a very good fighter. In fact, I was lousy. I'd already had a few fights and I'd lost them all. So I backed away when Octave called me bad names.

There was an Italian girl, named Maria, I kind of liked then. She was there when Octave called me a fat Jew boy.

"Alvin," she said, "aren't you going to fight him?"

"No, I don't think so."

"If you don't fight him, I'll never speak to you again as long as you live."

What we men don't do for women! I didn't want to go through the rest of my life with Maria not talking to me, so I said, OK, I'd fight him. I said, "Octave, you have insulted me. Let's fight."

The whole thing was arranged as the French used to arrange duels. It was all very organized. Octave and Alvin were going to have a fight. Three o'clock, tomorrow, at the cemetery. Bring three seconds. OK. I showed up, with three seconds, and I got knocked on my ass. Boy, did he give me a beating! But I learned that he who gets knocked on his ass gains a friend. From then on, Octave was my buddy. I think he realized that I had taken a stand, that I had fought even though I knew I was going to get whipped, and he respected that and therefore he respected me. We were pals all the way through high school after our big brawl.

It was Octave who shamed me into my first pair of long pants. In those days, the traditional thing was that a boy wore short pants until he went to high school. But times were beginning to change, and some of the kids got long pants in the sixth grade. Octave was one of those trailblazers. And he used to sneer at me in my short pants, and, naturally, I wanted long pants like his, too.

So I went home and said how I wanted long pants. I figured with my father a tailor that would be no problem. Somewhere he could come up with some long pants for me. But my mother was a traditionalist and she said no. No long pants for Alvin until high school. That was two years away, and two years, to an eleven-year-old, is damn near a lifetime. At the time, I had a paper route, and I think I made something like $2.15 a month. Well, I saved up and Octave and I went to a store and I bought me a pair

9

of long pants. But I couldn't show up with them at home—that much guts I didn't have. So I'd keep the long pants at school. I'd leave home with my usual short pants and change at school, then change again before I got home.

My other best friend as a kid was Harry Gitelson. He's now pretty famous as an artist; he calls himself Gittel. He was Jewish, and the two of us started doing the things that our parents expected of us, as good Jewish boys. We went to Sunday school and we met some nice, respectable Jewish girls. Only problem was that Harry and I were poor kids, from the wrong side of the tracks, and the girls we met were from well-to-do families, from the right side. The girls didn't want to have anything to do with us. We weren't good enough for them.

So Harry and I rebelled. We knew there were parties going on, to which we were conspicuously uninvited. We said to ourselves that we didn't care, but, God, how we cared! It's never fun to be on the outside, looking in. Here all our Sunday school friends were going to these parties and we weren't.

We found that we were welcome in other circles. The Irish Catholics, the Italian Catholics, the Orientals—they were happy to have us in their homes. Our own kind rejected us, while those our parents considered outsiders didn't. I used to listen to my parents talking.

"Hattie," my dad would say, "I ran into Sam Goldfarb today. He tells me his daughter is engaged to Milton Rothman. You know Milton Rothman. He's a doctor, a Shriner, drives a Buick."

Harry and I didn't think we'd ever qualify. We were Jewish, sure, but a doctor? A Shriner? A Buick-owner? Those were beyond our wildest dreams. So we figured that if you can't join 'em, go somewhere else. We went. And we had fun. But the whole thing bothered me, being totally isolated from my own group. We were rejected by our peers, by our own cultural unit. I think maybe both of us were spurred by that early rejection. I know a fire began burning inside of me, feeding on the fuel of discontent and unhappiness and looking for a way to blaze brighter.

This is not to say, of course, that I dedicated myself at a tender age to the pursuit of fame and fortune. It wasn't that conscious. It was just a need to get out of that rut I was in, to prove that I was as good as Milton Rothman, the doctor-Shriner-Buick-owner.

But, in the meantime, I had some growing up to do. And life wasn't all depression and rejection. I had plenty of happy times. Early in my life, I developed what has become a permanent infatuation—with sports. I was never much of an athlete myself, but I quickly found that I liked nothing better than watching a baseball game. The park where the Oakland Pacific

Coast League team played was about ten blocks away from where I lived. My friends and I would wait outside for home-run balls to sail over the fence. If we got one, we could take it around to the gate and they'd let us in. The team had some sluggers, fortunately. Guys like Buzz Arlett and Hack Miller. And a short fence. So there was plenty of business for the kids gathered outside. I got my share.

One day, I raced up to the gate with a ball and a man there said, "Kid, we're short of hustlers today, want a job?"

I knew a hustler was a vendor. So I said, "Sure," and I began selling peanuts and Z-nuts, which was some kind of nutty confection which wasn't as important as the baseball player's picture wrapped inside.

Pretty soon, I graduated from peanuts and Z-nuts to hot dogs. But my enthusiasm got me fired. I began piling extra hot dogs and mustard on each roll and the word got around the bleachers, wait for that kid, Al, he'll give you a lot for your money. I sold plenty of hot dogs, but my generosity was breaking the concessionaire. They took me off hot dogs, but they rewarded my ambition by making me an usher. That was a proud day, when I first put on my usher's uniform and took up my post behind first base. Now I was making some pretty good money for those days—a couple of bucks a day. I felt that I was really contributing at home. I'd give my mother a dollar, and keep a dollar for myself. So I had plenty of money for whatever I wanted, and I was helping out at home. After the baseball season, I hooked on at the Berkeley Coliseum—Tightwad Hill—where the University of California played its football games.

All my young life, I think, I wanted a bicycle. For a long time, it was out of the question, and I knew it. When there's barely enough money for food, obviously there can be nothing left for frivolities like a bike. Besides, my brother Harold had once had a motorcycle and had fallen off and gotten hurt pretty badly, so my mother was dead set against a bike for me. When I was young, though, I was normal, which meant that logic and reason meant little. I wanted a bike, that was all I knew. They used to give me fifteen cents a day for lunch. With that, I could buy a pot of beans, some potato salad, a bottle of cream soda, a piece of pie and a couple of pieces of candy. One day this kid with a bike came up and said he'd rent me the bike for a couple of hours for a nickel. So, from then on, I'd buy only a ten-cent lunch and use the other five cents to rent the kid's bike. And I'd ride up and down Echo Avenue, next to Piedmont Grammar School. It wasn't quite the same as having my own bike, but it was the next best thing. Then, one day, I fell off—and it took eight stitches to close the cut in my lip. I still have the scar. My mother gave me a good beating—she never spared the rod—and that was the end of my bike rental adventure. But, when I was an usher, I was able to save up enough and I bought myself my own bike.

I was beginning to have a taste of independence, and I liked the flavor. I enjoyed having my own money to spend on what I wanted. More and more, I resolved to be somebody, somehow. I knew I wanted a better life than my dad had. I looked around and I saw those people who had rejected Harry and me, and I frankly envied them their material possessions. I was going to get my share, one way or another.

It began with a few pennies, delivering newspapers, even before the few dollars, peddling peanuts and ushering at the ball games. My mother didn't want me to deliver papers, for some reason. So I had to tell a fib— I said I wanted to go out for the team at school, and I had to practice. That got me away from the house and I'd deliver the *Oakland Post-Enquirer* and the *Oakland Tribune*. I remember it clearly—I had thirty-two papers to deliver. It took about an hour. It gave me enough to buy myself an ice cream or some candy. It gave me a first, tiny taste of financial independence.

That was one of my early drives. The other, as I've said, was to get some recognition. I sure wasn't getting any in those early circles I found myself. Harry and I got snubbed, that's about all. At least, our own crowd snubbed us. In school, there was a club called the Nuggets, the big shots. Harry and me? No way. They didn't ask us to join. Fraternities? No sale, boys. Parties at the big homes of the Jewish kids in school? Sure—for everybody else but those poor kids, Harry and Alvin, with their made-over pants and those shirts with the frayed cuffs. So we'd be invited to Christian kids' homes, for parties, and we'd be welcomed by kids named O'Hara and Simpson and Bjornsson. No questions asked. Frayed cuffs and all.

The whole scene combined to make me—and I guess Harry, too—determined to show them. Sometime, somehow, someplace, I'd show them. I'd have money and fame and I'd be damned before I'd invite them to my parties. The only problem was to find the key that would unlock the door to all those goodies.

And I found it in music.

Nobody in the family was musical, unless you could call the wailing my grandfather did at synagogue and at funerals a kind of singing. It was just something that came to me through some freak of genetics. The only connections the Morrises or Smiths ever had with show business was that my Uncle George, for a while, worked as a projectionist. I'd often go with him and watch the movies from his stuffy booth. And my brother, Hal, used to do Chaplin imitations, but every kid everywhere did Chaplin imitations in those days. Mike, my dad, sang, after a fashion, but he wasn't my real father so I had no hereditary gifts from him. Maybe, though, it was hearing him sing that kindled the spark in me. We had a player piano in the living room and, as a kid, I'd make believe I was playing while he sang the songs.

I always sang. I always played some instrument or other, real or imagined, until I got that soprano sax that time for going to religious school. At first, of course, my music was just for my own fun. I didn't recognize it right away as my passport away from poverty.

Maybe the first time I thought that music might be more than just a way to kill time came one day when my mother was having some friends in for whist. I have said that she wasn't very social. Her one violation of that habit was her whist club. There were ten women in the group, and they'd play once a week, rotating homes. That meant that every tenth week they'd be at our house. All the women would bring some food, and I looked forward to the times the whist game would be at our house, because there was always some left-over food for me. And I always had a pretty good appetite.

One day, I came home from school and the women were sitting around our living room, playing whist. My mother always asked me to put some music on the player piano, and I did. Then, this day, she said, "Alvin, please sing something for my friends."

"Ah, Mom, I don't want to. I'm embarrassed."

"Alvin, do as you're told."

"Please, Mom, I don't feel like it."

She grabbed me by the hand and led me into the kitchen.

"You have to sing, Alvin. I told all the girls you would. They're very anxious to hear you."

"Well, OK. But I don't want them looking at me. I'll sing, if they all look the other way."

So she went back in and gave them their instructions and then I came out and sang. When I finished—I think I sang "Does Your Mother Come from Ireland?"—they all applauded. I guess I had a nice boy soprano voice. Anyhow, the sound of that applause was pleasant to my ears. The next time the whist club met at our house, I didn't have to have my arm twisted. I asked if I could sing for them. And they didn't have to look away, either.

I began looking for more places to play and sing. As a freshman in high school, I started playing the sax in the school band. A man named Trautner ran the band, and he was very nice and encouraging to me. He was the first man I ever saw with long hair; in those days, only musicians and artists wore their hair long. I got a big kick out of being in the band, out of feeling myself part of a group dedicated to creating music. And I liked the fact that a band is totally unsegregated. It didn't matter to Mr. Trautner what color you were, what religion you were, or whether or not your cuffs were frayed. He just handed out the music and all he asked was that you played your part. So I was part of a group, and it was good. We played at football games, we played at school assemblies. I had found the place where I was welcome, where I belonged.

I don't believe I ever consciously said, "I am going to be a musician when I grow up." It just happened. One thing led to another. And I enjoyed it, so I went along with the way my life was drifting.

One problem. My instrument. That little soprano sax my grandmother had bought me was fine, for a kid, but it was little more than a toy. I needed something better, now that I was in the school band, now that I was taking lessons. And I got it—the hard way.

Mike had made some clothes for a musician, a tuxedo for him to wear when he played. But then things got tough for him and he couldn't pay for it.

"Mike," the musician said to my father, "I haven't got any money. I just got laid off. I'll have to give you the tux back."

"That's too bad."

"Or, I tell you what. Didn't you tell me your son wanted a saxophone?"

"Yes, Alvin; he's getting pretty good."

"Look, Mike, maybe we can make a deal. I've got an old C-melody sax I don't need. It's old, but it's still very good, I take good care of my instruments. I'll trade you that sax for the tuxedo."

I think, knowing dad, that he inspected the merchandise before he agreed to the swap. But the deal was finally made—the sax for the tuxedo. Dad called me at the Piedmont Avenue School, and said I should come to the store right away, he had something to show me. They let me out of school and I ran over and he handed me the sax, the first full-sized, genuine musical instrument I ever owned. I took the sax and played a song on it, right there in the store. I couldn't play very well then, no matter what my proud father thought. But, with that instrument, I knew I could learn. All I needed were lessons.

So I began studying. Somehow, my parents scraped together the three dollars a week it took for me to study the sax. Every day, from 3:00 to 4:15, I had my lesson. All my friends were outside playing. I suppose I should have envied them, but I didn't. I liked taking those lessons. So I took them for a few years. My dad was bringing home something like twenty-five or twenty-six dollars a week—thirty dollars was a whopper—but he always peeled off three dollar bills for me to give my teacher each week.

The teacher told my parents I had promise.

14

"He has a good ear for music," he said.

So, naturally, everybody was encouraged. They kept on shelling out that three dollars a week, and I kept on studying. It brought me several benefits, immediately. I had acquired an identity. I was no longer just Alvin Morris, the tailor's kid. Now I was Al Morris, the one with the saxophone. It also gave me a direction for my ambition, my drive to make something of myself. Maybe I could do it through music. Maybe I could become a professional musician. At first, I thought of my future as playing the sax in an orchestra. Singing never occurred to me, in those early days. I always sang, but that was for fun, nothing else.

I had sung in my grammar school glee club. I liked that. We sang, of course, at the Christmas program. Christmas carols are happy songs. I preferred them to the sadness, the minor-key sadness, of the traditional Jewish songs. One year, the lady in charge of the glee club gave me a solo. That helped my ego, too. I remember another year getting a few of my friends together to form a little group, six or seven of us I think, and we went around singing carols. I think at a few houses we were given some money, and that was probably the first money I earned through my music.

I could read music, of course. I found it came easily. School work was hard; I did pretty well in school, but it was always a struggle. I found that square roots were very difficult, but E-sharp was a cinch. I guess we all gravitate toward what we do with the most comfort. If the square roots had come easily, I might have gone into engineering. But, with me, it was always music that was the simplest, so I stuck with it. I was also blessed from the beginning with a gift for it. For one thing, I had perfect pitch. Years later, Woody Herman and I made a lot of money out of my perfect pitch. We used to go to bars and Herman would be the shill and make the bets, and then I would come through. I was always right.

All through high school, I kept on with my music. And then, without even making a conscious decision, I became a professional. They used to have dances every Friday afternoon at school, from four to six. A few of us decided to start an orchestra, so we could play for those dances. We got together, rehearsed a few of the hit songs of the moment, and we began playing. I imagine it was pretty bad, but we kept the beat and the melody was recognizable so everybody was happy. Every week, I got a dollar and a half for those two hours.

We called ourselves Al Morris and His Four Red Peppers. The name came from our uniform. Everybody had to have a uniform, of course. We would have looked ridiculous if we'd tried to wear tuxedos or something like that. So we got white sweaters and our mothers sewed red peppers on the front of the sweaters. We got some beanies to wear on our heads, and we were in business. We had a drum, a piano, and two trumpet players and me on my sax.

Gradually, other jobs came our way. People would come up to me at the school dance and ask if we would play at a birthday party or some private function—one thing or another. One of the first jobs we got was to play for a gypsy wedding in Livermore. Later, Livermore became famous as the home town of Max Baer. I knew him then and, if my memory serves, he was at that wedding I played. He was sixteen then, just about my age. His father ran a slaughter house in Livermore, and we became pretty good friends. We took the bus to Livermore, and we played at the wedding. Gypsy weddings are different. They have a ritual of two tents. The bride is in one, guarded by her relatives, and the groom in the other. The groom has to fight his way into the bride's tent. And they fight for real. We played the musical accompaniment to the brawl. I doubt that anyone was listening to us, but we played as loudly as we could.

Over the years, my music has been my entrée into many different worlds. It all began with that gypsy wedding. It was fascinating for me, a kid from an Orthodox Jewish home, to see a new culture. I've been lucky, down through the years, and my career has taken me all over the world and given me the privilege of seeing many things and meeting many people, even a few presidents. I think I felt the first recognition that I had stumbled onto a way to get out of my rut that day in Livermore.

That also brought me my first windfall. The gypsies were generous. They gave us each six dollars. I came home and showed my fistful of dollars to my grandfather.

"Good for you, Alvin," he said. "You're learning how to look out for yourself."

I was learning about other things, too. Naturally, uppermost in my teen-age mind was girls. I've been very fortunate, as you will learn later in this book, and had romances with some of the greatest beauties of the world. I think it all began for me in the sixth grade. Her name was Carmelita Goldberger and her hair went all the way down to her waist. I used to sit behind her and dip her hair in my inkwell. That, my friends, is true love. I'd write her notes, with such original sentiments as, "I love you." But I was at that point very shy—I got over it—and I wouldn't sign my name. I did all the usual dumb-kid things. I carried her books home from school. I'd squeeze into the seat next to her in assembly. And then, in the seventh grade, our teacher had us make Valentine's cards. I made a beauty for Carmelita. And I ran six blocks in the rain to her house and rang the doorbell. I had screwed up my courage and was going to give it to her so she'd know how much I loved her.

But her mother answered the door. I just shoved my little Valentine's card into her mother's hands and ran away. I guess that was the first time I ever was prepared to tell a girl that I loved her. It happened many times afterward, but that was the first time that I really meant it.

After that, though, I was scared. What if I saw her? What if she saw me? What if our eyes were to meet? What would I say to her? I knew there was nothing more I could say, so I avoided her.

In the eighth grade, she came over to me in the schoolyard one day.

"Alvin," she said, "that day last year when you brought the Valentine's card to me, why didn't you come in the house and give it to me yourself?"

I mumbled something. But I did manage to ask her to have lunch with me that day, and even went so far as to buy her whatever it was she had to eat. And a Baby Ruth bar for dessert. I was too nervous to eat a thing.

"I have to tell you something, Alvin," she said. "It's very important."

"What is it?"

"I'm moving away. My folks are going, and I have to go with them."

"Oh, no." I was devastated. Here I had my first affair, and the party of the second part was leaving.

"I'll miss you," she said. "Write to me, please?"

I never wrote. I think I carried the torch for her for about three hours. At that age, what does one girl mean? Actually, it was important for me, however. I learned a valuable lesson from Carmelita Goldberger. I had found out, at that age, that I really liked girls. Perhaps more important, I had found out that they liked me back. For the next twenty years or so, girls would occupy an important part in my life.

In a way, I feel sorry for kids today. I think the girl-boy arrangement of my youth was superior to that of today. We had respect for girls. That seems to be totally absent from the boy-girl relationship now. The girls do as much pursuing now as the boys do, and the old respect is gone. It's like hunting. If the animal steps out of the woods and says, "Here I am, shoot me," it's no great challenge. And if a girl comes to a boy and says, "I'm yours, buster," that's not as much fun as if there was the old game of catch-me-if-you-can. All in all, I'm glad I grew up when I did.

Nobody told me about sex. I learned it all, as most kids did then, from the other kids at school. The older ones told the younger ones, and so it went, legend and fact passed down the ladder. The only thing there was at home was a couple of pictures on the wall. My mother called them art. I thought of them as dirty pictures. There were three prints of nudes, acceptable, artistic nudes but no matter how you sliced it, they were girls with their clothes off. They weren't big, I'd guess they were maybe a foot square or something like that. But, as I was growing up, those pictures occupied more and more of my attention. I'd come home from school and, if nobody else was home, I'd stand in the living room and look at those pictures, memorizing every glorious detail, drinking in each curve, each anatomical feature. If I'd only studied my lessons as closely as I studied those nudes, I might be a genius today.

One day, I was eyeing those pictures with my usual close attention when my dad came home early from work and caught me. As soon as my mother came home, he told her.

"Hattie," my dad said, "we'd better take those pictures down."

"Why? They're lovely."

"Sure they're lovely. Maybe too lovely. But Alvin is getting too old to appreciate them as females and not old enough to appreciate them as art."

So they took the pictures down. It didn't matter. I had seen them long enough, studied them closely enough. I had memorized each one. They didn't have to be on the wall for me to see them. They were my illustrated guideposts of things to come.

Like kids everywhere, I experimented. There is a normal, natural curiosity about the other sex. The first time I found out exactly how the two sexes differ, anatomically, was once when I was, I suppose, around ten or eleven. I had a girl in to play after school, and we played doctor. And we got caught. My grandmother found us there, in the examining room. She really whacked me around for that.

It was, I imagine, a few years after that that my dad decided I needed some practical sex education. As I say, I'd had none at all. I didn't even know what the dirty words meant. Kids at school used to say "Fuck," at least the bad kids did. The good kids said, "Honk you, Larry," and the medium kids said, "Uckfay ooyay," but the bad kids said "Fuck" loud and clear. I knew it was a very naughty word, but exactly what it meant I had absolutely no idea.

But things had changed since the times when I had carried Carmelita Goldberger's books home from school. Now I knew that girls were different and I ached to touch them, although what I would do if I had that chance was beyond me.

I guess my dad, understanding as he was, recognized the signs in me. Maybe it was my staring at those nude pictures that did it. Maybe it was something else. I'm not sure, not any more. All I remember is him coming to me one day when I was sixteen.

"Alvin, my son," he said, "you've been indulging yourself about girls. Fine. That's normal. That's as it should be. But it's time for you to join the major leagues, time for you to become a man. You've been *bar mitz-*

vahed three years already. You haven't had a girl yet, ain't it true?"

"Yes, dad, that's true."

"That's what I thought. Today is the day. Today you will have a girl."

I was scared. What did it mean? What was I supposed to do? How was I going to accomplish this mysterious business of "having" a girl?

"Maybe tomorrow, Dad."

"No, today. Right now. But don't you tell your momma. We'll tell her a little white lie. We'll tell her you're coming with me today to see about a summer job."

He took the day off. It was arranged that I was to take the ferry boat to San Francisco and meet him at a certain street corner. I told the little white lie to my mother and I'll never know if she believed it or not.

He took me to a house, a nondescript house like the others on the block. A lady let us in and my father whispered to her. Then he left, saying he'd be across the street and after I was through I should come over and then we'd go home together.

The lady led me up the stairs, a narrow staircase with worn carpet and creaking floors. I was looking down so I noticed the carpet. I heard strange sounds coming from the rooms in the hallway, but I didn't look right or left, just down.

"Here we are, sonny," the lady said, and opened a door and practically shoved me inside.

And there she was, my first physical affair. I forget her name. Maybe I never knew it. And, fortunately, I forget what she looked like. There is a vague memory of masses of white flesh and a pile of peroxide-blonde hair, but I'm not sure if that's a true memory or just the tricks the years have played on me. I do remember, clearly, that she sort of smiled at me and said, "You're a cherry, right?"

I knew what that meant. I nodded.

"OK, kid," she said. "Come on over here and take your clothes off and I'll do the rest."

I tried. I took my clothes off and she pulled me down onto the bed. And I did my best, but I was scared to death. I never completed the act. I couldn't. I was way too frightened, too embarrassed, too conscious of my own innocence and ignorance. I recognized, somehow, that this wasn't the way it was supposed to be. I guess, in my subconscious mind, I missed the romance that somehow I knew should have been there, but wasn't. I remember her getting up once to look out the window to see if there were any cops, and that didn't help matters any.

"OK, I guess that's about all we can do today," the girl said. "Come back again when you're a little older."

19

I dressed as quickly as I could, not even tying my shoelaces in my haste to get out of there. Then it was back across the squeaky floors, hearing more of those sounds behind the closed doors, and back down the staircase with the faded carpet. And I ran across the street to where my dad was waiting for me in an Italian restaurant.

"*Nu?*" he said. "How did it go?"

"Fine," I lied. "Gee, Pop, thanks a lot."

"Now you are a man."

And I think I felt like a man, once I had gotten over my embarrassment and my feeling of revulsion about the whole affair. I only knew that I had gone to bed with a girl and I guess I bragged a little to my friends. I neglected, of course, to tell them the details, sticking only to the plain, absolute fact that I, Alvin Morris, was no longer a cherry.

The fact that my father had taken me to a whorehouse was, when I thought about it, really out of character for him. Whenever the subject of sex came up in our house—which it did very seldom—the opinion was usually expressed by everybody that it was vulgar. Everything sexual was considered vulgar, and people who talked about it were vulgar. Worse were women who indulged in and derived pleasure from it. Time after time, my mother would say—and my father would sit in his chair and nod his agreement—that a boy left himself open to a dread disease if he had anything to do with women who enjoyed sex. So, when I reflected on it later, I was surprised that my father had taken me on that great adventure. Most likely he knew that, at sixteen, I was beginning to have the urge to try sex, and he felt it was part of his parental duties to initiate me.

I think the fact that I had lost my virginity gave me more self-confidence around girls. By the time I was seventeen, which was only nine or ten months later, I was indulging in the normal pleasures in the normal ways. And I found, of course, that with the element of romance added, sex became a thing of beauty and a joy forever.

I dated more and more. I was reasonably manly to look at, I suppose, and the fact that I was a professional musician of sorts gave me a little added glamour. So I had no trouble finding willing females. In fact, I became pretty popular with the girls at school. When I'd go to pick a girl up, invariably her father would say, "Just be sure you get my daughter home by one minute to midnight."

It was a simple time, I think an easier time. There was no pot, no booze. The idea of drinking never occurred to most of us and, of course, the word "pot" hadn't even been invented then. If we were daring, there was a little necking in the rumble seat—and a lot of wishful thinking. We'd go to a movie and then to Edie's Ice Cream Parlor for a milk shake. At the door, a couple of kisses, maybe a pat on the fanny if I felt daring. That's all there was. It was a different era. I guess my old-fashionedness is showing, but I think it was a better era. I was luckier than most of my classmates, because of my music. I was making what was a lot of money by then, playing with my Red Peppers, and some weeks I'd come home with fifty or seventy-five dollars. My Uncle Willie, who was still alive then, bought me my first car. So I had wheels and I had money in my pocket and I was a free spirit. It was a good time.

Then I came face to face with what I guess was my first big decision. Should I go to college or just continue with my musical career? My family, of course, wanted me to go to college, and I finally went along with that. They said I could continue playing while I was studying, and their arguments about the need of an education made sense to me. Then came the second question—which college?

And, of course, another big question. Money. How would I be able to afford a college education? They didn't give scholarships to saxophone players, at least not in my day. The second question was solved when, surprisingly, my grandmother produced some money. Out of my grandfather's modest income, she had somehow saved enough to pay for my tuition. It still amazes me how she did it. These days, people make thousands a week and still can't save a dime. But my grandmother put aside a quarter here, a dollar there, and it mounted up.

Since she had the funds, the family figured it was only right that she pick the college. Another surprise. She wanted me to go to St. Mary's, a very Catholic university. And she was such a devout Jewish lady. I asked her why. It was fine with me, but I was naturally curious about her reason. She told me a story I'd never heard before. It seems that when she was a young wife, and had the baby who turned out to be my mother, she was having problems nursing. She wasn't producing enough milk. There was, at the time, a Holy Name Society across the street and they helped her, finding a midwife to nurse my mother.

Apparently, they had done other kindnesses to my grandmother, those Holy Name Society nuns. Whenever there was a sickness in the family, they would trot across the street and do what they could. So the nuns and the Jewish family had become friends. My grandfather would bring them bags of fruit when he could. If they needed a hand, he'd run across the street and help. When his barn needed a thorough cleaning—that was when he was still peddling fruit and had a horse and wagon—the nuns would pitch in. And, as long as they lived there, the Smiths and the Holy Name Society nuns were good friends, good neighbors.

St. Mary's was a school run by the Christian Brothers, one of the

Catholic orders. My grandmother felt that would be a good place for me.

"I want you should go to a Catholic school," she announced. "I want you should know what it means for people to believe in their own religion, whatever it is."

I guess she had seen me drifting away from Judaism, as my mother had drifted away. She must have felt that exposure to an institution, no matter what faith, where there was still a strong belief would be a good thing for me. She had been a witness to the way the generations of Jews in this country had moved away from the Orthodoxy of her heritage, and she didn't like it.

Harry Gitelson went to St. Mary's with me. Maybe his folks felt the same as my grandmother, that any religion was better than none. And, looking back on it, forty or so years later, I think it was a wise choice for me. I didn't become a Catholic and I'm certainly not what you'd call a devout Jew, but I believe I qualify as a God-fearing man. I love God. I believe in Him. I respect His teachings.

St. Mary's was a great part of my life. There was, first, the religious experience. Every afternoon, we were required to go to the chapel for a meditation service. All my Catholic friends genuflected when they entered the pew. I didn't have to do that, but I did have to go. And I found myself looking forward to that restful hour every day. It was quiet there, in chapel, quiet and peaceful and somehow it was good for the inner man. I would sit there, surrounded by tranquillity, and stare up at the figure of Jesus, in the stained glass window behind the altar, and reflect on that man, that Jew, who thought the world needed a new direction. And had sacrificed everything to spread his ideas.

I came home once and told my grandmother about how good I felt in chapel.

"You see?" she said. "You're learning. Wonderful! That's what I wanted for you."

There was never any prejudice toward me at St. Mary's. Later, I met it. Head on. Many times. Once some friends wanted to get me into the New York Athletic Club. No Jews allowed.

"What difference what I am?" I said. "I promise I won't use the bathroom."

The same thing happened in reverse when I tried to get my friend, Leo Durocher, into Hillcrest, the all-Jewish country club in Los Angeles. No dice. But I wouldn't let it lay. I got up a petition and everybody signed it and Leo got in.

There isn't as much prejudice as there used to be, but it's still around. The Los Angeles Country Club won't take a Jew. Of course, they're very fussy there; they won't even take an actor. God forbid their sacred soil should be defiled by a lowlife like Jimmy Stewart or Charlton Heston. The Bel Air Country Club is another one. But I played there several times. They're very big about opening up the club on Yom Kippur and Rosh Hashanah, when Hillcrest is closed. On those two Jewish high holy days, Bel Air will let Jews play. Big deal. Maybe this has changed now.

Why is it that golf clubs are the holdouts, the last bastions of bigotry? So many of them have their prejudices. I once shot a movie at St. Andrews, the great golf course in Scotland. Anybody can play there—Jew, gentile, Hindu, Shinto, no matter. Anybody, that is, who is male. No women allowed. That's their hang-up. And no women even permitted on the grounds. I had a woman doing my make-up then. She had to make me up on the running board of my car parked outside the course.

But there was none of that nonsense at St. Mary's. I was one of the boys. Maybe privately they thought of me as the one who didn't genuflect in chapel, but, if they did, they kept it to themselves. I guess, like most men, I look back on my college years as probably the happiest of my life. I lived on campus one semester, but most of the time I stayed home and commuted to my classes. That made me popular with my friends. Most of them came from out of town, so they grabbed at the chance to come home with me. It became a ritual. Every Friday night was open house at our home at 4109 Terrace Street. I'd bring a bunch of boys with me and my mother would have a big spread, a buffet, and the fellows would help themselves. It got so the whole college knew about it. In fact, Slip Madigan, the football coach—and, in those days, St. Mary's was always a gridiron powerhouse—used to say, "If I can't find my team, I know where to look—they'll be over with Al Morris on Terrace Street."

They'd often sleep over, stretching out on the spare beds, the couches, the floor. My mother usually cooked some fish for them on those Friday sessions, knowing that ninety-nine percent were Catholics, and that was when Friday fish was in. All the guys called her mom. And they called Mike pop, too. He used to bring home bargain slacks and shoes and a lot of them, who didn't have much money, outfitted themselves at my house. There would usually be one or two who stayed until Sunday morning, and there was a Catholic church nearby, and my mother would wake them up so they could go to Mass.

I was kind of torn, in those days. I knew I loved music, and loved playing with a band, but the old message—"be a lawyer or a doctor"—had been drummed into my head so long that I semi-believed it. To my folks and their friends, if a young man didn't aim for the professions, he was a nogoodnick. Naturally, I wanted to make my family proud of me. So part

23

of me said, "OK, I'll be a lawyer and they'll be happy." That part of me pushed me into a pre-law program. The other part said, "Make yourself happy, stick with music." That part of me had me continuing musical studies, working with the college band, playing dates in my spare time. I hooked on with a local band of some repute, Tom Coakley's Orchestra. We worked weekends, playing fraternity and sorority dances. Then we got bigger and better, and got a steady gig at the Athens Athletic Club, in Oakland. I'd pick up twenty or twenty-five dollars a weekend, easily. And more during the week. I was making more than my father. Harold, my brother, was living with us then, naturally making no contribution. I was helping to support my family and studying besides.

The part of me that loved show business dragged me down to the Cocoanut Grove in the Ambassador Hotel in Los Angeles, whenever I had a chance. I wanted to catch Russ Columbo, who was my idol. Columbo played violin with Gus Arnheim's Band, and he'd fill in and sing if the regular vocalist, Bing Crosby, was out. Naturally, there was no money to pay the Cocoanut Grove prices, but we had a gimmick. We called it "lobby dancing." We'd all drive down from college in a Model T and we'd have dates. We'd all be dressed in our collegiate best, and we looked pretty decent. We'd sit in the lobby. And then, when the music started, we'd casually walk in and go over to the dance floor and dance. They knew what was going on, but as long as we looked and behaved like ladies and gentlemen—which we always did—the maitre d' wouldn't stop us.

I liked Crosby. But I preferred Columbo, I guess because his family came from San Francisco. He'd sing "I Don't Know Why" and "Everything I Have Is Yours." He'd sing the hell out of those songs. I guess it was listening to him that made me decide I wanted to sing, too. Columbo played the violin and sang, so I figured I could continue the sax and sing, too. I followed Russ Columbo around. Besides the Cocoanut Grove, he'd appear at a little place called the Pyramid Club, on Sunset Boulevard in Hollywood. Once in a while, a few of us would pile in a car and make the long trek down the coast to L.A., and go to the Pyramid Club to see Columbo. I think he began to recognize me. Maybe it was my imagination, but I don't think so.

All this talk of going to nightclubs and fooling around may give you the wrong impression of my college years. It wasn't all fun and games. I worked and studied, and applied myself to my class work. My grades were not magna cum laude material, but I did all right. I was still taking a pre-law curriculum, and it was difficult for me, mainly because I knew deep down —even shallow down—that law wasn't my bag. At the time, I was taking those courses for one reason—I figured law was my entrée to recognition, to being somebody. It wasn't Gladstone that turned me on, it was the chance to be something better.

But, gradually, I was getting the recognition everybody craves via my music. In my freshman year, I was still playing with Tom Coakley. Then I had a better offer. A band leader named Tom Gerunovitch heard me one night, and asked me if I wanted to join his band. Gerunovitch was big time in and around the bay area, so that was a great thrill. Tom and Frank Martinelli owned the Bal Tabarin nightclub, and his band was a fixture there. And the Bal Tabarin was considerably higher up in the social scheme of things than the Athens Athletic Club, where I played most of the time with Coakley. But still I felt a sense of loyalty to Tom Coakley. He had always been decent with me and I just couldn't walk away.

One night, after we had played, I took him aside and put it to him this way:

"Tom," I said, "I have an offer from Tom Gerunovitch. If you say no, it's no. I won't leave you if you don't want me to leave. But what do you think?"

"Hey, Al," he said. "Why would I stand in a guy's way? I think it's a good deal—go, with my blessing."

So I joined Tom Gerunovitch, and now I was in the big money. I made $72.50 a week, and I was in clover. I could give my folks a bundle and still have plenty left over for myself.

Naturally, with all this going on, there was an immediate desire to quit college. What did I need it for? Why struggle for years to become a lawyer, when I was raking it in with music? Anyhow, I was certain, now, that my future was in music, not law. So I announced to the family one night that I was thinking of quitting college to be a full-time musician. You would have thought I told them the sky was falling.

"You are to stay in college," my father said.

"Music? That's for nobodies," my grandmother said. "You should be a lawyer, get respect."

They ganged up on me, and I was still too young to be able to defy them. Besides, I loved them too much to go against them. Finally, we worked out a deal. I could play at night, with the band, if I went to college in the daytime and studied in between.

So it was back to St. Mary's. Still in pre-law. But taking a lot of other courses, courses that were fun and interesting. I took astronomy, I remember, and that has given me a lifelong interest in the heavenly bodies. I also took Latin, which was, I believe, required of all students. Plus the usual subjects. It was a grind. I'd get up early, cram for an hour or so, then rush off to classes. I'd get home generally around four or five, gulp down some

25

The pianist played the introduction, and I did that same combination, as I danced diagonally across the rehearsal hall. The class continued, and the other girls did their work, and Mr. Bolm and the visitors talked and watched. Then, the class was over and I was about to change when Mr. Bolm called me.

"Sid, would you come over here for a moment?"

I walked over to where he stood with the gray-haired man and the others.

"Sid, I'd like you to meet Colonel De Basil, of the Ballet Russe. Colonel, this is Sid Finklea."

"How do you do?" I said.

"It's a pleasure to meet you, young lady," the Colonel said. "I think you are a young lady of exceptional talent."

"Thank you, sir."

"Tell me, Miss Finklea. Are you serious about your dancing?"

Serious? I lived and breathed dancing.

"Oh, yes, sir," I said. "That's all I really want to do."

"Good," he said. "I was hoping you would say that. You see, I am the director of the Ballet Russe. And I think you are a dancer of great promise. I would like you to join our company. Does that interest you?"

I literally could not speak for a moment. Maybe two or three moments. What I had just heard was something as staggering as though they had asked me to become President of the United States. Join the Ballet Russe? That was the outstanding ballet company in the world, and I was just a skinny little girl from Texas. I had dreamed about a career in ballet, of course, and that was what I was working for, working hard, practicing every day, studying and sweating. But I thought I still had years of learning to go. And here this man had asked me if I would like to join the Ballet Russe. Or had he really said it?

"Did you say join the Ballet Russe?"

"Yes, that's what I said."

Of course, I wanted to join the Ballet Russe. What aspiring dancer would not? But I was not in the position of being able to say yes, right off.

"Oh, I would love it, Colonel," I said. "But I can't accept, until I talk to my mother and father. And they're not here."

"Where are they?"

"They're home."

"Where is home?"

"Amarillo, Texas. And I just couldn't say yes until I talked to them."

Adolph Bolm suggested I telephone them. I practically ran into the school office and I placed the call to Amarillo. As soon as my mother answered, she wanted to know if I was all right.

"Yes, Mother, I'm fine. Can I speak to Daddy, please?"

You see, I knew my father would understand. After all, he had always been a balletomane and his passion for the ballet had infected me when I was five or six. He used to drive all the way to Dallas, just to see a touring ballet company.

"Hello, honey," It was my father's voice.

"Daddy, guess what? Some men came to see me at the dancing class today and they're from the Ballet Russe and they want to know if I want to join the company."

"Join the Ballet Russe?" There was a long pause. "Well, that will require some thought."

It wasn't simple. My mother got on the phone. She wanted to know all the details. Then my brother, Ernest—we called him E.E.—got on the phone. And my Aunt Bobbie, and even Lindy, the black woman who had practically raised me. They all wanted to say hello, and they all had questions to ask about my joining the ballet company. Where? When? And, most important, who would look after me?

"Darling," my mother said, "we just can't discuss this properly over the telephone. There are too many things to consider."

Bolm and Colonel De Basil got on the telephone, and talked to my father at length. It was eventually decided that I should go back home, to Amarillo, and thrash the whole thing out.

Colonel De Basil said that was fine with him. The company was going east in a few days, anyhow, and if I could join the company, I could meet them later.

So I went home, back to Amarillo, the city where I was born and where I had grown up, where I had first become interested in dancing.

Amarillo. It's in the Texas Panhandle, and my family on both sides had been Texans for generations. One of my father's great-grandmothers, Matilda Smith, had been one of the area's earliest settlers. In fact, she had received a grant of land—they called it "a league and a labor of land"— that amounted to 6,666 acres before there was much of anything there. On my mother's side—her maiden name was Norwood—they were East Texans. Way back in time, there was a Captain John Norwood who, with his wife, Mary, had a plantation in South Carolina. That was lost in the Civil War, so the Norwoods had moved to Erath County, Texas. My grandparents had lived in Austin and then in Ranger, and then, after my grandfather died, my grandmother struck it rich. This was Texas so, naturally, the source of her wealth was oil. A book called *The Roaring Ranger* was written about the oil well that Grandmother Norwood brought in. At that time, it was the largest oil well that had yet gushed up through the Texas soil.

The riches lasted less than a generation. Some of the money slipped through the fingers of my mother's older brothers and sisters. She was one of seven children. My grandfather had died and my grandmother, Lily Norwood, was left alone with her brood. This must have been around the end of World War I. There was still plenty left from the oil fortune so they had one of the first automobiles in that part of Texas, and they decided to take a trip. It turned out to be a fateful excursion for my mother, Lela.

In the small city of Plainview, their car was hit by a train. My mother, who was nineteen at the time, was driving. Her mother was killed instantly. Two of her brothers and sisters were critically injured. They were all hospitalized for varying lengths of time. My mother was one of the least seriously injured.

Plainview was very near Amarillo. In fact, Amarillo was the big city to the folks in Plainview. While my mother waited for her brothers and sisters to recuperate, she often went into Amarillo, to buy them things, to see a movie, to kill time. One day, she went into a store to pick up a package. But she must have been daydreaming or something, because she made a mistake and went into the wrong store. She found herself in Ernest Finklea's jewelry store.

A few months later, Ernest Finklea and Lela Norwood were married. He was thirty-three, settled and successful. She was nineteen. Despite the disparity in their ages, the marriage was a good one. They stayed together, a happy couple, until my father died.

Ernest Finklea was, as I imagine most daughters feel about their fathers, probably the most wonderful man I have ever known. He was kind and gentle and loved me very much. He had had a good, Texas kind of life, before he met my mother.

His family, French Huguenots, had come originally from Canada, up around Hudson Bay. Then they had migrated to Maine, for reasons nobody now recalls. But that proved too harsh a climate and some distant ancestor pushed south, in search of warmth and more tillable soil. During the Revolution, there were Finkleas in Georgia and I'm told they had a hotel somewhere in Georgia that was an important institution at the time. But they were, apparently, a restless lot, and they had kept on the move, eventually making the covered wagon trek to Texas.

As a young man, my father had worked for the railroad, in a town called Pecos, as a dispatcher. But then he apparently decided to go into business for himself, and opened his jewelry store on Polk Street, Amarillo's main street.

Ernest Finklea's Jewelry Store was successful. He was not a wealthy man, but he made considerably more than a comfortable living. We were always well off and we never wanted for anything, as long as I can remember.

Soon after they married, my father and mother moved into the house at 1616 Tyler Street, which was my home as long as I lived in Amarillo. I was born on March 8, and that was my first and only home. I was even born there. It was the very epitome of small-city American living. It was on the right side of the tracks. It was large and comfortable, with a big porch sprawling across the front, shaded by lovely old trees, a swing and exercise barns in the back. Inside there was that typically Texas touch, the double living room. There was a grand piano. On the wall were the paintings of ships, under full sail, that my father loved to stare at. And, out in the kitchen, there was always Lindy.

Lindy Lee came into our lives before I was born. The story is told in the family that one day my dad was driving down a street in Amarillo and saw this young black girl—we politely called blacks "colored" when I was a girl—standing on the sidewalk.

"Would you like a job?" he asked her. He must have seen something in her and the question just popped out of his mouth.

"Yes, sir, I sure would." I guess she saw something in him, too.

So she jumped in the car and he took her home, and Lindy was a fixture in the Finklea family from then on. Lindy lived in the back, in a small house behind ours, and there were always several others living with her and her husband and son—from time to time, aunts and sisters and her mother. They would come and they would go. We never knew who was back there with Lindy, and we didn't ask. Lindy was pure goodness. If any of Lindy's friends in Amarillo were hungry, the word was out—go over to 1616 Tyler Street and see Lindy for a free meal. My parents knew about it, of course, and it was fine with them. There was always plenty to go around.

I can never think of my childhood without thinking of Lindy. She practically raised my brother and me, because my mother became busy— she often helped out in the jewelry store, and she had other activities, her charities and the P.T.A. and such, so Lindy was the one who was always there. She was the one who fixed my breakfast, before I left for school. She was the one ready with milk and cookies after school. She was the one with the kind words and gentle hands if I hurt myself.

Lindy's husband had a job somewhere, but he also helped out around our house, mostly in the garden. The chief feature of our garden was a small fish pond in the back yard, and it was Lindy's husband's job to clean it out every spring. It used to become full of algae and it took an annual scrubbing

31

to get it clean. One year, he cleaned it and, we later found out, he was bitten by some insect. At least, that's what the doctors came to believe after he was hospitalized. They said he had typhoid fever and it must have come from being bitten by an insect when he was cleaning our fish pond. They put him in the hospital, and we all went to see him. I was very small, but we were all concerned for him—he was Lindy's husband, after all, and I loved her so much—so I went to the hospital, too.

I remember walking into the hospital room. I don't know what I expected, but it wasn't that. For some reason—fear, perhaps, or embarrassment—he pulled the sheet over his head and he would neither look at me nor talk to me. I kept trying to talk to him, but all I could see was his hands clutching that sheet over his head and all I could hear was his heavy breathing. So I said, "Goodbye, I hope you feel better real soon," and I left and went home.

Two days later, he died. It was my first experience with tragedy of any sort. It took me days to get over it; I know Lindy never did.

There wasn't much sadness in my life, at that time. I suppose there were tragedies. Every family has them. Mine was a large family, full of aunts and uncles and cousins, but if there were any unpleasantness, I was shielded from it.

Two national tragedies imprinted themselves on my consciousness, however. The first was the Depression. It was never a very real thing to me, of course, because I was too young. And we were not personally affected too seriously. It did bother my father a great deal. Just before the market crashed, he had decided to branch out. He had opened another, larger store. Besides jewelry, the new store had appliances—refrigerators and radios. But then came the Depression and the new store folded. He went back to his original location, and that survived. I think he had some investments in the stock market which cost him some money, too, but we were never without food or clothing—or Lindy. Actually, until my father died, he was always successful and well-loved by his many friends. And he always had his Packard automobile, at that time the status symbol of success in Texas.

The other major problem of the outside world which penetrated my secure inside world was the Dust Bowl of the thirties. The Texas Panhandle is freaky country. Amarillo sits on the top of a plateau, flat as a pancake. You can drive for miles and miles without seeing a tree, nothing but mirages of water swimming on the road ahead. So there was nothing to stop the wind. In winters, the storms piled up enormous drifts, which became great heaping mountains of snow we played on as kids. But, when the drought came and there was no moisture, that plateau became nothing but a breeding ground for dust storms.

I can remember sitting in school and looking outside when it was pitch black, as black as though it were the middle of the night. They said we should go home. We would walk home from school with our handkerchiefs clutched around our noses. At home, my mother would soak a towel in water and then swing it around the living room, to collect the dust. She and Lindy would walk through the house, twirling those wet towels about them. The windows were closed tight, of course, but the dust would blow in anyway, and eventually we all took to swinging wet towels to keep the dust from settling on everything.

Mostly, though, I remember the good things about being a child in that time, in that place. In some ways, it was right out of a picture book. There was Christmas, of course. What a delightful day that always was, when I was a child.

Both my mother and father had big families and, since we had a large and roomy house, 1616 Tyler Street was always the Christmas headquarters. Family would come from all over Texas to be with Uncle Ernest and Aunt Lela on Christmas day. The preparations began days before. My father and my uncles were all hunters, and they would go out and bag a few pheasant and quail. But those were only side dishes. The main event was a roast pig, complete with an apple in its mouth. The smell would be so tantalizing that it would wake me up on Christmas morning.

E.E. and I knew, from past bitter experience, that it didn't pay to get up early and sneak into the living room and try to get a head start at opening presents. No, we weren't allowed to touch anything until everybody got there, which wasn't generally until around noon or so. Maybe, if my mother was in a good mood, we could each open one little present first, but that was rare. Ordinarily, we had to wait, smelling the roast pig and trying to guess what was in all those fancy-wrapped packages. Then, when the house was packed with uncles and aunts and cousins, then and only then could we all begin to unwrap our gifts.

Easter was almost as important. I can still see Lindy, in her fluttery apron, boiling dozens of eggs in the big cast-iron pot on the stove. Then E.E. and I would color them, and somebody—I imagine it was my father —would hide them, and we would have to hunt them out. And always in our new Easter clothes. That was a ritual, too. We would go down to Polk Street and get me a new dress the week before Easter.

Everybody would say how pretty I looked. But, as a child, I never felt pretty. Actually, I hated the way I looked. I have never had any daughters,

33

but I understand from friends who have that most girls feel the same way. I know I did. I would stare at the mirror and wonder why my mother was so pretty and my father so handsome and yet I was so plain. More than plain: I thought at the time that I was out-and-out homely. My mother made me wear my hair in a Dutch bob with bangs, which I hated. Every week, she would stand me on the kitchen sink and wash my hair—and then, the final indignity, she would pour vinegar on my hair to "make it shine like a star." Maybe it was the vinegar that did it, but my hair was as straight as a string—but, I must say, it shone! I was the only girl I knew with straight hair. Everybody else had curls. I wanted curls, too.

My family would say, "Sid, you are so pretty," but I knew better. How could anybody as skinny as me and with hair as straight as mine and with those dreadful bangs be pretty? I was homely and I knew it. I would often cry about it. Still, I kept hearing, especially when I had on my new Easter dress, "Sid, you are so pretty."

They always called me Sid. My real name is Tula Ellice. Tula after an aunt, Ellice after an uncle whose name was Ellis. But, when I was a baby, my brother tried to call me "sister" and the closest he could come was "Sid," and that stuck. I've never been anything else, although Hollywood changed the spelling years later.

I thought I was unattractive during most of my growing-up years. But I didn't dwell on it. It was just one of those things I took for granted, like my name and my house and my parents and my brother. It was one of those facts of life I accepted. But I wasn't a brooder. I had too many other things to do.

My mother was beautiful, I thought. She had black hair and blue eyes and she walked straight and smiled a lot. And my father was handsome, too. His hair was thinning and he wore eyeglasses. But the thing that intrigued me most about his physical make-up was the diamond stickpin he was never without. It was in the shape of a kite. Whenever I remember my dad, I remember that stickpin, worn proudly in his tie. He was literally never without it. When he died—he was only fifty-two—my mother gave it to me. I had it made into a ring and it was one of my best-loved pieces of jewelry. Years later, Tony and I were robbed in Miami Beach, and the robbers took all my jewelry. I think of everything that was taken—and they stole many very valuable items—I missed that ring most of all.

Dad was well-loved by everybody, not only me. He was a good man. And a good man, as the song goes, is hard to find. He was very sensitive, artistic, interested in everything and everybody. As far as I know, he never had any enemies. Even in Amarillo, which was a city in the heart of the South, he had no prejudices. And, because of him, neither did I. As a girl,

I knew no difference in people because of race or religion. They were either good people or bad people, and they were never labeled as to their race or their religion in our home. He did business with everybody and had friends who were black and friends who were Jewish, Catholic and Protestant. There weren't too many Jewish families in town, but there were a few. One owned the dress store which was next door to my father's jewelry store. They were good friends of ours. And, after my father died, I think that dress store owner had a crush on my mother. Nothing ever came of that, as far as I know.

Even today, I often run into people who knew and liked—or loved— my father.

When I'm performing somewhere, occasionally someone will come up to me and show me a necklace or a ring or a pendant and say, "I bought this from Ernest Finklea. He was a wonderful man."

Everybody liked him. When he died, the city mourned, literally. But none was more stunned nor mourned as deeply as I. I had loved him very much, and he had returned that love. Or maybe it was vice versa.

So, as a child, I was surrounded by a wall of warmth, a thick layer of love. It made growing up, which is never an easy thing for a girl, reasonably easy. I had my shares of injuries, both physical and mental, but the warmth and love I knew at home protected me and shielded me from those harsh experiences.

Injuries. I was accident-prone as a young girl. Our front porch had a concrete floor. It was great for roller skating, but one day I took a bad fall and broke my arm. My brother, who was the big one, pulled it and set it himself.

And there was the time, when I was still a pre-schooler, that I fell out the window. We had a long breakfast room that overlooked the driveway. I would sit at the window of the breakfast room, watching for my brother to come home from school. I was so jealous, because he could go to school, and I was too young. I would lean out, farther and farther, as the time approached when I knew he should be appearing down the street. One day, I leaned out too far, and fell through the glass and landed on my backside on the hard driveway. I still have a scar to show for my rashness.

But the worst thing, physically, that happened to me was as a result of a vaccination. In those days, they used to cover vaccinations with a celluloid shield. Somehow, the one on my arm became terribly infected, and I was very sick for days.

"Ernest," the doctor said to my father, "I'm afraid there's nothing more I can do. That infection has gone too far. We're going to have to take this child's arm off."

My father, thank God, wouldn't hear of anything of the sort. He grew pale and his eyes flashed behind his glasses.

"Absolutely not," he said.

"But I have no choice."

"No. I'd rather not have a daughter at all than to have one who had to go through life without an arm." So the doctor, of course, bowed to his strong will. And he and my mother nursed me and I recovered. I have an enormous scar on my arm, even now, but I do have both my arms.

So there were the injuries and the frights and, of course, there were the usual childhood ailments. There were the tonsils that had to come out; that was fashionable in Texas at that time. E.E. and I had our tonsils out together. We did most things together in those days. The two of us were taken to the doctor's office for the operation—and were back home the same day. We didn't know what hit us. At least we had each other. We were still sleeping in the same room at that point in our young lives. There were duplicates of everything, although sometimes in different colors. We each, for example, had our own rocking chair. His was brown, mine was white. And I remember waking up the morning after I came home from having my tonsils out and looking over at my rocking chair, and there was a pair of bright purple silk pajamas draped across it. My father had brought them back from Nieman-Marcus in Dallas with him. He often went to Dallas on business trips, and never came home empty-handed. I don't remember many of his gifts, but for some reason those purple silk pajamas are permanently etched in my mind.

Aside from all those momentary discomforts, life was really smooth. There were no real emotional problems, certainly. I had the chief ingredients of a contented life—I had love, security and plenty to eat. Not that I ate much; it seems to me the sound of my father saying, "Please, darling, take one more bite for me," will forever echo in my mind. I was a poor eater. And, as a consequence of that and my predilection for physical activity, I was thin to the point of scrawniness.

And I did run around a lot. With an older brother, a girl has a tendency to become tomboyish, and that was me. I'd run around with the boys, rather than the girls. I preferred baseball to dolls, any day. My best friends were my brother and the boys across the street, Roy Vineyard and Billy Adams. Billy is now Captain William Adams, and he's in the Navy, the skipper of a nuclear submarine.

Mostly, though, it was E.E. who inspired me. I tried to keep up with him, do everything he did. He ran, I ran. He played baseball or football or roller skated, so did I. I'm told some big brothers hate to have their kid sisters dogging their footsteps, but I don't think E.E. minded. He never said he did. We were pals, not just siblings. In fact, there was a time when he was grateful for my presence.

There was a place across the street from school where we would sometimes eat lunch. It was a cafeteria. My mother was not one to pack lunches, so when we didn't go home for lunch, we were given some money and we would have our lunch at the cafeteria. And one day, over some long-forgotten matter which, at the time, was of dreadful importance, he got into a fight with some other boys. I didn't hesitate a minute. E.E. was in trouble. I waded into the brawl, my bony fists shooting out at every face in sight. I forgot whether we won or lost. But I do remember that both of us, and I imagine our foes, too, were hauled up to the principal's office for stern sermons. He called my mother, too, and she had to race down to the school to plead our cause.

The principal was a man named Mr. King. To give you an example of how small our school was, Mr. King moonlighted during the daylight. Every recess, he would come out of his principal's office and become, for the duration of the recess, Mr. King the Ice Cream Man. He would sit in the hall and sell ice cream bars. I seldom had any money for such treats —I'll tell you where my allowance went in a little while—but Mr. King would give me an ice cream bar, anyhow.

"That's all right," he'd say, handing me one of those little gems. "Your folks will pay me later." And, of course, there was always a day of reckoning and they always paid.

That reminds me of another childhood accident. One day, I was swinging on the playground swing and, of course, I wanted to go higher and faster than anybody else. I did, but paid the price. Off I flew and landed on the ground, which was covered with sharp gravel. I was bleeding from several cuts on various parts of my exposed body. They took me to Mr. King's place of business—the ice cream stand—and he closed up shop and took me into his office. Mr. King had one remedy for any injury: he kept a large bottle of iodine in one of his cupboards, and would pour it liberally over any wound. He doused me with the iodine, and, naturally, it stung like fury. I screamed. I had a very loud scream. He got frightened. And, once again, he called my mother and, once again, she had to race to school to calm me. That little incident left a scar, too. I seem to be a mass of scars.

I was pretty good in school, although not as good as E.E. He was— still is—a whiz. He went on to high school and then Texas A & M and became an engineer. He's very successful and now lives in Ridgefield, Connecticut.

What helped both of us get along well in school was our father. We had a ritual. After school, we would come home and do our homework and then we would have our daily session with dad. He even bought a blackboard and put it up on a wall in his room. He'd call us in and we'd have to go over our work with him. He always made a point of leaving the jewelry store so he'd be on time for those little lessons. It helped me, and I think it was even more helpful to E.E., because he was always so interested in math.

Dad always took such an interest in us. Mother was different, entirely different. It wasn't that she ignored us, because she didn't. But her theory, apparently, was that we should grow up independently. She was very free with us, totally free. We could do almost anything we wanted to do within reason. I sometimes look back on that facet of my upbringing and it frightens me. God, what trouble I could have gotten into, and I sometimes wonder how I avoided it.

I was totally innocent. Nobody ever told me the facts of life. Certainly, my mother would never dream of such a lecture. Maybe my father talked to my brother, but he never talked to me. I grew into adolescence and beyond without the foggiest notion of what went on.

We were seldom punished. If there was a disciplinarian in the family, it was my mother. Once in a while, if we were very naughty or had done something absolutely horrible, she would spank us. Generally, her philosophy was if something went wrong, she'd spank both of us, both E.E. and me. I think she was guided by the idea that if one of us was naughty, it followed that the other must have been bad, too. She was usually right about that. So she'd whack us both and we'd both go off, crying our eyes out.

My father only hit me once in my life. I guess I deserved it. It happened one summer. The highlight of the summer for me (a harbinger of things to come) was the annual appearance in Amarillo of a traveling troupe of players, The Hardley Sadler Company. It was a tent show. I lived from summer to summer, just so I could go down to the tent with my dad and see the play. On this particular day, my father came home and we had dinner and he said he was very sorry, but he had some business to attend to, and he couldn't take me to the tent show as he had promised.

"You have to," I screeched. "You promised!"

"Sorry, sweetheart. I simply can't."

And then I said something fresh, something like "I hate you," or words to that dreadful effect. And I climaxed that by stating, in a voice that could almost be heard in Dallas, "I *am going whether you like it or not!*"

That did it. He slapped me across the face. But that was the only time he ever disciplined me. The other ninety-nine percent of my childhood, he was a man without visible temper, without meanness, with nothing but absolute love for me and his family.

I grew up, in the normal course of events. I had everything I wanted, except for one thing. That was a doll house like Catherine had. Catherine Monning was the girl next door. There was a vacant lot between our houses, and we used to play on that lot all the time. As I began to outgrow the tomboy stage, I took an interest in Catherine because her father had made her a doll house big enough to walk into. It had all handmade doll furniture and it was beautifully decorated and fixed up. I wanted one just like it, but for some reason I never got one. So I made miniature doll houses from the satin-covered jewel boxes my father would bring home from the store. They sufficed until I found a greater passion.

My father loved the ballet and music. It seems strange, looking back at it now, how he ever developed that love. After all, he had never been exposed to the cultural centers of the world—certainly Pecos, Texas, is far from that. Yet he had developed this fascination for the dance. Whenever a ballet troupe came to Dallas, he would make that long drive to see them. He also made my brother and me take piano lessons, and E.E. moved on to the organ.

He encouraged me. I learned how to do a simple pirouette, and he arranged a place for me, in the center of the living room, where I could pirouette on the hardwood floor away from the dangers of rugs and the sharp corners on tables and chairs. If I did the pirouette to his liking, he would give me a nickel. I liked dancing. I liked the nickels, too.

When I was about five or six, the doctor suggested I should do more dancing, for the sake of my health. I was very thin. And it grew worse one summer, almost to the point of my being considered frail. I was very sick. Doctors I have consulted recently tell me I probably had polio that summer. One side of my back is slightly atrophied. So that fall, the doctor said I should do something to improve my physical condition. He thought dancing might be the best thing. That was fine with everybody, especially me and my father.

There is so much luck in people's lives. Things often happen for you, not because you make them happen, but because of external factors over which you have absolutely no control. I suppose I might have gone into dancing anyhow—I can't imagine my life without dancing—but the impetus came from that summer's illness. Without that, I might not have started studying ballet until I was considerably older, perhaps too late to make a career of it.

There was a further bit of luck for me, too. By a strange coincidence, there was at that time a very talented teacher in Amarillo. When I began my studies, Amarillo was a small city, hardly the place you would ordinarily expect to find a genuinely qualified ballet teacher. But she was there.

Her name was Constance Ferguson. She had had a reasonably successful career as a dancer herself. She had even trained with the great Russian star Maurice Koslov. Now retired, she had come to Amarillo because she had a sister who lived there. So when our doctor suggested dancing for the sake of my health, my father took me to Miss Ferguson. I think it was the doctor who knew of her, and that's how the contact was made.

She was my first teacher. At the very beginning of my lessons, she was almost afraid to have me do anything, because I was so thin. I know, because she told me later, that she wouldn't touch me. She was frightened that if she touched me, I might fall apart. But, although I was so skinny, I was strong and well-coordinated—those times of playing with my brother had helped—and I learned quickly.

Her classes were held in the Paladuro Hotel ballroom. There was a bar and mirror, of course, and I can still remember those first lessons in that drafty old ballroom. I went to the bar, and, within a week or so, I had mastered the first five positions. I found I loved it. I couldn't wait until it was time for my lesson. And, gradually, Miss Ferguson realized that I wasn't as frail as I looked—or maybe the lessons did the trick and I became stronger—and she made me work harder.

The lessons and my practice at home filled up my hours. And there was school, most of the year. Saturdays would be my big treat, no school, no lessons, just a day for fun. My allowance, during most of my childhood, was twenty-five cents a week. I'd spend it all on Saturday to go to the movies, but it would be enough for a ticket and some popcorn and candy. The quarter was supplemented by those nickels I managed to wheedle out of my father, doing pirouettes in the living room, and any other way I could. He used to call me "The Nickel Consumer."

Sunday there was Sunday school. My parents were not heavy into religion, and that was unusual because most of Amarillo was. My father's family had been strict Baptists and my mother had come from Methodist roots. She changed to the Baptist church when she married my father, but they were not regular church-goers. They did think that it was very important for my brother and me to go to Sunday school, however. So, on Sundays, they would take us to the church and then come back later and pick us up.

One Sunday, I went to Sunday school in the Baptist church, as usual. I had put on what few pieces of jewelry I owned—I have always loved jewelry—and that was not usual. But, after all, jewelry was my father's business. The minister noticed me and my pathetically few pieces of jewelry.

Looking straight at me, he launched into a hellfire-and-brimstone sermon about the sins of wearing jewelry and dancing. He knew I danced, he could see the jewelry. Everybody else in Sunday school turned to look at me as the dire words from the pulpit rained on my poor head. I began to cry. My brother took me by the hand and led me out, with the whole Sunday school staring at us as we left the church.

We waited outside, on the curb, until my father came along in his Packard to pick us up. I was still crying and my brother was trying to console me.

"What happened?" my father asked. "Why are you crying?"

I blubbered something, but couldn't talk, so my brother explained about the sermon the preacher had delivered.

My father didn't say anything, but I could see he was angry. Nothing more was said—but the next Sunday, they took me to the Presbyterian church for Sunday school, and we became Presbyterians.

Some weekends we would go on trips. With family all over, there were many people to visit. One aunt had a house at a place called the Pacific Palisades, which was twenty or thirty miles from Amarillo. That was where the plateau, on which Amarillo sat, fell off. There was a creek there, and we fished for perch and catfish. I loved going to my aunt's house there because, when it was hot enough, we slept outside, on the verandah, on blankets. And that was fun, mosquitoes and all.

My favorite weekend excursion, however, was to my uncle's ranch, the Goodnight Ranch. The big thing there was the buffalo herd. In those days, buffalo were scarce and the Goodnight Ranch's herd was one of the last remaining. Now, of course, there are breeding herds, and the buffalo are no longer in danger of disappearing.

When we went to the Goodnight Ranch, my brother and I and our cousins would go off by ourselves, carrying bags of lunch, for our own private picnics. They just told us to avoid one particular gully, where the buffalo ran through. So, naturally, that gully was the place we headed for first of all. We would creep down in the gully and wait. And then, when we heard the ground begin to rumble, heralding the approach of the galloping buffalo, we would quickly scramble up out of the gully and watch them roar by, raising huge clouds of dust. We got to be pretty fast at scrambling.

We often went there in the summer, too, when my father would close the store and take his vacation. But, generally, we would drive to New Mexico for those two-week trips. Both my mother and father loved trout fishing. At first, we would go wading, but the long hikes got boring. E.E. and I would sit on a bank downstream with our Lindy for hours and hours. I grew to hate fishing as a result—and I still do. The area where we went to camp is now part of the ranch which Buddy Fogelson and his wife, Greer Garson, own, and I now realize how beautiful it is.

As I grew older, dancing became more and more important to me. I continued my studies with Constance Ferguson, and went to her more frequently. My father built a bar and mirror in my room, and I would practice by the hour in the evening. I still had my friends and my family, of course, but increasingly I was by myself, practicing. And every good dancer I've ever known has the same story to tell. You can't become an accomplished dancer without that youthful dedication.

So, as a consequence, I grew inward. I have never been an extrovert and I wasn't, even as a child. But now, as the urge to dance grew stronger, I became more and more the loner. In the first grade, I remember, I had had boy friends. I used to leave my books at home, forget them deliberately, so the teacher would make me sit with one of the boys—Henry Seamon or Roy Vineyard—and share their books. And my brother's friends were always hanging around the house, too. If it hadn't been for dancing, I suppose I would have had a pretty active social life in Amarillo as I grew into the dating age. But that was not to be. I chose another way of life, the way of the dedicated dancer.

I never went to a prom. I never really went out with a boy until I met the man who was to become my first husband. I had no teen-age life, none of that existed for me. It was school, home, dance. And, more and more, I practiced on weekends, too. I'd still go to the movies, though, especially if there was a dance picture on the local screen. I had never seen a real ballet. My dance horizons were limited by what I could see at the local theater on Saturdays.

It was Astaire and Rogers, Eleanor Powell, even Shirley Temple and Bill Robinson and their little tap-dancing routines. (Incidentally, I was so rabid for Shirley Temple that one Christmas I simply had to have a Shirley Temple doll, and, of course, I got one.) To me, that was what dancing was, those elaborate and improbable numbers I saw up there on the screen.

Naturally, I saw all the recitals Miss Ferguson's pupils put on. And, equally naturally, I participated in all of them. The very first one I was part of I danced the role of a snowflake. It was the same sort of thing every dance teacher puts on at every dance studio in every city in America. All the little children perform and all the parents are there, beaming with parental pride, as their little darlings prance about the stage in their costumes. Those recitals were always a thrilling experience for me. I found that I enjoyed

42

performing, and enjoyed feeling the audience reaction surrounding me. I was, I suppose, the only child there with natural ability, so I was always the star of the show. That is a delightful feeling and one I never tire of.

When I danced at those recitals, there was always a big contingent from our house. There were my parents and my brother, first of all. But we generally had others living in our house, too. My Aunt Bobbie—Roberta Finklea—lived with us for years. She had a bad leg and couldn't get around too well, but she always managed to limp her way down to the ballroom to watch me dance. Another boarder for a long time was an Englishman named Robert Taylor. He was a jewelry salesman my father had befriended and it was typical of my dad that he had asked Mr. Taylor to stay with us for a while. The "while" stretched into years. He was almost one of the family and he, too, frequently watched me at one of those Constance Ferguson recitals.

As I grew older, my life changed little. The routine grew comfortable —school, dance lessons, practice, a little time for fun. My mother and her friend, Mrs. Scott, started what they called their "Preventorium," a home for tubercular children, and mother got all her friends to chip in fifty cents at the beginning. She had hundreds of friends, from her work at the store, her work with various organizations such as the P.T.A., her endless bridge games. The Preventorium flourished, and she began spending more and more time there.

It all changed for me when I was twelve. As I have said, our summer vacations were ordinarily spent in New Mexico, although we did go to Colorado once or twice. But the year I was twelve we came to California.

There is some family mystery to why that change was made. I have never really understood it completely. All I know was that it involved my Uncle Clarence. He was a tragic figure. He had served in the Army during World War I, had gone to fight the Germans, and had been gassed. I'm not sure what happened, but suddenly the house was full of whispers and they kept me close at home for a while. The snatches of conversations I overheard mentioned words like "kidnapping" and "threat" and "danger." I gather that my Uncle Clarence had talked wildly about kidnapping me, for whatever reason, and so the family decided to vary its usual vacation schedule.

We came to California and rented a place at the beach in Santa Monica. I wanted to continue taking dance lessons, of course, so the first day my parents asked people for the name of a reputable studio. They were directed to the Fanchon and Marco Dance Studio, and they took me down there and I was duly enrolled for the duration of the vacation.

The studio was on Sunset Boulevard in Hollywood. And one of the teachers was a dashing figure named Nico Charisse. I don't think I developed a crush on him at that time, but I loved to watch him dance and he was an excellent teacher. Perhaps I might have entertained some romantic visions toward him, except that that was the summer my brother became so ill. All my thoughts were directed toward him.

It began with an earache. But it was something much more serious. It was a mastoid problem, an infection in his ear, which mushroomed somehow into spinal meningitis. He was taken to the hospital and the doctors told my parents to be prepared for the worst. That was, of course, before penicillin or the sulfa drugs.

"We are very afraid," they said, "that this boy won't survive."

My mother refused to accept that verdict. She is a very strong, very determined woman, and she was not going to allow her only son to die. She and my father sat for hours in front of the hospital. I assume they were praying. I know I prayed, too. My mother had become friendly with a woman, a Mrs. Strauss, who was a Christian Scientist. Mrs. Strauss had some of her friends, who were practitioners, come over to the hospital, and they all sat with my brother.

He pulled through, astounding the doctors. My mother, as a result of that experience, became a Christian Scientist and still is. I cannot say, of course, whether it was their efforts or the doctors' medication or my prayers or just the will of God that saved my brother. But it was such an astounding development that the doctors had my brother appear at seminars to show other doctors his recovery.

My father's vacation was over, so he went home. My mother stayed with my brother, while he recuperated. When he was well enough, she drove back to Texas with him. She put a mattress in the back seat of the car, and he made the trip from California to Texas in a prone position. He was fully recovered although, some years later, it was learned that the bout with disease had left him with a slight heart murmur.

I didn't go back to Texas, either with my father or with my mother and brother. I think that disturbance with my Uncle Clarence was still hanging over our family, so they decided to let me stay in Los Angeles and continue my studies with Nico Charisse and the other teachers at Fanchon and Marco. They also felt, I suppose, that I had learned all I could from Constance Ferguson in Amarillo and, if I was to go on in dance, it was time for me to have more advanced instruction.

So they found a place for me with a family in Los Angeles, and, for the first time in my life, I was alone. It was a terrifying experience. I was only twelve, and totally inexperienced. From the cocoon of a warm, loving family and good friends in a relatively small city, suddenly I was thrown into an alien world—a big city, no family, no friends.

To make matters even more miserable, I didn't like the lady I was staying with. I went to my classes and my dance lessons, and then I would come home and go to my room and cry, feeling very sorry for myself. I remembered Amarillo, the world I knew and loved. And here I was, in an unfamiliar world, in a strange room, with nobody I knew or cared for around me. I poured out my unhappiness in letters and telephone calls. It was a case of extreme homesickness.

I don't remember exactly how long I stayed in California, that first time, but it couldn't have been too long. Maybe a month. Then we couldn't stand it any more—I couldn't stand being away from home, and my father couldn't stand hearing me sob over the telephone. So I went back home to Amarillo.

But two years later, I had changed. Now I was fourteen and now I knew that I had to go on with dancing and must have better teachers. By then, too, I was mature enough to feel I could cope with being away from home. So back to California I came, back to Fanchon and Marco. This time, they found a home for me with a woman—her name was Mrs. Ray Crumly—she was wonderful. She had two daughters, Caroline and Marilyn, who became good friends. I went to the Hollywood Professional School, but I didn't like that very much. I was completely disinterested in studies at that time. Dancing was my whole life. I'd spend all my time dancing at the studio, in any empty studio that was available, then race home to my little apartment to sleep a few hours.

I went to see my first professional ballet at the Los Angeles Philharmonic Hall. I sat there, with my eyes popping open, and watched the ballets —Les Sylphides, Aurora's Wedding, Prince Igor, Swan Lake—thinking they were the most magnificent things I had ever seen. To me, it was fairyland. I couldn't believe there was anything as beautiful as that. It made me more determined than ever to be a ballerina.

When I had gone back to Amarillo, after my bout with homesickness, I had learned a very important lesson for me. That one summer and those few weeks when I had stayed there by myself had been turning points in my young life. Even though I had yearned to go back home, when I got there I found I had outgrown it. I no longer fit in. I had somehow moved beyond that insular life. Oh, for a few weeks I was so glad to be home that I thought I was happy, but it gradually dawned on me that I wasn't. I hadn't fallen out of love with my family; far from it. But I came to understand that there was something gnawing at me. I had had a taste of the big, bright outside world in California. I had seen truly professional dancers. I knew that there was a lot more to life than I could find on Polk Street and Tyler Street.

So, when I went back to California, I knew that I had reached a major milestone in my life. From now on, Sid Finklea was going places!

I had been bitten by ambition. It wasn't the driving ambition of some girls, to be big, glamorous stars with lots of money. Mine was a more single-minded ambition. I wanted to become a great dancer, that's all. There was, I suppose, the yen to see the world, to have a heart-stopping romance, to love and be loved. But, primarily, it was the honest goal to dance, to soar across the stage and to feel my performance bringing great emotional surges to those who saw me.

And so, when I came back to California that second time, I really worked. By then, Nico Charisse had left the studio and had joined the San Francisco Opera Company. I had liked him and had felt he was a superb teacher, but that was the extent of my feelings for him at that time. I was too busy to think about things like that. Besides, there was Adolph Bolm to replace him, and he, too, was an extraordinarily talented man.

I danced. I went to school, but my heart wasn't in that. I had no dates, no time for that nonsense. It was, I realize now, a terribly one-track existence, but, at the time, dancing was all I could think of.

And then came that wonderful day when Colonel De Basil visited the school, and asked me to join the Ballet Russe. Another part of my life was about to begin.

3

MUSIC
AND
MARRIAGE

". . . and now, Ladies and Gentlemen, here is Al Morris to sing 'Lady of Spain.' "

I'd leave my sax on its stand, step down front and center, and sing my heart out. For an eighteen-year-old kid, that was the height of class. I was a pro, singing and playing with one of the top bands in our area, making good money and having my moments in the spotlight.

Being with the band gave me status, gave me balls. I knew now that, forever more, I could make a living with my music, that I was my own man. I guess, since it happened to me relatively young, at an age when I hadn't the maturity to cope with it, I became somewhat arrogant about it. I was a cocky kid. Gone forever was the shy little boy who had tagged along after the big kids. Now I was somebody, a professional musician, making $72.50 a week. I was a big shot, junior grade.

I made friends among the rest of the band. I was accepted for what I was, a good saxophone player and a good singer, part of the band. Musicians don't worry about race, creed or religion. They've always been integrated.

Woody Herman had joined Tom Gerunovitch's orchestra about the same time I did, and we became the closest of friends from the beginning. We did many things together, grew up together, chased girls together. I was still living at home then, and Woody often came home with me for dinner. I was still bringing a lot of money into the family treasury, so I figured I had the right to bring guests.

My folks figured I was still a kid, however, and expected me to spend my nights at home, after my night's work was done. But I wanted a little freedom, and my boss cooperated with me.

"Hello, Hattie, this is Tom," he'd say. I'd put him up to it, and he'd call her after we'd wrapped it up at the club.

"How are you, Tom. Will Alvin be home soon?"

"That's why I'm calling, Hattie. We've got to do a little rehearsing now. So Al will be late. In fact, I think it would be better if he stayed at my place tonight."

And I'd step out, generally with Woody and maybe some of the others. It was a fast time in San Francisco then, around '31 and '32. Prohibition was the law, but there were plenty of speakeasies and we found them all. One night we got caught in a raid, four or five of us with some girls. But the local cops knew us and let us go. It was part of the era, and we didn't think anything about it.

There were plenty of girls around, too. As a semi-star, I was the object of their attentions. And, being a normal teen-ager, I responded. Sometimes, it would be several days in a row that I asked Gerunovitch to alibi me with my mother. I have a feeling she knew what was going on. Tom would call her, day after day, with that tired story about rehearsing. Then, when I would finally come home, after a few days of carousing with some girl, she'd greet me with a knowing look on her face. "You know, Alvin, I think maybe you're rehearsing too hard," she'd say.

I was learning—music as well as girls. We played at the Bal Tabarin every night, and I was getting a chance to work and work hard. I tried things, different types of songs, experiments in phrasing and breath control. I had studied the saxophone but I'd never had a singing lesson in my life. It was the constant practice of singing with the Gerunovitch band that taught me. I felt myself improving with every song, every night. It gave me self-confidence and my ego another boost.

Then, in 1933, Tom told us we were going to go to Chicago to play at the World's Fair. Kay Kyser and his orchestra followed us into the Bal Tabarin. Tom decided that this move would be a good time for him to shorten his name, which was a mouthful. He announced that from now on he was Tom Gerun. When he mentioned that to his mother, she turned her back on him.

"Get out," she said to him. "You are Gerunovitch and you will always be Gerunovtich. I don't know anybody named Gerun."

But he stuck to his guns, and it was Tom Gerun and His Orchestra that went to Chicago. We had some time between closing at the Bal Tabarin and when we were due to be in Chicago at Pabst's Blue Ribbon Casino, so Woody and I decided to drive from San Francisco to Chicago.

I was excited about the trip, my first outside California. We piled our instruments in the back of Woody's car and began our big adventure.

We drove from San Francisco across northern California and into Nevada, through Reno and on into Utah. We stopped in Salt Lake City and discussed what we should do. We were being paid twelve dollars per day and I figured if we kept on going, we could pocket that money. Woody argued that he was tired and we should take a room. But I finally persuaded him that twelve dollars in the pocket was better than a few hours in the sack, and we pushed on.

We had gone about thirty miles beyond Salt Lake City. It was dusk. Woody was driving. He hit a curve too fast, the fading light somewhat obscuring the road, and he stepped on the brakes hard. The back wheels slipped and I felt the car hurtle into the air. We flipped four times, finally landing right side up.

"What happened? Are you OK?"

"I think so, how about you?"

"I guess I'm all right. I'm bleeding."

I held Woody's head in my lap. There was blood all around, some his, some mine. For some time—a few seconds? a few minutes?—we sat there like that.

And then, suddenly, he jumped up.

"Oh, my God," he said.

"What's the matter?"

"My sax!"

He ran to the back of the car, opened the trunk, and dragged out his sax case. The instrument looked all right, but he wasn't taking any chances. He took his sax out of the case and played a few bars.

He gave me a big smile.

"It's OK," he said.

And then he fainted. But that was typical of Woody. He was more concerned with his music than he was with his own personal well-being. He'd given only a fleeting thought to his own condition, but his chief worry was how his saxophone had survived the crash.

We managed to get the car back into Salt Lake City, chugging along a few miles an hour, and had it fixed the next morning. Then we drove— very carefully—on to Chicago where it was completely repaired.

Chicago, during that World's Fair summer of 1933, was a big and wonderful experience. All the great musical aggregations of the time came through, and I heard them all—Ben Bernie, Ted Weems, Buddy Rogers. And, of course, Tom Gerun and His Orchestra, with Al Morris. Sally Rand was doing her fan dance just down the street from where we were playing.

Virginia Hill, just up from Mississippi, was working there. I got to meet Paul Whiteman and Hal Kemp, Coon Sanders and Earl "Fatha" Hines. Perry Como was Ted Weems' vocalist, and we were introduced and talked about singing. The musicians would all meet, after we had finished playing, at a place called Thompson's, where you could get a sandwich and all the milk you could drink for twenty-six cents.

When the fair was over, we were booked into the famous Chez Paree in Chicago. This was really the big time. Our band, besides playing for dancing, accompanied the big stars, and they were the big ones. One who made a great impression on me was Helen Morgan. She was a terrific entertainer, and a great lady, besides. Helen was one of the most liberal people I ever met, in the sense of being generous. Whatever she had, she gave away. A man from Detroit was smitten with her—it happened all the time—and had given her a three-quarter-length mink coat.

One night, one of the ponies—short line dancers—admired her coat.

"Gee, Miss Morgan," the girl said, "that's the prettiest coat I've ever seen!"

"Here, it's yours," Helen said. She had had a few drinks, of course, but still.

"Oh, no, I couldn't."

"I insist." She took the coat off, draped it around the girl's shoulders, and walked off.

The next day, that pony went up to Mike Fritzell, who owned the Chez Paree with Joey Jacobson, and told him what had happened. The coat, she knew, was worth somewhere around $20,000, and she was worried.

"She had had a couple of drinks," the girl told Fritzell. "I'm sure that today she doesn't remember giving it to me. I don't want any trouble. You'd better give it back to her."

Fritzell took the coat back to Helen. She became incensed.

"Look, Mike," she said, "I gave that girl that coat and I want her to have it. If you don't tell her to keep that coat, I won't go on tonight."

So the pony got herself a $20,000 mink coat, and Helen Morgan never looked back. She had others.

I fell in love, again, when I was at the Chez Paree. But the girl I was in love with never knew it. Her name was Irene Coleman, and she was one of the showgirls. The revue had six showgirls and fourteen ponies, and Irene was one of those tall, gorgeous showgirls. I was absolutely crazy about her —beautiful face, superb figure, exquisite legs. I'd bring her sandwiches and coffee, just so I could get close to her, and hear her say thank you. She would smile at me.

"You're a good-looking boy, Al," she said. "I bet that some day you're going to be in pictures."

She was dating a very wealthy man then. All the girls were dating very wealthy men. Those were the days when the Stage Door Johnnies were outside the dressing room door every evening, carrying bouquets of flowers as if they were rifles. I kept expecting somebody to shout out a command, "Right shoulder, bouquets!" So I would watch as my Irene was met by this rich guy and they would walk out to his block-long car and drive off.

Once she asked me for a favor. Her boy friend was out at the airport, she said. He had just flown in and had to fly right out again. But, if she could get to the airport, she could see him for an hour or so. Would I? Of course, I would! It gave me a chance to have her at my side for a while. I was a sucker for beautiful women. I drove her out to the airport and waited around while she had her rendezvous with her boy friend, and then I drove her back again.

That was all there was to that great romance—a few favors, a few smiles. I never asked her for a date, or anything else. She was out of my class, out of my league. I just looked at her, and dreamed of the day when I might have enough on the ball to pursue a girl like that. That day would come.

Irene Coleman would come into my life again, a few years later. And, that next time, she would be very important to me.

Things moved swiftly for me at that period in my life. I was still with Tom Gerun, at the Chez Paree, when the next step up the ladder was thrust at me. Dick Stabile came to me and offered me a spot in Ben Bernie's band —at $132.50 a week. That was a big jump, both financially and professionally, because, in those days, Ben Bernie was very big. He was playing at the Hotel Sherman and had a radio show, too.

"Tom," I said to Gerun, as I had said to Tom Coakley only a couple of years before, "I have an offer to go with Bernie. What do you think I should do?"

This time, there was more than mere loyalty involved. There were two other factors I had to consider. One was a rumor that had been floating around that Gerun was about to dissolve the band. The other was the fact that, once again, I was in love.

The vocalist singing at the Chez Paree then was the incomparable Frances Langford. I had fallen in love with her, and it was a warm, rich, wonderful romance. I sort of wanted to hang around Chicago, so we could be together. The Hotel Sherman was just a few blocks away, but you know how it is—when you're in love, a few blocks is as remote as Casablanca.

So, before I accepted the Bernie offer, which Dick Stabile relayed, I

51

had to satisfy myself that I'd still have some time to be with Frances. And, also, I wanted to know what Tom Gerun's plans were.

"What's Bernie offering you?" he asked.

I told him.

"That's good money, all right," he said. "But I'll tell you what you should do. I'm going to go out of the orchestra business in a little while. I've had it. And I think you're the right guy to take over the band."

"Me? Lead the band?"

"Sure, why not? You'd be perfect. You look good, you sing good, you hold the saxophone OK."

That was one idea that hadn't occurred to me. Oh, I suppose I'd daydreamed about someday having my own orchestra, fronting a band, but someday was, I thought, a long way away. I was only eighteen, not quite nineteen. That's pretty young to be dreaming big dreams. But Gerun seemed to think it was right, and the other men in the band seemed to think it was right, too. They all agreed to stay with me. Tom said we'd make the change when we got back to San Francisco. So I turned the Bernie offer down.

We stayed on at the Chez Paree a while. I was able to see Frances during that period, which was nice, and then, as these things usually do, it ended. We stayed friends. I might mention, at this point, that I have been in love many times and most of those affairs have come to their inevitable end. And yet none of the girls have ever wound up angry or unhappy with me. Every one of them—and that even includes an ex-wife —is still on good terms with me. I think that's something to be proud of, the fact that there has never been any acrimony. There have been a few torches carried—mostly by me—but no hard feelings.

Playing at the Chez Paree was fun. The best acts came through and the band would have to accompany them. We played music for the DeMarcos to dance by, for Martha Raye (Woody Herman was seeing her while I saw Frances) to clown by, for Helen Morgan to sing with. Harry Richman, then one of the world's foremost entertainers, came through and played for a few weeks and we became good friends. Harry brought along his own special mike, and let me use it in my numbers. That's when I became conscious of the value of having the finest equipment. I've been fussy about it ever since.

That was when Chicago was pretty wild. I knew "the boys," of course. They were often at ringside tables, in their flashy clothes with the fur-clad gals. They didn't interfere in my act, so I didn't interfere in theirs. We let each other live. Actually, they were always an appreciative audience. There was never any trouble when the boys were there. They never bothered entertainers.

I never took a day off. I was too hungry. I tried to figure out someplace to work, where maybe somebody else would see me. Even later, when I was down in Los Angeles, that habit persisted. I remember that Sunday nights at the Trocadero were very important. They opened the place up on Sunday nights, and new acts were allowed a shot. These weren't amateurs, of course, but pros who were looking for a place to perform, to be seen. There were so many young acts trying out that you almost had to fight your way on to get your shot. I remember one night working with Martha Raye, Dixie Dunbar and some comic. The four of us were all relatively unknown then—and three of the four amounted to something in a short time.

Finally, the Chez Paree engagement was over, and we moved back to the Bal Tabarin in San Francisco. Now, instead of Tom Gerun and His Orchestra, the sign read Al Morris and His Orchestra. I must admit that was one of the greatest thrills of my life, seeing that sign. Going out there the first night, in my tuxedo and waving my hand and having the whole band follow my lead was a top-flight thrill. Gerun gave me his whole library of music, and gave me my big chance.

That was really something, to come back to my home town with my name up there in big letters. My folks came to see me and they saw the sign "Al Morris and His Orchestra," and I doubt there were prouder people anywhere. I felt like busting a few buttons myself. I wasn't yet twenty.

I began appearing regularly on radio, too. The NBC Blue Network had remotes from many night clubs, and they picked up ten minutes or so an evening from the Bal Tabarin. I was always careful that there was an Al Morris solo somewhere during those ten minutes.

One night, Irene Coleman, the show girl I had been crazy about in Chicago, came in. She was with a date, naturally. After the show, I went over and sat with her and she introduced me to her date. He turned out to be an executive at MGM. He said complimentary things about me and my singing.

"How can we get in touch with you, Al?" he asked.

I gave him my number. That was all there was to it. I wasn't naive. I knew the kind of idle talk people make sitting at a night club table. This wasn't the first time some Hollywood big shot had said he was going to get in touch with me. But Irene winked at me, as if to say, "Remember when I told you you'd be in pictures someday? Well, someday is here." It was a very profound wink. But, wink or no, I forgot about it. It had given my ego a little momentary zing, and that was enough.

53

But, the next Sunday, the phone rang. The long-distance operator said it was Malibu calling. Malibu? I didn't know anybody there.

"Is this Al Morris?"

"Yes."

"Hold on. Mr. Louis B. Mayer is calling."

I knew a rib when I heard one.

"Why don't you shove it?" I said. And hung up. That'll teach those wise guys, whoever they were, that I didn't bite on gags like that. All my friends, all the guys in the band, knew I was movie-crazy. I went to every movie I could see. I was dying for a crack at a movie. I could just see them —it could have been Woody—chortling over the gag, over how I'd jump down the phone when I heard the name Louis B. Mayer. Well, I didn't fall for it.

The phone rang back, a few minutes later.

"We must have been cut off, Mr. Morris."

"Who's this?"

"My name is Nat Goldstone. I'm calling for Mr. Louis B. Mayer of MGM. I'm in personal management. Mr. Mayer heard you singing on the Blue Network and has been told about you."

"You're not kidding me, are you?"

"No, no. I'm very serious. This could be a very important moment for you. Mr. Mayer wonders when you could come down to take a screen test."

"What's today, Sunday? I'm off Monday, the place is dark. How's tomorrow?"

"Tomorrow will be fine."

He told me where to come, and when. I later found out it was all true. Mayer had heard me sing "Poor Butterfly" on radio, which was a big number for me at the time. And he'd heard about me, too, coincidentally, from Irene Coleman's friend. The combination had been enough for him to get in touch with me, via Nat Goldstone.

I knew it was real when somebody from United Air Lines called me, a little while later. They had been instructed by MGM in Los Angeles to arrange transportation for me the next day from San Francisco to Los Angeles. Everything would be done to facilitate the trip. It felt good, getting that first taste of Class A treatment. It's enough to spoil a guy for reality.

The next day, I flew down. It was a flight to Burbank, which was the terminus then for most West Coast flights. Nat Goldstone met me. It was the beginning of a long and happy association between us. He took one look at me and laughed.

"That hair style of yours," he said, "may be OK when you're leading a band. But L.B. would have a stroke. Before we see him, we have to make a few changes."

We went directly from the airport to Westmores'—they were the famous family of make-up men and hair stylists—and they gave me a haircut, with Nat overseeing every snip. He wanted me to have the All-American-boy-next-door look; that was what Louis B. Mayer wanted on everyone.

My clothes didn't fit that image, either. I dressed then the way most musicians dressed. It was pretty wild for the boy-next-door, no matter what door he was next to. Nat took me to the wardrobe department, where they gave me a conservative suit, conservative shoes, conservative shirt and conservative tie.

Now I was ready to meet the great man. After all that, the confrontation was something of a let-down. We just shook hands, he glanced at me for one very brief second, said, "Is he ready?" and that was the end of it. I was ready, so there was nothing more to be said.

I found out, as they hustled me from Mayer's office to a soundstage, that I was being tested for a role opposite Joan Crawford. I forget the name of the film—I didn't get the part, so I guess I let the name slip out of my head. I do remember the test, however. Who wouldn't remember his first Hollywood screen test? That's daydream-come-true time. Nobody could ever forget a moment like that.

Irene Hervey, who was pretty important as an actress then and later became the mother of the fantastic Jack Jones, was delegated to appear opposite me in the test. I was a rookie, scared to death. She was very kind to me, tried to calm my jangling nerves, gave me a few pointers. I had to sing, of course, and the song chosen was "Every Day I Think of You." The whole test was me singing that song to Irene, and then kissing her. I got through the song part OK—after all, that was my business—but I botched up the kiss. I'd never kissed professionally before. I kissed her too late or too early, I forget which. So the director worked out a system. He had them tie a string to my leg, and when it was the opportune moment to do my kissing, he'd pull the string and I'd present lips. The next pull on the string meant stop already.

So the test was made. I responded on cue to the tugs of the string, did my song and my kiss, and went home. I hung around a day or two—Nat had arranged a room for me at the Hollywood Athletic Club—and then got the news that they decided not to use me. Some guy named Gene Raymond got the part I'd tested for. OK. If you have to lose out, might as well lose out to the best. Nat Goldstone drove me to the airport. I remember the date—it was May 15, 1935. The reason I can remember the date, but not the picture I was testing for, is because we made a stop on the way from the Hollywood Athletic Club to the airport. Nat's wife, Bernice, had just given birth to a son, Eddie Goldstone, and his birthday is still clear to me. We stopped off at Cedars of Lebanon Hospital so Nat could meet his son.

As we parted at the airport, Nat Goldstone told me not to be down-hearted. He said he thought I still had film potential, and he would see what he could do for me. I may have flunked the MGM test, but I passed my exam with Nat, and he became my agent and remained that for thirty years —without a written contract.

So it was back to San Francisco, back to the same old stand—the bandstand. It was kind of a letdown. I'd gone down to Los Angeles with such high hopes, and came back feeling pretty blue. All the guys in the band tried to cheer me up, told me that there would be another shot at it. They helped. But not much.

As it turned out, my depression lasted only about three weeks. Nat Goldstone called to tell me he'd arranged another crack at Hollywood for me. This time, it was better than a test, it was a firm deal. The studio was RKO. Nat had shown them the MGM test, and they had liked it. They were making me a genuine offer, he said—$135 a week. That may sound like peanuts and I guess, compared to what the big stars were making then, it was. Still, it was a start.

So it was back down the coast to Los Angeles again. But I wasn't about to burn my musical bridges behind me—not yet. I wanted to have some-thing to fall back on in case the RKO deal turned sour for any reason. I called Tom Gerun and explained the situation. And he agreed to come back and take over the band again for a while, just in case I fell on my face in Hollywood. He said he'd run the band until I decided one way or the other. If it was OK for me at RKO, then he'd get rid of the band. If things didn't work out, I could come back to the band. I felt good about that. I wasn't putting all my eggs in one basket, even though the basket looked pretty solid.

It wasn't much of a rise in my standard of living. I'd been getting about $120 a week, with my band, and this was only fifteen dollars a week more. But the potential was so much greater that I didn't argue. I was pretty cocksure in those days, and I figured in a year or so I'd be a big star, making thousands a week. I went back to the Hollywood Athletic Club. Lots of actors lived there, then; I got to know some of my neighbors at the Club, men like Duke Wayne, John Ford and Ward Bond.

My second invasion of Hollywood was a little more successful than my first—but not much. First I was given a couple of small parts and songs in

56

a couple of two-reel shorts. I didn't mind. I knew that a lot of stars had gotten their breaks in shorts. Two-reelers were a Hollywood staple then, and they were a respected first step up the ladder. So I did them, waiting for the second step. It came, but somebody pulled the ladder out from under me.

Producer Pandro Berman asked for me, after seeing one of those two-reelers, to do a big part in a big picture. It was a lavish (for those days) Fred Astaire musical called *Follow the Fleet,* with Harriet Hilliard and Randolph Scott. There was even a big song for me to sing—"Let's Face the Music and Dance." For a few fast days, I was on top of the world. Doing that number in that picture would surely establish me as a movie comer. But it never happened. I think the thing was that Fred Astaire, or, more probably, some of his advisors, felt he should do all the songs in the picture. All I know is that director Mark Sandrich took me aside on the set one day and said that I wasn't going to sing "Let's Face the Music and Dance," that Fred was going to sing it himself. They had to rewrite the script so it would make sense for him to sing it. I was still in the picture, however, Sandrich said.

OK. So there wasn't a big song. At least I was still there, and maybe I'd make my impact as an actor, not a singer. Then I could always sing later. But, when the script was rewritten, my part got chopped to ribbons. If you see it now on the Late Late Late Late Show, you'll see. I'm there all right —but I have only one line. That was all there was left of my big break, of my second crack at Hollywood.

Even though I was finished at RKO, I didn't go back to the band. That part of my life was over. I knew now that I could do more, that leading a band had been great fun but I had outgrown it. I was working regularly on the big radio shows—and that gave me more than enough to live on. And I wanted to stay in Hollywood, wanted to be a part of the grand and glorious world of movies and movie-makers. So I turned my back on the past.

There was one positive change in my life which I owe to my brief stopover at RKO—my new name. That came about when I made a picture there that I didn't make. It confused me, too. I was supposed to play John Carroll's brother, but I found out that the character I was supposed to play had been killed before the picture started. All I was was a picture on the piano. I spent a day in the studio photo gallery, getting my picture taken so it could sit on the piano. That was the extent of my participation in that picture, whose name, happily, I've forgotten.

But, still, my name presented a problem to them for that picture. Besides Carroll, the cast contained Chester Morris and Wayne Morris.

And then I came along and my name was Al Morris. That was one Morris too many. They told me they were going to change my name and, since I was then under contract to them, I had no say in the matter.

Perry Leiber was then the studio's publicity chief. One of his duties was to arrange for bodies to be present at big affairs, to hype whatever picture they were pushing at the moment. He had me go to an opening at the Biltmore, and set Anne Shirley as my date for the evening. So I was a good boy, and showed up on schedule. Afterward, I took Anne to the Cocoanut Grove, where Freddie Martin was playing. I was still Al Morris that night—but it was Al Morris' last night to howl.

The next day, the studio brass called me in. The big problem was what they were going to call me.

"I kind of like Martin," I said, because the name Freddie Martin was still vivid in my mind.

That seemed to be all right with them. Now the problem was—should it be Martin Somebody or Somebody Martin? They played around with a few combinations for a while, without hitting on anything that pleased either them or me. Then I remembered the name Tony, from some recent magazine story I'd read. The character was rich and stylish, and I sort of liked that image. Tony seemed to me to be a name that conjured up that rich, stylish picture.

"How about Tony Martin?" I said.

They tried it on their lips for a while and they liked it, and that's how I was reborn as Tony Martin.

The first thing I did, when I had my new name, was call my mother. "Hello, Mom?"

"Hello, Alvin!" she said.

"Mom, I'm not Alvin any more. I'm Tony."

"Tony is a horse!" my mother said, and hung up.

I don't think she ever really liked the name Tony Martin. She called me Alvin until the day she died. But Tony Martin became my legal name, when I had it changed legally in the Superior Court in 1936. For a while, when I was at Fox, Darryl Zanuck had me use the name Anthony Martin, but that never did sound right. I liked Tony Martin from the start, and I've always been happy that I made the change.

My third crack at Hollywood films came when Darryl Zanuck either heard me or saw me, and had me come in. We talked for a while and he signed me to a contract, for $140 a week, plus acting lessons. Two other actors signed contracts with Fox that same day—young men named Tyrone Power and Don Ameche. It turned out to be one of Zanuck's better days.

They immediately put me to work. Producer Sol Wurtzel stuck me in a B-picture, one of the Jones Family series. At Fox, that was the training ground, those B-pictures, that's where they saw what they had.

Then they asked me if I could fight. There was a prize fight film they were putting together, and could I handle myself in the ring? I'd never even had a pair of boxing gloves on in my life. But, of course, I said I was a helluva fighter. Why not? A part was a part, and I had a few weeks before the picture started. That was plenty of time to learn how to be a boxer. Somebody told me about Jackie Fields, Jr., who had been a world welterweight champ, and I went to him and he gave me a crash course in fighting. I learned my lesson well. I did the movie, and the big fight scene had me in the ring with an actor named Kane Richmond. We sparred, and then I threw a left—and hit Richmond in the arm so hard I broke several blood vessels.

That was a B-picture, too. So were my next few. I worked in one with Joe E. Lewis and Joan Davis. It was the only film Joe E. Lewis ever made. It almost put us all out of business, it was so rotten.

Then came what, at the time, looked like my big break. This was going to do it for me, and make Tony Martin a household name. They called me for a major part in *Poor Little Rich Girl*, with Shirley Temple and Alice Faye. I was living at the Montecito Apartments then, in a six-by-eight cell, but it was a good address. Lou Schreiber, the studio's casting director, called me to come in for the part. I had heard about the picture and knew there was a great song in it, an original Gordon and Revel song called "When I'm with You." I figured I was going to sing it. But it turned out I didn't.

Another singer had already done it. But then Darryl Zanuck decided this fellow didn't look the way they wanted him to look. They liked his voice all right, but his appearance wasn't what they wanted. So I was supposed to mouth the words to the song this other singer had already recorded. And here I was, a singer by trade. So I showed up, and opened and closed my mouth while this other fellow's voice was piped over the recording system. What a thrill that was!

Then came the premiere, at Grauman's Chinese Theater. Everybody was there. It was a major Fox film, and that was a big event back then. People stopped me in the lobby—"Hey, Tony, you were great, what a voice, great set of pipes"—all that. Doc Martin, Louella Parsons' husband, grabbed me, saying I had to come with them to a party later at the Trocadero. Everybody was rushing up to me, shaking my hand, saying nice things. I was in—but I felt ashamed because I knew that wasn't my voice they were praising. And, later, the reviews came out and they compared me to Gable and Crosby and said I had a big future as a movie singer. That made me feel even worse.

So I called this other singer.

"On account of you," I said, "I'm a star."

He was very nice about it. He said it was one of those things, and he didn't begrudge me the attention coming my way on the strength of his singing.

"Look," he said, "we do what we can. If I could do Rin Tin Tin's part, I'd grab it."

He wished me luck. I wished him luck. I don't think I ever heard of him again.

The excitement of the *Poor Little Rich Girl* opening didn't last long. I quickly learned that all that hoopla in the lobby afterward, all those gushing words—none of it meant much. Hollywood is a place where people are quick to say things, but slow to do things.

Alice Faye was in *Poor Little Rich Girl*, but I didn't meet her then. I had no scenes with her in the film. I had, of course, seen her around the lot, and liked what I'd seen. And I'd met her at some of the parties we'd all gone to. She seemed to me certainly a stunning creature, and full of vivacity. But, at that point in our respective careers, she was a major star and I was small potatoes, so there was no point in even giving her a second look. That was way out of my league. I was dating plenty, anyhow. Whenever Frances Langford came to town, we'd see each other. And there were other girls—girls who were actresses, girls who were in the wardrobe department, girls who were just girls. At that point, I was just looking for fun, not for names to date, not for wife material. And I had plenty of fun.

Anyhow, there wasn't much I could do on my salary. The studio was paying me relatively little. I was making some more through recordings and radio, but still, compared to other Hollywood people I hobnobbed with, I was decidedly in the lower income brackets. And I was still sending a lot of what I made home to my mother and dad. I didn't even own a car then. I rented a Packard 120, and that set me back a large chunk of my weekly earnings. But I had to have something to fool around in, and that was it.

My folks were, of course, proud of my progress. I had become something of a celebrity in Oakland, and some reporters came over to the house to interview my mother and ask her what she thought about my career. I laugh now when I look at what she told them:

"I am proud and glad," she is quoted as having said, "with one provision—if anybody tries to cast my Tony for a gangster movie, I'll put my foot down and I'll put it down hard. I won't have him be a criminal, even on screen."

That was my mother talking, all right. She never minced a word in her life. I had to play a few crooked parts later, but I guess she forgot what she'd told those reporters, because I never heard a word from her about it. As far as I know, her foot stayed up.

Pretty soon, I was doing OK at Fox. I actually got to sing on screen in *Sing, Baby, Sing.* Fox wanted to put Tyrone Power in a role in the picture, but Sidney Lanfield, the director, didn't think much of Power. "Where the hell does Zanuck find these bums?" Lanfield said, and turned Power down. Ty and I were friends, so I commiserated with him and he congratulated me. We knew that it all evened out. That was the way it was in Hollywood then. A bad break one day, a good break the next. Now it was my turn. Power was out and they gave his part to Michael Whelan. Whelan was OK, but Power became a legend.

Alice Faye was in *Sing, Baby, Sing,* and so were the Ritz Brothers, who became lifelong friends of mine, and Patsy Kelly and Adolphe Menjou and Gregory Ratoff. The song they gave me to sing was called "When Did You Leave Heaven?" The scene called for me to sing it at an audition, and I was supposed to be dressed in absolutely dreadful clothes. I wore the worst stuff I had, but it still wasn't bad enough. They wanted something so flashy as to be laughable. They sent me down to the wardrobe department and dredged up a wild and gruesome outfit—a plaid suit with extra wide shoulders and lapels, awful shirt and tie. As I put everything on, I noticed the labels in each garment; everything had originally been made for a famous actor. The suit I was wearing said "Jack Oakie" on the label, the shirt said "Maurice Chevalier," and the shoes said "Ricardo Cortez."

(Incidentally, it was Cortez who gave me the best advice about being a Hollywood actor I ever got from anybody. He once told me that I'd be "up and down like a yo-yo, so you'd better find some good friends and keep them.")

Anyhow, when I came back out on the stage I looked awful—which was just what they wanted. Alice came over and said, "Now you look better," and winked at me.

"Yeah," I said, "and if I could only find Valentino's tie, I'd be in business."

Everybody laughed, except Lanfield. He didn't have much of a sense of humor. He was one of those directors who carried a crop.

It was my first real part in a real movie. I was nervous. My usual self-confidence left me for a time. Then Alice came over and talked to me, told me that it was all a game everybody was playing. She put me at ease, and I was OK after that. She and I became good friends, but, at that point, that's all we were. Later, that would change.

Along about that time, another big break came my way. Nat Goldstone called me one day and he had some good news for me. Jack Benny's regular singer, Frank Parker, was sick. Jack was doing a tour, playing in Los Angeles at the Paramount and then going to the Pantages in San Francisco. It would be for three weeks. Would I be interested in filling in for Parker for those three weeks? You're damn right I was interested.

It was a great three weeks—until I got fired. What was especially gratifying was coming home to the Bay area, in front of my home town family and friends, in such fast company. It was almost like retribution—the kid who didn't get invited to the parties was now a big-timer, working on the same stage with Jack Benny. I must admit that made me feel great.

It was fun, working with that group. Mary Livingstone, Jack's wife, was especially good to me. She's a wonderful lady, always ready to help a newcomer along. She helped me a great deal. In fact, our rapport became too good.

The three of us—Jack, Mary and I—had one skit in the show. And we began breaking up when we did it. Jack called it "tea-kettling," when you try to suppress a laugh and you start going *tss-tss-tss*. It got so whenever Mary and I would look at each other, during that skit, we'd go into that tea-kettling business. And the more Jack reprimanded us, the worse we got.

"Now cut that out," Jack would say, and you know how Jack said it.

That's all Mary and I would need to hear. Off we'd go, with more outbreaks of laughter.

For almost the whole three weeks, that went on. And then it came the night before we were to close. Jack called me into his dressing room.

"Look, Tony," he said, "I want to thank you for stepping in like you did. You were great, just great. But this business of you and Mary tea-kettling in that skit has got to stop. Look, we're closing tomorrow. Now either Mary goes or you go—and I can't fire her, because I'm married to her. So you're fired—after tomorrow."

Since we were closing the next day, it wasn't a real firing, of course. But he meant it, and I can't say that I blame him. Jack was always good to me, from then on, and he called his friend George Burns and told him about me, and that's how I became a regular on the Burns and Allen Show.

The Burns and Allen Show rehearsed at a hotel across Vine Street from the Brown Derby, and that's where we'd eat lunch. When it came time to pay, George would always pick up the check—and then find that he had nothing smaller than a $100 bill. So I'd pay.

I didn't mind. It was worth it, just being with them, being part of their circle. They took me to New York with them, and it was my first visit to the Big Apple. We had three radio shows in New York, and that was exciting. I was feeling my oats and wanted to make a big impression on everybody. One night, I took them all out, Burns and Allen and Henry

King, the bandleader, and some others. I spent $210 that night, and that was about all I was making for a week. So I was broke. Gracie, bless her heart, loaned me $10 here and there to get through the week. I don't think George knew about that.

I took an heiress to the Stork Club, still in my Tony-the-big-shot period. Eddy Duchin was at a nearby table, and I sent him a bottle of champagne. George and Gracie were along and, again, I picked up the check. But I found I was a little short. I whispered to Gracie, could she slip me some money? She edged a $20 bill into my hand, and I was able to pay the check.

Gracie was a love, but she wasn't inherently funny. Week after week, she'd say to me, after the show, "I didn't know that line was funny." But, the way she had said it, it had been.

I was gradually widening my circle of friends. I now had the Ritz Brothers and the Bennys and George and Gracie and lots of others. People were always good to me, ordinarily. Hollywood people are kinder and more generous than they are given credit for being. I remember when I first came to Hollywood, and was staying in a tiny room at the Hollywood Athletic Club. Thanksgiving came and I had no place to go. Johnny Weissmuller —Tarzan—used to hang out at the Hollywood Athletic Club in those days.

"Hey, kid," he said, "what are you doing for Thanksgiving?"

"I don't have any plans, Johnny," I replied.

"Well, Lupe is making dinner. She wants you and Runyon and all the guys to come to dinner."

So we did—me and Damon Runyon, Jr., then a struggling writer, and whoever else in the place was at loose ends for the holiday. Lupe was Johnny's wife, Lupe Velez. That's the way it was, then; people were good to each other.

One of the places we'd hang out, especially those of us at Fox, was a restaurant called Sugie's Tropics. It's still there, but now it's called the Luau. A guy named Harry Sugarman ran it, and he was a good host and ran a good restaurant. We'd go there for Chinese food and those exotic rum drinks. I'd go there with Ty Power or Don Ameche or the Ritz Brothers. And, most of the time, I'd see Alice Faye there. She was usually with her brother, Bill.

I got to know her during those evenings at Sugie's Tropics. She was easy to know, easy to like. I think that's where I fell in love with her, and I think Ty Power fell in love with her about the same time I did. So, since we were all chums, the three of us began going out together. I suppose he and I knew we had become rivals for the same girl, but it didn't affect our friendship. I always envied him, in a way, because I thought that there was

63

a man who had everything—so handsome, in addition to being charming and witty and decent and a fine actor and a great athlete. And, on top of everything else, a real fine man.

So we competed for Alice. She was worth competing for. There's no need to describe her physical attributes here; anybody who's ever seen her knows what she looked like. But that was only half of her, or maybe even less than that. She was one of the queens of Hollywood, at that time. She was making, I guess, around $5,000 a week. It hadn't affected her. She was a real girl, not one of these paint-and-powder dolls that were all over Hollywood then. Alice Faye was a person.

I finally got lucky—Ty Power left town. He had to go to Cincinnati to do a play with Katherine Cornell. That left the field clear for me, and I went after Alice with everything I had. Because of who she was, we were invited everywhere. Parties. Openings. Screenings. We went together to affairs at Errol Flynn's house, at Cesar Romero's house, at Joan Crawford's house. We were part of the scene, and in those days that was some scene. Hollywood was a small town that was the envy of all the big towns. All the most beautiful and talented people in the world were in Hollywood, or so it seemed to us. And we were not alone in that opinion; the press of the world concentrated on our doings. The fact that Alice Faye and Tony Martin were seeing each other was news in every city in the entire world.

We couldn't care less about what the world thought. At least, I couldn't and I'm pretty sure Alice felt the same way. I just knew that I loved being with this girl, and I'd never felt quite the same way before. I had enjoyed Frances Langford's company and worshiped Irene Coleman from afar, but this was different. This was what I always figured true love would be like. I was desolate when we were apart, and only lived for those hours when we could be together. Isn't that what love is all about?

We got along. I danced well and she loved to dance. I treated her with respect and she demanded that. I think maybe she was tired of those swinging rich guys she'd been seeing, and felt more at home with me. I was simple to talk to, easy to understand. I had no pretenses—I wasn't rich enough or eccentric enough to have any.

She was a sex symbol. She didn't act like one. The world knew her as the blonde beauty. I knew her as a laughing girl who insisted on being home and in bed by ten if she had an early call the next morning. Our dates were generally simple affairs—a couple of drinks, dinner, maybe a movie, a kiss at the door. That was it. I was doing the Burns and Allen Show then, and she'd often come down when I did the show and visit me at the studio. She and Gracie liked each other. After the show, the four of us—George, Gracie, Alice, me—would go out to dinner.

It got to be a habit, and I liked it. So, naturally, I began thinking in terms of marriage. Looking back on it now, I don't know why I hesitated, but I did. I guess it was a couple of things. There was the idea of intermarriage. Alice was an Episcopalian. Intellectually, that didn't make any difference to me and I knew, from our talks, that the fact that I was Jewish didn't make any difference to her. Still, all that crap that had been hammered into my head as a boy—*shikseh!*—was hard for me to overcome. Intellectually it was one thing. But traditionally and emotionally it was something entirely different. I hesitated, too, because of the difference in our stature. She was a $5,000-a-week star—a genuine big star. And I was, comparatively, nobody. I'd just gotten a raise and was up to $185 a week, which was peanuts. I made another $150 from Burns and Allen. Still, it was nothing next to what she made.

I tried to overcome the first source of my hesitation, the religious thing. I went to George Burns. Burns had married Gracie, a Catholic.

"George, I'm in love with Alice," I said.

"No kidding?"

"I'm serious. I really love that girl."

"Well, then, marry her."

"But she's not Jewish."

"What is she?"

"I think she's Episcopalian."

He gave me a long look, and toyed with his cigar for a moment.

"The big question, Tony," he said, "is whether or not you love her."

"Yes, I love her. Very much."

"Do you light up whenever you think about her?"

"Yes."

"Do you only live for those moments when you can be with her?"

"Yes."

"Well, then, there's only one thing for you to do."

"What's that?"

"Become an Episcopalian and marry her."

So I guess that conversation helped me resolve my doubts about the difference in religion. And the question of the relative status of our income I just sort of shunted into the back of my mind.

The biggest issue, however, was my mother. Let's face it, I hadn't yet cut through those powerful apron strings. That's the truth, hard as it is for me to admit it, even today.

I wanted to marry this girl, but I was afraid of what my mother would say. And, what's worse, I couldn't think of getting married without her approval and blessing. So I procrastinated, and pretty soon Alice recognized what was happening—or, rather, what was not happening.

I knew I loved her. But I had this thing in my head about my mother. I wouldn't dare get married without going through the whole business of checking it out with her.

That cooled it with Alice. She began being hard to reach on the phone. Then I heard she was dating George Brent, who was pretty stiff competition. I got panicky. What if I lost her?

So I screwed up my courage and called my mother in Oakland.

"Mom," I said, "I'm in love and I'm going to get married."

She wanted to know all the details, of course, and I told her it was Alice Faye and I went into rhapsodies in describing her charms and her attributes and what she meant to me.

"Sounds like a lovely person," she said. "You ask Grandma, if she says it's all right, it's all right. I'll put her on."

So I had to speak to my grandmother. She was, as I have said, the boss of the family.

"I'm really in love with her, Grandma," I said, summing it all up.

"You're a very lucky young man," she said. "You see, Alvin, I was a picture bride from the old country and I didn't fall in love until I'd been married for five years. Are you sure this is love, this thing you feel for this girl?"

I explained it all again.

"I'll tell you what, Alvin," she said. "When you open the door to your house, there's only going to be two people there—you and the woman inside. If you love this girl and want her to be the woman inside your house, marry her."

So I had her blessing. Now what was I supposed to do, go back to Alice and say, "My mother and my grandmother say it's OK for me to marry you?" Wouldn't I look like the prize idiot! But I had to do something. It had gotten to the point where Alice wouldn't even see me any more.

I'd rented a little house on Swall Drive, maybe in the hope that it would be our honeymoon cottage. And I'd hired a Filipino house boy, Marcella. It was a bad time for me. Alice wasn't talking to me. I'd literally cry and Marcella would try to entertain me—he'd show me some pitiful little magic tricks he'd learned to try to take my mind off my problems. It didn't help much. And neither did reading the gossip columnists who were reporting how Alice Faye and George Brent were a big item these nights. I knew I'd lost a lot of points with Alice by my shilly-shallying about my mother, and it would take a lot of action to get back to where I was before.

So I started out, stalking her again. Maybe stalking isn't exactly the right word, although it felt to me as though I was in some kind of jungle.

Everybody was against me. All her friends and her family, with one or two exceptions, kept telling her to stay away from me. The gist of their objections was that a girl like Alice, who was at the top of the heap, could do a helluva lot better than Tony Martin, who was pretty near the bottom.

But, undaunted, I waged my campaign to win her. I had a couple of allies. Her brother Charley was on my side. Her other brother, Bill, was against me, but Charley was a big help. And her best girlfriend, Betty King, who was her stand-in and who later married Walter Scharf, was on my side, too. Alice and Betty had come up together, from the days when they danced together in a New York restaurant. For some reason, Betty liked me and she kept telling Alice that I was a good guy. But the rest of her friends bad-mouthed me, and for a while it looked as if they were winning. I couldn't get near her.

Finally, I prevailed on her brother Charley to arrange it so Alice would be at Sugie's Tropics one night. And I was there, too. And that's how we got together again.

"Alice," I said, "I love you. I really do. And I want to pick up where we left off."

She was rather surprised at my sudden decision. No matter what happened in my relationship with Alice Faye, there is one sure thing, and I'll always be grateful to her for that one sure thing. And that is that she made me grow up. I would never again ask anybody for permission about what to do. My own judgment would be my guide forevermore.

We began going out again. It was just like it had been, only more so. Now I was in command of myself; I had no more qualms about anything, about religion, about the relative differences in our place in the Hollywood scheme of things. I knew I loved this girl, and I knew she loved me, and the only thing that remained was to set the time and place and get married.

One evening, it all happened.

"Let's get married," I said.

And she said, as she smiled as only she could, "I've waited a long time to hear you say that. I'm ready." We laughed together.

So I called Paul Mantz and chartered a plane, and made the arrangements. It was September 5. We flew to Yuma, Arizona, and Alice became Mrs. Tony Martin. Ty Power wired me: "I'm glad one of us got her."

We went on our honeymoon, to Hawaii, and stayed at the Royal Hawaiian, on Waikiki. In those days, before World War II, Waikiki was a lovely, underpopulated beach, an ideal spot for a honeymoon. Today, it's like Coney Island with palm trees, but then it was magnificent. We met people—everybody wanted to meet Alice, of course—and had a wonderful time. Duke Kahanamoku, the famous Hawaiian athlete and entertainer, was hospitable to us, and Duke and I became friends for life. We danced, we ate, we swam, we lay on the beach. And we made love. It was a honeymoon to remember.

Then it was back to Hollywood, back to work, back to reality. And back, primarily, to that period in any marriage of getting acquainted with the merchandise. When you first marry and have your honeymoon, you're still governed by passion and ruled by love. Afterward, though, you have to get to know your partner, the good things, the bad things. There are bound to be surprises. Sometimes, they can be unpleasant.

I can't speak for Alice, but I can tell you about my reactions to learning who the real Alice Faye was. I came to like her, as well as love her. She wasn't a very complex person. She was open and honest and, basically, a simple girl. She wanted a nice life without any problems. She didn't have grandiose ambitions—she'd already made it—and she didn't have expensive tastes. She liked a few luxurious things—orchids, good clothes, hats particularly—but in most things she preferred the ordinary to the exotic.

I knew a lot about her before we were married, of course. I knew she wasn't a flirtatious person, that she was a one-man woman. I knew she spoke her mind, and if something was bothering her, she wouldn't brood about it, but she'd say it and say it loud and clear. And her language could be pretty interesting, too. She had told off the studio bosses—Zanuck, Schenck, that crowd—and she had told off guys on the street who made passes at her. She used the same language to both, and everybody understood what she had to say. There was a facade of toughness, but underneath she was kind and generous and a very good person.

She stood up for me, too. Once, when we were shooting *Sally, Irene and Mary,* soon after we were married, director Lew Seiler made a snide remark to me.

"It's too bad you can't sing your part," he said.

Alice turned to him, and said, "It's too bad you can't direct."

I really didn't need anybody to fight my battles, but it felt good realizing I had somebody like Alice on my side.

It was a good time for us, at first. For one thing, we were together during what was probably the best time for America. The Depression was over, the coming war was only a vague shadow on the horizon. There didn't seem to be any problems for America, and the two of us were sitting on top of the world, too. Alice Faye was at the pinnacle of success, a glowing star in a land where glowing stars were adored. I was at the threshold of similar success, and things began going pretty well for me, too. The night club circuit beckoned; they wanted me and were willing to pay good money

68

to get me. More and more, I had to go out of town to fill these lucrative engagements.

But, always, I would rush home to Alice as fast as I could. I wasn't jealous of her, although I knew other men were flocking around her. Why not? She was beautiful, famous, popular. It was understandable. It would have been odd were it not so.

Still, it was sometimes annoying. The phone would ring and I'd answer, and there would be a man's voice, asking to speak to my wife.

"Sorry," I'd say. "She's out."

"Well, tell her Johnny Smith called," or whatever his name was. Johnny Smith wouldn't have the decency to realize he had been talking to Alice Faye's husband, or the courtesy to ask if he was talking to me. No, it was just as though I didn't exist. Still, as I say, it rolled off my back. It was one of those things that happen when a guy marries a movie sex symbol, and I had to learn to live with it.

Much of our life together revolved around work, hers and mine. Very often, when she was shooting, she would leave for work early in the morning and, as she left, she'd say, "Tony, why don't you invite some friends over tonight?" So I'd invite some pals—the Ritz Brothers, Sid Tomack, the Reese Brothers, the gang—and send out for some deli. Then she'd come home, after shooting and staying to see the rushes. If she'd liked what she'd seen, she'd be in a good mood and come in and kibbitz with my pals. But if the rushes hadn't pleased her, she wouldn't even say hello. She'd come in, walk right through and on upstairs and go to bed. That was how much her life was governed by her career.

I had to learn to live with that. I was married to a star, with a capital S, and that went with the territory. But it was difficult to adjust to the kind of marriage I found myself half of. My only other marital experience had been as an observer to my folks' life together, and that was so different. I guess I had halfway expected Alice and me to have a relationship like my mother's and father's, and, of course, it couldn't be. My wife was one of the great glamour girls of the moment, and she couldn't be just Mrs. Tony Martin. She had her own identity, and I tried to adjust to that situation.

For a while, it worked. We both tried hard. And I have to give Alice a lot of credit, because she really did her best to make it work. One of the things we both did was to try to make a go of it with our respective in-laws. I think my folks went more than halfway, in embracing her as a member of our family.

Alice said she wanted to meet my grandparents, because I had spoken of them so much and so lovingly. So, one day, we made the trek north, to

69

Oakland, and visited them. She brought a present for them, a beautiful Crosley radio that cost her around $1,200—the best they made, in the finest cabinet. I had told her what a big part radio played in their lives. She gave them the radio and they adored it, and they adored her.

My grandmother took me by the hand, led me into the kitchen and gave me a big hug.

"Alvin," she said, "your wife is very nice. I don't blame you an inch."

On the other hand, Alice's mother was never too choked up with me. Curiously, her mother and mine got along fine and became good friends and used to call each other and talk about "the kids," but Alice's mother never did warm up to me. I guess it was part her feeling that Alice could have had anybody, and chose somebody who wasn't in her star category.

We had fun together, despite our problems. We were in each other's corner, and that's what marriage is all about, I think. When I had problems, she went to bat for me. She didn't have too many problems, herself, but there were a few.

One night, I picked her up at the studio—Fox—as I did when I wasn't working and had the time. As she got in the car, she was crying. I asked her what the trouble was.

"That miserable so-and-so, Zanuck," she said. "He didn't like the dailies and said I was no good."

I managed to calm her down. Then I wondered what I should do about it. Should I go busting into his office and tell him off? Alice said no, I'd only get in big trouble and it could hurt me and my career. So I didn't do anything, and that diminished me in my own eyes—maybe in her eyes, too.

We were invited, once, to a big ball at the White House, and met Franklin D. Roosevelt. He liked us both, he said. He was the consummate politician. As I was introduced to him, he said how much he liked my latest record, and named it. He had been well briefed, and remembered every detail.

While I was at the White House, I was invited to a very special occasion—a White House poker game. F.D.R. and some of his cronies— Sam Rosenman, Alben Barkley and Bernard Baruch are ones I remember —played regularly and I kibbitzed. F.D.R. smoked like a chimney. And those important men, who guided the destiny of our country, used language from one of today's X-rated movies. I like to play poker, too, and I asked if I could sit in.

"Sorry, no outsiders," they told me.

One Christmas, Alice and I went to Armonk, New York, because I'd been mentioned as a replacement for Lanny Ross on his radio show, *Show Boat*, and he wanted to meet me. He was having a pheasant hunt and asked if I could handle a shot-gun. I said sure, even though I'd never had one in my hands. He was very gracious, and said, "OK, Tony, take the first pheasant." So I waited until the first bird took to the air, and I raised my shot-gun and fired.

I knocked Lanny's hat off.

So there were wonderful experiences, which Alice and I shared. When we were together, everything was fine. Alice was a girl who liked the simple life. She was very happy, going out and getting a cheeseburger for dinner. Or, maybe, some Chinese food a couple of times a week. Her eating habits were very simple, not what you'd expect of a star. She was just an ordinary girl, who happened to be blessed with stardom. I remember lots of times I'd have lunch with a good friend, director Norman Taurog, and we'd go to a delicatessen over on Western Avenue. And I'd always bring Alice a kosher pickle, and she loved it.

We had our own circle of friends, and we had a good life as long as we stayed with them. While we were married, she was loaned out by Fox to Universal to make a picture called *You're a Sweetheart*, with Dave Butler directing. Dave and his wife, Elsie, were both heavy into thoroughbred horse-racing. Around that time, he bought two yearlings and they were both fillies. He said to Alice that he was going to name one after her.

"But not the best one," he said. "I'm sure you understand, but I have to name the best one after my wife."

So he named the more promising of the two fillies Elsie B. and the other one he called Alice Faye. Well, Alice Faye turned out to be a champ and won a couple of big races at Santa Anita, while poor Elsie B. was never heard from again. We enjoyed that whole experience, and it was fun rooting for Alice Faye to win at the track.

Those were the good times. There were times that weren't so good. The fact that Alice's male admirers kept admiring her, as though I didn't exist, began to get to me. Joe Schenck, at the studio, was one of that crowd. He kept sending her flowers. It was as though he had decided not to recognize the marriage. The flowers kept coming. Alice laughed about it. I didn't.

But I guess the worst thing for me was that old cliché. To many people around town, I was Mr. Alice Faye. Don't forget, she was a big star and I was trying to catch up to her. We were both young and yet she was one of the top stars around. They never let me forget that.

There was one incident that really tore me apart. I took her to the premiere of her film, *In Old Chicago*. We'd gone to other premieres, of course, and Alice was always careful about my feelings. At the post-premiere party, she made a point of making sure that I had a good seat at a good table with the right people. And we'd always have the first dance together. But this night turned out to include one event I've never forgotten. We had seen the movie and were standing in the lobby, and, naturally, the whole world flocked around her heaping praise on her pretty blonde head. So I was off to one side, talking to Benny Oakland, the songwriter, and some of my own friends. Everybody was waiting for the cars to be delivered by the parking boys.

"Mr. Clark Gable's car."

"Mr. Tyrone Power's car."

"Mr. Spencer Tracy's car."

And then it came.

"Miss Alice Faye's car."

So I got in our car with her, but it was like my tail was between my legs. I had never been so humiliated in my life. When we got home, I said, "Alice, I don't think I can make it like this."

She understood. It wasn't her fault, I knew that, and she apologized and said there wasn't anything she could do about it. She knew that I had my pride, that I was suffering. And I think if she could have rectified the situation, she would have. But she was right; there wasn't a damn thing she could do about it.

I knew I had to make it on my own, I had to scratch and claw my way somehow up to her plateau. So I told Nat Goldstone to get me some good bookings back east, where I could be on my own, not Mr. Alice Faye.

I did pretty good. Because of my radio work and the few films I did, I was now able to command a pretty good weekly fee from clubs. I went to the Royal Palms in Miami Beach and made $1,500 a week. I called Alice a couple of times a day. It wasn't the same as seeing her, as touching her, but I had my own ego, and my own pride, and I felt I was becoming successful.

Still, that was another wedge driven between us. She wanted a husband at home, naturally. And I was across the country. I was just a voice on the phone.

I have a feeling some of her "friends" began gossiping about me. These were the people who had tried to persuade her not to marry me in the first place. Now, I am convinced, they were telling her that I was running around in Florida. I'm no saint, and I guess I flirted a little and responded to the flirtations of others. But, on my honor, I didn't have a serious romance while we were apart. I was still in love with Alice and thought she was in love with me. But I know that she was getting the word from some of those so-called friends, mostly men who figured that with me out of the way, they'd have a clearer field. I know who they were, too. The late Sidney Lanfield was taken with her, and never troubled to cover up his feelings. He was constantly bum-rapping me. Joe Schenck, he of the constant barrage of flowers, never cottoned to me, either. And many others played the same tune.

Still, when I called her from Florida, it was all lovey-dovey stuff. I told her how much I missed her, how I'd love to take her in my arms and all that. She responded in kind. She missed me very much, too, she said, and couldn't wait until I was home again and we could be together. We gossiped about what we were each doing and exchanged stories about our lives apart. I never had a clue that anything was seriously wrong. I knew that there were problems—mostly the career clash that kept us apart—but they hardly seemed insurmountable.

I should say, at this point, that there were many people who spread the word that I had married Alice Faye only to give my career a boost. There are always people around ready to accept the worst. These people believed the stories, that I had married Alice for her money, her fame, her reputation, and I was cashing in on all that. It wasn't that way at all. I had married her for love, that's the simple truth.

At the Royal Palms, I shared one huge dressing room with Abe Lyman, the bandleader, and Tony DeMarco, the dancer. And, at that time, Walter Winchell was in town and he'd come over to our dressing room to write his column. That was when Winchell was the king of the gossip columnists and we were flattered to have him there with us.

He'd be there when I called Alice and he eavesdropped shamelessly.

"Give Alice my best," he'd say, and I'd relay his regards.

So this one night, as usual, I called her and we talked and Winchell listened. And he said how nice it was that the two of us were getting along so well. I smiled and said something about how much I loved that girl. It was a very pleasant thing, because her call that night had been especially warm and loving.

The next morning, I got the paper and there was a headline: ALICE FAYE FILES FOR DIVORCE.

I looked at it in utter disbelief. There must be some mistake, that was obvious. How could she file for divorce and not at least tell me? No, somebody goofed. In a few minutes, she'd call me to tell me that somebody had misinterpreted something she said. That was probably what happened. I thought about calling her, but figured it would be better to let her call me.

But she didn't call. Instead, there was a steady stream of calls from reporters, asking me for my comment, and from friends, sympathizing with me. To the former, I could give no comment. How could I, when I was certain the whole thing was a hoax, a phony? And to the latter, I just said it was all news to me. I tried to make light of it, but as the hours wore on, it got harder and harder to do that.

And then Winchell called.

"You're ungrateful," he said.

"What do you mean?"

"After all I've done for you, after all the nice things I've printed about you, that's what I mean."

"But, Walter—."

"Don't give me that crap. Here I was, sitting with you last night, and you pull that phony business of calling Alice and making with the lovey-dovey stuff. And all the time you knew it was all over, and you wouldn't even tell me. Why didn't you give me the scoop?"

"What scoop?"

"About the divorce, you creep. You knew about it, and you wouldn't tell me. All right, if that's the way you want it, that's the way you've got it. You're on my list from now on."

And I was on his list, which was a bad place for anybody in show business in those days. Try as I could, I couldn't convince him that the divorce story was as much a surprise to me as it was to him. He wouldn't even talk to me for several years after that, and he never wrote a kind thing about me during those years, either.

What he failed to realize, of course, was that his anger didn't upset me. I was sitting there, with my heart breaking, and I could care less about Walter Winchell's pique. It became clear, as the hours passed that dreadful morning, that the story was all too true. We had been married about two years. Now it was over.

I am convinced, to this day, that she did not initiate the idea of splitting from me. No, it was the people around her who planted the seed of her discontent.

I learned about newspaper columnists, too. Winchell's behavior taught me. No matter how they may react to you, cater to your wishes, when the chips are down the only thing they're really and truly concerned about is their own story. Winchell didn't care about me, about Alice, about anything except his precious "scoop." Well, I wouldn't be suckered in like that again. From that moment on, I began guarding my own feelings and thoughts, and I recognized gossip columnists for what they were—people to whom a "scoop" is everything.

You know that old cliché about the clown who has to go on, despite his broken heart? Well, that was me that night in Miami Beach. It was no cliché then, it was the real thing. I still had no direct word from Alice, only that newspaper story and all the phone calls from people to confirm its veracity. But I was expected to go on that night, to do my act, to entertain the people and give them an hour or so of escape from their own problems and miseries. Nobody cared how miserable I felt. In fact, because of the story, the place was jammed that night. I guess they all wanted to look at me, to see my wounds, to watch me cry. Well, I went on all right. The show must go on, and all that. I believed that then, so I did my thing, and I poured my heart and soul into my act. They weren't going to see Tony Martin crying. And they didn't. Instead, they saw me at my best, because I think I never sang as well as I did that night at the Royal Palms, the night my heart was broken.

I never had any animosity toward Alice, and she never had any toward me. For my part, as I have said, I knew the whole thing wasn't her doing. I may have been momentarily angry toward her, but that passed. And, as for her, I obviously can't speak for her, but I know down through the years she has always maintained a friendship for me, as I have for her. Anyhow, as has been said so often and so truly, time heals all wounds. And, eventually, what you remember are the good times and the happy moments, and you forget the bad.

Some nine or ten years ago, I was working at the Roosevelt Hotel in New Orleans. I came down the elevator one evening with my conductor, Hal Borne. When we reached the lobby floor, the door opened and there was this girl standing there, waiting for the elevator. I thought I was seeing a ghost. It was Alice Faye, as she was when I had first met her, when she was a beautiful young girl. She recognized me.

"You're Tony Martin, aren't you?" she said.

"Yes, but who—."

"I'm Alicia Harris, Alice's daughter."

It gave me the wierdest feeling, because she was an exact duplicate of her mother. She came to see me several times during the week I played at the hotel.

And there was another funny thing that happened to me, which fits in at this point. Long after the divorce, I was playing in a golf foursome, with Artie Stebbins, Dick Arlen and Phil Harris. Phil married Alice and they have had a long and happy marriage. Anyhow, after we finished the round, we went to the clubhouse for the usual nineteenth hole round of drinks.

As we were about to leave, I said to Phil, "Please give Alice my best."

Phil looked at me for a moment.

"Do you know Alice?" he asked, and then it dawned on him. "Oh, for Chrissake!"

We had played eighteen holes of golf and he had forgotten that we had both been married to the same girl.

The divorce really rocked me at the time. It had come out of the blue, out of darkest left field. I had had no time to prepare myself emotionally or practically for it. So I was very mixed up inside. I didn't understand what had happened to me. I was young, I wasn't sure how to cope with it. Actually, it came at a time when my career was finally falling into place. My salary in clubs had jumped to the $2,000-per-week level, which isn't a bad level at all. My work on radio was increasing, and I found myself flying all over the map. I'd be singing in a club, but would have to commute to New York or Los Angeles every week to do a radio show. And, besides, I was finally making a sizable dent in the recording field, too. So I was going pretty strong on all three burners.

It was my first real taste of honey.

So, just when I should have felt great, I felt awful. And, the next time I got back to Hollywood, I could feel the reaction of people. Hollywood, let's face it, is a small town. It's like living in a tiny midwest town where everybody knows everybody else, and everybody else's business. I've always said that Hollywood has a little Chinese wall around it. Inside the wall, it's a world of people who know everybody else and all the gossip about everybody. And do they love to gossip! I'm convinced that Hollywood stars and starlets gossip more than anybody else. They claim they hate gossip about themselves, but they do it all the time. And you have to be very careful about Hollywood gossip. It has a way of growing, like crab grass, until ultimately it can choke out the truth.

It gets ridiculous sometimes. Take, for example, Hollywood parties. There's always a problem of who talks to whom—or, more important, who doesn't talk to whom. And who used to be married to whom. So you wind up with a lot of people who aren't talking to each other. That's just like it is in a small town, isn't it? When your potential guest list is small, you can't help but invite some people who don't get along.

It happened to me, after Alice. I came back to Hollywood for a while. Some people sort of shunted me aside, figuring that as Alice's ex, I was yesterday's news. But more of my friends were behind me, and I went to the parties and there were the behind-the-hand whispers, "Isn't that Tony Martin? And didn't he used to be Mr. Alice Faye? And what do you suppose will happen to him now? And I wonder how much he took her for?" And all that crapola.

The divorce, for a long time, was uppermost in my mind. I tried to see Alice, tried to talk to her. I asked people to intervene for me with her —Harry Sugarman, Ty Power, some others. Nothing helped. She was a strong lady and she'd made up her mind and there was no changing it.

I began hearing that she was out on the town again. The columns carried items about her and George Brent. I'd never met the man, but I sure was jealous of him. Then, to crown the jealousy, came one awful incident.

I was in Oviatt's, a fine men's store. The proprietor, whom I knew well, spotted me and came over to where I was looking through the shirts.

"Tony," he said, "you've got to do me a favor. Greta Garbo is here and she wants to buy an overcoat for George Brent. You're about his size, would you try it on for her?"

I didn't much feel like doing a favor for George Brent, but I wasn't about to turn down a chance to meet Garbo. So I went over to where she was holding a cashmere overcoat with great big buttons. I tried it on.

"No," she said, "I don't think that's right."

What with one thing and another, I decided that I had to get out of Hollywood. At that time in my life, it was all too depressing. So I packed up, got Nat to book me into the Paramount Theater in New York, and went on a tear.

Charlie Barnett was the band at the Paramount. I was the featured attraction. We packed them in. I was getting bigger all the time I played —out of Hollywood, that is. I was really ripping things up now. A lot of money, a lot of fame and adulation. Hit records, too. My records of "Begin the Beguine" and "I Hadn't Anyone 'Til You" suddenly shot me to the top of the recording heap. And I was still a fixture with Burns and Allen on radio, which was a red-hot show.

It was 1939. War drums were rumbling across the Atlantic, but we felt safe. Nobody I knew gave much of a thought to the war. We all hated the Nazis and Hitler, of course, and maybe in the back of our minds we had a hunch that we would have to go over there and stop the sonofabitch, but it was way off.

I didn't give world affairs much thought. I was too busy with Tony Martin's affairs. In New York, I made friends with the jet-setters. After my stint at the Paramount, I'd go over to El Morocco, and there I'd find Henry Fonda or Aly Khan or Pat DiCicco or Cubby Broccoli or Bruce Cabot or Porfirio Rubirosa. We'd sit around and the girls would come buzzing. We called ourselves The Stud Farm. It wasn't an inappropriate name.

We all had money, looked pretty good. We did some pursuing but I guess we got pursued as much as we pursued. We weren't hard to get. We were normal men and we were ready, and the girls were beautiful. We were gay blades. There was a period there, maybe fourteen or sixteen days, when I don't think I got home once.

You know how it is. When things are going badly, you have a tough time finding a job. When everything is breaking just right, you have more shots than Annie Oakley. That's the way it was with me back then. Everything started to come my way—clubs, radio, records, everything. And I must say that cocky me, I figured it was only right that it was happening to me. I had it coming, after all the lean years.

I was doing very well on radio, which was a major industry in those days. I appeared regularly, for a while, with André Kostelanetz and Lily Pons, on their show. Kay Thompson and I were regulars, and Ethyl was the sponsor. Kostelanetz and Lily, his wife, were fascinating people. For one thing, she picked out all his clothes and he would wear what she bought, without question.

"Kosty," I'd say, "I think your coat jacket is a little too short."

"Don't bother me," he'd say. "Lily picked it."

The two of them seemed to drink nothing but champagne. There was always a bottle on ice in their dressing room. He'd invite me in, from time to time. That was rare, I learned, because ordinarily he didn't let people get close to him. He was rather aloof and, through most of our association, I called him Mr. Kostelanetz. But I learned a lot from him. I learned punctuality and respect and discipline, because those were his keystones.

Another radio show I was on for a long time was the Texaco Star Theater. One small and curious fact about that show: when I began, one of the ushers was an ambitious young singer named Gordon MacRae. When I finally left the show, they hired another singer to replace me— Gordon MacRae.

All that experience on radio made me a major name in the industry. So, when Hollywood called me again, I figured that was as it should be. This time it was MGM, where I had had my first shot. The studio was going to make a film called *Ziegfeld Girl* and they had a big production number and they thought I should do it.

Great. Why not? The way things were going, I knew this time it would work. I was relaxed now, not pressing, and that's the winning attitude. I had a what-the-hell way of looking at things then, born of my steady stream of success with everything I touched lately. If this didn't work, what the hell, something else would come along tomorrow. So I came back out to Hollywood, reported to MGM, and Busby Berkeley handed me a song to sing, a song by Nacio Herb Brown and Arthur Freed called "You Stepped Out of a Dream." It was a beautiful song—it's become a standard—and the scene worked out well.

I was kind of at loose ends, away from what had become my familiar stamping grounds, The Stud Farm at El Morocco. That didn't last long, however. I found myself presented with a choice such as men dream about.

It was Milton Weiss, in the MGM publicity department, who gave me what was probably my most difficult moment.

"Tony," he said, "we're having a premiere Friday night, and we want you to go with one of the girls in the picture. It's up to you, kid. Which one would you like to take—Hedy Lamarr or Lana Turner?"

That's like asking a cat if he'd like a white mouse or a brown. They're both tasty, it's just a question of which flavor he prefers. It was the same thing with me. As Weiss waited for my answer, I considered the possibilities. It was the most beautiful brunette in the world or else the most beautiful blonde in the world.

"Come on, Tony, make up your mind."

I guess I was still in my blonde period at the time.

"What the hell," I said. "I guess I'll take Lana."

"OK," he said. "I'll fix it up."

Naturally, the word got around the studio fast. By that evening, everybody knew that Tony Martin was taking Lana Turner to the premiere on Friday night. I went to Lillian Burns for my daily dramatic lesson. I think it was about four o'clock. She gave me a funny look.

"So you're taking out the blonde bombshell," she said.

"Yeah. How about that?"

"Just watch yourself, Tony. Don't get hung up on her."

"What do you mean? I can take care of myself."

"Sure you can. That's what Napoleon said before he marched off to Waterloo."

I thought about what she had said. "Don't get hung up on her." Me? Fat chance. I was free now, and I aimed to stay free a while. I would never get hung up on anybody.

So I went out with Lana on Friday—and got hung up on her so bad you wouldn't believe. I'd only been divorced from Alice for five or six months and here I was in stupid fascination again. I suppose I could plead that it was one of those rebound things, but that doesn't matter. The only thing that matters is that it happened. In one miserable, beautiful night.

The depression I'd been in since the divorce vanished. Maybe you think I'm being funny. How could I be depressed when I was swinging with the El Morocco Stud Farm? Well, I was. Oh, I'd go out and go through the motions of having a good time, but I was depressed underneath it all. I'd been cancelled by my wife and it takes a while for a guy to build his ego back up after something like that.

I tell you what. If you have a bruised ego, let Lana Turner tend to it. She's the best little ego-builder-upper I've ever seen. She had a way of

79

looking at you, of concentrating on you, that was unique. Her eyes never wandered from yours. She shut the whole world out. There were just you two, just those blue, blue eyes to drown yourself in. And who could have a dented ego after a night of that kind of therapy?

Literally, in one night I was a different man. She swept me off my feet. I'd never heard of the expression at that time, but it's a good one to describe what happened to me—I went bananas over that girl.

Let me try to explain. Lana Turner could do everything well, better than anybody else. She knew that there was more to love than just the physical, although there was that, too, of course. But lots of girls are good lovers; that comes naturally. What doesn't come naturally is the rest of it, the technique of being a total woman. And that Lana had in spades. She was warm and tender and thoughtful and unselfish. When you were Lana's guy, you were a king. She never looked at anybody else, or anything else. Her eyes followed you around the room. She was always there, ready to do things for you, ready to love you. We'd be out strolling around and she'd spot a jewelry store and take me by the hand, lead me inside, and proceed to buy his and hers diamond pins. Or a clothing store. In we'd stride and she'd order us matching suits. While you were with Lana, it was as though she had been put on earth for one purpose and only one purpose—to serve you and to love you.

At the time we met—or, rather, MGM pushed us together—Lana was going around with Victor Mature. Maybe when she was with Vic, he felt the way I felt. I'd heard about Mature, but when we were together, Lana and I were so close that she pushed everything else out of my mind. I couldn't believe there was anybody else in her life but me, or that she had ever felt toward anyone the way she felt toward me. She looked up at me with those dewy blue eyes and they were so worshipful, so puppy-dog worshipful, that I knew I had to be the only man in her life, past, present or future. That was all there was to it.

Some movie critics said Lana Turner wasn't much of an actress. They should have met her in real life. Although maybe I do her an injustice. Maybe it wasn't acting when she fell in love as often and as completely as she did. Perhaps that was just her nature, and when she fell in love with me or Vic or Steve or Artie or the rest of them she really meant it sincerely at the moment. Maybe. Nobody but Lana knows.

At the height of our romance, I went to San Francisco, to entertain at the World's Fair there. Lana was there, too. That's when I introduced the Jerome Kern song, "All the Things You Are." Judy Garland was there at the time, too, with her husband, David Rose. We became friends. Then, suddenly, Victor Mature was around.

"What about Vic?" I asked Lana.

"Oh, that doesn't mean anything," she said, looking up at me with one of those makes-you-want-to-melt expressions. "Vic and I are just good friends."

Good friend Vic didn't stay in San Francisco very long. He was there a day or so, then departed. I never did find out what he was doing there or why he left after he showed up. I was too busy to ask.

When I finished working in San Francisco, Lana and I flew back to L.A. together, and we drove over to her house. As we walked up the driveway, there was Mature, coming down the driveway, carrying a couple of overstuffed suitcases.

"Hi, everybody," he said, with a big grin on his face.

He and Lana kissed, in a brotherly-sisterly fashion. Then Lana went inside the house and there we were, Vic and me and his suitcases.

"Hi, old buddy," he said.

"How's it going?" I said.

"Look, Tony," he said, "all I can tell you is that I want to wish you a lot of luck."

4

TROUBLES
AND
TRIUMPHS

At fourteen, a girl knows only one thing—if there is something she wants, that's the only thing that matters.

I wanted to join the Ballet Russe. It was an overwhelming desire and I wasn't about to pass the opportunity by. If I had been older, perhaps I would have weighed the pros and cons more deeply. I imagine I would have reached the same decision, but not as rapidly, not as totally.

I went back to Amarillo, for the family conference which would decide whether or not I could accept Colonel De Basil's offer to become one of the Ballet Russe. I knew my father was on my side. And, together, we worked on my mother until she agreed.

Even my father had a few reservations, however. He wanted some assurances that his daughter—after all, I was only fourteen and a very naive fourteen at that—would be looked after properly. He was worldly enough to know that ballet companies live a Bohemian kind of existence, and he wanted to make certain that I didn't get involved in that sort of un-Texas behavior.

Colonel De Basil gave him that assurance. He promised that he, personally, would keep a fatherly eye on me. He said they would arrange for me to keep up with my school work, through correspondence courses. Whatever objections my mother raised, the colonel was able to answer to her satisfaction.

At last, my mother reluctantly gave her permission. She was far from the stereotype of that awful person, The Stage Mother. Actually, she was the direct opposite. She said she could not come with me. She had her life in Amarillo with her husband, her son, her family, and she wasn't about to leave it to go traipsing around the world picking up after me.

"If Sid wants to do this thing," she said, "she'll have to do it on her own."

That was fine with me, of course. By now, I was feeling that typical teen-age surge of independence, and the equally typical teen-age desire to be out on my own. This was my chance.

It was finally decided. I would join the Ballet Russe on a certain date, when they would be playing in Cincinnai, Ohio. My father would go with me to Cincinnati, to see that I was settled in properly. There was a frantic few days of packing, of saying good-bye to friends, of taking what might be a last look at those familiar sights. As the day to leave neared, there was some cold feet, but always that was effectively countered by the excitement of anticipation.

At the Amarillo train station, as I left for my big adventure, tears flowed. My mother and I hugged each other, and we both cried. Lindy cried. Aunt Bobbie cried. I think I even detected a tear or two in my brother's very-mature-for-fifteen eyes, too.

"So long, Sid," E.E. said.

"Goodbye, child," said Lindy. "You be a good girl, now."

"I'll miss you very much, darling," said my mother.

And then the conductors said, " 'Board!" and we were on our way. I looked out the window and waved as the train began to pick up speed. It was farewell to my childhood. But, more important, it was hello to my future.

We got to Cincinnati, and I officially became a member of the Ballet Russe. My dad saw that I was in good hands and then, after a few days, he left for home. More tears. And then I was alone.

But this was a different kind of alone. Now I was one of the group. I met all the dancers and had to begin to cope with all those Russian names.

Colonel De Basil was, at the time, one of the most important men in the ballet world. Some time earlier, he had taken over the world-famous Diaghileff Ballet Company, which had fallen on hard times. Through the force of his personality and his brilliance, he had completely rejuvenated it. He had attracted some of the greatest dancers in the world—people like Olga Marozova (I soon learned that she and the colonel were living to-gether) and her sister, Nina Verschina; David Lichine; Tatiana (Tanya) Riabouchinska; Tamara Toumanova; and so many more. Most were true Russians but some were English and Canadian, although they all had Russian names—all except for the Japanese-American ballerina, Sono Osato.

And, I think it was the second day I was there, I got a Russian name, too. The colonel came to me and said, "Miss Finklea, from now on you will be Felia Siderova." That was all. Nothing about whether or not I would like to change my name, or whether or not I liked the name he had chosen for me. So "Felia Siderova" was listed in the program, as one of the corps de ballet.

That first night in Cincinnati, I sat in the audience with my father, watching my new company perform. I have forgotten what ballet they danced that night, but I know that the repertoire then included *Swan Lake, Aurora's Wedding, Prince Igor, Les Sylphides, Scheherezade, Le Coq d'Or, Petroushka* and *L'Apres Midi d'un Faune.*

Then, after my father had left, I settled down to a routine. During the day, I worked with the others in the company, rehearsing, practicing, learning. In the evening, when the company performed, I would watch them from the wings, totally absorbed in studying each of the dancers, noticing their techniques, their virtues and even their faults. Generally, one of the company would be standing beside me, pointing out the good points and the bad points.

The colonel took good care of me. As he had promised my father, he supervised my school work. Each week, from a correspondence school, a sheaf of papers would arrive. New lessons. Old corrected test papers. I did my work, but I must admit it was reluctantly, at best. Every moment that I had to spend with English and math and history was a moment taken away from the ballet. And I was, at that time, one hundred percent absorbed in the dance. Nothing else could possibly attract or interest me. So those hours when I had to pore over lessons were, to me, lost hours. But I did what I had to do.

We moved on, from Cincinnati to Cleveland, to Pittsburgh. I began to make friends in the company, friends who have remained friends down through the years. David and Tanya Lichine became particularly close. They were good people and they took a friendly interest in my career. They helped me make the adjustment from a serious student to a rookie ballerina, and it's a hard adjustment. They showed me the ropes, so to speak.

I learned how to budget, for one thing. The pay was next-to-nothing. I made barely enough to live. My parents sent me money to help out, and gradually I learned to live with the money I was earning.

I learned how to take care of my equipment, particularly my shoes. Like all the dancers, I was issued three pairs of ballet shoes. It was Tanya who showed me how I should crochet them, to reinforce them so they would last longer. I began crocheting the toes with silk yarn, otherwise they would wear out quickly and I would have to buy new ones. In common with

84

the others, I spent a lot of time from then on taking care of my shoes, my tights, my costumes.

I learned many things, those first few weeks on the road with the Ballet Russe. And I was so busy learning and doing that I had no time to miss my home and my family. Besides, I had a new family now. And there were the intrigues, the romances, the politics that exist in every large family.

Colonel De Basil was true to his word to my father. He saw that things went smoothly for me and, above all, that I was taken care of properly. I think some of the other dancers were jealous of the time he spent looking after me, feeling that, since I was just a newcomer, he shouldn't give me special attention and special favors. But he did, because he had told my parents that he would.

In every city we visited, he made sure that I had a nice room in the same hotel where he and Olga stayed. And he kept a paternal eye on my welfare. It helped me through the rough period of adjustment.

But the company was a stern one, artistically. Where Colonel De Basil might make sure that my personal comforts were taken care of, when it came to the actual dancing I was on my own. I was just one of the crowd. And that was brought home to me with great force the first night I went on stage and actually performed.

My earliest assignment with the company was dancing in the *Swan Lake* corps de ballet. I learned from another dancer, while we stood in the wings and watched the company. I had never even rehearsed when Grigorieff, the company's *regisseur*, or artistic director, informed me that I would be dancing that night. I think this was in Pittsburgh, and I was terribly nervous.

I was shaking, but, I went on. It was a thrilling experience. The orchestra played that lovely, sweeping music and there is no feeling quite as exhilarating as being one of a group of dancers, all executing intricate steps simultaneously. The only problem was that one of the dancers wasn't quite as simultaneous as the others. That one was, of course, me. At one point, all the dancer's legs went one way in a *rond de jambe en l'air*, and mine went the other way. I felt every eye in the audience was on me.

When we danced offstage, Grigorieff was furious.

"Miss Siderova," he said, "how dare you make a mistake in *Swan Lake?* This is the Ballet Russe!"

I was fined. Deducted from my already insignificant pay, that left me that week with practically nothing except money from home. I learned, however, that that was the company policy—a mistake onstage resulted in a sizable fine. I learned, consequently, not to make any mistakes.

85

As the weeks wore on, and the tour continued, I found myself getting a liberal education in sex. Not from any firsthand experience, but from observation. There is the myth that most male dancers are homosexuals. Forget it! While it is true that many American male dancers are homosexuals (I'll have more to say on this subject later), in Russian companies it is not true. There may be some, but not many. Of course there are myths about all people even in sports today. In Russia and in many other countries, dancing is a very noble and masculine career for a man. And so the Ballet Russe was populated with men with normal desires, and an equal number of girls with equally normal desires. Many of them paired up, both to satisfy those desires and to cut down on living costs. I came to know who was sleeping with whom, who was jealous, who was on the make, but I came to take it all in stride. It was an education, perhaps as important as that I was getting in the dance or from my correspondence courses. Ever since my time with the Ballet Russe, I have learned not to be shocked by anything I saw or heard, and I accept people as I find them.

Some of the girls took me into their confidence. I guess they recognized that I was too young to be a threat to them. They would tell me their romantic troubles, in the broken English that was typical of most of them. I'd just murmur, "It'll all work out, you'll see," and they'd go away satisfied. I think they probably only wanted someone to talk to, a friendly ear. But it all helped me learn about life, and particularly about the wrenching impact of a love affair. In the years to come, that knowledge would be valuable to me when it came time for my own romances.

The company moved on, eventually reaching New York. It was my first trip to the city and it was tremendously exciting. I couldn't believe all those tall buildings and all those people, rushing about. I went with the colonel and Olga, as usual, and they were staying at the St. Regis, so I had a room at the St. Regis, too. The colonel was still keeping his word to my father, that I would stay near him so he could keep an eye on me.

The others in the company had to fend for themselves. I remember David and Tanya coming to visit the colonel, Olga and me the day after we checked in. They couldn't get over the elegance, the European chic, of our hotel.

One of the events of that first visit to New York that stands out clearly in my mind is a dinner the whole company had. There is a famous restaurant in New York called The Russian Tea Room, and it is the haunt of people in music and dance. It is close to Carnegie Hall and all the great stars of the opera, the concert stage and the dance dine there when they are in the city.

The Ballet Russe had a dinner for all of us at The Russian Tea Room.

86

I think it was a custom that they had always followed. And the colonel insisted that, since I was the newest member of the company, I sit at the head of the table. There was caviar—my first taste. And champagne. And all sorts of elegant, delectable and exotic dishes. It was a glorious evening, and the warmth of the company made me feel, finally, as though I had arrived. I was one of the group, an in-group, and it's always comforting to realize that. Even Grigorieff toasted me and smiled at me, and my poor performance in Pittsburgh was forgotten.

And we performed. I danced with the Corps de Ballet, my legs moving with every other pair of legs. I was ecstatic. I was getting to know the choreography of other ballets, going on almost every night with the other girls. I couldn't have been happier. Oh, there were times when I wondered what my old girlfriends in Amarillo were doing, times when I thought it would be fun to be back there in high school, going to the dances and trying out my wings on flirtations. But then I measured that life against the life I had—dancing, caviar, champagne, friends among the dancers—and mine seemed to be by far the more glamorous and exciting of the two.

I had my life all mapped out. I would stay with the Ballet Russe, move up slowly to small parts and, eventually, to prima ballerina. Nothing could stop me now.

But something stopped me. And it happened when the company arrived in Washington, D.C. and it happened with stunning suddenness.

There was a telephone call, a long distance call from Amarillo. That, in itself, didn't frighten me, because one or another of my family called often to see how I was. But this was different and as soon as I heard my mother's voice, I knew something terrible had happened.

"Sid," she said, and that's all she needed to say. There was something in the way she said it.

"Mother, what happened?"

"Sid." She couldn't say anything more.

My brother got on the phone. "It's daddy, Sis. He's had a stroke or something."

My heart stopped.

"Is he all right?"

"Well, he's alive but, no, he's not all right. He's very bad."

"I'll be home as soon as I can."

"Wait, Sid. Mr. Jones said you should call him in Washington, he'll get you home quickly."

Marvin Jones was a state senator who was influential in Washington. He was our state senator and he and my father were very good friends. My mother called him in Washington. And he made arrangements for me to fly home from Washington to Amarillo. In those days, airline service wasn't as good as it is today and senator Jones' help was invaluable.

First, of course, I had to tell Colonel De Basil. He was very sympathetic. He had grown to like my father in the brief meetings the two men had had, and he was very kind to me when he heard the news. He told me to take all the time I needed and that I would always be welcome back with the company whenever I was ready to return.

I rushed home and went directly from the airport to the hospital. Thank God, he was alive. My father was sitting up in bed, weak, but he smiled at me when I came into the room. We had a very short visit and then I went home.

I learned that some weeks before, my father had been out hunting with some friends. They had been shooting quail. My father was riding on the running board of a car as it jounced over rutty roads, and he had been bumped off the car when it went over a particularly rough stretch. He had landed on his spine. He wasn't injured, but, my mother told me, the doctors felt that perhaps that accident induced the stroke he had just suffered.

It was a strange homecoming. In my fantasies, I had imagined that my return to Amarillo would be different. I had daydreamed about coming home as a great ballerina, with everybody there to welcome me. But this was far from my fantasy. The house was quiet, the faces drawn and tear-stained, the voices hushed. They were glad to see me, but they hardly asked me anything about my experiences or my life. It was only natural. Everybody's only concern was my father and his chances for recovery.

The doctors were optimistic. He seemed, they said, to be making progress. He was young—only fifty-two—and relatively strong. They had high hopes that he would eventually regain total use of his faculties and be able to resume a normal life.

After a few days, they let him come home from the hospital, and we brought him back to the house happily. Gradually, he did seem to be getting better. He was able to sit up in bed. He was talking normally. Every sign indicated that the doctors had been correct in their prognosis. One by one, the nurses who had attended him around the clock were let go, until only the night nurse remained.

Then he was able to get out of bed. I came in to see him one evening, and he was sitting by the fire. But he didn't look right. His pallor was unhealthy, gray and pasty. Still, he seemed cheerful. As always, he wanted to know everything about me and the company, and he asked questions and was delighted to have me home and hear, firsthand, about my experiences with the Ballet Russe. So I told him everything that I could think of, and sat with him for several hours. I held his hand and recounted my adven-

88

tures, such as they were, and told him of the intrigues and the gossip and the affairs, and he relished every story. When I had run out of true stories, I made some up; anything to keep him amused.

It was the last conversation we ever had.

That night, as he slept, he had another stroke. In the morning, he was in a deep coma, from which he never recovered.

Our grief was real and, it seemed at the time, eternal. I think I was in a state of shock. I tend to believe that his death was harder on me than anyone else, but I suppose everyone in a loving family feels his own sorrow is the greatest. We had been so close, had shared the same love of the dance, and I knew that his interest in my career was all-consuming. I wondered for a few days how I could go on without him. Even when miles had separated us, I felt that he was with me and that feeling had always comforted me. Now I was alone. Of course, my grief was selfish. I had no real idea of how deeply my poor mother was affected, how great was her suffering.

I stayed in Amarillo a few months after my father died. I had to. They needed me, to help them over that rough period of adjustment. My brother needed someone to talk to. And most of all my mother needed someone to consult with. There are always, after a death, decisions to be made concerning the lives of the survivors, who have to go on. In our case, there were big questions—the house, the business, his possessions—to be settled. We conferred, hashing over the pros and cons. Eventually, mother decided to sell the house. It was too big for just my mother and my brother, who would be off to college in a year or so anyway. And, after some serious soul-searching, my mother elected to try to run the jewelry store business herself. She had been working there, off and on, for years and knew it well.

When those questions were settled, I found I had a decision to make regarding my own life. So I searched for some alternative. The company was on tour, I think in Australia. That was too far for me to go to rejoin them.

I heard that Nico Charisse was back in Los Angeles and had opened his own ballet school. I remembered him as a fine teacher and, perhaps, as something more. I decided that I would go back to Los Angeles. For a dancer, there is no such thing as not dancing. I knew I had to work and work hard if I was to progress with my career.

My mother objected. It was one thing to be with the company, where there was somebody to look after me. But I was still too young in her eyes —I think I was only sixteen at the time—to go to Los Angeles on my own. She suggested I take Lindy with me. In the apartment she was now in, she wouldn't need a full-time maid. Lindy could come with me and take care

under the stars, which somehow always seem to be brighter and closer when you're at sea.

There was another passenger on the ship I came to know. His name was Hans. He was a young Dutch boy, who was, I guess, my first conquest. At any rate, it was the first time in my life that I realized the power a girl has over a boy—and the first time, too, that I ever thought of myself as beautiful. Hans courted me furiously, first on the boat and then when we were both in London. I had never really considered that I was anything special in the looks department. As a child, as I have said, I believed myself to be downright homely. But Hans' compliments were so effusive and his courtship so relentless that I was forced to reassess my own raw material. As it turned out, maybe I wasn't so bad, after all.

Actually, he was, I suppose, a catch. He was young, good-looking, very pleasant—and rich. His father was in the diamond business, to cap it, and I have always loved jewelry in general and diamonds in particular. Maybe if I hadn't been still so single-minded—dancing was my life, my total, entire life—I might have listened to his entreaties. He invited me to come to Holland with him, to meet his parents. The implication was plain—there might be a proposal in the offing—but I chose to ignore that involvement. There was nothing that could possibly be more important than dancing in my life. Even diamonds, lovely as they were, would have to wait. And even Hans, charming as he was, would have to wait. Very sorry, but that's how it was. He left my life.

The great Fokine was with the Ballet Russe when we performed in London. He was a legend in ballet circles and I was thrilled to meet him. Grigorieff, who was still *regisseur*, introduced us.

Fokine bowed, royally.

"*Krasavitsa,*" he said.

I knew enough Russian by this time to know that meant "beautiful." I was flattered, and even more when, some time later, Fokine singled me out for my first solo part. It wasn't big, but it was something. He was choreographing *Paganini*, which turned out to be the last ballet he ever did. And he came to me one day and said he had a part for me in *Paganini*.

It was, actually, a very simple role. I was supposed to be a mother-figure. I had never seen myself in that way, and I suppose I looked disappointed. But he told me that he thought I conveyed emotion in my dancing and that was what he wanted. I had to walk across the stage, in a semi-circle, while others in the corps were running around me. Then I was supposed to gather them together about me, as a mother would gather her children. It was really nothing much, a few moments of movement that required little dancing skill but perhaps some emotional content. Still, it was more than I had done before and I was grateful for the opportunity. Later, when we performed the ballet at Covent Garden in London, I received a lovely review in a London newspaper for that small bit.

That London engagement will linger in my memory as long as I live. The Covent Garden season was probably the most important single stop on the Ballet Russe tour. The English were tremendous balletomanes in those days, and they still are, and we stayed for six weeks. The auditorium was jammed every night. On many occasions, the Royal Box was packed, too, and King George VI and Queen Mary attended on several evenings.

One night, the King and Queen were there when Baronova was dancing *Les Sylphides*. Her performance ended with an arabesque and then a run off stage. That night, as she ran off, her feet slipped out from under her and she landed, ungracefully, on her fanny. I was in the chorus, and all of us watched, astounded. There was a collective shocked gasp. Poor Baronova. She was humiliated. To fall on her bottom, in front of the King and Queen! I don't think she ever got over it. After the performance, she had a tantrum—she was, as many dancers are, highly temperamental—and then dissolved into tears. We all understood, and we all thought to ourselves, "I'm glad it was she—and not me!"

But her disgrace was a joy to some of the others. Ballet companies are hotbeds of petty rivalries and jealousies, and ours was no exception. There was a tremendous rivalry in our company among our three prima ballerians —Baronova, Toumanova and Riabouchinska. (I still take lessons from Tanya Riabouchinska, who has a studio in Beverly Hills now.) But I had no time to get personally involved in those affairs of temperament. Besides, as a lowly member of the corps de ballet, I was too insignificant to matter. I was too busy learning ballets, watching and learning, to be concerned with those intrigues. But it was fun to see them fume and watch their spats. The very beautiful Tamara Toumanova, who later made a few movies herself, wasn't so bad as was her mother. Tamara's mother was the typical stage-mother; she never left her side and schemed and connived for her to get the cream of the roles and the most attention.

Fokine seemed to pick on me, at least I thought he was picking on me. At first, that made me downcast, until David Lichine told me that Fokine only picked on people he liked and thought had ability. After that, I was elated when he singled me out for criticism.

It was a lovely six weeks, there at Covent Garden. The English fans would invite the whole company out for supper, for parties, for all sorts of things. One Sunday, we all went to a magnificent home in the country for tea. Although we all had Russian names, there were two American girls (myself and Sono Osato) and a sprinkling of English and Canadian girls, too. The English fans were always surprised when people with names like Maria Istomina spoke English.

The only thing to dampen our spirits during that English engagement was the threat of war. It was the summer of 1939 when I was there, and everybody was saying that war was imminent. There were a few appeasers around, but most people felt that Hitler and his hordes could not be appeased, short of total war. More and more, our audience was dotted by men in uniform as the English nation began—with painful slowness—to get ready for what seemed inevitable.

After we finished those memorable six weeks at Covent Garden, we were given a month's vacation. And we were told that we would all reassemble in September—in Berlin. That was to be our next engagement.

I had nowhere to go, nothing to do for that month. I thought of going home, back to Amarillo, but two things argued against that trip—the expense and the fact that when I got there my father wouldn't be there. I would have liked to travel around Europe, since I had never seen anything but London, but again the money problem raised its ugly head. Besides, the company was going to tour Europe in a month, so why not wait and go with them?

Two of the Canadian girls in the company suggested I stay with them. They both had family in London and offered to put me up at first one place and then the other. Lonely and homesick and pretty nearly broke, I seized their offer eagerly.

As the month of August wore on, the war drums were beating louder. Every day brought new and more ominous headlines. The U.S. consulate issued warnings, advising Americans to go home. But I had my commitment to join the Ballet Russe again in Berlin in September and that was what I was going to do. With the eternal optimism of youth, I figured that somehow all this war talk would blow away and, anyhow, it didn't concern "the company." So I ignored the warnings and stayed in London.

One day, without any advance notice, Nico Charisse was knocking at my door. He said he had discovered that he missed me, that he wanted very much to see me, that he had come all the way from Los Angeles to London just to meet me again.

How romantic! Any girl would have been swept away by that notion, that a man would travel halfway around the world to visit her. And, at the time, I was terribly vulnerable. I missed my father deeply, and yearned for a mature man—Nico wasn't as old as my father, but he wasn't my age, either—to talk to. Then, too, I was so far from home, with few friends and literally nothing to do all day.

I practically jumped into his arms. I told myself I was very much in

94

love with him and I knew I was at the time. I had always liked him very much and had always been very intrigued by him. The accent, the way he moved, the chain around his fingers—they all made him, to me, a most romantic figure.

"Sid," he said, "I love you very much. I just had to find you again."

"Oh, Nico," I said. "I'm so glad to see you. I love you, too."

And so it happened, that suddenly, that unexpectedly.

He suggested that we go to Paris. I had never seen Paris, of course, and he was very French, as he had been born there—although his parents were Greek. He said he could show me the real Paris, the Paris that tourists never get to see. There was certainly nothing keeping me in London, so I quickly agreed. We went to Paris.

I suspect he recognized that my Texas sense of morality was operating overtime. I had gone with him, willingly, but I imagine he could sense that I had some reservations about the whole situation.

"I tell you what," he said, when we had settled in Paris. "Why don't we get married?"

"Married?"

"Sure, why not? A wedding in France would be a wonderful thing, something we could always tell our grandchildren. And I know a lovely little town, a picture-book town."

"But married?"

I hesitated. I loved him, he loved me. At the time, I was certain of that. But I hadn't planned on getting married for years. I wanted a career first. It would be a long time before I'd be ready to be a wife and mother. Nico assured me he didn't want any children yet, either, that he wouldn't interfere with my career, that he would help me and guide me and be proud of my dancing.

Finally—a day or two of wrestling with myself—I agreed.

We were married in the town of Virchinny, which as they say there, is *"tout pres de Valence."* Nico was right; it was a picture-book town. We were married in the Catholic Church, of all places. My Baptist forebears would have had what we used to call a conniption fit. But, to me, it was a charming wedding. I would have liked my family there and I would have liked a white wedding gown, but, still, there were compensations. The church was picturesque and the priest right out of a Hollywood movie. And the little children, after we came out of the church, threw almond candies at us.

I didn't understand a word of the ceremony, as it was all in French and I didn't speak the language. Nico translated it for me as it went along.

I was Mrs. Nico—or, I suppose, Mme. Nico Charisse would have been more appropriate. I had some misgivings—what bride doesn't?—mostly because of the difference in our ages. Nico was sixteen years older than I and, I'm sure now, I married him because of my desperate unhappiness over the loss of my father. At the time, however, I would have argued that point.

We had very little time for a honeymoon, although we did have a few romantic days, bicycling around the countryside, eating cheese and drinking wine in out-of-the-way restaurants. August was wearing down and the war clouds were blacker. The American consuls everywhere were saying that we had to get out now, while we still could. But still I had my plans to go to Berlin in September and rejoin my company. But, on September 1, Hitler and the Nazis invaded Poland, and, two days later, France and England declared that they were at war with Germany.

The United States was still neutral, but it was obvious that the tour could not continue. Nico and I rushed to leave and we made it. We sailed aboard the S.S. *Bremen,* which turned out to be one of the last ships to leave Europe safely. It was a thoroughly miserable trip back to New York. The ship was blacked out, all the windows painted over so no lights would show to guide any submarine to our position. It was overcrowded. We took what accommodations we could get. I had to share a stateroom with two women and Nico was in another cabin with two men. But we just felt that we were fortunate to get out of Europe at all, so we endured the unpleasant crossing without complaining.

The Ballet Russe had disbanded. I learned later the members had gone to the four winds. David and Tanya went to Australia. The others went wherever they could.

With a new husband to show off, I took Nico to Amarillo. My mother was, understandably, shocked. In fact, she didn't believe it.

"You can't be married," she said, over and over. "You're too young. I don't believe it for a minute."

When she finally came to accept the truth, she insisted that we be married again—"married properly," was the way she put it—and we all drove one day to Tucumcari, New Mexico, where we were remarried by a judge with my mother and my brother present. Now, in her eyes, we were decently married.

I shocked the entire city of Amarillo. Sid Finklea, married—and to a man much too old for her. The tongues wagged and I could see people looking at me as though I were something very peculiar. I think the whole episode hurt my mother and she said that I wouldn't have done it if my father was still living.

Very soon, Nico had to go back to California to see to his school, and

I found myself back in Los Angeles, too. I didn't know it, but it would be my home from then on. Nico's studio was on LaBrea Avenue, close to where Charlie Chaplin still had his studio. It was wartime, and the city was dark at night, dreary and depressed in the daytime. My life was not too exciting either, during that period. I was totally wrapped up in dancing. I'd study with Nico or one of the other teachers. I'd work by myself for hours. And, for the first time, I began to do some teaching myself, handling the beginners. One of my pupils was a young girl who, some years later, would be Nico's second wife.

But I thought I was happy. I had my dancing, and that was the main thing. I also had Nico and we were newlyweds and he was romantic, exciting and kind. We rented a small house and I began to become some-what domesticated, although the housewifely arts have never been my strong suit. I did what had to be done, passably, and we got along.

Gradually, our household expanded. My brother, E.E., was in college and had married his high-school sweetheart, Elaine. There was no longer anything to keep my mother in Amarillo, and she was lonely for her children. She eventually sold the jewelry store and most of her things, packed up, and moved west to live with us. At that point, she was very fond of Nico. Lindy came with her, too. And pretty soon Elaine, my brother's wife, joined the westward trek, when E.E. went into the Army. We had a full house.

It was a sad time for my mother. She had loved my father very much, and she was only thirty-nine, and very attractive, when he died. Yet she never married again nor, as far as I know, did she ever even consider marriage. I imagine she felt that she had had her one allotted romance and it had been so perfect that she would not even consider another one. So she came out, and joined us, and freed me from domestic duties, with the constant help of Lindy, of course.

Nico tried to join the Army; like so many Americans who have come from other countries, he was terribly patriotic. But, because of the physical condition of his fingers, and his age, they turned him down flat. He then got a job in a defense plant, figuring that at least he was doing something for his adopted country. I did more teaching at the school, to help take up the slack caused by his absence.

It was a frantic time, with so many people to look after now, and the school to run. And then, to compound my troubles, I discovered I was pregnant. Nicky was born in 1942. Nico had decided he wanted a child very badly, so he was elated. I was happy, too, although my happiness was tempered by my realization that now, as a mother, I would be pretty well tied down. I saw my dream of a ballet career fade, but my adorable little son helped make up for that disappointment. He was, without a doubt, the most beautiful baby there ever was.

Fortunately, David and Tanya came to Los Angeles from Australia to teach at the school. Business was good. We had more pupils than our small staff could handle. And the two assisted me, and now I had my friends with me again. Much of the burden of teaching was lifted from my shoulders. I spent more time at home with Nicky, less time at the school. But, of course, I danced every day. I was still determined that, somehow, somewhere, some day, I would dance again. And a dancer must keep in shape, physically, if he or she can entertain any dreams of professional work. That's one thing about dancing; you can never lay off for an extended period. If you do, it's hell to get back in trim again.

David Lichine's return to Los Angeles was important. As a great dancer and even greater choreographer, he was almost instantly in demand by the Hollywood studios. As soon as the news slipped through the grapevine that he was here, there were offers. Everybody wanted him to do dance numbers in their films. He agreed to do a film for Gregory Ratoff at Columbia, a dance number in a movie to be called *Something to Shout About*. It was to star Janet Blair. Ratoff wanted a big ballet production number, and David was to choreograph it and star in it. He asked me to be his partner in the number. Fine. Why not?

We did the number together. It was shot on a stage in a downtown theater, because David wanted the real look of a theater. I remember I had a costume with many veils. Despite the title, the movie was nothing to shout about, but people seemed to like that number, and many singled me out for particular praise, which was pleasant to read and hear. Actually, over the years, the public has been my biggest booster, bigger than the critics or the producers. No matter what I did, they seemed to like me. I could always tell from looking at the cards they fill out at previews, and they have always been kind to me.

That delightful trend began with *Something to Shout About*. I had never been before a camera before, and nobody knew me. My name, incidentally, in the brief credit in that film was Lily Norwood; Ratoff had given me that when we had discussed names. The Lily was from my grandmother, the Norwood was my mother's maiden name. I thought it sounded pretty, but nobody ever called me that. I was still Sid to family and friends and to the people on the set. But it was "Lily Norwood" that the fans who saw the previews talked about.

And, naturally, Hollywood's moguls—who were always ready and eager, in those days, to find new cattle for their herds—were quick to notice the public reaction.

I had just done that number with David as a favor to him. Honestly, the idea of working in movies had never once entered my head. I was a dancer, not an actress. I had no delusions about myself. I couldn't act—I never had acted—so how could I be a movie star?

And yet, after *Something to Shout About* was premiered and reviewed, my phone began ringing. People were calling for me to do more things.

I had to reassess myself, my capabilities, my dreams. Did I want to take a shot at movies? Nico said I should. My mother said I should. Elaine said I should. David and Tanya said I should.

I could think of no really powerful reason why I shouldn't. OK, then, I'll do my dancing in the movies.

HOLLYWOOD
AND
HEARTBREAK

I think outsiders have the feeling that, of all show business types, singers are the greatest lovers of them all. I guess it began with Columbo and Vallee and the myth has been perpetuated by Sinatra and others.

But it's about time that somebody set the record straight in this area. Maybe we singers didn't do too badly in the romance department, but let me tell you that the comedians were the ones who always got the cream of the crop. I've watched them operate, and those comics know how to work with lasses as well as with laughs. Maybe that's why I've always had such a high regard and respect for comics. If there is reincarnation, I'd like to come back a comic.

Even in the area of a band, however, singers are not the romantic king-pins. Let me tell you—compared to drummers, singers are nowhere. Show me a guy with a drum and I'll show you a guy with eight girls waiting for him somewhere. I don't really understand it, because I've always found drummers to be somewhere in another world, but the girls apparently like that kind of character. I've never yet met a drummer who didn't have a way with the women. Compared to drummers, man, I'm out of it.

Well, not out of it completely. I got around, both before and after (and sometimes a little bit during) my time with Lana Turner. I dated some of the greatest beauties in Hollywood, in the age when there were great beauties around. Remember Marguerite Chapman? I think Maggie Chapman had one of the most exquisite faces that ever came along. I dated Maggie a lot, and I dated others—Ann Miller and Ida Lupino and Yvonne DeCarlo and Marilyn Maxwell and Carole Landis and Linda Christian and Sonja Henie.

I was a single man then. And even after the war, when I came back a different man from when I went in, I was a single man. And single men are always in demand in Hollywood. I was always invited to the big parties, the Jack Warner parties, the Jack Benny parties, the Mervyn LeRoy, the Goldwyn, the Zanuck parties, all the biggies. They needed single men, especially guys who looked presentable and who could hold their own on the dance floor. So I'd be invited and so would the others who happened to be bachelors at the moment. Cesar Romero, Ty Power, Hank Fonda, Pat DiCicco, Franchot Tone, Burgess Meredith—whenever any of us were between marriages, we were very popular with party hostesses. Romero was probably the most popular of any of us, because he was such a great dancer. Cesar could make any gal look like a Charisse on the dance floor, he was so good.

Before the war, most of us would go to the Trocadero on Sunday nights. It was something of a Hollywood tradition in those days, and Hollywood was a town that loved traditions because it was so new, and really had none. So that "Sunday night at the Trocadero" thing quickly caught on and became a brand-new old tradition. Hollywood was then really a small town, and everybody knew everybody else. You'd see the same old faces and the same new faces week after week.

It was a tough life, for all its glamour. In those days, before the war, we had to work Saturdays in pictures. It was a six-day work week, and a back-breaker. So the only day you had to play was Sunday, and you tried to cram in a week of playing in that one day. Monday mornings you'd go to work with enough Murine in your eyes to float a battleship. Of course, we had a little legal help in trying to keep our health. In those days, there was a curfew for public drinking. The last drink was poured at one o'clock, and then that was the end—unless, of course, you moved on from the Trocadero (or Ciro's or the Mocambo) to a private party somewhere. And we usually did, because we were having so much fun and there would be a natural reluctance to call it quits.

That took care of the evenings—drinking, partying, dancing, womanizing.

Sunday, during the day, was a time for sports. There were all kinds —some of the men like Tracy and his cronies even played polo. That wasn't for me. I was more of a golf player. But there was a period, in the good old pre-war days, when croquet was the "in" sport. I think it got its impetus from two sources—the English set (Ronald Colman, George Sanders, David Niven and that crowd) and, as a strange counterpoint, Sam Goldwyn. Who would have thought that Goldwyn, the glove salesman turned moviemaker, would share the same interest as the urbane and sophisticated

101

British? But he did. And Sundays he'd invite a bunch of us over to his place for a spot of croquet, including most of Hollywood's English colony.

Tennis was another game that had its adherents, and that group included me. It wasn't the big industry it has lately become, but those who loved the game were really nuts about it. There were no public tennis courts then, at least not in Los Angeles; the courts were all private, and you had to know somebody before you could even get a chance to swing your racquet. Most of the courts were owned by non-show-business people, and they wouldn't let actors near them. There was still some of that vestigial feeling in the minds of the non-actors, in the pre-war days, that there was something vaguely unclean about actors. They still thought we were second-class people. They wouldn't let us defile their tennis courts. So what I did, and what dozens of others did, was to join the Racquet Club in Palm Springs, and that was what helped make Palm Springs the popular spot it became. We'd drive down there for the weekend, if we weren't working on Saturday, and have a ball, playing tennis, soaking up the sun, having a few flirtations and generally behaving like movie stars.

That business of how the non-show-biz types looked down their noses at actors was always ridiculous.

Of course, there are a lot of actors I'd turn down if it was my club, too. Actors and entertainers. There is a deplorable tendency on the part of anybody in show business to become an egotist. I suppose it's part of the qualifications for our trade, and I may be as guilty of it as the next guy. But most of us can see the next guy's faults and overlook our own. And I've often seen such monumental egos operating in show business that they become thoroughly offensive. It's a shame, but it's true.

Not all, of course. And there are just as many egomaniacs in other businesses. But, somehow, in show business, they become worse, I suppose because they are so often the types who are always on.

One of the things I guess I am conceited about is the number of great men that I can proudly call my friends. To me, the opportunity to meet and come to know the most extraordinary men of our generation is one of the great plusses of our business. I've talked to presidents—Roosevelt, Kennedy, Johnson, Nixon—and I've entertained them, too. I've become friends with generals, business leaders, writers (Harold Robbins has become one of my best friends), educators, industrialists, college professors—wherever I go, I am introduced to the important people and then it's up to me. I have a knack for talking to people—I guess that's the show business in me—and I can quickly cut through the natural reserve we human animals have for each other. So I make friends easily, and I can manage to talk to people in their own language, be it politics or big business or sports or whatever.

I had a beautiful relationship with Jerome Kern, dating from the time I appeared in his life story, *Music in My Heart,* at MGM in 1939. I sang "All the Things You Are," one of my favorites, in that film. He would play the song for me, to show me how he thought it should be interpreted— but never forcefully, never dictatorially. He suggested, that's all, but I was delighted to get the suggestions of the man who created the song.

I knew George Gershwin, too. For a long time, I had a reserved ticket to the Friday night fights in Los Angeles, and Gershwin was a big fight fan, too. He'd sit in the seat right behind mine every Friday night. We became good friends even though he often pounded my back in exciting moments.

Once I did a TV special, and I was asked to sing the Rodgers and Hammerstein number about the theater, "That Big Black Giant." Richard Rodgers worked on the special, and he was more of a dictator than the others. He would brook no changes in his song. It had to be sung exactly as he had written it down, as though it were the national anthem. I tried to reason with him, to say that every singer was bound to have a different interpretation of a song, but there was no discussion permitted.

"But, Mr. Rodgers," I said, "I have to be myself when I sing."

It didn't matter to him who I was. If I was singing his song, I'd sing it exactly the way it was written down, without any Tony Martin style superimposed on it. There was quite a to-do about that, but I had to do it his way.

Among my fourteen gold records, six or so were songs written by Cole Porter. I was always lucky when I recorded his songs. I was singing at the Copa in New York around 1955 when my old pal, Ethel Merman, called to say she was bringing Cole Porter in to see me that night. It was his birthday. She cautioned me not to mention his presence—"for Chrissake, don't tell anybody," was the delicate way she put it. So I told Al Sendrey, who was then my conductor, to be particularly careful with "Begin the Beguine" that night. But, when it came time for me to sing the song, the inevitable happened. Halfway through, I forgot the words—and I'd only sung it a million times before. So I did what I always do at times like that, I made up some words as I went along.

You can imagine how I felt, with Porter out there listening to me. After the show, I was so disgusted with myself that I just went back to my room at the Hampshire House and threw myself in a chair and sat there.

The next morning, I got a telegram from Cole Porter.

"Dear Tony," it read. "You are a super magnificent artist. I appreciate your translation of my music on your records which have been successful for both of us. Pleased to have seen you last night. Cole Porter. P.S. Personally, I prefer my own lyrics."

Not everybody I met was a revered figure, however. In the days when I sang regularly at the Copacabana in New York, I often had a few hours after the show with Frank Costello, the boss of bosses of the mob.

"Frank wants to see you," they'd tell me, after I'd finished my act. I'd change, wash, take a deep breath and go upstairs. I wasn't frightened. Costello was not a frightening figure.

"Frank wants to see you." It happened many nights. He'd be sitting quietly in a corner of the upstairs room, and he'd gesture me to sit down next to him. So I'd sit, and we'd have a bite to eat, a few drinks, a little talk.

He called me kid. I don't know if that was because he couldn't remember my name or because he called everybody kid.

"Siddown, kid," he'd say. "Take a load off. How'd it go tonight?"

"It went OK, Frank," I'd say.

"That's good. So what's new?"

We'd talk about safe subjects, subjects we both knew and enjoyed talking about, subjects that wouldn't incriminate him or get me in trouble. Mostly those were sports and show business. In those days, both of us were rabid Brooklyn Dodger fans. So we'd talk about the Dodgers, and some non-Dodgers we both admired, such as Carl Hubbell, Stan Musial and, above all, Joe DiMaggio. Sports was the safest of topics. Show business was next, but there we might disagree, so we stayed with sports.

It wasn't easy for him to talk. He had a bad throat, even then, and had trouble talking. He used to warn me about smoking.

"Don't smoke, kid," he'd say. "It's bad for the throat."

And he'd point at his throat, grin sheepishly and shake his head, as if to say, "but it's already too late for me."

I knew Virginia Hill, too, while I'm on the subject of the notorious people I've run into. We'd had a platonic friendship for a long time, starting from the World's Fair days in Chicago. I knew who her benefactors were, who was paying her bills—a gentleman from Chicago and another gentleman from New Jersey who got himself deported back to Italy. But I always liked Virginia, and she liked me.

During the war, when I was with Glenn Miller at Yale, I got a call from Virginia one day. She was staying at the Waldorf Towers in New York and I guess she had a surge of patriotism and wanted to do her bit for the boys in uniform. Anyhow, she invited our whole outfit, Capt. Glenn Miller and the Air Force band, to a party at the Waldorf. We used to go into New

York and do a show, *I Sustain the Wings*, every Saturday. So it was arranged we'd have the party afterward.

She took over the place. Xavier Cugat played for our dancing. She had the finest foods and wines. There were about forty of us—the band plus our wives or dates. Glenn Miller was at the head of the table and I was at the other end. We danced and ate and drank until dawn and, as we left, Virginia gave each one of us a solid gold cigarette lighter from Cartier's. She'd made her contribution to the war effort. She was a "good broad."

A lot of singers had problems with the "Boys." I won't mention any names, but there were plenty of them. The boys would move in on them, buy up their contracts and operate them from then on. I was lucky. They never bothered me. I don't know why, really. I used to think it was because early in my career, I'd done a lot for Jimmy Petrillo and the Musicians' Union. I'd done many benefits and things for them, and maybe that's how I stayed clean. I don't know. Maybe if I'd ever gotten into a bind and needed money and had gone to them, it might have been different. That was one way they got their hooks into you. But I was lucky that way and, no matter how bad off I was, and there were days when money was a problem, I never was quite so bad off that I had to go to them for a loan. I knew that that way lay disaster, and I stayed away from that trap.

So my sessions with Costello and the other boys I met were always friendly, but reserved. We were from two different worlds.

Still, it was part of my continuing education to get to meet a Costello, along with the greats in more respectable fields. It's like a zoologist; if all he studied were the nice animals he wouldn't be doing justice to his science. He has to get to meet a crocodile once in a while. Well, the same with me and my studies of men and women. Costello was my "crocodile," even though he looked as if he could have been in the Cabinet, had the manners of a peer, the dignity of a statesman and the honesty of a saint.

It was funny, though. Only two people that I can remember called me kid regularly. One, as I have said, was Frank Costello. The other was Al Jolson. That's about all those two had in common, of course.

"Al," I said to Jolie, one day at Hillcrest Country Club, "why do you always call me kid? Can't you remember my name?"

"Sure I remember your name, kid," he said. "But, let me explain, I only call the people I like kid. When I don't call you kid, that's when you should complain. That means I don't like you."

I remembered that conversation some time later, when Al Jolson and Frank Sinatra were together. I eavesdropped and, all through their conversation, Al Jolson called Sinatra "Frank." Not once did he say "kid."

You can't like everybody. Some people come along and they rub you the wrong way, for one reason or another. I get along pretty well with most people. I can overlook a lot of human faults and frailties, but I cannot overlook gross ingratitude. To me, that's one of the cardinal sins, especially in show business, where most of us owe our careers to the helpful assistance of others. I know I got many boosts along the way and I'm always ready to admit it. But there are some who think they did it all themselves.

I've always taken a great deal of joy in finding young people I think have talent and nurturing that talent, helping them and watching them make it big. One day, I got a call from a personal manager named Harry Adler. He knew I was in a position in those days to take a comic with me when I appeared in clubs. I could take anybody I wanted. I used many young comics—Jackie Kannon, Alan Drake, Jack Carter, many more.

"Hello, Tiger," said Adler, who always called me Tiger for reasons he alone knew. "I've got a great young comic for you to use in Vegas. How about giving him a break at the Flamingo with you? His name is Alan King."

So, sight unseen, I took Alan King. I went to the bosses at the Flamingo, and they went along with my recommendation.

I consider myself responsible for his career, but not for his talent. He always was and still is a superlative comedian, one of the wittiest men around. But, I think, if it hadn't been for me and my intercession, he might still be working in Sheboygan.

When I took him under my wing, he was totally unknown. His style was raw and unpolished. But I sensed his brilliance, although it needed a lot of work. I began taking him on the road with me. I'd work with him, day after day, week after week, working on his material. I'd help him edit his act. I gave him tips on his delivery. He was smart and recognized he was improving, thanks to my tutelage and his opportunity to work steadily.

He called me Zeke, and still does. And Zeke and Alan became close, for a long period. I had him go to a dramatic coach. I sent him to my tailor, so he'd improve the way he dressed. When we were between engagements, he'd stay with Cyd and me in our home. One day, he borrowed my wristwatch and my Cadillac—he wrecked the car and, in the excitement, never did return the watch. And it was a gift from Eddie Cantor that I treasured for its sentimental value.

Over a period of a few years, the unpolished lump of talent that was Alan King became the intensely professional comedian he is today. I even got him a role in a movie; I had Joe Pasternak write in the part of a sailor for him in *Hit the Deck*. I enjoyed the experience. I'd done it before, and it is always rewarding to watch young performers advance in skills and in the reception they get from audiences.

Once I was playing in Las Vegas, at the Flamingo, and I'd brought Alan with me. Sid Luft came over and said that Judy Garland—they were still married then—was going to London for her first concert appearance there.

"I need a good comic for the first half-hour," Sid said. "Got any ideas?"

"Come on over and catch the show tonight, Sid," I said. "I've got a very funny young kid on the bill with me. I think he'd be just right for London and Judy."

So Luft came over and caught Alan King's act, and he liked what he saw. They made the deal, and Alan King went over and was on the bill with Judy when she made her sensational appearance in London, her first shot there. And he was a hit, too—which was due, in a large part, to something I had told him before he went.

I had played London. I knew it and loved it. And I knew the English were sick and tired of every American performer coming over and saying, "I'm so glad I'm here," and gushing over everything British.

"Look, Alan," I said, "for a guy with your style, your great gift for sarcasm, it would be great if you came out and did just the opposite. Say how much you hate it in London and how you hate the English. They'd eat it up."

"That's a fantastic idea, Tony," he said.

So he did it. And, as I said earlier, Alan King has a great talent and, once pointed in the right direction, he did that reverse approach perfectly, and the Londoners loved him. He immediately became a great personality in London. And he was interviewed right and left and whenever anybody asked him who was responsible for his success, my buddy, Alan King, had the answer ready: "Judy Garland," he'd say.

Not a mention of Tony Martin. Never. Not once. It was as though I had ceased to exist. Through the years, whenever reporters ask him who helped him along the way, he'll say, "Judy Garland."

Before that London trip, he would always say to me, "I'll never forget you, Zeke." He always called me Zeke. So he'd say he'd never forget. But he forgot. It happens that way sometimes.

Later, after he had made it big, I went to a major Hollywood party and I took him with me. Right inside the door, there was Jack Benny. Alan went up to Benny, without even waiting for me to introduce him.

"Hi, Jack."

Later on in the evening, Benny said to me, "I don't like that guy you brought with you tonight. I've never met him and he calls me Jack."

The year before Jack died, he and I and Alan happened to be in

Chicago at the same time, and we were all on Irv Kupcinet's show there. After the show, Jack and I were outside the studio, waiting for cabs. Alan drove by in his big chauffeur-driven limousine, and he had the driver stop. And he pushed the button and the window slid down.

"Hey, Jack. Let me give you a lift."

"No thanks," Jack said. "I'll wait for a cab with Tony."

Even though it didn't turn out the way I would have liked, I'd do it again tomorrow. I have a great deal of inner satisfaction, knowing that I recognized that spark of talent in Alan King before anybody else, and nurtured it and fostered it until it became a forest fire of fun.

I've always loved comics. And I have something of a flair for it. For one thing, if the voice goes, it's not so bad if you're a comic. Look at George Burns—he can't sing a lick, but nobody cares.

Over the years, I've recognized many unknown and unsung comedians and helped them. Don Rickles and Redd Foxx are two more. I didn't help them as directly as I helped Alan King, but I used to lead the cheering for them when nobody had ever heard of them. I'd get parties of Hollywood people together, and take them down to a little club, Slate Brothers, where Rickles and Foxx were working. I'd say I want them to catch my latest discovery. It helped them. Everything helps at that stage in a career.

I don't expect any great outburst of love and affection for what I did. I don't expect more than a "Hello, Tony."

It's always fun to be around comedians. I remember back in '46, I guess, I took Buddy Hackett with me to meet a man named Sam Freedlander, a big supermarket tycoon, who was building a Miami Beach hotel called The Diplomat. I liked Buddy, he was funny and easy to be around. But he couldn't get a job. So I figured if I introduced him to Sam and Sam liked him, maybe he could work The Diplomat when it opened.

But I knew Sam was a stickler for cleanliness and neatness, and those weren't two of Hackett's outstanding qualities. So I made Buddy dress well for his big meeting, had him put on a nice suit, a shirt and a tie. He looked pretty good, for Hackett. And I cautioned him to keep the conversation clean, because Sam was something of a prude. Between the two things— the suit and tie and the need to watch his language—it was a tough time for poor Buddy. But he did it, and the meeting went smoothly. We had met Sam at his hotel, and we were sitting by the pool, and I guess the combination of what he was wearing and what he wasn't allowed to say began to get to Buddy.

"Why don't you fellows take a swim?" Sam said.

Buddy stood up and bowed and jumped into the pool—with that suit and tie and everything else.

Alvin Morris, in uniform.

The Five Red Peppers.
(Al Morris, in front.)

Sailor Tony Martin and his mother. "There was one positive change in my life which I owe to my brief stopover at RKO— my new name."

In India, Tony Martin with the Maharajah of Cooch-Behar. (Tony is in the Maharajah's clothes.)

The photo Tony sent to his parents as he left for India.

Tony (seated, third from left, front row) as part of Glenn Miller's wartime band.

L. to r.: Tony, Alice Faye, and Glenn Miller.

Tony enters London's famed Palladium, where he topped the bill.

L. to r.: Alan King, Tony Martin, and Joe E. Lewis. On Alan King: "If it hadn't been for my intercession, he might still be working in Sheboygan."

L. to r.: Milton Berle, Tony Martin, Eddie Fisher, and Robert Merrill.

Rita Hayworth and Tony Martin. "I can't go to Del Mar with you, Tony,' she said. 'I've decided to go back with Orson.'"

Tony dabbles in politics with Wendell Willkie.

L. to r.: Lana Turner, Hedy Lamarr, Tony Martin, and Judy Garland, in *Ziegfeld Girl*.

Tony chums it up with Nat Goldstone and Peter Lorre.

L. to r.: Tony Martin, Dean Martin, George Jessel, Jack Benny, and John Raitt.

L. to r.: Phil Harris, Dinah Shore, Betty Hutton, Tony Martin. "Phil looked at me for a moment. 'Do you know Alice?' he said, and then it dawned on him. 'Oh, for Chrissake!' We had played eighteen holes of golf and he had forgotten that we had both been married to the same girl."

Jamming it up with (l. to r.) Fred MacMurray, Dick Powell, Tony Martin, Jack Benny.

Tony, with his first Rolls-Royce.

Around the same time, I was working with Sophie Tucker and Joe E. Lewis, and that fabulous character, Swifty Morgan, was hanging around. Joe E. Lewis had been so good to me, I figured I should buy him a nice present, and I mentioned my intention to Swifty.

"I got just the thing, Tony," he said, and went to his room and came back with a magnificent pair of cufflinks. "Joe E. will love these."

He was right. The cufflinks were perfect. We haggled over the price and I finally bought them for $400.

The next night, at the show, Joe E. and his piano player, Austin Mack, were there, and this was the right moment to give Joe E. my big present.

"Here, Joe E.," I said. "These are for you—a small token of my thanks for your many kindnesses to me."

Joe E. Lewis took the cufflinks and studied them.

"Gee, that's very nice of you, Tony," he said, and started to put them in his pocket.

"Hey, let me see them a minute, will you?" said Austin Mack, and Joe E. handed them over.

"I hate to tell you this, Joe E.," Mack said, "but these are your own cufflinks. I've seen them on you many times."

Well, I guess that qualifies as my most embarrassing moment, if my teacher ever asks me to write a composition about that. I stood there, my face getting redder and redder. Then Mack asked me where I got them, and I said I bought them from Swifty Morgan. They both laughed, then. It seems Swifty did that a few times, taking some of Joe E.'s things and selling them. But this time he got caught at it.

Fat Jack E. Leonard was another of my all-time favorites. We worked together a lot and always had fun. He was a funny man, in many ways. One of his peculiarities was that he would get genuinely hurt if he didn't hear from you, if you were out of town for any length of time. On one of my trips to London, when I was making the movie *Let's Be Happy*, I was awakened one morning about four with a call—collect, yet—from Los Angeles. Emergency, the operator said. So, of course, I accepted the collect call.

"Hello, Al? You're full of shit," a voice said, and hung up.

I knew it was Leonard. He still called me Al. I called him back and asked him what that was all about. He said he was mad because he hadn't heard from me, and that was his way of displaying his anger.

My friendship with Fat Jack goes back many years. It was in 1949, I think, when we were both working at Bill Miller's Riviera, across the Hudson River from New York in Fort Lee, New Jersey. At the time, there was some kind of jurisdictional labor dispute involving the New York cabs, and they weren't allowed to go across the George Washington Bridge to New Jersey. Jack and I were staying in a hotel in New York and to get to work became quite an involved procedure. We had to take a cab up to the bridge, then hitch-hike across the bridge, and then grab a Jersey cab to take us to the club. And then reverse the procedure to get back to the hotel after we had done our shows. After a few days, that became a bore. So I said to Jack that I thought I'd be better off buying a car and he agreed with me.

Right across the street from the hotel was an English car showroom, so that day I went over and bought a little MG. Came time to go to work that night, and I got in the front and Fat Jack got in back. Well, he was so heavy that the car's front wheels were lifted off the ground. Obviously, we couldn't drive across to New Jersey like that. So I traded the MG for a Riley, which was a little bigger and heavier—but still not big enough. It was a two-seater and when Jack tried to get in the passenger's seat, he couldn't make it. He had too much girth. So the Riley had to go. But I was still dealing with the same dealer, and the next step up the ladder was a Triumph.

That wasn't too bad—for a few days. But then one day, we were off and decided to go to Yankee Stadium to see the ball game. On the way back, the gear shift lever came off in my hand, and I had to drive all the way back to mid-town Manhattan in first, because that was the gear the car was in when the lever came off. I had it fixed and, when we were through at the Riviera, I had the car shipped to California. Somewhere between New York and Los Angeles, some hoodlums found it and totally stripped it. That ended my Triumph career—but I was still in an English car mood, so I traded what was left of the Triumph for a Jaguar. Three days later, I totaled that. The remains were traded in the next day for a Mercedes-Benz, the 300 SL, the one with the wing doors that went up. Cyd couldn't get out of that car and, after a few attempts, announced she would never ride in it again. So I traded the Mercedes in on a Rolls-Royce.

The point of the whole thing is that Fat Jack Leonard always insisted that he was responsible for my getting my first Rolls-Royce.

"If I wasn't so fat," he used to say, "I wouldn't have upended the MG and you would have kept it and that would be your car today."

We were working together once at Bill Miller's Riviera and Leonard was on too long. That happened with him once in a while; when he was on he just kept going. So I began heckling him from behind the curtain, loud enough so the audience could hear me.

"Get off," I said. "You're on too long."

The audience laughed, of course, and Jack E. made believe he was angry. He got off, finally, and I went on. Right in the middle of *Begin the Beguine*, he sauntered on stage again, wearing nothing but his underwear and carrying a huge towel.

"Hey, Al," he said. "Where's the soap?"

Comics are a strange, wonderful breed. You never know what to expect from them. When I got together a party and went down to the Slate Brothers Club, to introduce all my friends to Don Rickles, he was in his glory. He insulted everybody—but he made Cyd freeze with one line.

"Well, there she is, Cyd Charisse," Rickles said. "What's wrong with Alice Faye's legs?"

We thought that was a little below the belt, especially Cyd, and we wondered what kind of man could say something like that in public. He must be heartless. But, then, after the show, he was a different man. He insisted that Cyd have a picture taken with his mother, who was there.

Alan Drake was one comedian I saw in circumstances that weren't particularly funny. We were working the Lotus Club in Washington. After the show one night, we were sitting around my hotel room and I was hungry, so Drake volunteered to go out and get some Chinese food from a restaurant he knew. I turned on TV, relaxed, waiting for him to come back with the food. The phone rang. It was Mimi Weber, an agent, who lived next door to Drake on Long Island.

"Alan's wife was just murdered," Mimi said. "He'll have to come back to identify the body."

She had been shot, we later found out, with some New York mobsters. I quickly arranged to charter a plane for him and I got out a bottle of Scotch. I was ready for him when he came back.

"Hello, sweetheart," he said, flinging the door open and holding the bags of food high, like they were trophies of the hunt. "Have I got food for you! It's a feast!"

I poured him a tumbler full of Scotch.

"Drink this down, Alan," I said.

"What's the matter?"

"Just drink it. No questions."

"Is there something wrong with my son?"

"No, you're son's fine."

"It must be my wife."

I told him the story, then. I gave him $500 and told him that the plane was waiting for him. He left. I was so upset by what had happened that, for the first and maybe the only time in my married life, I forgot to call Cyd. She called me the next morning, worried that something had happened to me. I couldn't tell her the story; it was still too much for me to talk about. So she figured I must have been loaded the night before and got sore.

"Can I call you back, Cyd?"

"I don't care if you never call me back."

When she found out, of course, her anger dissipated. Generally, with comics, life is full of laughs. I guess I've gotten to know most of them. There was Rodney Dangerfield, who wore underwear ten times too big, and would sit in that floppy underwear, writing his act. There was Jackie Clark, who had a fetish about his clothes; he'd keep everything. So Tom Turner, who worked for me and still does, and I would throw his shirts out the window. There was Jackie Kannon, who used a rubber chicken and a real egg in his act. Tom and I would substitute a live chicken and a hard-boiled egg.

I think the most comical man I've known, however, is Dean Martin. We had something in common from the beginning—neither of us were ever afraid of a drink. Dean and his martinis, me and my Scotch. But we'd always be on time for our shows and the drinking never affected our acts. We also had a mutual reputation as skirt chasers. We were out one day playing golf on the Desert Inn course in Las Vegas. I said, "Dean, I hear you're going through the line at the Sands."

"Well," he said, "I hear you're doing the same thing with the line at the Flamingo."

We laughed.

"If you and I did all the banging we're given credit for," I said, "there'd have to be two big statues in the cemetery with our names on them."

I worked with Sophie Tucker, too, and she was one of my all-time favorites. What a lady! I worked with her the last time she ever appeared, when we both showed up for Ted Lewis' fiftieth wedding anniversary party. She had a bad back, but she wouldn't miss that party, so they gave her a shot of something and she went to the piano and did her act.

We used to have a running gag going, Sophie and me. I'd tease her.

"How about you and me, Soph?" I'd say. "Just once, OK? Tonight, after the show, OK?"

"Aw, come on, you little cocker," she'd say, but she would be smiling. "You've got enough to handle at home."

As the years went by and my career prospered, I made friends—and a few enemies, I suppose—all over the world. But Hollywood was my home and that was where I hung my hat and so, naturally, I had more friends there than anyplace else.

Another of my Hollywood friends was the late Sonja Henie. The thing that I'll always remember about Sonja was that she never called me Tony —to her, I was always Tracy Brown.

That happened because when she first came to this country, I was at 20th Century-Fox and that was the studio that imported her. They asked me to make the test with her—although "asked" may not be exactly the right verb to use. I think "told" would be a little more precise. Anyhow, I did Sonja's screen test and I was happy to do it. As a sports fan from way back, I had always admired her—I still think she was the greatest figure skater who ever lived—and I looked forward to the chance to meet her and work with her.

It was a pleasant experience, too. She was cute as a button, bright and sharp and charming. Anyhow, the test we did was a scene from some minor movie, or maybe it was a movie script that had never been made. I don't know exactly, but I do know that the part I played was a man named Tracy Brown. For some reason, that name tickled her. She giggled over it. And, from then on, whenever we met, it was always, "Hello, Tracy Brown" and never Tony.

Sonja and I dated once. Maybe twice. We never had a romance, but we did have a rapport. She'd often call me—"Hello, Tracy Brown"—and we'd talk about things, about her career and her romances and her problems, and sometimes about my problems, too. It was a good relationship and I valued her friendship—but I could never get her to say my name. I was always Tracy Brown to her.

Hollywood was—is—a strange place. I knew everybody and that was a help getting parts in films. But sometimes it was a hindrance, too. I'll never forget the day that Mervyn LeRoy called me.

"Tony," he said, "I need your help."

"Anything, Mervyn."

"Look, I'm casting a picture. And I need a fellow who looks like you and sings like you."

"Yes?"

"Well?"

"Well, what?"

"Well do you know anybody like that? Anybody who looks like you and sings like you?"

I don't remember what I told him. I only remember feeling frustrated. Here was one of the top directors in town, calling me for the name of somebody who looked like me and sang like me—but it never occurred to him to ask for me. Maybe I should have said something, like Paul Douglas once did. That's how Paul got his big break in *Born Yesterday.*

The men who were going to produce the play were having lunch at Twenty-One in New York, and Douglas happened to be with them. They were in the middle of casting the play at the time. So they asked him if he knew of an actor who looked and sounded something like he did.

Douglas was quiet at first, but after the third Bloody Mary, he had the nerve to speak up.

"What about me?" he said.

They were stunned. They never would have thought of asking him. That simplest of ideas would never have occurred to them. But Douglas spoke up—and he got the part.

I didn't say "What about me?" to Mervyn LeRoy that day. I've never regretted it. Maybe my problem is that I'm too shy about pushing myself. Maybe if I hadn't been, I might have gone on to bigger and better movies. But I am what I am, and I can't change that. I'll break walls down for other people, but not me. There are two parts to Hollywood—the dining room and the shooting stage. I've never been able to sell myself in the dining room.

As we moved into the forties, the war in Europe was paramount in most people's minds. We weren't in it yet, but if we were realistic, we knew our involvement was only a matter of time. I know I felt that way. I'd gone out and performed for various war-related groups—Greek war relief, R.C.A.F. recruitment, other things. I read everything I could get my hands on about what was going on in Europe, listened to all the radio news and the radio commentators, puzzled over what would happen next. We all wondered how the war was going to affect us and our careers.

When the Lana Turner affair ended, I was pretty down. After Alice, now this. I had plenty of time and nothing to do with it, both professionally and socially. Coupled with the war news from Europe, this combined to put me into a state of serious depression. I began asking myself tough questions. What was I doing with my life? Where was I headed? Could I ever find someone who loved me for myself, someone I could love for herself? None of those questions was unique to me, but that didn't make them any the less baffling.

The coming war began to look to me like a way out. Maybe I should enlist, go off to war, and, at the same time, perhaps I'd find the answer to some of those nagging questions.

As our entrance into the war neared—anybody who thought it would bypass us was kidding himself—I grew more and more serious about it. My draft call wasn't until May, 1942, and I suppose I could have stalled beyond that. But I couldn't stall myself. I decided I had to do something. The Navy appealed to me more than the Army—my Uncle George had been a Navy man.

I decided the time had come for me to enlist in the Navy.

6

ROMANCE
AND
RENAISSANCE

When it happened, it happened suddenly. One day, I decided I'd give this acting thing a whirl. Within a week, I was dancing with Fred Astaire.

After my number with David Lichine in *Something to Shout About* made people interested in me, I had quite a few calls from various people. The one that seemed most exciting was from Bob Alton. I knew the name. Robert Alton was dance director for the Arthur Freed unit, the group that did all those outstanding musicals at MGM. He told me they were working on a big one there, *Ziegfeld Follies,* and they needed a dancer to work with Fred Astaire on a couple of production numbers. Astaire! I had grown up watching him on the screen in Amarillo.

Nico told me I should do it, that it would be a wonderful opportunity. His persuasion helped, but I think it was the idea that I would be working with Fred Astaire that really sold me. I still wasn't thrilled about the idea of being a movie personality, but what dancer didn't want to work with Astaire?

So I told Alton that I would come in and we would talk about it.

It was like a scene from one of those early girl-makes-good movies. I went to MGM and I danced for Alton. Even before I was finished, he was on the phone, talking to Freed.

"I've got a girl here, Arthur," he said, "and I think she's the one we've been looking for."

They whisked me up to Freed's office. He talked to me about ten minutes and then offered me a seven-year contract. Just like that. It was all too fast. I really didn't know what he was talking about, what was going on.

"Look, Sid," he said, "you really should get an agent. Then have the agent come in and talk to me and we'll work out the terms."

I said I would think about it, and then I went home. I know most girls would have given everything they had—and quite a few did—to be in my shoes. But I truly wasn't impressed. If I had grown up dreaming of stardom, that would have been one thing. But none of this had ever entered my head. All it meant to me was maybe a chance to dance with Astaire but, also, it meant months away from my own dancing.

Nico, again, talked me into it. He found me an agent the next day. And before I really knew what was happening to me, I was under contract to MGM and getting ready to do *Ziegfeld Follies*—with Fred Astaire.

There was one thing to be settled. My name. Arthur Freed asked me what my name was, of course, and I said, "Well, I've had quite a few names." And I explained that I was Sid Finklea, now Mrs. Nico Charisse, but I've also used Felia Siderova and Maria Istomina and, in the one movie I did, I was Lily Norwood.

"So you're really Sid Charisse," he said. "I like the sound of it. But I don't like the spelling S-I-D. That's too masculine."

He doodled on his desk pad for a few minutes, then said, "How about if we spell it C-Y-D? Has an exotic look to it, but it'll still sound the same. OK with you?"

Yes, it was fine with me. I knew many young people, who signed contracts, were given outlandish names. This wasn't bad. At least my name would sound like it had always sounded. And that's how Cyd Charisse came into being.

From then on, Arthur Freed was to play an important role in my life. Through him, I met and worked with the very greatest—the elegant Cole Porter; the brilliant Alan Jay Lerner; Roger Edens, who practically orchestrated all of Judy Garland's songs; Howard Dietz; and so many more creative people who clustered around Arthur. There were set designers, costume designers, musicians—the cream of the creative crop. Arthur was always my great champion, and I was very fond of him and listened carefully when he gave me advice.

So, within a week, Cyd Charisse reported to work. And, suddenly, there I was, in my little tutu, dancing with Fred Astaire.

It turned out that I did two numbers with Astaire for that picture, but one was cut out. The one that stayed in was called "Here's to the Beautiful Girls," in which I worked with Fred and Lucille Ball. This was long before Lucy became the major star that she is, but she was so kind and warm toward me, when I was just beginning, that I will always have a soft spot in my heart for her. That was just a big, big number without any special effects or business. But it was the first time I felt a spark, that maybe I had stumbled into a business that would be good for me.

The other number, which was left out of the final film, was a shambles. It was called "There's Beauty Everywhere," and it had me and Astaire and Lucille Bremer dancing while James Melton sang the song. It was a whopper of a production number—showgirls on a mountain with water and bubbles cascading down. I was supposed to dance down the mountain, through all the water and the bubbles, on point. Alton should have known that it was physically impossible to dance in water on point, because toe shoes are made of satin and satin and water don't mix too well. But nothing was impossible in Hollywood in those days, so we did it. It took weeks to shoot. The bubbles were too bubbly one day, not bubbly enough the next. My shoes would shrink until I could barely stand. We'd have to wait until I could get new shoes. Everything that could possibly go wrong went wrong. Still, at MGM in 1944, no expense was spared and when they decided to do something, they did it. Damn the dollars, full speed ahead.

And yet, when it was all done, the decision was made to cut it out of the film as it was eventually released. That's the way money was wasted in Hollywood in the forties.

I did my two numbers and waited. But my waiting hours were full. I was now a contract player, and, in those days, the studios took good care of their contract players. I had a schedule, the same sort of thing every other contract player had. I would have hours for speech, for acting lessons, for singing and dancing. I studied speech with Gertrude Fogler and acting with Lillian Burns, who was to become a good friend through the years. And I would be required to show up for interviews and to shoot publicity shots. I did my share of cheesecake in those days. You had to do it. Before every holiday, they would have you pose—with a turkey for a Thanksgiving shot, in a Santa Claus hat for a Christmas shot, with a great big heart for a Valentine's Day shot. It was all part of the job.

But I had a private life, too, and it was a full one. Nico was working in the defense plant, so I had to oversee the operations of the school. Elaine, my sister-in-law, was pregnant now, and she had to be watched over. Nicky was a growing boy, and I had to be sure that someone was there to see he didn't toddle into trouble. And there was my mother, too, and Lindy.

A few months after I finished *Ziegfeld Follies*, Arthur Freed asked me to make a test. It wasn't for anything particular, just a general test so they would see what I looked like, what I could do, how my acting lessons were progressing. He got the fine director Bobby Lewis to direct the test, and that was fortunate for me, because Bobby believed in me. Lillian Burns, at that point, didn't. She felt I was fine, doing what I did, which was dancing, but she didn't see me as an actress. Lucille Ryan, who was the assistant to Billy Grady, the casting director, was another one who thought I had talent. And Lucille arranged the details of the test.

They found a small scene for me to do, a dramatic scene set under a tree. And Lewis directed it brilliantly and the test turned out to be a smash. From then on, I had something to show producers and directors, and they were always impressed. Over the years, that very early test was terribly helpful to me, and brought me several important parts.

It paid off immediately. As a result of that test, I was given my first speaking part. It was just a small part, but I did get to say some words. It was in *The Harvey Girls*, with Judy Garland, John Hodiak, Ray Bolger and Angela Lansbury, which George Sidney directed.

It was while we were shooting that picture that things began to turn sour at home. Nico and my mother had started off liking each other, but that changed. Now they didn't get along at all. And one day, my mother fell in the kitchen and broke her back. She was hospitalized for a long time. At the time, we lived on a ranch—really a small orange grove—in Encino. (If I'd have kept it, I would have been wealthy now, because it was in the path of a great deal of future growth.)

It was difficult for me, trying to keep peace in the family and trying to work at the same time. When my mother went to the hospital, Nico refused to visit her and that just compounded the problems. There were money worries, too. My mother had invested money in Nico's school. Now, with him working in the defense plant, it wasn't doing too well. After all, it was Nico Charisse's School of the Dance, and the pupils logically expected Mr. Charisse to be there. He wasn't. So the pupils dropped out, at least many of them did. Mother and Nico were constantly arguing about that, among other things.

I was in the middle. Nico wasn't a businessman, he kept saying, he was an artist. My mother would say, fine, then don't try to run a business. He blamed my mother for her interference. She blamed him for his absence. I tried to keep peace between the two, but it went from bad to terrible. The whole situation made me very nervous, and I felt I wasn't performing as well as I could in *The Harvey Girls*.

We decided that we had to live apart from my mother. Maybe if she was away from us, things would improve. So we sold the orange grove. My mother bought a small house for herself in the San Fernando Valley. Nico and I bought a place in Cheviot Hills, far from the San Fernando Valley.

It didn't help much. Nico, when the war ended, left his defense plant job and tried to interest himself in teaching again. But he really did very little, and he was left at home, bored and frustrated.

I finished *The Harvey Girls* and went immediately into another film, *The Unfinished Dance*, for producer Joe Pasternak. That, too, was a direct result of the Bobby Lewis test. Pasternak had seen it and wanted me. It was my first really major part. There was one funny aspect to *The Unfinished Dance*. I was playing one of two ballerinas, with Karin Booth playing the other. Karin wasn't a dancer at all; I think she got the part because, at the time, she was going with an important MGM executive.

Yet she was playing a dancer, and she was supposed to dance. My friend, David Lichine, did the choreography, and he and the director, Henry Koster, had to figure out ways to make it look like Karin was a skillful dancer. And she had trouble even moving her feet. They wound up placing her on a machine that whirled her around, so it looked like she was dancing.

But that was the only funny facet of my life in those days. For one thing, life on the set wasn't too happy for me. Henry Koster, the director, was something of a tyrant. I wasn't too sure of my acting ability then; I'd never really studied, except for those lessons at the studio, and that left me feeling somewhat inadequate. I was still in the process of losing my Texas twang. Gertrude Fogler of the studio's speech department was helping me do that. But I still had to think of how I talked, as well as everything else. And Koster was a dramatic director and he made it very clear to me that he regarded me as poorly prepared for the role. He gave me a very hard time, and it got so I dreaded going on the set. He had a thick German accent, strong and harsh, and he tongue-lashed me in front of everybody and I'd be left shaking.

Then, too, at home it was all falling apart. Nico and my mother weren't speaking at all now. And he had virtually abandoned the school. I believe he was finally rebelling against his mother and the way she had forced him to become a dancer. I think that, deep down, he never even wanted to dance. The only thing he really liked to do was go out hunting. It was sad, because he was really a very talented man, but something inside him refused to let him use his talents. A few sessions with a psychiatrist might have straightened him out, but he laughed at that notion. He didn't like where we were living. He wanted to sell our house and buy another ranch out in the Valley somewhere, where he could go hunting more frequently.

I'll always be grateful to Nico. I think he gave me a certain quality that set me apart from the run-of-the-million dancers. It is relatively easy for a dancer to acquire the technical ability to dance, to perform all the steps in a pure textbook fashion. But I watched Nico dance—and he could be positively brilliant—and some of what he did rubbed off on me. He had a very fluid way of dancing. He never came to a full stop, he was always in motion. He imparted that quality to me.

He was a brilliant dancer, a brilliant teacher—when he wanted to be. But, gradually, he got bored with the whole dance picture. His boredom led to frustrations and he took them out on me.

He came to me one day and said he had sold the school. What would he do now? He didn't know, he said. But what he did was go out hunting, when he could, and the rest of the time he spent at home, with his frustrations gnawing at him, eating him up. Naturally, I suppose, he became more and more irritable and edgy. He had always had a temper, but he came to have no control over it now.

I grew to be very afraid of him. He would get angry over trivial things and threaten me. He accused me of becoming "a movie star," of neglecting him, of any manner of untrue actions. All these temperamental outbursts hurt me. I would go to work on *The Unfinished Dance*, but my mind would be at home and on the scene I was certain I would encounter when I got there.

Then he got a call that his mother was dying of cancer. My mother helped her for a time; the two mothers had gotten along well. But Nico had to be with her, which was only natural. While he was away, helping his mother in her last weeks, I moved out of our house and moved in with my mother in her house. As far as I was concerned, my marriage was over. There didn't seem to be anything keeping us together any more. I had once thought I was very much in love. Time taught me that I wasn't. It was, I think, only a reaction from the death of my father, and that is far from enough to sustain a marriage.

But there was more to come. When Nico returned, the scenes really began. He yelled and shouted, blaming everything and everybody for what had happened—blaming my movie career (which he had encouraged me to begin, of course), blaming my mother, blaming everyone but himself. The one thing he couldn't accuse me of—and he knew it—was seeing another man. I hadn't, and I wouldn't. I didn't believe in going with anyone else while I was married. I had always been very moral and Nico knew that, at least. But the scenes continued until I finally had to tell him that I was going to get a divorce and I didn't want to see him again. He finally understood that I was serious. If he brooded, it wasn't for long, because he married again soon after our divorce became final.

There was one other problem for me during that time, and I really didn't need another problem.

One of my co-stars in *The Unfinished Dance* was Robert Sterling. Bob was then married to Ann Sothern. At the time we were filming, Ann was out of town. Bob asked to take me out. No, I said, I can't do that, because I am married and so are you.

"Just for dinner?" he said.

"No, not even for dinner. That's just the way I am."

"Well, at least let me walk you to your car."

I laughed, and we walked to my car in the parking lot. He called me several times at home, too, but there was nothing in the whole silly little business to arouse even the hint of suspicion. A walk to a car, a few phone calls, a request for a date that was turned down. Period.

But one day, Howard Strickling, MGM's publicity head, called me in to his office.

"I have something to tell you, Cyd," he said. "You're about to be named co-respondent in a divorce case."

"A divorce case? Whose?"

"Bob Sterling and Ann Sothern."

It later developed that she had tapped their telephone, and our few innocent conversations were all recorded.

"Howard," I told Strickling, "I want you to know the truth and you've got to believe me. I've never even had a date with the man."

"I believe you, Cyd," he said.

Ann was furious about the whole thing, but Howard believed me and the lawyers believed me and nothing ever came of it, as far as I was concerned.

My life changed dramatically, however, as soon as the word went out that Nico and I had separated and that a divorce was in the offing. Now I was fair game. And, for the next year and a half, I had my lost teen-age years.

I had never really been through what most girls go through, in their teens. None of the calls, the dates, the excitement. I'd missed all that. Now I was having my chance. Flowers, phone calls, dates, the works. It was, in some respects, the gayest period in my life. It made me realize that I was a girl that men liked to look at. I'd never known that before, and it was a delicious feeling.

I suppose I overdid it. I'd be out all the time, sometimes seven nights a week. I know my mother thought I was going out too much. And my director in *The Unfinished Dance*, Henry Koster, who wasn't exactly the soul of tact anyhow, hurt me deeply about my socializing. I was getting many calls on the set, and almost every day some flowers would be delivered, and very often there were male visitors.

"It's like a dog in heat," Koster said, growling as he turned away from me. The coarseness of that remark shocked me deeply.

But, despite those little unpleasantnesses, that year and a half was a great time. I suppose I was living every girl's dream—a Hollywood star (well, perhaps not a star yet, but nearing that pinnacle) and being courted by some of the most glamorous and eligible men in the world. Actually, I had really led a shy and almost a cloistered life. My dancing had been everything to me and I had never cut loose. If girls sow wild oats, and I guess they do, I didn't. There were some wild oats in my system that were just crying to be sown. Until that period in my life, I had never had a drink, except for some wine in Europe and the annual Christmas eggnog at home. And I knew some four-letter words, but I never used them, except in French. For a girl who had been married and had a child, I was certainly innocent.

I was still protected. At that time, every studio player was protected. It was almost like a family, and they were especially protective of me because they knew I was still pretty naive. So they would watch over me, make sure I was all right, cluck like a bunch of mother hens. I had my responsibilities—classes when I wasn't shooting, watching the big stars at work when there were no classes. The whole thing finally got to me, and, at last, I was excited at being part of it. At first, since I had just sort of accidentally drifted into movie work, I had been somewhat blasé about it. It wasn't as important as ballet, I thought to myself. But the atmosphere around MGM in those days was thrilling. How could I remain blasé when I'd eat lunch in the commissary and spot people like Gable and Tracy and Garson and Turner and Gardner and Pidgeon and Kelly at nearby tables. As I became more important, they would nod at me, and then say hello, and eventually pause for some idle chitchat. I caught the spark and I became ecstatic at being part of that scene.

For that year and a half, I was one of the more popular girls in town. My ego got a nice boost. There were all kinds of men I dated—and many more I didn't. And several proposals.

There was one important writer, Robert Riskin. For a while, some other dancers and I ate lunch together in the commissary, and he would come over and join us. One day, after lunch, he walked me back to where I was rehearsing a dance number. When we got there, he grabbed my arm and thrust a little box in my hands. It had an engagement ring in it.

"I am terribly flattered, of course," I said, "but I—."

I didn't know what to say. So I put the box with the ring in his hand, patted him on the cheek and turned and walked away.

Something of the same sort happened with the doctor who had delivered my son, Nicky. One day, he sent me a long and passionate letter, proclaiming his love for me. It came out of the blue. Before I had a chance to marshal my defenses, he appeared at my front door, surrounded by flowers and candy. It was such a surprise. One doesn't expect one's family doctor or even obstetrician to suddenly come around, saying things about love and marriage. I had to explain to him, calmly, that I appreciated his attentions but, no, I didn't think I could marry him.

But I did enjoy my new-found popularity. I went out with producer Jack Cummings, with writer Sidney Sheldon, with actors such as Peter Lawford and Barry Nelson. My mother would shake her head as a different man would show up at my door every night.

"I think you've lost your mind," she would say.

No, I hadn't lost my mind. I had simply found my youth. I loved it. I would be taken to all the great restaurants and nightclubs, to the premieres and parties, to the "in" places and sometimes the more intimate "out" places, too. It was great fun.

One evening, my agent, Nat Goldstone, called me an asked me to go to dinner. I knew that wasn't a date, because Nat was happily married. I just figured he had some business to discuss with me and I said I would.

He picked me up and escorted me to the car. Then he quickly left and I noticed there was a man in the back seat.

"Get in, Cyd," the man said.

It was only after I had gotten in the car that I realized that the man in the back seat was Louis B. Mayer, the boss of the whole studio, himself. I had met him once or twice before, and, as was the custom in the MGM family, I had had my picture taken with him. But I had never met him socially, and I had never expected to. But there he was, patting the cushion next to him and saying, "Sit right here, dear." I was totally tongue-tied, but I sat down and we went somewhere for dinner.

Nothing came of it, thank goodness. It was only years later that Nat told me Mayer had come to him later and said, "She's a nice girl, but she's not bosomy enough for me."

Another time, Howard Strickling said he wanted to arrange a meeting between me and Clark Gable. I know Howard liked me, particularly after that squabble with Ann Sothern during the Robert Sterling business. So I said I would like nothing better than to meet with Gable. Howard arranged for the two of us to meet on the lot one day. We did meet, but, again, nothing came of it. I never went out with him. I think the problem was that we were both basically shy people and our conversation never left low gear.

I guess like every American girl, I had a crush on Clark, but we never even dated once. Curiously, now, long after he is gone, his widow, Kay, has told me that "Daddy thought you were the end." It was mutual.

There were two real romances for me during those eighteen months or so of being single. One was with the man who would eventually end that state, Tony Martin. The other was with Howard Hughes.

Shortly after World War II ended, Nat Goldstone asked me to have dinner with him and Bernice. Again, I thought Nat had some career matter to go over, but it turned out he was playing cupid for me. We had dinner at the Bel Air Hotel and then we went on to Ciro's afterward. But it wasn't just the three of us. Nat wanted me to meet another of his clients, Tony Martin. He had only recently been discharged from the Army and was footloose and fancy-free. It wasn't exactly love at first sight. Far from it.

Tony never even sat down at our table. The total extrovert, he was table-hopping all evening. For some reason I can still remember what I was wearing that evening—a beige-and-white satin outfit—and I can still see myself, sitting there at the table in Ciro's in that dress, fuming. I got madder and madder.

"Nat," I said, "what have you done to me?"

"I'm sorry, Cyd," he said. "The poor guy is just out of the Army, he's been over in India for God knows how long, he's still enjoying his freedom."

"That doesn't excuse common rudeness."

Finally, Tony asked me to dance. We had barely begun when he noticed Rita Hayworth on the floor, and immediately steered me over to her and we stopped dancing while he gave her his undivided attention. I went back to the table.

When I went home that evening, I was very quiet. My mother knew something was wrong. When I'm angry, I get very, very quiet.

"Feel like talking about it?" my mother asked.

"I met a man tonight," I said, "who I hope I never see again, that's all."

Curiously, it was Tony who introduced me to Howard Hughes. A few months after our disastrous first meeting, he called me one night and asked me if I'd like to go with him to the premiere of *Black Narcissus* that evening. I think it was Nat who put him up to making the call; dear Nat didn't like to see two of his favorite clients hating each other.

It was one of the very few nights that, for one reason or another, I had no plans. My first inclination was to say no. I wasn't out to set a record for most-consecutive-evenings-seeing-different-men. Besides, that first evening had been so unpleasant that I didn't want to subject myself to another dose of the same misery. But, on the other hand, I did want to see the movie. Moreover, Tony tried to persuade me by saying that we would be going with Nat and Bernice, a foursome, and they were always good company. If Tony reverted to his routine of not paying me any attention, at least I'd have somebody to talk to. Finally, I shrugged my shoulders and said, what the devil, give him a second chance.

"All right, Tony," I said, "I'll go with you."

It was evident from his behavior that night that Nat had given him a stern lecture. He was the complete opposite from the way he'd been during our first encounter—kind, solicitous, attentive, just what I'd hoped an escort would be. We went to the movie and, afterward, we all went to one of those inevitable post-premiere parties, and I found myself having a very pleasant time. And I told myself that first impressions can be wrong. I had always prided myself on making snap judgments that were accurate, but this time I may have made a mistake.

So I began seeing Tony.

And then, one evening, Tony hosted a party of his own at the Mocambo, and I was with him. The party was in full and glorious swing when I noticed a man edge over to Tony and whisper in his ear, and then they both turned and looked at me and whispered some more.

"Hey, Cyd," Tony said, when the man had gone. "There's somebody having dinner in the other room who would like to meet you."

"Who was that man?" I asked.

"No, not that guy. That's Johnny Meyers, he's Howard Hughes' assistant. It's Howard who wants to meet you. Come on, I'll introduce you."

But that wasn't the way it was. Before we could go into the other room, Hughes came over to where we were sitting. Tony introduced us, and we got another chair for Howard and he stayed with us for the rest of the evening.

At the time, Howard Hughes was an important man in Hollywood, but he wasn't quite the institution he became. He was wealthy, of course, and somewhat eccentric even then, but his eccentricities had not become the total peculiarity they eventually reached. He was known as quite the man about town, and he did produce movies, so he was good to know. I had, naturally, always been curious about him.

I found him, from the outset, to be a tremendously talented person, a man who could do almost everything and do it well. Talent is one quality I have always admired, no matter what direction it takes. And so I developed an instant respect for him. I came, eventually, to believe that he was more than just talented; I think he was a genius at what he did.

He began calling me often and we became good friends. He sent me masses of roses and, after he got to know Nicky, he would send him huge toy airplanes. Nicky liked that, and I did, too. I thought it showed him to be a very considerate and thoughtful person.

Still, he had his quirks. He kept strange hours which I learned to adjust to. He was the absolute night person. I learned that, if he was going to ask me out, the request would come in the form of an abrupt telephone call sometime after eight in the evening. I found out that that was when he got up; he would sleep all day.

He'd call me soon after eight, ask me if I was free. If I was, he'd pick me up and we'd go out to dinner in some out-of-the-way place. It was breakfast for him, and he'd always have the same thing—steak and tomatoes. I could eat whatever I wanted, but he never varied his order.

After that dinner/breakfast, the routine was that we would then go to see his plant. Many people criticized him in those days for ignoring his plant and his business in favor of the movie business, but he didn't ignore it, it was just that he did his inspections late at night. Everyone else would be gone, but he would go through the plant carefully, looking at every detail, and I would tag along. He tried to explain things to me, but most of it was far beyond me, because it was all highly technical.

I suppose that doesn't sound like a very romantic evening, but the force of his personality made up for the drabness of the locale. He was an exciting, electric man, and I looked forward to those strange post-midnight tours of his plant. If any other man had suggested I spend my evenings in an industrial complex, I would have crossed him off my list with enthusiasm. Somehow, though, Howard Hughes could make inspecting an airplane factory a charming way to spend an evening.

It wasn't always that way, of course. There were exceptions. One of the most memorable of those exceptions started out the same as always, the eight o'clock telephone call and the usual request.

"Are you free, Cyd?"

"Yes, I am tonight."

"Good. Let's go to dinner. Pick you up in about a half-hour."

"I'll be ready."

And I was. Even though I expected it would be another of the usual evenings, I dressed up in my newest outfit. I always looked my best. And, incidentally, he did, too. Maybe he came to wear sneakers, appear unshaved and dress like a bum later on, but in our time together, he was always neat and clean and well-dressed.

He showed up, right on schedule. But instead of heading for one of his usual tiny restaurants, this evening he drove to the airport.

"Where are we going?" I asked.

"San Francisco."

That's all. No further explanation. And he piloted us to San Francisco, and there was a car waiting there and he took me out to dinner. Again, a small, out-of-the-way place. He had his usual steak and tomatoes. Then it was back to the airport. But we didn't fly directly back to Los Angeles. He wanted to stop off in Las Vegas, and we did. There weren't as many hotels there then as there are now, and we only went to one, The Flamingo, caught the show, and he made his usual bet—one dollar—at the blackjack table. He won, but quit immediately.

It was, of course, very late when I got home that night. In fact, it was almost time for me to go to work at the studio. When I walked into the living room, I found my mother pacing the floor. And, keeping step with her, was Tony.

"Where have you been?" my mother asked.

"We had a date, remember?" Tony said. "I don't like being stood up."

I didn't know which one to answer first. Actually, I had forgotten. When Howard called and asked if I was free, my engagement with Tony had completely slipped out of my head. He was angry, and I can't blame him, and he stayed angry for a week or so. But, I'm delighted to say, he got over his anger and called me again.

Howard was generally predictable and a man who liked to do the same things over and over. But, once in a while, he enjoyed cutting loose and doing something completely out of character. That impetuous night of going to dinner in San Francisco and then stopping off to bet a dollar in Las Vegas was typical of him. It didn't happen often, but the fact that it might happen at any time made him somehow mysterious and exciting.

Then it was back to the old routine. Once or twice, he would take me to his Goldwyn screening room, after dinner and the plant tour, to see some footage he was especially interested in. I remember once he said he wanted to see rushes on a new girl he had discovered. That turned out to be Faith Domergue, who had a lot of publicity and a brief flirtation with fame.

At that time, during the months I was dating Howard and the others, I was continuing to work. In fact, I was working very hard. I was lucky, in that I had both Lindy and my mother to look after Nicky. We had a little house in the valley and life was, basically, very good.

But it wasn't all roses and sweet music. I had my share of setbacks and pain, too.

Nico was still in the picture. The divorce was in the works, but it took time and he was still, legally, my husband. He would, of course, come over to see his son, and I had no desire to interfere with those visits. The two adored each other, which was right and proper, and I certainly wanted

Nicky to have those visits with his father. But Nico would take advantage of those visits to berate me, to yell and harangue and threaten. He was jealous of my social life—which, of course, was always the subject of gossip in the newspaper columns. He was bitter over my success, I think. He was frustrated in his own life. The combination made him skittish and erratic, and I grew to be afraid of him.

He would threaten me. And he would also threaten to take Nicky away from me. He never did hit me, but he would double his fist and start out as though he were going to give me a shot in the jaw. Then, at the last second, he would hit the wall instead.

I was making a big Esther Williams musical at MGM called *On an Island with You.* Jack Donohue was the choreographer and I was due at the studio for a huge production number. I was supposed to leap down the multi-level set, from one level to the next, and I knew it was a difficult thing to do. But, on the morning when I was to shoot that number, there was an especially difficult scene with Nico. There were bitter words, tears, wall-pounding. By the time I got rid of him and calmed myself down, I was late reporting to the studio.

When I got to the set, Joe Pasternak, the producer, and Donohue and everybody else was waiting for me. And, to compound my sin of lateness, there were a group of exhibitors there. They had been invited to watch the dress rehearsal for the big dance number and the fact that I was late, thus holding up production, made the brass very edgy.

"Cyd, where have you been? Hurry up, we have a lot of important people waiting to see this number."

"I'm sorry. I'll hurry."

I ran to the dressing room and changed into my costume, a very brief affair which covered me here and there with a lot of shimmering beads. I had problems putting it on, because I was shaking from a combination of leftover anger from the scene with Nico and nervousness because I was late.

"You'd better warm up a little," Donohue said.

"No, it's too late," I said. "I'm ready."

I knew I should warm up, to get my legs limber for the strenuous leaping I was about to do. But Pasternak's stern expression and the restlessness of the exhibitors and the fact that every minute I delayed was costing the studio thousands of dollars made me decide that, this once, I would forego the customary limbering up exercises.

I ran up to the top of the lofty set. I signaled I was ready. The other dancers and showgirls got into their positions. The playback with the music started. Donohue gave me my cue and I turned on my best smile and started.

I began the leaps down. One level. OK. The next level. Still fine. Then I leaped down to the third level and as soon as I landed I knew something was very wrong. My knee bent—the wrong way. I fell down and stared at my leg, with the knee twisted peculiarly. I felt no pain, not right away. I guess I was in a state of shock. Donohue yelled, "Cut," and ran up to where I was sprawled on the hard wood of the set.

"Oh, my God," he said.

Then he took my leg and bent it back to a more normal configuration. The studio first-aid department had been called immediately and they were there in a few minutes. They loaded me on a stretcher and gingerly carried me down the rest of the way. I was conscious but writhing on the stretcher. Terrible thoughts popped into my mind—was this the end of my dancing career? I had heard of other dancers who had to quit because of serious knee injuries. At one point, the people carrying the stretcher slipped, and I rolled off.

"For God's sake, be careful!" somebody yelled, as they picked me up and put me back.

They had called an ambulance and took me directly to Good Samaritan Hospital. I was there only a few minutes when Dr. Francis McKeever arrived. The studio had sent for him, because he was the man who had treated L.B. Mayer, when he had had a serious accident which damaged his hip.

He examined me, gave me a shot of something, had X-rays taken. Then, later, he came to my bedside.

"I don't think we'll have to operate," he said, and that was a tremendous relief. "I think what we'll do is immobilize you so you can't move that leg at all. You're young. Those ligaments will grow back."

"Will I be able to dance again, doctor?" That was my primary concern.

"It's too early to know for sure," Dr. McKeever said, "but I think you will. You're young and strong and, unless there are complications, I look forward to seeing you dancing again."

I was able to rest, then, with that load off my mind. Then I called my mother—"Mom, I've had a little accident"—and she was there at my side very soon.

But even before she got there, there was a telephone call from Howard Hughes. I don't know how he heard about it, but he did, and he was on the phone immediately.

"Why didn't you call me immediately?" he said. "I'll have my doctor over there right away."

When Howard took over, Howard took over. And he decided to take

Baby Sid Finklea.

The little girl.

Sid's first ballet recital,
as a snowflake.

As a ballet student in Los Angeles.

Cyd Charisse, in *The Unfinished Dance.* By this time, the spelling
of her name had been changed to the more exotic C-y-d.

Cyd, in *Ziegfeld Follies*.

Cyd, as an Indian girl, with Stewart Granger in *The Wild North*.

Cyd, opposite Rock Hudson in *Twilight for the Gods.*

Cyd and Barbara Stanwyck in *East Side, West Side.*

"The Gypsy Dance," from *Sombrero*.   *Party Girl*.

From *Meet Me In Las Vegas*, Johnny Brascia, Cyd Charisse, and Liliane Montevecchi.

Cyd and Fred Astaire, in *Band Wagon.*

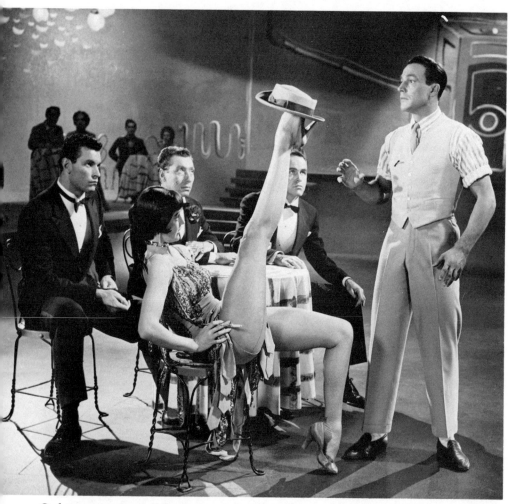

Cyd, opposite Gene Kelly in the "Broadway Melody Ballet," from *Singin' in the Rain*.

Again, with Gene Kelly in *Brigadoon.* "I think the only time I
was ever really angry at Gene Kelly was on *"Brigadoon."*

Cyd Charisse, in the opening number of *The Silencers*.
"That was a Matt Helm film . . ."

over. His doctor, Dr. Vern Mason, arrived within an hour and gave me another examination. His diagnosis and his prescription corresponded with Dr. McKeever's. Howard must have told the hospital he was interested in me, because from that moment on, whatever I asked for was immediately forthcoming. I remember I mentioned to a nurse, idly, that it would be nice if the room were cooler. Within fifteen minutes, there were a couple of mechanics in the room, installing an air-conditioner. All I had to do was request something, no matter how big or how small, and it happened. And, as if by magic, dozens of roses appeared on my bedside table.

I was in the hospital three weeks, but I was never lonely. There was a constant stream of visitors and even more phone calls. (And, since the studio paid all the bills, everything was first-class, or as first-class as it can ever be in a hospital.) Jimmy Durante, who was in *On an Island with You* with me, visited me several times. What a wonderful man! His visits left me cheered up for days. Howard came by to see me a few times, too. After the first week, he would come and they would bundle me up and carry me out to his car—not his usual little car, but a limousine to accommodate my immobilized leg—and he'd take me for rides. I knew, from reading the gossip colums in the newspapers, that he was seeing other girls as well as visiting me, but that didn't bother me. I had no claim on him. I also read in those gossip columns that Tony was seeing Rita Hayworth. He called me a few times in the hospital, but, because of knowing about him and Rita, those calls were brief and rather cool. Maybe that should have told me something about my own feelings.

The studio called to tell me they were keeping me on salary until I recovered, which was nice. When I first signed, I made $150 a week, but that had gradually been going up. They had torn my contract up and given me another one, with a sizable raise. But I was still far from being in the upper brackets of Hollywood salaries.

Eventually, those three weeks in the hospital ended and I went home, in a cast from hip to ankle. Carefully, I tried putting my weight on my bad leg and, over the next few weeks, I grew more confident in its strength. But it would still be a long while before I could dance again. I was faced with a lengthy period of convalescence, and I didn't know what I would do with myself. Having always been active, the thought of inactivity filled me with dread. I decided that I would be terribly bored for the next month or however long it would take.

The first time Howard came to see me, after I had gotten home, I grumbled about not having anything to do.

"I tell you what," he said. "Why don't you learn how to fly?"

"Fly? An airplane?"

"Sure. It's wonderful fun. And you do it all sitting down, so it can't possibly hurt your leg."

I had never even thought about it, but it was something to do at a time when I had nothing to do. So I agreed. And the very next day, I went out to the field with Howard. He knew a pilot who had a school directly across from Hughes' hangar. Howard introduced us, and said that "This girl wants to learn how to fly."

I learned to fly with my leg still in a cast. Whenever I went up, Howard was there to watch me land. I enjoyed the experience very much—there is nothing to compare with being up there in a plane alone. That first solo flight was one of the most thrilling experiences of my life. The adrenalin was really flowing that day. I flew to Palm Springs and back one day and began to get real confidence at the stick.

But, even though I was qualified, I never did get my pilot's license. By the time I was ready for it, I was dancing again and never had the time to take my examination. I sometimes regret not getting my license, and I may still do it someday.

One day, when I had been taking flying lessons for some time, Howard met me as usual when I came in for my landing.

"Very nice," he said. "Now I want to show you something."

And he led me across the field.

"Here's your plane," he said. And he pointed to a little Cessna parked there on the strip.

"What do you mean, my plane?" I asked.

"It's your plane. I give it to you. Here are the keys."

I had to laugh—and decline. How could I even afford the gasoline? That gesture, however, was typically Hughes—generous in the extreme and very thoughtful.

My recovery was more rapid than I had expected. I was home only three weeks after I was discharged from the hospital. Howard would take me to the airport, for my flying lesson, then back to see Dr. McKeever who checked on my progress. And the knee mended quickly, so quickly that, in just about two months from the day I tore the ligaments, I was dancing again. This time, it was with Ricardo Montalban and Ann Miller in a number in *The Kissing Bandit.*

Being back at work was a great feeling, because when the accident happened, I had genuine doubts I would ever be able to work again. So it was a very special day when I got up and danced, and everything went well. The knee seemed, at the time, to be as good as new. As it turned out, it wasn't.

I still kept up my giddy social whirl. Tony. Howard. Peter. And all the rest. But it gradually narrowed down to Tony and Howard, Howard and Tony.

Howard continued his generosity. One thing he said he liked about me particularly was my ears. That explains what happened one night.

We were in his screening room, where he was watching a new movie. As he always did during such occasions, he had sent out for a gallon of ice cream, and was spooning it up as the movie ran. When the film ended, he took me into his office. On a table were stacks of jewelry boxes, piled six high. And each one contained a pair of earrings, one pair more fabulous than the next.

"Take what you want," he said.

My Amarillo morality was still operating, however. I had been taught that a lady didn't accept expensive gifts from a gentleman. So I said that the earrings were lovely, but that I couldn't accept even one pair. He just smiled and had them taken away. I think, however, that I went up in his esteem that evening.

I always enjoyed my evenings with Howard Hughes. We did many things together. I was down at the port with him the day he flew his huge wooden plane. I helped him when he was in some sort of legal trouble, too. They wanted him to testify—it seems they always wanted him to testify —and he was hiding out. Subpoenas were issued for him, but nobody could find him. That was because he was spending most of his time with me. He had a small house nobody knew about in the valley, only a block or so from where I was living. He would drive his funny little old car over to my place, and we would have dinner together and listen to the reports on the radio saying that everybody was looking for him.

Our relationship was not a source of gossip. Whatever we did—those evenings at the plant, at his screening room, at my house and those days at the airport—were always far away from the usual Hollywood haunts. The first time it became common knowledge that Howard Hughes and Cyd Charisse were seeing each other was on one Christmas Eve, which also happens to be his birthday. (Curiously, Tony's birthday is Christmas Day, which is something of an oddity.)

Louis B. Mayer always had a Christmas Eve party, and he liked his "family"—his MGM stars—to show up. So I felt it behooved me to make an appearance. Howard and I had a date that night and I persuaded him to go to the Mayer party. We walked in and you could see the shocked looks on everybody's faces, especially Mayer's. We stayed only about twenty minutes; that was all Howard could stand of Hollywood parties.

I was fascinated by Howard Hughes and certainly intrigued by him. But I was never in love with him. I don't know why not, because certainly he had all the raw materials that a girl looks for in a man. He was brilliant, attractive, obviously not a pauper. He could do so many things at the same time—wheeling and dealing and giving orders and making things happen—that he was always exciting to be with. One of his problems was that he didn't hear too well. My own opinion, based on nothing more than a good dose of feminine intuition, is that his hearing problem is one reason he became the man he was when he died, hiding out from the world. I learned to talk at a louder level than I normally do whenever we were together.

He was a good friend and remained a good friend, to both Tony and me, after our marriage. But, at first, the two men were competitors. I was seeing Tony most of the time that I wasn't seeing Howard. It would be one one night, the other the next. I think they were each jealous of the other.

"Cyd, Tony's all right, but he's not the right man for you," Howard would say. "Don't get involved."

I think he liked Tony, but there is that jealousy factor inherent in all of us. It makes us say such things, so we can maintain our proprietary interest. I knew Howard was seeing other girls, just as he knew that I was seeing other men, and I imagine I got in some digs about those other girls, just as he did about my other fellows. It's part of the courtship process.

At the time, he didn't have to urge me not to get involved. I had no intention of getting involved. I was just getting out of a marriage that had produced very little happiness for me, except for bringing me my son. The last thing I wanted was another marriage, at least not right away. There was still a lot of lost time to catch up with, a lot of living to do.

The divorce finally came through. Actually, it was Howard Hughes who facilitated it. He sent me to his own law firm and they handled it. I neither asked for nor wanted anything from Nico, merely my freedom. The grounds were that usual staple of Hollywood divorces, incompatibility. Beverly Behr, a good friend who had been one of Nico's pupils, was my witness. At the end, Nico raised no contest; he knew now that it was inevitable.

So my life was now totally free. I had my work and my social life and I enjoyed both. At home, my mother was there to take care of Nicky. Lindy was homesick so she returned to Texas and my mother, who had never had to cook in her life, suddenly became a gourmet cook. There was nobody else to do it, so she learned.

I was learning things, too. I had never had more than a glass of wine, as I've mentioned. But now, out on the town, it became something that was expected of me. When I first started going out, I had heard of only one drink—a martini—so that was what I ordered. I'd take only a few sips, so it never bothered me. I think it was working with Esther Williams that taught me about drinking. But I still stuck with martinis when I was out —and, to this day, a martini is all I drink. Now, though, I make sure it's made with vodka.

The more I dated, and the more different men I saw, the more Tony Martin appealed to me. That wrong foot we had started out on turned completely around. I began to feel more and more comfortable with him. Of all the men I knew, Tony had the best sense of humor, for one thing. I liked that. I enjoy laughing. And I felt comfortable with him. That's the most important quality, I think, when you're contemplating marriage. It's just the feeling that it's right and good, that the two of you belong together. Besides, he was—and is—so handsome!

I felt that Tony really and sincerely cared for me. I didn't stop to analyze it. I didn't wonder what had gone wrong with his first marriage. I only knew that I found myself comfortable with him, that I had this wonderful warm glow when we were together. Of all the men I had been seeing, he was the one I wanted to be with.

If you love someone, don't analyze that feeling. Just enjoy it. When you really are in love, you don't concern yourself with the good and the bad, but merely with the overall effect. To me, the effect of Tony Martin on me was a pleasurable one.

Gradually, I began seeing more and more of Tony, less and less of the others. This attracted attention around town, of course, and everybody tried to warn me not even to think of Tony as a husband.

Everybody talked against him. Joe Pasternak and Benny Thau at MGM called me into their offices, and said that I shouldn't marry him. I tried to find out what they had against him, but there really was no concrete reason, just a feeling that we were wrong for each other. My mother, too, was against it. I think her reason was that she felt I shouldn't rush into anything.

The one person who seemed to believe we could make a go of it was Lillian Burns.

"Tony is a wonderful man," Lillian said. "If he asks you, go ahead and marry him."

I had pretty much reached that conclusion, too. I had, originally, felt that there was no reason to marry again for a few more years. I was still young and I had a beautiful child, so there was no purpose in marriage right away. But the more I saw of Tony, the more I felt I wanted to spend all my time with him. Life was never dull when he was around, that's for certain. So I began thinking that, if he proposed, I would accept. And I had reason to believe that a proposal would be forthcoming. He had said, on one of our first dates, that he was going to marry me. I assumed it was just one of his jokes, maybe part of his line with the ladies. But he kept saying it, and I came to believe he was serious. Still, he never actually asked me to marry him, just kept saying, "You know, one of these days I'm going to marry you."

Then one day, we were out in his car, driving to dinner. He turned to me and there was something new in his face. The funny man was gone and there was a very serious, almost sad, expression in his eyes.

"You know," he said, "I'd like very much to marry you, but you wouldn't."

"Why on earth not?"

"Because I'm Jewish."

"You've got to be kidding. What difference would that make?"

It would make no difference to me. Why should it? I was brought up to believe people were people, no matter what religion or color they were. And I believed it. I've found, over the years, that Jewish people are more sensitive, more aware of their religion than others are. There is a tendency to become defensive about it. I suppose it's a natural product of centuries of persecution, and they have learned to suspect and expect intolerance. Too often, they find it, too. But not from me, and I told Tony that. In fact, that was the last thing that would have occurred to me.

"The only thing that matters," I said, "is that you love me and I love you."

"You mean it?" That sad, serious expression vanished and the laughing man I loved so much was there again. "Oh, honey, I'll be very good to you, I promise."

And that's how it happened that I agreed to become Mrs. Tony Martin. But the actual event didn't occur for some time. We were both terribly busy, working, and then he had to go back east for some engagement or other. I think, when he left, he was still uncertain that I really would marry him. When he came back, he was loaded down with jewelry —an engagement ring, a necklace, a bracelet, a pin.

We set a date, then had to cancel it. That happened a few times. My mother was still telling me I was making a mistake. I think it's possible that the difference in religion was behind her objections, although she never came out and said so. But she pointed out that I had married out of my faith with Nico—he was a Catholic—and that hadn't worked. She kept saying, "Cyd, it's all too fast, much too fast."

I was pleased about the way Tony and Nicky got along. If they hadn't, I'm sure I would not have married Tony because Nicky's happiness and well-being were paramount to me. But the boy and the man became good friends. Nico was still popping in to see Nicky, of course, and I tried to be

136

out and when he came, because if he caught me at home, there would be more acrimony. He had heard about my impending marriage and, naturally, he wasn't happy about it. It gave him another reason to argue with me.

I don't think Tony's parents were too happy with his choice, either. In their words, I was *goyim*—a gentile. And with a child, too! Tony, naturally, was anxious for me to meet them, in the hope that if they met me, they would come around. So, one day, he took me over to the apartment on Olympic Boulevard where they were living. They were polite but cool. Tony's mother had cooked a big dinner. Afterward, she took me in to her bedroom, on some pretext. But there, on the dresser, very prominently displayed, was a picture of Alice Faye, Tony's first wife. And it was inscribed in a large, flowing hand. "To Mom." She pointed to the picture, which I couldn't possibly have missed.

"That Alice," Mrs. Meyers said, "was a wonderful person and a wonderful wife to my Tony. And a wonderful daughter-in-law."

I bit my tongue and said nothing.

"You have a child, I understand?" she said.

"Yes, I have a son. His name is Nicky."

"So Tony would be supporting a wife and a boy, as well?"

I said no. I said I would and could easily support my son.

Tony came in and rescued me, but it was an unpleasant few minutes, there in the bedroom. I can understand it, of course. A mother only wants the best for her son, and she had some doubts that I was the best—a different religion, a woman with a child, all that.

Between his parents and my mother and the flak we were getting from the studio, it was all getting to be too much. So I said to Tony that if we were going to get married, we had better get married and get it over with.

"OK, when?"

I pulled a date out of my head.

"Good. Where?"

"I don't care where. You take care of that."

He did. On May 15, Tony and I, together with Nat and Bernice Goldstone and Charles Carroll, Tony's right-hand man, drove to Santa Barbara and we were married. We wanted a civil ceremony, and Tony felt that Santa Barbara was beautiful—which it is—and far enough away to be apart from the Hollywood commotion, but still a fairly easy drive.

And so I had a new name. Tula Ellice Finklea Siderova Istomina Norwood Charisse—and now Mrs. Tony Martin.

We drove from Santa Barbara to Carmel. Tony had made reservations for us at Pebble Beach. But because we'd switched the dates, when we got there we found the hotel was completely booked. They were terribly sorry, obviously there had been some mistake, but there was simply no room for us. There we were on our honeymoon, with no place to stay. The manager of the Pebble Beach hotel was nice. He said he knew of a small hotel in the hills that had a room. It was, he said, pleasant. So we drove up there and it was hardly pleasant. Decrepit would have been a better adjective.

We climbed into bed—a very small double bed—and it promptly crashed to the floor. Worse, there was a large hole right in the center of the bed. When we came out in the morning, there was a crowd of children camped around our cabin—word had gotten out that we were there, and they had come from miles to see us and gather autographs.

We didn't stay another night. We went into San Francisco and had a proper, comfortable honeymoon at the Mark Hopkins.

Everybody said the marriage would last a week. As I write this, that was twenty-eight years ago.

7

UNDESIRABLE
AND
UNFIT

The coming war and the departing Lana made my life pretty grim in the beginning of the Fearful Forties. I had to get away, find a new life. All my friends said I was flaky. The fashionable thing in Hollywood then was to see how long you could delay the inevitable, namely, getting drafted. The draft board's net was getting closer every day. Most of the men I knew were shivering in their patent leather oxfords at the thought of serving. I might have been shivering right along with them, but when Lana and I broke up, I felt the need to change things drastically and the war and the service seemed like a heaven-sent opportunity.

Because of the specter of the war, too, my professional life was hurting. I wasn't alone, but that was little comfort. I was up for the leading male role in a big MGM musical with Eleanor Powell. They wanted to know how I stood with the draft. I said for all I knew I was 1A. So they said, sorry, they couldn't take the chance of giving me that part and then having me hauled off to serve in the Army in the middle of shooting.

That was the last straw. I did what any red-blooded American dummy would do: I joined the bar—but not the legal one, any one I could get to.

I went on a toot that lasted quite a while. I really don't remember much about a period of roughly four months. It was as though those four months were torn out of the calendar. They never existed. I don't know where I was or what I did. Lost beyond recall. Not lost weekend—lost season. All I know is that my bank account showed I'd spent $164,000 in those four months.

When I told MGM I figured I'd be 1A, I really was kidding. I had problems with my ears, but I didn't want the studio to know; I'd be uninsurable. I thought they'd never take me, not if they really administered a sound physical exam. But I knew two things that made me think such was not the case. The first was that they needed bodies and, unless a man was virtually a wreck, they'd take anybody. Secondly, they had it in for Hollywood types. The public was watching what happened to us, and the slightest hint of special treatment or favoritism brought howls of indignation. Uncle Sam Wants You, read the sign. They thought Hollywood stars in uniform would attract others.

So I figured I'd be drafted, even though I was far from the perfect physical specimen. I went for my physical exam, summoned by the Beverly Hills draft board, and what I expected to happen happened—only worse than I imagined.

I have long had ear trouble. Otosclerosis, it's called. It's hereditary. Later on, it got much worse, but even then I had problems with my hearing. So the doctor the Draft Board sent me to hollered out a series of numbers at me.

"Fifty-two! Forty-nine! SIXTY-EIGHT!" He screamed.

"What?" I said, because I honestly hadn't heard him. He said, "Are you trying to duck something?"

It didn't matter. My hearing was checked as OK.

Then it came time to examine my eyes, which were not so hot, either.

"You're not an ordinary person, Mr. Martin," the eye doctor said, "so I have to be very careful with you."

He was extra careful. Kind, too. Instead of having me stand where everybody else stood to read the eye chart, he let me stand right up close to the chart. I started off standing in the usual place.

"Read the top line."

"FZWXQ."

"Wrong. Move closer."

And I moved closer, then closer again, until I was practically nose-to-nose with the letters. He gave me a funny smile and said, "That isn't going to help you." He passed my reading.

So I was railroaded into 1A, along with a lot of other Hollywood stars. Don't get me wrong—I was glad to be accepted because I wanted to be a part of the action, but, still, it was patently unfair. They did the same thing to many of my Hollywood peers, just so there would never be an accusation that they had let Hollywood stars off easily. It isn't always a good thing to be famous, you know.

Of course, there was another side to that picture, too. I must admit that there were many stars I could name who would go to their doctors the day of their physical and get a pill or two to shoot their blood pressure up.

140

And there were other tricks pulled to get deferments. I didn't want a deferment, because, as I've explained, I wanted to get the hell out of town. Nevertheless, in all fairness, I think my eyes and ears were such that I should not have been placed in the 1A category.

But I was. And now I had to make a choice. Should I wait around to get drafted? Or should I see what I could do, as so many stars were doing, about getting a commission and enlisting?

Maybe my decision was influenced by the low opinion I held of the Beverly Hills draft board. The man running it was some insurance man from downtown, who had it in for movie people in general and especially successful Beverly Hills movie people. He was the man who turned down MGM's request for a three-month deferment for me so I could do that musical. No way would a Hollywood star get a break from him. He had as much right running the draft board as a bookmaker would have being named president of a college. The draft board was supposed to be made up of "a group of your peers," or some such wording. Peers, my ass. That reminds me of George Burns and the Internal Revenue Service. Once an I.R.S. man questioned George about deductions he had claimed for Gracie's clothing. George had carefully itemized all the dresses she had bought for their act, showing still pictures to substantiate the claim.

"Why is this dress listed as $1,750?" the I.R.S. agent asked.

"Because that's what it cost," George said.

"My wife has the same kind of dress. It cost her only $250. How do you explain that?"

"Because," George said, "your wife has no goddamn talent."

I had the talent so they moved me up close to the eye chart so I could see and hollered the numbers louder and louder until I could hear. It was a railroad bigger than the Union Pacific. They wanted anybody in show business, and the bigger the star, the more that particular draft board went to work until they grabbed him.

While I considered what to do—wait and be drafted or try to get a commission—I had engagements to fulfill. I had no permanent home at that time, so I gave the draft board Nat Goldstone's office as my address. And I blithely went off to Chicago, where I was doubling—the Chicago Theater and the Chez Paree nightclub. One morning, I got a call from the F.B.I. They wanted to see me about evading the draft, about hiding out.

Hiding out? My name was splashed all over the Chicago newspapers, it was spelled out in lights on two Chicago marquees. That's hiding out, to the Beverly Hills draft board? I'm doing ten shows a week, between the theater and the club, and thousands of people see me every week, and they say I'm hiding out? What a crock of shit that was.

I had to get a lawyer in Chicago to represent me, and he finally convinced them that the problem was simply I had never gotten whatever communication the draft board had sent me. If it was sent at all, it went to my agent's office, and his secretary had just forgotten it or overlooked it or something. But before he persuaded them of my innocence, I was taken to the F.B.I. headquarters, photographed and fingerprinted. A good friend on one of the papers there managed to get the photograph killed, or else the news of that little incident would have been all over the world. Still, some of the F.B.I. underlings were gung ho about handcuffing me and booking me on some charge or other, but the head man considered all the facts for a fast two minutes and said, "This whole thing stinks. This man is not hiding from anybody." And they let me go—after they had first questioned me for six hours.

That incident made me determined to beat the draft board. I didn't want that bunch of shitheels to get their hands on me. I'd go into the service I wanted and, if possible, with some rank better than the lowest. It wasn't that I wanted any special favors, it was simply I felt that my name meant something and perhaps I could do some good in recruiting as Tony Martin with some kind of title in front of it.

I decided the Navy was the life I wanted.

Finally, Nat Goldstone called me. He said a Commander Herman Spitzel, of the Navy's officer procurement department in Washington, wanted me to call him. I called him. In turn, he had me call Lieutenant Commander Maurice Aroff. Now that was a name I knew. Maury Aroff was a man around town I'd known very well from the time I'd arrived in Los Angeles in 1935. I called him. He was in San Francisco, with the Navy's 11th district, serving under Captain White, who was the chief of the district's naval officer procurement program. He said if I went through the proper channels he'd see what he could do for me.

But I didn't stop at that. I'd heard that line—"I'll see what I can do for you"—before so I wasn't about to put all my eggs in one ask-it. I knew I could do a job as an officer—I was mature, I had leadership ability (I'd done all right leading a band, which was more leadership experience than most officers had), I was healthy and I had no black marks against me.

For weeks, the whole thing hung in the balance. Finally, Commander Aroff came through. He said he was able to get me a rating as a Chief Specialist, the same rating Bob Feller had gotten.

"It's the best we can do for you, Tony," Commander Aroff said. "And I think you'd better join the Navy now."

He made sense. So I said OK. I was to report to San Francisco on January 2, 1942, to become a Chief Petty Officer, Specialist rating.

I had a final fling in New York which turned out to be sadder than I had expected. There was one incident that made it sad, and that haunted me for years—and still does.

I stayed at the Sherry-Netherland, and wandered around Times Square and my old haunts. Whenever I was in New York, I always made it a point to get my shoes shined at Doc's. Doc had his shoe-shine stand around the corner from the Palace theater. He'd been there for years. So on this last trip I went to Doc's, and I climbed up on the stand and put my feet on the iron pedestal and his grizzled old head bent over my shoes and he began polishing.

Then I noticed he was crying. Tears were falling on my custom-made alligator shoes.

"What's the trouble, Doc?"

At first he just shook his head and couldn't talk, but I persuaded him and it all poured out.

"My wife left me, Mr. T," he said, "and she took our two kids and went off with my brother."

And look who'd been feeling sorry for himself. His problems were so much worse he put mine in perspective. I realized at that moment that material things weren't as important—could never be as important—as love for your family and your fellow man.

"Doc, close up shop, you're coming with me," I said. I gave him fifty dollars, so he wouldn't lose any money, and took him to Twenty-One for lunch and we commiserated with each other.

"Nobody ever died of heartbreak, Doc," I said, and I had reason to remember that later on in my own life. And I think I helped him. At least, when we parted, he had stopped crying. He helped me, too; I felt now I could face the future, whatever it was.

I had one last date, playing at the Cosmopolitan Theater in Boston with Gene Krupa and his orchestra. It was kind of sad for me, realizing that this might be the last time I sang before the public. I knew that my assignment in San Francisco wasn't exactly front-line duty, but I also know that being in the Navy made me subject to transfer anywhere, even where people were shooting at other people, so I knew that I could damn easily be killed before this whole war was over. So I sang, up there in Boston, with everything I had. I always do, but this time I gave it a little extra. When there may be no tomorrow, you give it all you've got today.

Gene Krupa came to me the day before I closed and said that one of the Boston boys had approached him and wanted me to stay over an extra day to sing at his daughter's first communion.

"I can't, Gene," I said. "I want a day or so at home before I go into the Navy. I have a date with Lana for New Year's Eve, a last good-bye kind of thing. I'm not about to miss that to sing at some stranger's daughter's communion."

"Do me a favor, Tony," Krupa said. "Talk to this man. He's a very tough person. At least talk to him."

So I said I'd talk to him. I explained my situation—going into the Navy, needed a few days at home to see my folks, see my girl, clean up my affairs. He wouldn't take no for an answer. He had to have me sing at his daughter's first communion.

Krupa had told me the only way out of it all was to ask for so much money he'd refuse. So I decided to do that. I said, OK, I'd stay over and sing for him—for $5,000 cash.

"You got it," he said. Not an eyelash was batted.

"One more thing. I can't stay late. I'll have to catch the midnight plane, so I can get back to California in time to see my girl that next morning, give her a few presents I've got for her."

"You got it."

"I'll need ten violins."

"You got it. Is that all?"

"That's all."

So I was stuck. He'd agreed to all my demands. Ben Oakland, the songwriter who was my friend and conductor, came to me horrified when I was about to do the show. He said all they had in the way of an orchestra was ten violins. This guy had misunderstood me—when I said I wanted ten violins, I meant ten violins in addition to the regular orchestra. He thought all I wanted was the ten violins. So I had to sing for an hour with just ten violins accompanying me (I told them to play *soli*—together—and it worked pretty good).

That was my last professional engagement for more than four years. The guy was nice, gave me a couple of gifts besides my $5,000 and wished me luck and had his car and driver take me to the airport.

I reported to duty in San Francisco on January 2, 1942, as ordered.

I was glad it was over. It had become something of a cause célèbre. People had become very nervous in both Los Angeles and Washington, because I was a celebrity and the whole thing had gotten out of hand. Now, at least, it was over and I was in the Navy and I could do the job—whatever it was.

When I was sworn in, Commander Aroff explained my duties to me. I was what was called a specialist. It was a rating they had created for athletes and entertainers. Chief Petty Officer was the Navy's equivalent of the Army's rank of master sergeant. I was to be something like window

144

decoration for the Navy, to attract young men into the service. Aroff said I was to report to a Commander Walters, whose office was in the Ferry Building in San Francisco. I saluted neatly, turned on my heels and went over to the Ferry Building, where I presented myself to Commander Walters.

"OK, Martin," he said. "For the time being, all you have to do is stand around and watch and learn."

The Ferry Building was the place where they gave physical exams to would-be officers. They figured that if I was there, and the public saw me, I would be something of a come-on and lots of young men would join the V-5 or V-12 programs. There was a lot of competition between the services then, and the idea was for me—and others like me—to be the bait that brought more bright and talented young men into the Navy than went into the other services. So I really had nothing much to do, except to convince them that the Navy was a great service. As I remember it, my only real job was to go out every afternoon about two-thirty and bring a chocolate milkshake back for Commander Walters. He was a pleasant enough man —he'd had an ulcer and hadn't asked for a waiver—but I didn't exactly feel like I was contributing much to the war effort. I had them put extra cream in his milkshake, and that made me feel like I was doing my part.

It was, of course, a difficult adjustment for me, as it was for any dedicated civilian when he joined one of the services. From the casual, undisciplined life to the rigid discipline of the Navy overnight was bound to be a traumatic experience for anybody. But, I think, it was especially tough on anybody from the Hollywood crowd. Let's face it: we were an elite group. The money, the fame, the adulation all combined to make us think we were something special. Take me and my cars, for example. At the time I was sworn in to the Navy, I owned three cars. I had a $22,000 Darron Packard, a brand new Cadillac and a Studebaker which had been given me when I did a radio guest shot on a show the Studebaker company sponsored. Then, overnight, I was a Navy man—no cars, no nothing. Formations. Saluting. Chow lines. It was as though I had turned a corner and found myself in an entirely alien culture. And, as I have said before, I was very cocky at the time—success has a way of making you that way. When success is taken away, the period of adjustment is hard, but I managed.

It grew a little easier as the weeks went on, particularly when I began to expand my duties. Going for milkshakes was one thing, but then I started actively recruiting and that was better. I was doing something that bore fruit, and that made me feel that I was becoming part of the war effort. They sent me on trips to Wyoming, to Colorado, to Nevada, to Utah. I took along a slide show about Navy life, and gave my presentation to young men in various colleges. They asked me as many or more questions about Hollywood as they did about the Navy, but I guess that was the whole reason for my being there. I was the Judas goat, and my job was to lure the kids into Navy blue.

Then I began putting on some shows, too. The USS *Pennsylvania*, one of our big battleships, steamed into port on its first trip since surviving Pearl Harbor. I was assigned to put on a show for the boys from the *Pennsylvania* at Vallejo Naval Base, the big ship's home port. There were still a lot of badly injured boys, and I went around the various wards, singing for them. I can still smell that dreadful stench of their burned flesh and see those poor guys, swathed in bandages with their tortured eyes looking up at me.

It wasn't all work. I had been friendly with Maury Aroff and we resumed our friendship. He was a millionaire and kept a suite at the Clift Hotel in San Francisco. After hours, he'd frequently host big parties and I'd be invited—in effect, ordered—to appear and be the resident Hollywood star. Commander Walters, too, made use of my familiar face and name. He lived in Palo Alto and he'd often throw lavish parties weekends and invite me there to sing for his guests.

I didn't know it at the time, but those shenanigans of my commanding officers were causing some friction. There were jealousies building up. Some of Aroff's and Walters' subordinate officers thought this wasn't proper wartime behavior, these parties with a Hollywood star as one of the attractions—an enlisted man, to boot. As I say, I was unaware of all these undercurrents, but they were there. They must have been, judging by what came later. That probably kicked off all the spying. And there was spying, as it turned out. Aroff's Clift Hotel rooms were tapped and all his telephone conversations monitored by Naval intelligence officers.

Aroff wasn't very popular around San Francisco's Naval headquarters. He was a millionaire civilian with a reserve commission, not an Annapolis graduate, and that was two-and-a-half strikes against him right there. And that extra half-strike came quickly, when he showed them he wasn't about to play ball. He was no pushover. They wanted him to give commissions to favored people, like sons of admirals and high officials, and he just wouldn't do it automatically like a good guy was supposed to do.

I remember being in his office one day when his second-in-command said to him, "Commander, they don't like you around here. Why did you turn down Admiral John Doe's son?"

"He's no goddamn good, that's why. He's been picked up for drunk driving twice, for one thing."

A good reason, but not good enough to satisfy the Navy brass. And he kept doing it, kept sticking to his standards which he felt were for the good of the country, not for the pleasure of the Annapolis social set.

The shit really hit the fan when he turned down the son of a very important admiral. Aroff was stubborn. He could have saved us a lot of grief if he'd just given this kid an ensign's stripes, but he didn't think the boy was good enough for them. He said no. And then, realizing that his situation had become precarious, he put in for sea duty. His boss, Captain White, turned him down. He said Aroff was only doing his job and was doing it well, so he said no to the transfer request. That was the beginning of the end.

It didn't happen right away. Things seemed to be normal for quite a while. I kept going on trips for the Navy—and, I might add, I often had to spend my own money because they examined my expense chits as though they didn't believe me, and I didn't enjoy that feeling. Often I'd have to go to Los Angeles, too, to take some high-ranking brass down and introduce them around in the Hollywood crowd. That, too, came out of my own pocket, but nobody seemed to notice. In fact, those Navy brass were never reluctant to let me, a C.P.O., pick up the checks when we went out to dinner in Los Angeles. Show me an Annapolis officer, and I'll show you a no-tipper. It's been said that professional ball players are cheap tippers. No way, I've seen ball players tip just for a smile.

My fellow chiefs resented me, I began to discover. Most of them were reserve ratings from World War I days who had taken years to get their chief's stripes. They couldn't understand why I, a man with no Naval experience whatsoever, was the same rating they were. And the rated men resented me, too. I tried to make friends, but it wasn't easy.

I was very eager to be a good sailor. I didn't know the etiquette of saluting so, rather than not salute people who deserved it, I saluted every-body. One day, I saluted a man who turned out to be a Filipino mess boy. I saluted doormen, policemen, everybody in a uniform. I was going to do the right thing, that's for sure. I think I'd have even saluted a fireplug with stripes.

Actually, Aroff was the only real friend I had then. I had more in common with him, anyhow, than with the others. We had shared the same sort of life-style before the war, and were trying to stay with it during the war. Aroff still drove his Cadillac around, still kept his luxurious hotel suite, ate well, drank moderately, liked girls. I drove that gift Studebaker up with me after a while, and I'd often do my recruiting tours in it. Maury and I were trying to be civilians at heart. That was our mistake.

One day, one of the doctors, a wonderful guy named Lt. Cmdr.

Peterson, took me aside and put his arm around my shoulder.

"You'd better tell your friend, Aroff, that the heat's on," he said. "It doesn't look good for him."

"What doesn't look good? What's wrong?"

"Him with his Cadillac and his hotel suite and his girls."

"OK. It's his car, his hotel suite, his girls, his money. What's the beef?"

"Look, Tony, you've got to understand. The man's in the wrong job. White has him chief of naval office procurement—and he's a Jew, he's rough. They don't like that."

It seemed incomprehensible to me that this kind of thing could happen in the 1940s, in the United States, especially in the Navy. But politics and prejudice, I guess, know no boundaries of time and country. So I got together with Maury Aroff and told him what Peterson had told me. He laughed about it. I said that from what I'd heard it was no laughing matter and he should take it seriously.

"OK, Tony," he said. "What do you think I should do?"

"It's not just what you should do, but what we both should do," I said. "I think they're gunning for both of us. The first thing we have to do is start living simpler. For a starter, get rid of your fancy car."

"Whatever you say."

So he did that. Me, too. I bought a broken-down used Chevvy for $410 and began driving that. And Maury sold his Cadillac and I made a deal with him for my Studebaker.

"Maury, I've known you eleven years now," I said. "I'll sell you my Studebaker—I got it for nothing, so it's no big deal. Drive the Studebaker instead of the Cadillac. It'll take some of the heat off."

"OK, what do you want for the Studebaker?"

"I don't give a shit. Just give me something. It lists for $684, I don't care what you give me. Just so it looks right."

He had a $500 U.S. bond, and he signed that over to me, and said he'd give me some more later. I said I didn't need any more. That was fine with me. So the deal was made and I thought that was the end of it. But it was only the beginning. That little deal between two friends, which was really so innocent, became the source of all my future troubles. As it turned out, I'd never hear the end of it.

We kept a low profile after that. We drove our less gaudy cars. Aroff gave fewer parties at the hotel and I wasn't invited. There wasn't as much high living. We kept our noses clean. But it was too late. When people are out to get you, they don't give a damn about anything except getting you. And they already had what they thought was enough evidence to get Aroff.

148

I kept on with my duties, going around to the various western colleges with my story of how great Naval aviation was, and I think I did a good job. One day, my travels took me to the University of Nevada, at Reno. And it was there that I woke to read a headline in the local newspaper: AROFF RELIEVED OF DUTY; MARTIN WANTED BY NAVAL INTELLIGENCE.

And there was a big story about how the Navy had accused Commander Maurice Aroff of accepting a bribe of a car to give entertainer Tony Martin a commission in the U.S. Naval Reserve. Aroff was to be court-martialed, and Martin was being sought as a material witness for the Navy.

There were only a couple of things wrong with that whole messy story. In the first place, I never did get a commission in the U.S. Naval Reserve. And, in the second place, I had never given him a car as a bribe. Other than that, the Navy's story was completely accurate.

It had all been leading up to that terrible story. A few weeks before it all broke wide open, a junior officer, a graduate of Annapolis, working with me on the Naval Aviation Cadet Selection Board, had approached me with a sad story. He was about to get married, but he found himself on orders to go to sea, and wanted to bring his fiancée out so they could get married before he left to report to the USS *Lexington*. Would I lend him $250 for his girls' train fare? Sure, why not? I had the money and he was a nice man. So I wrote him a check for $250 as a loan. I found out pretty quick that that was the wrong thing to do. When it came out, the poor kid came that close to being busted. Even though he had paid me back when his paycheck came through, they threw the book at him. And they bawled me out for my part in the affair. Dum-dum me. I didn't know anything about those regulations that prohibited me from doing that. I found out, from that experience, that the Navy frowned on any financial dealings between enlisted men, which I was, and commissioned officers. But by then it was too late; I'd already concluded the deal with Aroff for the Studebaker.

I reflected on all that as I went back from Reno to San Francisco. I knew in my heart and soul that I had done nothing wrong and, as far as I knew, Aroff had done nothing wrong, either. Our arrangements about the car had nothing whatsoever to do with my becoming a Chief Petty Officer. That had happened on orders from Washington. I had gone into the Navy with no promises, no threats, no muscle—and certainly no bribe.

It didn't matter. I reported back to San Francisco and they hustled me into a session with some Naval Intelligence people, at their office on Market Street. Talk about the OGPU or the Gestapo and their interrogations! They had me in there for twenty-two hours straight, with no let-up.

149

No sleep, of course. No rest from the incessant questions. A cup of coffee, a glass of water, that's all. Not a bite to eat.

They'd throw in fresh teams of officers to question me. Some of them, in the style of police departments everywhere, were rough and others tried to open me up by being buddy-buddy.

"Look, Tony," said the buddy-buddy type, giving me a cigarette and an arm around my shoulder, "we got the goods on Aroff. Are you going to go along with the Navy, or are you going to go down with this Jew? It's your choice."

They didn't know I was Jewish. A few months before, I had filed for officers's school and Aroff and other officers had advised me that when I filled out the questionnaire, where it asked for my religion—Catholic, Protestant or Jewish—not to put anything down. He had said that there was a quota system in the Navy for Jews going to officer's school. I wasn't ashamed of my heritage, but I figured there was no point in bucking unnecessary odds. So I'd gone along with all this advice. Thus, on my records, I wasn't a Jew and the Naval Intelligence questioners figured they'd take advantage of my non-Jewishness and thus turn me against Aroff, who was undoubtedly Jewish.

I kept asking them, during those twenty-two hours, what the charges were against Aroff.

"He's going to get twenty years," they kept telling me. "We've really got him dead to rights. He's been taking gifts and favors from everybody."

As it later developed, those "gifts and favors from everybody" boiled down to two things—the famous Studebaker car he supposedly got from me, and a pair of fourteen-dollar cufflinks he received as a gift from an ensign from overseas.

The questioners took turns hammering at me.

The rough ones: "You gave him that car, didn't you?"

The buddy-buddy ones: "Come on, Tony, might as well tell us the whole story. We have tapes of you and Aroff and your friends whooping it up at the Clift Hotel."

The rough ones: "How come you wound up a C.P.O.?"

The buddy-buddy ones: "When you were supposed to be recruiting in Denver, we have reports that you stayed in a fancy suite at the Brown Palace Hotel. Tell us about that."

(That was true—but I paid for that suite, not Uncle Sam. I paid for a lot of things those days, because I had my own money. Anything over my per diem came out of my pocket.)

And so it went. On and on. Questions and questions, the same ones, the same answers. Finally, they let me make a couple of phone calls. I called

150

my manager, Nat Goldstone, and my press agent, Mack Millar. They both told me the same thing. This thing was all over the papers, and it was giving me a bad name. It looked to the public as though I had colluded with Aroff to get a soft spot in the Navy, and that was all the public needed to hear about a star in wartime. My name would be ruined, Nat and Mack told me, unless I cooperated and went along with the Navy.

After twenty-two hours, my head spinning and my eyes heavy with fatigue, I surrendered.

"Yeah, that's right," I said. "Whatever you say is OK with me. I'm tired."

They shoved some papers under my nose and I signed them. I was never on trial, so I had no lawyer. I didn't know what I was signing. I never did see a transcript of what I signed that day, and that document was never used in Aroff's court-martial. So as of today, I still don't know what I signed, and I guess I never will.

They let me sleep then. When I woke up they assigned me to Treasure Island, with orders to report to a Captain Culp. I was ordered not to discuss the pending court-martial of Commander Maurice Aroff with anyone, but to hold myself in readiness to testify.

I hung around for a month or so. It was, I guess, one of the worst periods of my life. My friends in Los Angeles kept telling me that I was big news, but certainly not the kind of big news I wanted to be. It caused major repercussions in Hollywood, too. During that period, many top stars were going into one service or the other. Arrangements had been made— Clark Gable was going to become a major, Tyrone Power a Marine lieutenant, Henry Fonda an ensign in the Navy. But when my case hit the papers, all those commissions were withdrawn hastily. They weren't going to risk any more charges of favoritism. So those guys all had to start out lower in rank. Gable had to go to O.C.S., make his way to his commission through the obstacle course and all the rest. Fonda went to Seattle as a Seaman 2nd Class. Power started out as a Marine private. All because of the news about Tony Martin.

For weeks, it was a major event in the newspapers. With the war going badly for us at that time, there was little to cheer about. So they wrote about my problems, and the insinuations were evident. I was branded a slacker. Maybe not in so many words, but that was the clear implication. The impression was left in the minds of the public that Tony Martin was that lowest of the low, a man who had bribed his way to a soft spot in the service. Everybody else went in and took his chances but not Tony Martin—he gave a Navy officer a car so he'd get a commission and save his own skin. Let me repeat again—I never bribed anyone, I gave nobody a car, I never received a commission. Those were the positive facts, but I had no forum through which I could defend myself. The public got that dreadful picture of me, and, as I will show later, that picture hung around in people's minds for years.

It may still be there. And that's one reason why I wanted to include this story in this book, so I could tell my side of the story completely and totally and with absolute honesty at last, without the Navy telling me to keep my mouth shut. No bribe. No commission. I went in as a Chief Petty Officer Specialist, so they could use my skills properly. After that, I was subject to orders like everybody else. And I was ready and eager to do anything they assigned me to do.

While I waited for Aroff's court-martial, I was given the most menial jobs around Treasure Island. I remember one day when some of us had to repair an admiral's putting green. He had this private little putting green behind his quarters, and some other men and I spent a whole day working on it, so it'd be as smooth as glass.

I was in a sort of limbo there. Aroff was there, too, but we couldn't communicate. I was advised, forcefully, not to speak to anyone. I just waited.

Finally, the court-martial was convened. The site was Yerba Buena, one of the Navy's small island installations in San Francisco Bay. It was a scene out of a bad novel.

Only answer yes or no. But I could tell from the questions that everybody's mind was made up, that Aroff, that poor man who had just been trying to do his job, was being railroaded. He had stepped on some sensitive toes, that's all. Just answer yes or no, Chief Martin. OK, I answered yes or no. But I told the truth. I shocked a few of them, because I wasn't about to play ball. When they asked me if Commander Aroff had accepted a bribe from me, I said no. I was under oath. The twenty-two hours of torture were behind me. I could tell the truth. I told the truth. No, sir, I bribed nobody and nobody accepted a bribe from me. No. No. No. Emphatically, no.

They went so far as to call my mother to testify. I still don't know what they expected to get out of her. As I remember it (the Navy will not release the transcript of the court-martial), her testimony went something like this:

Q: What is your name?
A: Hattie Myers.
Q: Where are you from?
A: I was born in Oakland long before you bastards were born.
Q: Could you please tell this court—

A: There's a war going on, why don't you go out and fight it instead of picking on these nice American boys?

Q: Thank you, that will be all, Mrs. Myers.

I didn't even have a lawyer. They called Nat Goldstone, for some reason, and he was represented by a lawyer. He knew all about it, he had been around when I worked out the deal for the car with Aroff, when he gave me the $500 bond as partial payment for the car. But he never said a word about that in court. Maybe he forgot, because it had been so insignificant.

The trial dragged on. When I wasn't in court, I got a few rather suspicious telephone calls.

"Chief Martin?"

"Yes."

"Hello, Chief. Don't say anything, just go out to a pay phone and call me back at this number."

The voice gave me a number in Washington. I went to a pay phone and called the number. The voice answered.

"We know you're not involved, Chief. This is Admiral So-and-So. You can't mention my name, but relax. We'll take care of you. Everything will be OK if you play ball. We'll get to Jacobs [Admiral Randy Jacobs] for you."

All very mysterious. As it turned out, they didn't mean a word of what they were saying. Take care of me? They sure took care of me, all right.

The judge advocate was a Lieutenant Commander named Klein, a Jew —a token Jew, I suppose, so the Navy wouldn't look prejudiced. All the judges were full commanders, captains and admirals. The trial had been going a week or so, when the presiding admiral rapped the table with his gavel.

"I see no serious evidence of any wrongdoing here. Perhaps some slight misconduct, that's all. I suggest we put an end to this affair and go on about the war. Any objection?"

The other judges nodded and, of course, the defense was agreeable. But not Lieutenant Commander Klein.

"I have more evidence, your honor," he said. The trial was his way of adding another stripe to his sleeve.

They had no choice but to continue with the travesty. Klein figured this was a juicy case and if he could get a conviction, it would look good for him. The hell with justice and fair play and the war itself, all he cared about was his own self-aggrandizement. The trial continued.

After the war, late in '46, Klein called me. I was staying at the Bel Air Hotel, trying to put the pieces of my life back together.

153

"Hi, Tony," he said, cheerful as a sparrow. "This is Commander Klein. I'm out in California for a few days, and I'm so happy you're doing well again. We should get together for a drink, how about it?"

"Fine," I said. "Where are you staying?"

"I'm at the Beverly-Wilshire."

We set a date. I went over to his hotel—and hit him in the mouth and left. It was one of the most satisfying moments in my life. The man had ruined a few lives to get his extra stripe.

The court-martial lasted, I think, for three months, from August through October of 1942. It was a long, hard time for me. There were varied reactions from the men I was living with on the base. Some of them knew what was going on and were friendly and tried to give me moral support. But they were a minority. By far the majority were eager to believe the worst.

They'd greet me with a wink and a knowing smile, some of them.

"I'd have done the same thing if I were you," they'd say. "You have to look out for yourself. Why the hell not get a commission if you can swing it?"

Then they'd wink again, give me a poke in the ribs, and walk off. That kind of approach didn't make me the happiest guy in uniform. In fact, from that grew several fights. There were a couple of older C.P.O.s who seemed born to provoke me. That was the only fun they had in life. They'd have a few drinks and start in on me.

"Hey, listen, Tony," one new C.P.O. said, "I know where you can pick up a nice Studebaker cheap. How about it?"

I took it as long as I could, and then whacked him. He was a big man, too, but I knocked him on his ass. We were going at it pretty good when the officer of the day and one of the top-rated chiefs came by and broke it up.

"Look, you men," the officer said, "I'm not for this man or against him, but I think he's taken too much punishment around here. He hasn't been convicted of a damn thing."

Somehow or other, the chief I tangled with was sent overseas the next day.

The court-martial was preying on my mind. I began to fear for my sanity, seriously. I went to see the base psychiatrist who was, as I remember it, a Mormon from Salt Lake City. He knew who I was and why I was there.

"I don't know what to do, Commander," I said. "This whole business is killing my mother, ruining my father, and driving me out of my mind. I'm going crazy, and I think, more and more, that the only solution is to take myself out."

"You think you're going crazy?"

"I sure as heck do."

"That's good," the psychiatrist said. "That's very good. When a man can realize his mental state, that means he's actually OK."

That was some consolation. Not much, but some. He wasn't able to help me, really. A few words, a pat on the back, a smile. It was more than I got from anyone else, as a matter of fact.

Day after day in the anteroom, waiting to testify if they wanted me again. Just sitting there, and worrying. And I had plenty to worry about. My profession—singer and actor—was a public profession, and my success or failure depended totally on public acceptance. I knew that the public had been given a warped impression of me, as a malingerer or worse. Would I ever be able to perform again? I had nightmares of getting up on some stage and the audience booing me, yelling obscenities at me, calling me "coward" and "briber" and all kinds of things.

It preyed on my mind and made me sick. Not only mentally sick, but physically sick as well. I'd always been pretty robust; not any more. My weight fell from around 175 pounds to below 145. My uniform billowed out in the front and back. I was pale and haggard. Sleep? Forget it. I'd doze off, one of those nightmares would come along and that would be the end of sleeping that night. Eat? I couldn't stand the sight of food.

What was the worst part of it all, I think, is that I was deserted by everybody. Not my mother and father, of course; they stuck by me and believed in me always. But Hollywood had crossed me off its list. To them, I was a man without a country—or a studio. I was taboo, dirty, untouchable. Oh, there were exceptions and at least one of them deserves a mention here.

A U.S.O. show came to play at Treasure Island. One of the troupe was a great guy, one of the finest, Pat O'Brien. We'd known each other, before the war. And I wanted to go backstage and say hello, but that wasn't allowed. Very little was allowed for me in those critical days. I guess word reached Pat that I had tried to come backstage and he sent word out that he wanted to see me, too. They said, sorry, but Chief Petty Officer Martin could not come backstage. Off-limits to witnesses, or some ridiculous reason.

"If Tony Martin can't come backstage," O'Brien said, "then I'm not going on. And if I don't go on, this whole goddamn troupe doesn't go on."

It didn't cut any ice. We still weren't permitted to meet. O'Brien finally went on—he was too much of a trouper not to, and I was glad he did. But that was typical of the way I was treated.

The Navy psychiatrist stopped me on the base one day, a little while after I had consulted him.

"I finally figured out what I should do if I were you," he said.

"What's that?"

"I'd get a bottle of whiskey and go home and drink it with your mother and father over in Oakland," he said.

I tried. It gave me an hour or so of surcease from my troubles, but when I sobered up nothing had changed. I was still Tony Martin, the untouchable.

I think the best advice I got during that period was from another Navy officer, one who thought I was getting the dirty end of the stick. He said that this whole business was throwing me for a loss and I had to fight it.

"You're starting to believe that you're a criminal," he said. "And, Tony, you've done nothing wrong. But if you begin to believe it, you're doomed."

"That's easy to say, but how do I go about changing my own self-image?"

"Act like the old Tony Martin. I remember you before this happened. You strutted pretty good. Go out, get a date, go to the Top of the Mark Hopkins, make like nothing has happened, live it up."

I tried that, too. I got a date, I got a shave, a new uniform, shined my shoes, the works. And we went to the Top of the Mark and I bought that girl the best dinner you could have. And I did feel better afterward. He was right. I was no criminal. I searched my soul, my conscience, my inner self, and I knew I had done nothing wrong. From then on, I held my head high, I walked like a gentleman, I threw my salutes with the air of a Cary Grant in a Foreign Legion picture. Inside, I may still have felt insecure, but I'd be damned if anybody would know it but me.

The court-martial of Maury Aroff was a farce. At least, it was for me. I was being tarred with a dirty brush and I had no chance to defend myself. I asked some of the officers if they would please have me court-martialed, too. At least then I would be able to take the stand with a lawyer representing me. I could defend myself against all these hints, these whispery insinuations which floated around my head. They were like mosquitoes— I heard all those buzzing rumors but my hands were tied. I couldn't swat back. They told me there was nothing I could be court-martialed for. So I just had to hang around and wait while they gave Maury Aroff the business.

I just sat in the anteroom, outside the court, every day from nine in the morning until six in the evening. Sat and waited, as witness after witness was called. I never heard any of the testimony, except my own. And that didn't amount to anything; just yes and no, as I have said. And I couldn't talk to anyone. Reporters were hanging around, but they got nothing from me. And they were really ganging up on me, too.

"What happened in there today, Tony?" one reporter asked me after one session.

"I can't talk. Sorry."

"You'll be sorry you treated me like that," said the man from the *San Francisco Examiner.*

What a joke! I'll be sorry?

"I'm already sorry, you sonofabitch. I can't be any sorrier."

Well, it finally ended. It was a waste of time and money. The shame of it was that it happened in wartime, when all these people could have been doing something to defeat our enemies. Aroff wasn't guilty. Oh, they saved face and allowed him to resign his commission with honor. He resigned. It was the end of the Naval career of a great, great man. I think it was one of the blackest episodes in the history of the United States Navy.

And me? For a few days, I thought it was over for me, that I would be reassigned, shipped overseas, and the whole matter forgotten. I remember now all those mysterious calls from high-ranking officers who promised they would take care of me. They sure took care of me.

Three days after the court martial ended, I was called into headquarters.

"Martin," an officer said, "you will turn in your uniform. You have been found undesirable and unfit for further Naval service. Of course, you will suffer no degradation or loss of time. Furthermore, you will report to your local draft board within forty-eight hours."

Undesirable and unfit! I said those words to myself a hundred times. Undesirable and unfit! Me? What kind of shit was that? Nobody likes to think of those adjectives applied to him, and I had done nothing to warrant them. I started to protest. The officer held up his hand. There was nothing that could be done. The Navy had spoken, and that was that.

I turned in my uniform. They let me keep a pair of work pants to travel in. I had no money, nothing. I couldn't cash a check on the base. A seaman named Louis Facelli loaned me bus fare, so I could go home to my folks' place. My mother gave me some clothes, some money. I took the bus down to Los Angeles. It was all a nightmare. I couldn't talk to anybody, not even my parents. I just rode down in silence, in misery.

And, all the way down, I read in the newspapers the big news of the day: TONY MARTIN KICKED OUT OF NAVY!

I knew one thing. I couldn't face the Hollywood crowd, my old friends, with those headlines floating around. So I made a call en route to one man I trusted, John Steinberg, the major domo at the Hillcrest Country Club. I told him I was coming home. He volunteered to meet my bus in Pasadena. That way, I wouldn't have to see anybody. Steinberg picked me up in Pasadena and drove me into Beverly Hills, where I'd always kept a suite with Jimmy Ritz at the Beverly-Wilshire Hotel. Jimmy took me out and bought me a dinner at the Brown Derby. I ate pretty well, better than I had for months. At least it was over and the worst had happened. Now I knew what I was facing and I figured I could cope. There were no more shadows to fight; there was substance, and that's always easier to combat.

Those last few hours in the Navy had been harrowing for me. I was treated as though I were the worst kind of leper. I tried to get an explanation for those dreadful words—"undesirable and unfit"—but nobody could or would talk to me. They just sent some Shore Patrol types over to my barracks, and they watched me while I got ready to go. They followed me while I turned in my clothing and the rest of my gear. My last official Navy duty was to go to the Paymaster's office, where they gave me transportation expenses to Los Angeles. It amounted to twelve or fourteen dollars or something. Then they said if I'd wait a few minutes, they'd figure up how much money I had coming from my ordinary pay.

"I know there is some money due you," the chief in the office said.

"I tell you what you can do with that money," I said. "Send it to Halsey, with my compliments."

And that was the last word I exchanged with anybody as a Navy chief petty officer. Exit, Tony Martin, sailor. Enter, Tony Martin, soldier.

I had forty-eight hours of freedom, between my two military careers. I wish I could tell you I did something dramatic during those two days. I didn't. There was nobody I wanted to see, after that visit with my folks. And I doubted that anybody wanted to see me. At that point, no gal could have turned me on. I figured I was a pariah in Hollywood and I decided not to risk rejection until I had vindicated myself. And vindication was something I determined to achieve. I knew it would be difficult—the whole world against me. And time is the only vindicator. The whole affair had left a bitter taste in my mouth, and had made my name synonymous with unpatriotic behavior. I was determined to change that.

As it turned out, my two days became five. I reported to the draft board in the Beverly Hills City Hall. They told me their current quota was filled, that it would be two months before they would be able to take me.

"Oh, come on," I said. "You have to take me. You hounded me long enough before, and now I'm here. I can't sit around this town for two months."

"Sorry, Martin, our hands are tied."

But, three days later, they called. Somebody was sick or something and they had a vacancy. So that solved that problem, thank God. I couldn't have stayed holed up in a hotel room for sixty days; five days had been bad enough. And that's what I'd done, spent my whole time in my room. A few old friends came to see me, but not many. Jimmy Ritz came up a few times, and brought me sandwiches which was what I lived on. I never left the hotel for a second—I couldn't stand to see people whispering—other than to go to the draft board.

And so, on December 12, 1942, I was inducted into the United States Army. Nothing fancy this time, no stripes, no bars, nothing.

Just buck ass private Tony Martin, and they were waiting for me!

8

DELIGHT
AND
DECISIONS

I loved being Mrs. Tony Martin. Being married to Tony was so different from my first marriage.

When we came back from our honeymoon, we were faced with a few problems. We were both busy with our work, so that made the problems more difficult to solve. The big question was where we should live.

At the time, Tony had a bachelor house off the Sunset Strip, presided over by his marvelous Filipino houseboy, Marcella. But I quickly discovered that Marcella resented me. He was a man's servant, and he didn't relish the thought of taking orders from a woman. For Tony, living alone, Marcella had been ideal. But when I moved in, things were just not right. For one thing, I found that the repertoire of dishes he could cook was quite limited. He knew how to make only two things, both Oriental. Tony had rarely been home, so that had been fine. But now it got to be a serious problem, eating Marcella's limited creations night after night. So I spoke up, and Marcella quit.

There was another problem with the house. It had been fine for a single man. It was built on several levels and he'd enjoyed that. But it was no good for a family—and, remember, he'd become an instant father as well as a husband. There was no yard, no place for Nicky to play. So Nicky stayed with my mother while Tony and I, getting adjusted to each other's quirks and foibles, moved to the Bel Air Hotel. Tony had lived there before and it certainly is one of the most beautiful hotels in the world, so we both thought it would be a lovely place for our period of adjustment. But one morning I felt the walls of our room and they were damp. I told Tony, "My God, this room is soaking wet!" And he said, "No wonder I was always hoarse when I lived here." So we immediately rented a house from a writer in Beverly Hills. It was our first home together, the first of quite a few. Nicky came back and we all settled down to what has become, I think, a very good life for all of us. We were both working, as we have been through most of our married life, and quickly established a way of life that has stood us well over the years.

If we had a problem, it was Nicky. Not a major problem, but there are always difficulties with a divorce and a remarriage and the effect of those events on a child. He was, understandably, insecure. All the moving around had given him a feeling of impermanance to his life. We had to try to reassure him, to give him the solidity and security any child needs. He had grown dependent on Nana, as he called my mother, and it took a while for us to wean him away, lead him back into our own family circle. Gradually, we accomplished this and he rapidly became the well-adjusted person he remains to this day.

I give Tony a great deal of credit for that. He loved the boy as though he were his own son, and still does. And I know that Nicky considers him a father. The two quickly became very close and shared many experiences, as fathers and sons always do. Most people don't expect Tony to be as careful of people's feelings as he is. He would call Nico before every Christmas, until Nico died, and the two men would discuss what they were going to give Nicky as a present. Tony always wanted the prized gift to come from Nico.

Once those domestic snags were settled, our lives began to take shape. It's been a merry-go-round ever since, and I quickly learned that life with Tony was going to be one fun experience after another. I said we honey-mooned in San Francisco. Technically, that's true. But that was only the first of several honeymoons. That fall, we went on a second honeymoon. Tony is the greatest sports fan I have ever known, and, in October, we went to Cincinnati to see the World Series. I knew absolutely nothing about baseball and cared less, but it was fun to watch him become so excited. All I remember about the whole thing is that Bob Feller pitched. Tony had to explain to me what a pitcher was.

Our third honeymoon, soon after our second, was a trip to Europe. Tony had an engagement to sing at the London Palladium, which was a triumph. We met wonderful people and made lifelong friends. After that, we went to Berlin. It was during the time of the Air Lift, and we had to fly in, sitting on bucket seats and wearing parachutes and, as we approached the city, all we could see was rubble. Today, Berlin is thriving, but in 1948 it was still broken and defeated, a demolished city. It looked as though it was dead and I didn't think it would ever rise again. Tony entertained the troops there and later in Frankfurt. In Frankfurt, we were given quarters in a mansion which, we were told, had belonged to Hitler's banker. He was obviously somebody important, because I've never seen a place with so many gadgets—you pushed a button and the glass windows would slide open or closed.

In those days, we learned that the Germans would give anything for a cigarette. We had some with us, and did a little swapping. They preferred cigarettes to monetary tips.

Then it was back home, and, by now, we were both busy with our careers. We rented another house, this time in Bel Air, and it was there we had our first fight.

I love shoes. I had a pair of yellow shoes, which I particularly adored. For some reason, Tony developed a hatred for those shoes. Whenever I wore them, he growled a little. One day, I came home to find my beloved yellow shoes being chewed by our dog. Tony freely admitted he had given the shoes to the dog, as a way of permanently settling the issue. There was quite a scene about whether or not it was proper for a husband to toss his wife's shoes to the family dog. I held out strongly in favor of the negative of that proposition, while Tony argued for the affirmative. I don't think either of us won, but I'm happy to say our dogs, over the years, have never had any of my favorite shoes to play with.

Tony opened up a new world for me—the glamorous side of Hollywood. When I was married to Nico, we had never gone to any of the big Hollywood parties. Tony, however, was an entirely different sort of man— he is the epitome of gregariousness. He loves big parties and, even before we were married, he began taking me to some of them. I remember the first one I went to, at the home of Mary and Jack Benny. At the time, the Bennys were at the very top of the Hollywood social ladder, and their parties attracted all the most glittering stars. Mary is a fabulous hostess. And, at that first one I attended, I was overawed by all the people and their talent. It was the custom at Mary's parties for the talented guests to do something entertaining during the evening. And there were people like Danny Kaye, George Burns, Dinah Shore, Jack and Tony, who all performed a while. It was so exciting, and I felt a great joy at being part of that most fantastic inner circle.

Traveling, for us, has been a way of life since that first flurry back in 1948. If I can manage it, I go with Tony when he's working. That's not too hard now, but, at first it was very difficult to arrange. I was under contract to MGM and, obviously, I couldn't go if I was shooting a picture. Even if I wasn't actually in a film, however, I had to get the studio's permission before I could leave. They would generally give it, but I would be taken off salary for the duration of the trip. I also had to be sure my mother was free to take care of Nicky. Mostly, she was, and I could go with Tony.

I think that's very important. Many marriages—whether in or out of Hollywood—flounder when there are too many separations. So we've made it a policy to try to be together as much as we possibly can. When we're apart, we call each other often—our telephone bills have been astronomical.

People always wonder how we have managed to stay together for so long, especially when we are both in show business. The automatic assumption is that two show business careers can't mix. I don't think you can generalize about that subject, any more than you can generalize about any subject. It's just as unfair to say that two show business personalities cannot have a happy marriage as it is to say that all lawyers are honest. Some show business marriages can survive. I think ours did because we worked hard at it.

We had a few things going our way, to start with. We were never competitive—I was always the dancer and Tony was always the singer. So we didn't have to struggle with that potential complication.

And we early agreed that, whatever happened, our marriage was more important than either one of our careers. If there was the possibility of one of us working, and that possibility made the other unhappy for any reason, we'd forget that particular engagement. It wasn't that important, it couldn't be. We knew there would always be other engagements, other possibilities.

Actually, I think the fact that we're both in the same business has helped our marriage, rather than hurt it. We understand the problems, the dangers, the difficulties. It never causes me a moment's grief if Tony doesn't get in until three in the morning when he's working. I know he has to unwind after he's been singing—because I've been there, I've performed and I realize the situation. After he works, and he works hard, he can't toddle right off to bed. He needs an hour or so to get rid of the tension, a few laughs, a few drinks. A wife who had been, say, a schoolteacher might get very uptight about that, but I understand the problem and so when he gets home late, there's no scene.

Similarly, if I'm on a picture and I don't get home until eight or nine in the evening, he doesn't come running up and say, "Where've you been?" He's made movies, too, and knows that sometimes you shoot late or have to stay to see the dailies. Vincente Minnelli, for example, very often kept us until eight or nine in the evening. I'd come staggering home, beat and exhausted, and Tony would greet me sympathetically. If I'd married a

CPA, he might easily have made a big thing about it. People who aren't in show business find our lifestyle hard to grasp, so I believe the fact that we were both in the business helped make our marriage last.

Tony is a very sensitive and very understanding man. He can read my moods like a book, and knows how to react accordingly. I suppose I'm the same way about him. Whatever the reason, it's worked.

They—whoever "they" are—often say that love is better the second time around. Both of us had been married before. We'd had our heartaches. We knew that, this time, we would each have to bend a little. And we bent and it turned out to be easy.

One wonderful thing about Tony was that he had no objection at all to my having my own career. Nowadays, of course, that's the normal thing but when we were married, there were many men who believed women's place was smack dab in the middle of the kitchen. Maybe an hour or two in the bedroom. But I think Tony was proud of me and what I could do and he knew that my career was terribly important to me, too. So that helped. And I am very much of the opinion that a busy life is good for any woman. If she lives only a vicarious existence, through her husband's career, she can easily become restless and unhappy. One thing I've never been is restless. Maybe at times I've been too busy, but never not busy enough.

As I have said, it's worked, for whatever reason. I don't mean to say there haven't been some sticky moments, because every marriage has them. We've had to learn that we each have our quirks. Right from the start, I've had to adjust to Tony's peculiarities.

It began early. We rented for a while after we got married, then we bought our first house. It was at the corner of Sunset Boulevard and Beverly Glen, and it was a lovely Spanish house that had been owned by Bob Hope at one time. We bought it from Bill Castle, the producer. We had no furniture so for a while we lived in an empty barn. But, gradually, I furnished it. That was later, though. We had been in it only a few days when Tony announced, very casually, that we were "having a few people over tonight."

The few people turned out to be dozens of his pals—the Ritz Brothers, Jan Murray, his old cronies. There wasn't a stick of furniture in the place, except our beds and the stove.

And a record player. Which was fortunate, because that provided our entertainment. *South Pacific* had just opened in New York and of course we had the record and played it, and Harry Ritz, one of the world's funniest men, mimed to the lyrics. We were all laughing our heads off when Frances Lastfogel came in, with Fanny Brice. Frances is the wife of Abe Lastfogel, one of Hollywood's most important and most respected agents. She's a

Wedding day.

Tony and Cyd in England. She was pregnant at the time.

Entertaining in the Philippines.

In Mexico for the shooting of *Sombrero*, (l. to r.) Tony Martin, Cyd Charisse, and producer Jack Cummings.

In England for polo matches, (l. to r.) Maharajah and Maharanee of Jaipur, their son Bubbles, Tony and Cyd.

Alohaaaaa.

Tony, Cyd, and Tony Jr. "I was preparing to go into *An American in Paris,* with Gene Kelly when I learned for sure that I was pregnant. It was going to be a long shooting schedule. I knew that I couldn't do the picture and have the baby . . . I guess that was the toughest decision of my life."

A Hawaiian vacation with Nicky (left) and Tony Jr. (right).

The twelfth anniversary celebration for Tony and Cyd.

In Las Vegas for their first act together. Tony: "It's always been traditional in show business that the man's name comes first. So it's been Tony Martin and Cyd Charisse. I hope it continues forever. The billing doesn't matter, as long as we're together."

Back to front: Tony, Cyd, Grace and Harold Robbins socializing in southern France.

A rehearsal break.

Cyd, Tony, and
Wilt (The Stilt)
Chamberlain at a
party in San
Diego honoring
the tenth
anniversary of the
National Basketball
Association.

Tony Martin and
Cyd Charisse,
today.

lovely lady but something of the old-fashioned sort. She kind of turned up her nose at the scene—the lack of furniture, the record player blasting, Harry miming, all of us laughing. And then the music stopped and that crowd started talking and the language was pretty strong stuff. Harry's language was outrageous. And Fanny kept pace with him, syllable for syllable.

It was pretty rough to me, too. I was the girl who had never used a four-letter word in her life. It was too much for Frances, though. She picked herself up and walked out. Later, I found out her vocabulary could be strong, too; she had originally been a comedienne—and worked pretty blue at times, so she knew her rough words.

That was my introduction to one of Tony's little habits—the impromptu party. And to the quality of those parties. Pretty soon, I began to enjoy those evenings as much as anybody. I even learned to hold my own in the language department. But I quickly became unshockable.

When we got our furniture, Nicky moved in with us to stay. Nico was still living then, and he would come over on weekends and take his son hunting with him. The two of them loved military things—Nicky had a fabulous collection of lead soldiers—and guns and all that. At Nico's request, I sent Nicky to military school, California Military Academy. He lived at home, however. If I was working, my mother would come over and be there when he got home from school and see that he had dinner and did his homework.

I never cooked—at least not until very recently. Tony always said I was the only woman who could ruin hot water. Actually, it would have been impossible for me to, because of the hours I kept when I was working. So, from early in our marriage, we've always had domestic help in the house. In those days, it was easy to find. That's not true now, so lately I've done a little cooking. And I must confess I'm no cook. My hairdresser, Julius Bengtsson, suggested I try a crock pot and I did and the thing works. I take my recipe book to the market, buy whatever it says, come home and stick it all in the crock pot and, by dinner time, it's ready. And, miraculously, it's edible.

Tony never complains about that. He eats what is on the table. He's pretty even-tempered, although he can explode from time to time. So can I. The one thing that sets me off more than anything else is inefficiency. If somebody doesn't do his job well, I really lose my temper. I also blow up over inefficient things—stoves that don't work, telephones that don't work. I guess that's my pet peeve.

In 1950, we were scheduled to do a show in Puerto Rico, with Ed Gardner, the famous Archie of *Duffy's Tavern*. When we arrived, we found that Paulette Goddard had suddenly become available to do the show, so Ed asked us if we'd mind postponing our appearance for one week. He said he had a nice way for us to spend that week. He had a yacht, fully staffed, and we could take it and go anywhere we wanted to. We had no immediate plans and that sounded like heaven, to sit on a yacht for a week with a crew to take care of us. Mind? I should say not!

For a week, we cruised those blue, blue waters and it was a delight. The sun in the day, the moon at night. It turned out to be so romantic that I came home and found out I was very pregnant.

Ordinarily, I would have been thrilled. It was just that the timing was wrong. I was preparing to go into *An American in Paris*, with Gene Kelly. I was supposed to start costume fittings for that role when I learned for sure that I was pregnant. It was going to be a long shooting schedule. I knew that I couldn't do the picture and have the baby—I'd be too far along by the time we were into the heart of the shooting.

I guess that was the toughest decision of my life.

I had just done *Band Wagon* and things were really looking good for me in pictures. *An American in Paris* would, I knew, be a major film and I wanted very much to do it. And, yet, I did want to have another child, one with Tony.

"Tony, what'll I do?" I asked him. "This is going to be the most fantastic movie of all time. I want to be part of it so badly."

"OK, do the movie. You can get an abortion. No problem."

"But I don't want an abortion. I want to have the baby."

"OK, have the baby. There'll be other pictures."

"But I want to do the movie."

"Look, honey, you just can't do both. No way. You just have to make up your mind what you want to do the most, that's all."

That's all. One or the other. For days, I debated with myself. I wanted Tony to help me make up my mind, but he was smart enough not to commit himself. He felt it was my decision—my body, my career—and he was right. I had to make my mind up, one way or the other.

I went to see Arthur Freed at Metro, on the wild hope that maybe I could get my scenes done in the film before my pregnancy was so far advanced that it would show. He quickly dashed that hope. He told me they would be shooting at least six months and there was no way my scenes, my dances, could be all lumped together at the beginning. So I was back where I started, with a decision that only I could make.

I finally elected to bow out of the film and have the baby. I told Freed and he told Gene Kelly. It all worked out well—especially for Leslie Caron. Gene had recently been in France and had seen Leslie and knew her, and he suggested that she could do the part that I had been supposed to do. And she did. *An American in Paris* won an Oscar for best picture and made Leslie Caron a star and I loved it and cried all the way through it for what might have been.

But, on the other hand, I had my second child, my second son. Tony Martin, Jr., was born on August 28, 1950, and I've never regretted the choice I made. Like Nicky, he's a wonderful boy.

Both of my sons had a choice to make, when they grew old enough to understand. That was a choice of religion. We had carefully exposed Nicky to all three faiths—his father's Catholicism, his mother's Protestantism, his step-father's Judaism. Tony would take him to temple with him and I'd take him to Presbyterian Sunday school. When Tony, Jr., grew old enough, he followed the same pattern.

He is a stern father figure, not a tyrant by any means, but a man who is strict but fair. When they were young, Nicky and Tony knew that they could go only so far, and not an inch further, with Tony. I guess I'm a pushover, and they always could talk me into almost anything. But not Tony. He can be hard on them at times, but there is always justice there. And, at the next moment, he can be incredibly generous. He's been a terrific father, I think, and the boys turned out well, which is the proof.

It's been exciting to watch them grow up, two distinct and totally different personalities. We've had our problems, like all parents, but we all survived.

Nicky, when he got past the military school phase, wanted to go to school somewhere where there were horses. He always loved horses. So we sent him to the Judson School in Arizona. He was very bright and skipped a few grades. One day, when Tony and I were about to go to Las Vegas for an engagement, we got a frantic call from the school.

"Don't get excited," said the voice, which was enough to get me excited, "but your son has shot himself."

We immediately rushed to Phoenix. And we found that Nicky was shot, all right, but not seriously. He and his roommate both had guns, which was against the rules. They were allowed guns, but they had to keep them locked up. And these two reckless boys had kept their guns in their room. They liked to ride out in the desert and make believe they were cowboys, practicing their fast draw. Nicky drew so fast that he pulled the trigger before the gun had left the holster and shot himself in the leg. Fortunately, it was just a flesh wound.

Because he had skipped, he was only seventeen when he graduated and was admitted to Stanford. He was too young and couldn't handle it. He got involved with a girl, thought he was in love and didn't study. You can't do that at Stanford and expect to keep up with the rest. That summer, he took off in his car, which Tony had given him, and we didn't hear from him for a few weeks. I was frantic with worry. Finally, there was a call. He was in San Francisco, visiting his girl friend and staying with her parents.

"OK," Tony told him. "You're on your own now. I'm not sending you any money. You think you're big enough to go cavorting around the country, then you do it all yourself."

He did. He got a job fighting forest fires for the rest of that summer. After that summer, he was at loose ends. He had, not surprisingly, flunked out of Stanford. So he decided he wanted to be an actor, and he talked Tony into letting him go to New York to study. Tony went to New York with him and saw that he had an apartment and was enrolled with a good teacher. He stayed in New York for a year, but I think he spent more time bumming around than he did studying acting.

Then he came back to California, studied acting a bit, went to college (Santa Monica City College) a bit and chased girls a lot. I was beginning to worry that he was wasting his life. And then I really worried when he joined the National Guard, which was a hangover from his early fascination with military things. His unit was called to active duty during the Watts riot, and Nicky had to patrol the streets during those awful few days.

He began working part-time for Greg Bautzer, the lawyer, and that turned out to be a great move for him. For one thing, he met a girl there and Sheila was the best thing that could have happened to him. They were married and she wanted him to finish college and go on to law school. As I am writing this, Nicky has just taken his bar exam, and soon I can now say, "My son, the lawyer." Sheila has helped him through his learning years, by working. After she left Bautzer's office, she became what I believe is called a computer expert.

Tony, Jr.—we called him Little T until he grew to be six-feet-two, so now we call him Young T—has always leaned toward music. We were away so much, when he was young, that we sent him to boarding school when he was thirteen. He went to the Harvey School, in Katonah, New York, and we chose that school for a reason. Katonah is only ten minutes away from Ridgefield, Connecticut, where my brother, E.E., and his four children live. So we had someone close by to be there if needed, someplace for him to go on weekends and holidays. But Young T came back to Beverly Hills for high school, mostly because he wanted to be closer and, also, I felt the co-ed system was good for a boy.

At the moment, Young T is still unmarried. He has had some escapades that have caused us some gray hairs. Still, he's always been a charming and delightful person to be around. I think he's very talented.

He's written some lovely songs. He was under contract for a while to Motown, as a songwriter, and he's also worked with Terry Melcher and he's worked for RCA. Last year, he traveled with us on our tour, as a performer, and that was a pleasant experience for all of us. He's an excellent performer and I'm sure he'll have a fine future. Right now Tony Jr., with Desi Arnaz Jr., Dean Martin Jr., and their Beverly Hills Blue Band are recording for the Curb label, a subsidiary of Warner Bros. Records.

So my private life has been a good one, since I became Mrs. Tony Martin. There have been ups and downs and ins and outs, of course, but mostly it's been a remarkably even keel. Professionally, however, it was much different.

9

WAR
AND
WORRY

On December 12, 1942, I reported for service. Again. I was sworn into the Army. Buck private, naturally. If they could have come up with a grade lower than that, they would have given it to me. From the beginning, I could tell they were just waiting for me. Not everybody, of course, but most of them. I was a cheap target, the Hollywood star who had been kicked out of the Navy.

Right off the bat, it happened. This was at Fort MacArthur, where I went for induction. I think they jabbed the needle in my arm, for those injections, a little deeper than they had to. Maybe it was my imagination, which was working overtime, but it seemed to me that the kid with the hypodermic gave it an extra twist as he took it out. Then I moved on, along the Army's induction assembly line, to the quartermaster's barracks, where I got my uniform.

"What size shoe?"

"Nine and a half," I said.

Down the line.

"What size is your waist?"

"Thirty-three."

"Do you know your hat size?"

I'd bought enough hats. I knew. Seven and three-quarters.

All the stuff was piled in my arms. I went to a bench, as they told me, took off my civvies and put on my uniform. Or tried to. The pants were big enough for Primo Carnera. The shoes would have fit Wilt Chamberlain. The hat came down over my ears.

"Hey, this stuff is all too big," I said.

"We just gave you the size you asked for, Martin," the supply sergeant said. "It's all yours now."

So I walked outside in that wardrobe, looking like a jerk and feeling worse. I was wandering around when a major, a man who knew me, noticed me. He'd been chief grip at MGM before the war.

"Hey, Tony. Were those clothes just issued?" he asked me.

"Yes, sir."

"OK. Follow me."

He marched me back to the quartermaster barracks. He asked me to point out the person who had issued me the clothing. That was one trap I wasn't going to get into. I said I'd forgotten.

"Was it that master sergeant there?" the major asked, pointing to the creep who had told me it was all mine. "Or was it the lieutenant himself?"

"I'm sorry, sir, but I don't know."

The lieutenant said, "Major, I issued this man his clothing."

"Why?"

"Because he deserved it, sir."

"OK, lieutenant, if that's all the regard you have for the war effort, as of tomorrow you're on a shipping list."

And he was. They sent him to New Guinea. Somehow, I didn't shed a tear.

I got the usual indoctrination given a recruit for a few days—the shots, the uniform, the KP duty, the works. I hung around Fort MacArthur maybe a week, waiting to get a permanent assignment. Some of the others had had requests put in for them, in letter form, and these requests were honored. There was a request for me, too, by a tank corps outfit stationed in Palm Springs. A friend of a friend had felt sorry for me. That would have been nice duty, to be stationed in a familiar place. There was an envelope they had given me, with that request inside. All I would have had to do was to hand it to the officer in charge and I would have automatically been sent to Palm Springs. But I'd had enough by now. I never wanted it to look as if I was being favored again. I tore the envelope in half, looked up at God and said, "Lord, I'll take my chances, like anybody else."

The Lord has compassion. I found myself in the Air Corps, on a troop train heading south. That was OK. I'd heard the top IQs went into the Air Corps, so I figured maybe I was being sent to where I could do some good finally. We didn't know where we were going on that blacked-out train. Endless days, sleepless nights, lining up on that rocking train for meals. It

171

finally stopped and a grinning, red-headed master sergeant stuck his head in our car.

"Welcome to Shepherd Field, Texas, boys," he said. "Y'all are now in Squadron 405."

We piled out. We were in Texas, all right. Snow up to our knees, wind blowing our heads off. Wichita Falls, Tex., said the sign on the station. We called it "Itchy Balls." We loaded into trucks. The master sergeant kept looking at me, as though he were trying to place me. I didn't help him. I knew he'd figure it out sooner or later. He did. A snap of his fingers.

"Y'all are Tony Martin, ain't you?" he said.

"Yes, I am."

He laughed. He hit his thighs with the flat of his hand.

"Now ain't that somethin'." he said. "Well, let me set you straight right now, buckass private. Y'all ain't going to have it soft here, like y'all had in Hollywood."

I didn't say a word. I knew it was going to be tough, but I had confidence. After what I'd been through in the Navy, what was left for the Army to do to me?

There's an old saying about Shepherd Field, Texas. A man can stand in the wind all day and be up to his knees in mud at the same time. Very true. The climate in that part of Texas was invented by a madman. Wind, rain, heat, cold—all in a few hours. Whatever you put on, your flannels or your lightweight cottons, it was the wrong thing. You either froze or you broiled. And we were outdoors all day, taking our basic training.

Because I had learned the close-order drill in the Navy, I was made a drill instructor. I had a blue armband, with the letters D.I. on it. So all day long, from the crack of daylight until it got dark again, we were out in that crazy weather, marching up and down the dusty, muddy, snowy field. I was in with an outfit that came mostly from Laredo, Texas, and they were U.S. citizens, but their first language was Spanish. They answered the roll call with *"Aqui,"* not "Here." But they were good kids, cheerful, anxious to please. They were used to the weather, and that was a headstart.

We did all the other things that went with basic training. Classes in rifle nomenclature. Lectures on how to salute. We had to see all the V.D. movies although nobody had any chance to pick up any social diseases at Shepherd Field, Texas.

I was drilling a platoon of men one day when a captain came by and recognized me. One can always tell. The double take, that split moment to run the face through the brain's memory bank, then the sparkle in the eyes that shows the connection has been accomplished.

"Tony Martin!" he said. I acknowledged that that was who I was.

172

"Welcome to Shepherd Field. How about singing at the officer's club Saturday night?"

"No, sir."

"Why not? You can pick up a fast $12."

"Sir, I'm just a buck private, and I just want to do what the rest of the guys in my group are doing."

He paused. Then he put both hands on my shoulders.

"Yeah, the Navy gave you the shit, carry on and good luck."

I saluted him, did an about face. I felt like maybe the clouds would disappear. I felt good about that. All that mattered to me at that point in my life is that I was allowed to be just another guy. I had had enough of special treatment. Now I wanted un-special treatment. But I found out that being one of the boys can be lonely, too. I really had nothing in common with my barrack-mates. I was older than they were, from a different world, in many cases speaking a different language. So I had no friends. But, for the first time in a long while, no enemies, either. I had expected trouble from Army men who would pick on me because of that Navy fiasco. Nothing happened. I was grateful for that. I could take the loneliness—loneliness contains no animosity. They left me alone, because, to them, I was from a different planet, Hollywood. So I did a lot of reading, did hundreds of crossword puzzles, kept my shoes polished, my buckle shined, my foot locker in order and my nose clean.

But, no matter how much I wanted to forget my past for the duration of the war, it followed me. I was out on the drill field one day, shouting out the orders, when I saw a familiar face turn around and look after me.

His name was Joe Rifkin. He used to be an agent in Hollywood and he had, in fact, worked in Nat's office. He seemed stunned to see me out there in the Texas wind, barking out commands at the top of my lungs.

"Tony," he said, "what the hell are you doing? You'll ruin your voice like that."

I told him I was just doing what I was supposed to be doing. A drill instructor can't very well whisper. He said I should have told them who I was.

"Joe, I don't ask for favors," I said.

"Favors, hell. This war won't last forever. Your voice is your fortune. This is ridiculous. Come with me."

So he took me down to headquarters. Since he was a captain, I had to follow him. He took me into a colonel's office and explained who I was, what I was doing and why he thought it was dumb.

"All right, private," the colonel said. "What's this all about?"

"I was just following orders, sir," I said.

"From now on, you have new orders."

That was the end of my career as a drill instructor. The colonel had me reassigned, this time to headquarters, where I taught—but I didn't have to shout into the wind any more. I gave little talks on information and education, lectures on the progress of the war, instructions on military etiquette, lessons in the fine art of saluting and the chain of command. It was all very important stuff in winning the war. There was one particularly vital bit of learning I passed on to my men—how to polish their belt buckles.

There was only one part of my D.I. weeks that I missed. Those were the moments I spent with the chaplain. That came about when, one particularly bone-chilling day, a chaplain, a rabbi, had noticed me shivering out there on the drill field. Again, a face from the past. This rabbi had seen me at the Chez Paree in Chicago. He called me into his office, at the end of one of the barracks at the edge of the drill field. He poured me a glass of slivovitz. It warmed me. So, from then on, whenever we had a break, I'd go into his office. A little slivovitz, a little talk. It helped me survive.

Army life was a grind. I don't mean to sound spoiled, but I guess I was. After Romanoff's and Ciro's and Chasen's and Perino's, this bit of eating off an iron tray with the apple pie perched on top of the mashed potatoes and gravy was tough to take. The mess sergeant used to sing out, "All right, you guys, remember that whatever you take you eat." So I didn't take much. Then the guys with the big spoons dishing up the food would sneer, "Don't you like Army food, star?" I just smiled.

Every once in a while, we'd go on long marches and overnight bivouacs. Even after I was transferred to headquarters, I'd still have to do those hikes and bivouacs. Marching eight or ten miles with full field pack.

Once I went out with a bad cold. Everybody had colds, but nobody could get into the infirmary unless he had a fever of—I'm not sure, but I think it was 102 degrees. I missed that by a point or so, so off I went. Besides, I didn't want to run the risk of being tagged a goldbrick—a goof-off —and I knew they were just waiting for a chance to find some fault with my actions. I would have marched if my temperature was 110. The officer in charge figured it would be a good thing to have me lead some singing as we trudged along, so he set me in front of the column and directed me to sing "I've Got Sixpence," and all the other rousers. With my cold and my headache and my burning feet, I doubt if it was a particularly stirring rendition. Here I'm looking to die and I have to sing.

A top sergeant drove by in a Jeep.

"Hey, private," he said. "You're walking kind of funny. What's your problem?"

"I always walk like this, Sarge."

"What's your name and serial number?"

"Private Tony Martin, 39459073."

"Oh, I see. I guess you're looking for—"

"I'm not looking for anything. I just want to be left alone."

He drove away. Three miles down the road, they tell me I collapsed. This time, no matter what my fever was, they carted me off to the hospital. Double pneumonia. The doctors gave me hell for not going on sick call before, but I was scared. I had to prove myself. I nearly proved myself into my grave.

All I really remember about Shepherd Field was fear. After that Navy experience, I just wanted to keep out of trouble, do my job and be left alone. I didn't want any attention paid me. I didn't want to get into any trouble, any hassle. That's why I wouldn't go on sick call, even though I knew I was a pretty sick fellow. That's why, the night before Saturday inspection, I wouldn't sleep on my bed. I slept on the floor beside my bed Friday nights. I spent an hour or so getting the bed right, so it would pass inspection, and I wasn't going to ruin it by sleeping on it. I knew that the officer would be twice as tough on me as anyone else, just so it wouldn't look like he was going easy on me. Like I say, I wasn't taking any chances of fouling up. The same thing with my rifle. I took that damned thing apart over and over, cleaning it, oiling it, making certain when it was inspected it would be absolutely perfect. I was sure that whoever peered down the barrel of my piece would be twice as tough on me as on the rest of the guys.

I was always early. I was always neat. I was always polished. I was always right. Nobody was going to find any fault with Pvt. Tony Martin.

What sustained me was prayer. Sounds funny. I had never been religious, but now, with all this stress, if it hadn't been for God I would have cracked. I prayed a lot, maybe ten times a day. I repeated the twenty-third psalm so often the guys thought I was talking to myself. It was God, prayer and some sense of survival that saw me through all the bullshit. I survived.

There were moments of release. I'd get a pass once in a while, if it was coming to me. I never asked for one, but we'd get one automatically every few weeks. I'd take the bus into Wichita Falls with the other GIs, wear the issued uniform, take my doled-out pay. No special favors. I could have had more money. Nat Goldstone sent me a check every week, but I didn't cash them. What for? There was nothing in Wichita Falls to splurge on. I couldn't buy clothes or anything luxurious. I thought of taking my sergeant to dinner—he was a decent sort—but rejected the thought. Somebody might say I was trying to bribe him.

175

Then one day I found myself on a shipping order. It was the first of several shipping lists I made and, curiously, I was always on those lists by myself. Most shipping lists contained pages and pages of names. But I went solo. It was always:

"The following men will report on such-a-such day at such-and-such a time for shipping."

I had to report at three in the morning to catch a train which went, as it turned out, to Chanute Field, Illinois. My orders were sealed, as they usually were. I couldn't open them until the train had left Shepherd Field. I laughed. What a lot of crap. Sealed orders! You'd think I knew some dark secret, like maybe how to make bomb sights or something. But I dutifully kept my orders sealed until the train chugged along a while, then found out I was Illinois-bound.

And what was my job when I got to Chanute Field? Guess. Right. I lead the singing. Chanute is where they taught night flying, using the famous Link trainer. And as the neophyte pilots marched to and from their training sessions, the brass figured a little singing would be good for their morale. So they had me brought up from Texas to supply the lead voice. I'd sing one group from the barracks to the training building, and sing another one back the other way. "Private Martin, march the men to the mess hall." I'd sing them to chow, sing them back again. I was winning the war at the top of my baritone lungs. In the wind, the snow, the rain, the hail, the sleet. "Off We Go, into the Wild Blue Yonder." I don't imagine I ever got as sick of any song as I did of that one, although I never had disrespect for it.

My weekends were pleasant. I performed at the dances at the Officers' Club. They paid me an extra six dollars for that. And I got to sit in with the band, too, back in the reed section where it all began. The officers would sneak me a drink and let me eat off a plate instead of a tray, so I felt like a privileged citizen for a few hours.

At one of those affairs, a full colonel came up to me and invited me to come home with him Sunday afternoon. I hesitated. Would that be considered favoritism? He saw my hesitation.

"I'm a full colonel, Private Martin," he said, "and I am inviting you to my home tomorrow afternoon for a drink. That's all there is to it."

So I went. It was nice. He had seen me at the Chez Paree in Chicago. For an hour or so, I was a human being again. But, the rest of the time at Chanute, I just minded my own business, did what I was told to do, stayed out of trouble.

Most of the men were decent kids and I had no problems. And most of the officers were bright and upright citizens, but there were a few who were overly impressed with their own importance. Like most enlisted men, I guess I had a touch of anti-officer in my make-up, but it wasn't as virulent with me as it was with some of my buddies. Many of the officers had compassion, but there were a sprinkling—usually they were kids who had been auto salesmen or clerks in the hardware store—who just couldn't handle their first taste of power. They became toy bullies. But the backbone of the officer corps in both the Navy and the Army were service-educated —Annapolis or West Point—and their business was fighting the war. They weren't out to destroy us to satisfy their own fragile egos, as some of the others were. I learned to distinguish the good from the bad, the reserve officers from the regulars. I steered clear of the former group.

I had one three-day pass while at Chanute. I had long been interested in the Masonic order, and I requested a three-day pass from my commanding general to go to Indiana City and finish my Masonic work. And the general, who was, coincidentally, a Roman Catholic, immediately granted my request.

"I never hold any man back," he said. So I hitched a ride to Indiana City and went through my Masonic work through the 32nd degree.

My stay at Chanute was, I suppose, only a few months. Then it was off again. This time I was excited about my new assignment. A captain summoned me to headquarters and informed me that Captain Glenn Miller had requested me for his Air Force band. What a surge of excitement spread through me when I heard those words! Glenn Miller was then, as anybody over forty remembers, the king of the bandleaders. He had gone into the Air Force, been made a captain, and been told to put together the best band that ever was. He was in the process of doing just that. He was stationed at Yale University, in New Haven, Connecticut, and that's where I went to join him.

I was to be the band's vocalist. I reported to Captain Glenn Miller as ordered. He turned me over to his chief of personnel, Colonel Green, a thoughtful and kind man. After all the shit I'd been through, I felt as though I'd stumbled into heaven through a side door. I was with my kind of people, musicians, for a change. Some I knew, the others I quickly came to know. There was no unnecessary Army crap, although it was strictly a military organization.

They immediately made me a corporal. I wanted to throw a party at the Waldorf-Astoria! I was billeted in an old house for a while, then we were all put together in a dormitory. Durfee Hall. We called it Dirty Durfee. We rehearsed all day long. We had some duties to do, of a military nature, but not much and certainly not unbearable. It was a pleasant time for me. I began to think maybe I could survive the war—in mind as well as body.

Some time after I got there, I was called into Captain Miller's office. It was strictly a captain-corporal relationship, which was the best way to handle it during the war.

"Corporal Martin reporting, sir."

"At ease, Corporal."

He had me sit down, and then he told me he was going to London, where he was to organize the greatest band in history as the musical unit for the Eighth Army. He said he wanted me to be part of that, in fact to become one of his aides. But for that I'd have to become an officer. Was I willing to take a shot at O.C.S.? I pondered; I reminded him of my story. He said he knew all that. "Go ahead," he said, "I want you."

I had to appear before an Officers Selection Board and take an exam. I did, took the exam, passed it. Then there was a person-to-person interview with the Board. They asked me why I wanted to become an officer. It was a tough question for me.

"Officers," I said, "I am getting close to thirty years old. There are so many younger men all around me in service. I think they need someone older to help them, someone like me who has been through an awful lot, someone who is a God-fearing man, who understands humanity."

They seemed to like that answer. There were more questions, which didn't give me a moment's pause. Then they were finished with me. They dismissed me. I turned to go, then stopped.

"Sirs," I said, "before I go, I have a confession to make. I want this chance at Officers' Candidate School very much, but I want it without any blemish. So I must tell you something. It wasn't many months ago that I was discharged from the Navy as undesirable and unfit and—."

Colonel Green, who was in charge of the Board, interrupted me.

"We've seen your service record, Corporal. We know all about that."

"Yes, sir. I'm glad you do. But I wish you would take it one step further, have it probed through the F.B.I. and Army Intelligence. I don't want anything coming up in the future to knock me out of the ball game."

"Corporal," Green said, "we've known all about your record in the Navy. We've been in correspondence with Army Intelligence about you. You've been given a clean slate at the Pentagon in the matter. It's all out in the open. There's nothing in your service record to worry about."

A few days later, they told me I'd been accepted for O.C.S. I was elated. So was Glenn. He gave me a big hug as we separated.

"Don't let me down, Corporal," he said. "I'll be looking for you in

London in a few months with bars on your shoulders."

The officers' school was in Miami Beach, Florida, and that was my home for the next four months. I was in Class 44-A; funny how some things you never forget. I sailed through the training. It was tough, but I was bouyed up by the thought that, finally, I was going to make it in the Army on my own, and I knew that, when I became a lieutenant, I would have a happy experience from then on. I'd be part of the Miller organization, and that could only be a joyous time.

So I worked harder than I've ever worked in my life. The course was a combination of both classroom time and physical exertion. I buckled down for those four months and had no real problems. The first three months, actually, were a breeze. But, at the end of the third month, they called me in.

There was an officer from Army Intelligence. He said that they had "learned" about my Navy problems. He asked me to explain about what had happened in the Navy.

"But, sir," I said, "Colonel Green told me Army Intelligence was completely aware of that whole situation."

"It has just been called to our attention by the commanding general of the Air Force." That was Hap Arnold.

"Sir, everybody knows about me and the Navy."

"Tell me what happened."

So I had to go through the whole cruddy business again, answering the questions, explaining the motivations. He didn't show any expression on his face, one way or the other, and, after a few hours of questioning, let me go. But, for the last month of my O.C.S. course, the specter of that interview hung over me. Was I to never, ever to be let up?

I really worked. I don't think I've ever worked harder in my life. I wanted that commission, not for the bars on my shoulder, but to vindicate myself, to show everyone that Tony Martin, as a person, could make it. And I graduated in the top 140 of my class of 764 officer candidates. That last month was a back-breaker, because I had that burden on me, that extra feeling of knowing that any moment they could lower the boom. But it looked like I'd made it.

I stood a formation one day on the parade grounds. We were assembled to pay tribute to some foreign dignitary. I was standing there in the hot sun, at attention, when I felt something land on my shoulder. It was crap from some bird that had used me as target practice. I heard the guys in the rank behind me suppress a snicker. Later on, some of the fellows congratulated me. They said it was supposed to be good luck, for a bird to crap on you during a formation. It didn't turn out that way for me.

I had offered to resign when the Army Intelligence people quizzed me. They emphatically said no, that wasn't necessary. It was all under control. Just do your work, Cadet Martin, they told me. So I did. And when graduation day came, I graduated with all the others. The evening before graduation, they posted the list of assignments and there was my name: "Cpl. Tony Martin, assigned to 1 Park Avenue, New York, N.Y." That was, I knew, the way-station between O.C.S. and the Glenn Miller band in London. The next day, we were all to be sworn in and receive our gold bars, signifying we were second lieutenants, officers and gentlemen. There was going to be a party afterward. The men had invited their wives, their girl friends, their parents, whoever. I had nobody to invite, but they were all my buddies, then, and I knew it would be fun. I'd even arranged to sing a few songs for the party.

Then the bottom fell out of my world. An officer came to my quarters. I was told to pack my clothes, I was being shipped out. No commission. No gold bars. And no reason—but I knew what had happened. The Army and the Navy played ball. And the Navy had obviously told the Army that it would consider it an insult if they commissioned a man the Navy had kicked out as undesirable and unfit.

They told me not to say anything to anybody about it. And I didn't. But you can't keep secrets in the service. There's always somebody who finds out, and they found out and, in an hour, the word was all over the base. Tony Martin wasn't going to get his commission. And my friends almost started a revolt.

They quickly circulated a petition verbally—in an hour or so, 200 men had agreed to it. They said they refused to accept their commissions unless I got mine. All hell broke loose. The brass got all excited and turned the screws on me. I had to go out and talk to the ringleaders, tell them it was all some kind of bureaucratic mix-up, and I'd get my commission later. I told them to keep calm, accept their commissions, follow orders. I said the war was bigger than all of us, that our first responsibility was to our country. I'll be all right, I said. I put on a phony brave front, but inside I felt like I was in the middle of open-heart surgery.

One of my roommates in Miami Beach, a nice young boy named Baldrich, went to Walter Winchell. Winchell was then staying at the Roney-Plaza. Baldrich hadn't been too good a student, and I'd helped him, and now he figured he was repaying the debt. He told Winchell the whole story, and Walter wrote a paragraph in his column about it, and mentioned it on his radio show. It didn't make the services look too good.

But the Army didn't pay any attention to Winchell, to the protest, to anything. They had received what they called VOCG—Verbal Orders of the Commanding General. And those orders were to get Martin the hell out, and fast.

I was a buck private again. They didn't even let me keep my corporal's stripes. They had made us all turn in our enlisted men's uniforms the day before, preparatory to getting officer's outfits, so I had no military clothes. They quickly rounded up another ill-fitting outfit for me, told me to pack my things, hustled me on a train. The day I was supposed to become an officer and gentleman, I rode the train to Goldsboro, North Carolina, a nothing and a bum.

I am convinced to this day that the Army dumped me as a favor to the Navy. There was no other possible explanation. I had had no trouble in O.C.S., I'd done well in all my work, I was accepted by all the men. It was just that the Navy would have been embarrassed if I'd made it in the Army. So some big-shot Navy brass asked some big-shot Army brass to get rid of me. And they did. They lost me.

In Goldsboro, I was immediately put on an overseas shipment. I was in with an outfit of fuck-ups—ex-cons, men in prison who were trading Army service for a reduction in their sentences. We were going to be sent to some overseas assignment in a few weeks. I was convinced that this was some kind of suicide mission, and that the Army and Navy had figured the best thing to do with Martin was to put him somewhere where he'd get himself killed. End of embarrassment.

But God found me again. An old friend of mine was a man named Jerry Brady, who was then the secretary of the Hialeah race track in Florida. He read the paragraph in Winchell's column that told of my being sent to Goldsboro. By coincidence, Jerry's brother was General Francis M. Brady, who was the commanding officer in Goldsboro. Jerry called his brother, told him that I was being railroaded, and asked him to talk to me.

I didn't know any of this, of course. I just knew that this was the lowest point in my life. I ran out of tears on the train from Miami to Goldsboro. Grown men don't cry? Bullshit. Show me a man who had gone from the heights of excitement to the depths of despair in an hour, I'll show you tears. I sat in that train in the blackest of moods. Then the conductor tapped me on the shoulder and said there was an officer who wanted to see me in the next car. I figured some jackass wanted to rub some salt in my wounds. What else could it be? But at least it was a diversion, so I walked to the next car. And there was Lt. Robert Messervey, better known by his professional name, Robert Preston.

"What the hell are they doing to you, Tony?" he said.

I tried to explain, but I couldn't. He had a bottle of Scotch and we polished it off. He got me through the trip.

Goldsboro was like a P.O.W. camp. We were marched everywhere, even to the latrine. I began to think that the expected death overseas wouldn't be so unwelcome. It would be a release from everything I'd been going through, and was still going through. A day or so after I got there, as it turned out, was a Sunday. No formations. Nothing. I thought of calling home, but what could I tell my folks? So I just lay on my bunk in the barracks, brooding. I was emotionally distraught. I guess I was closer to a nervous breakdown that day than I've ever been in my life.

Along about four in the afternoon that day, a top sergeant came into the barracks looking for me. He told me to follow him. Outside was a general's car, and the sergeant told me to get in. I didn't know what was going on. As a matter of fact, I seriously thought they were going to take me somewhere and shoot me, and make up some excuse that I'd been trying to go AWOL. They drove me to headquarters and the sergeant told me to report to General Brady.

"Sir, Private Martin reporting as ordered," I said, saluting smartly.

"Forget all that, Tony. Sit down."

General Brady offered me a cigarette, poured a stiff belt of Scotch. He told me to relax.

"Tony, when did you talk to your mother last?"

"Three days before graduation."

"What's your home number?" I told him. He had his aide, a major, get the number and ordered that the call be charged to him personally. I had a long, wonderful talk with my mother and father.

I don't think I'll ever forget the kindness of General Francis M. Brady. He picked me up when I was down and being stomped. He rejuvenated me. From that moment on, I began to feel like a man again.

He asked to see my orders. He immediately had them rescinded.

He said, "Obviously somebody in the Pentagon hates you. But I don't hate you. I'm going to keep you here with me in headquarters. Effective immediately, you're a staff sergeant."

This was Seymour Johnson Field, Goldsboro, North Carolina. I was attached to headquarters and headquarters squadron. Brady had me produce shows there, and I even got several commendations for the shows I turned out. Hank Mancini, one of our finest musicians, was stationed there at the time, with the band, and he made several arrangements for me. I wasn't supposed to be eligible for a furlough for six months, but Brady got me one, and I went home to Oakland and saw my family, for the first time in two years.

Brady made me so much a man that I began to feel a tremendous surge of patriotism. I figured I wasn't doing enough for the war, just producing shows in some backwater camp. So I swung a transfer to a radar school in Boca Raton, Florida, but that still didn't satisfy me. I decided I wanted to go overseas. A buddy—a sergeant named Vince Haydock—and I applied for overseas duty and we got it. We were shipped to Kearns, Utah, where we were issued winter clothing. We figured we'd be going to Europe and that was OK with us. A sign there at the station read: "THROUGH THESE PORTALS PASS THE BEST SOLDIERS IN THE WORLD." We trained there for a while, then went to Hampton Roads, Virginia, where we shipped out on the U.S.S. *General Mann*. This was it! Look out, Europe, here we come!

We were on that ship for thirty-six days. My bunk was next to the head. Hardly a luxury cruise. I got off, expecting to find myself in England or France—but then I got a shock. Those couldn't be Englishmen or Frenchmen, those poor, dark-skinned people sleeping on the wharf. Somebody yelled out, "Where the hell are we?" And the answer came back from another dock—"Bombay, you fucking idiot!"

We were driven by truck convoy to a place called Kamshapara. But I didn't stay. Again, I found myself on a shipping order all by myself, and piled into a Jeep with my duffle bag. A lieutenant was driving. I asked him where we were going.

"I'll let you know," he said. And that was all.

We drove over a twisting road for some seventy miles and then he said, "This is it." It was a place called Hastings Mills, the headquarters of the ATC—the Air Transport Command—on the Oogly River. It had been originally a jute mill.

This was the ass end of the world, as far as I was concerned. I guess I couldn't have been any further away from home. There was a sign post: "ATTENTION: GIs. AWOL WON'T HELP. NEW YORK, 12,425 MILES, SAN FRANCISCO, 12,260 MILES." I don't know if the figures were accurate, but it didn't matter.

Still, as it turned out, it wasn't bad duty. I guess the thing that made it bearable was that I fell in love—again. Her name was Dotty Luft, and she was a WAC sergeant working in headquarters. I met her, I guess, the first or second day I was there. I kept smiling at her and I imagined she smiled back. As it turned out, she hadn't. The smile I thought was aimed in my direction was meant for someone else. Dotty had bad eyes and couldn't see very well without her glasses. So she was smiling at somebody else, but it didn't matter. Encouraged by that fleeting smile, I tried to move in. And, in no time, we were seeing each other.

From then on, it was always Dotty and Tony. We would go to Calcutta weekends, have dinner at Firpo's, go to a movie. There was a big

MGM theater near the French market. One night, they played one of my films. The Hindus laughed at the film and then saw me and laughed at me —and the damn thing wasn't even a comedy.

We'd go to the movies on the post during the week, Dotty and me. One night, I remember, we saw *Stanley and Livingstone,* and the picture broke. That wasn't unusual. The films were shipped from camp to camp and often they got film fatigue and snapped. Years later, I happened to mention to Mervyn LeRoy, back in Hollywood, that I never did see the end of *Stanley and Livingstone* because the film broke in India. And he arranged a special screening of it for me, on my birthday, at his home. That's been a running gag with Mervyn and me ever since; to this day he always calls me and says he's running *Stanley and Livingstone.*

The evening shows at Hastings Mills were always interrupted by PA announcements: "Squadron 54, please report." Ours was a very busy air field. And my job, reporting to General Bill Tunner, was to see if I could get some entertainment into the CBI—the China-Burma-India theater. All the big USO troops would go to the ETO or the Pacific, but nobody came out our way. I was supposed to see if I could use my influence to get some shows to visit us and, failing that, to see if I could round up some talent in the CBI itself and put together a couple of show units.

We were the Siberia of the war. They dumped all the flotsam in the CBI. I was a piece of flotsam, and so were a lot of the other men. If there was anybody who was an embarrassment or out politically, he'd wind up in India, China or Burma. I wasn't the only exile, by far. I flew one mission of mercy for General Bill Tunner and, going along with me, was Major Melvyn Douglas. His wife, Helen Gahagan, was very controversial, so he got the flotsam treatment. He didn't seem to mind.

I flew all over the CBI, bringing entertainers to distant outposts. And doing other odd chores for the general. One day he asked me and Sergeant Paul Benson, an old Broadway press agent and buddy, to represent him at a ceremony in Burma, to honor another general who was being replaced. It turned out to be a memorable trip. Benson and I were playing gin as we flew along in a B-24.

"Gin!" Benson called, and at that instant, some Jap Zero fighters zoomed in on our transport. To get away, our pilot dropped a thousand feet or so into the clouds, and the cards Paul and I were playing with scattered all over the plane.

"Did you say gin, Paul?" I said, when we leveled off.

"Yeah."

"Show me."

"Well, I had it, you sonofabitch, and you know damned well I had it."

"No good. You gotta show me."

We had a big argument, but there was nothing he could do. He lost —and I don't think he ever forgave me. But we're still good friends.

It was a screwy place, India in those days. One Sunday, I was on duty in headquarters. A captain and a master sergeant came in with a Top Secret dispatch. I watched as they opened it. It was a request for Ping Pong balls to be sent to Manila, immediately.

I had nice quarters to live in. There were six of us in a sturdy British tent. We had hot water for an hour a day, from six to seven in the morning. You couldn't drink the water—that way was excruciating sickness. If you got thirsty, it was either beer, if you were lucky, or a dash of powdered lemon in some bottled water. There were nets covering our cots, because of the mosquitoes, especially the anopheles which carried malaria. When we went to the post movie theater at night, some medics were stationed there with flashlights, checking to see that we all had anti-mosquito salve on our wrists, necks and ankles. Those anopheles mosquitoes in India were big enough to bite an elephant's head off. And they carried dysentery and yellow fever and all kinds of awful things. I was lucky. The only thing I came down with was love.

Dotty and I became very close. At that point, American propaganda was that the war might last ten years or more. The atom bomb was just a dream in some scientist's mind. We were told the war would go on for a long time, and that we were all stuck out there in India. So, naturally, we made the best of things, and the best, for me, was Dotty.

I think I might have married her, there and then, but she had a boyfriend from her home town—Wilkes-Barre, Pennsylvania—and she was very faithful to him. She was still wearing his ring. He was an Air Force mechanic. One day he wound up at a nearby base, Dum Dum. He'd gotten himself a transfer, so he could be close to his fiancée. It was tough on Dotty. She had the two of us to juggle. She managed it, but the boyfriend and I were both jealous. He'd seen her first, so, for a while, it all ended.

I was too busy to feel too bad about that. There was always something going on. There was one day that Colonel Ed Hastings—he's now head of the Far East operations for Sheraton Hotels—called me in. Hastings, head of G-2—intelligence—and some other officers were there, and they were worried about the low morale in the theater. It was true, all right. We were in what they called a "stalemate" command—the war was all around us, but we weren't in it. Most of our job was flying Chinese soldiers to the

185

front, and there's not much kick in that. I went on many of those flights, to break up the monotony. There was once when I counted off sixty-five Chinese soldiers getting on the plane, but there were only sixty-one getting off. I asked the Chinese officer in command what happened to the other four. He spoke English fluently.

"Got airsick," he said, with a big grin. "Made sure they didn't suffer."

He had literally thrown four soldiers off the plane. Stories like that were common, and that contributed to the lowness of our base's morale. And that was what Ed Hastings, Col. Jim Austin, Col. Teague and Col. Ledbetter wanted to see me about that day. They said they'd appealed to the U.S.O., but still couldn't get any shows out there. Wasn't there anything I could do, any sort of show I could put together? I said I was sure that in the CBI there must be a lot of guys with talent. But I had to be able to look through every 201 file—the history of each soldier's civilian life —to find out who and what was available. Jim Austin, who was head of personnel, agreed and gave me the OK. So I spent a few days reading the personal history of every soldier in the CBI, and it proved worthwhile.

I assembled a troupe of talented guys. One of my first acquisitions was the great concert pianist, Leonard Pennario, who had been a clerk in some remote headquarters. There was my old friend, Vince Haydock, a fine dancer. Honey Coles, a dancer out of vaudeville, was marooned somewhere in Myetkina, Burma. I found a magician and another singer. I got them all together, found a place to rehearse, and began assembling the CBI's first entertainment unit. Eventually, there were sixteen different companies of entertainers, all home-grown from the CBI itself, touring the theater and playing from cities like Calcutta and Bombay to tiny crossroads where sometimes the only audience was two GIs and a sacred cow. I performed a lot myself, but most of my efforts went into assembling these companies, cutting orders, booking them, arranging transportation, seeing to their housing. I was the Abe Lastfogel of the CBI.

I was really running a pretty large booking agency. I had to organize the troupes, cut the orders, figure out how to get where we were going and back again, plan for food and housing for my men, beg and borrow and wheedle microphones and speakers. It was tremendously hard work, but rewarding. And I received many a commendation for my efforts. When I left the theater, I received a Bronze Star.

My troupes performed everywhere—hospitals, bivouacs, airfields, big bases, small bases, for the British, the Aussies, the Free French. As often as I could, I went along because I enjoyed going to the various places and the singing was good for my voice—except when mosquitoes flew into my mouth. Once, a comic named Leon Fields and I went to a little base outside

Chungking and found ourselves performing for Navy men. I wondered what the Navy was doing so far from the ocean. They told me they had set up a radio intercept station there. After we'd done our show, we had some time to kill before we could catch a plane back to Calcutta. We had a Jeep and we asked the Navy men what was interesting to see around there. They said there was a little city called Luliang, which, they said, was "cute." They said there were some fine artisans in Luliang who worked in pressed silver. So we drove to Luliang in our Jeep. Fields was expecting to go home soon, and wanted to buy something for his wife. We were in one little shop, looking at the silver. Fields leaned too heavily on a showcase and it broke into a thousand pieces. He got scared and started running and I ran with him—and five hundred Chinese chased us. It cost 100,000 cian—$100 American—to square it with the shopkeeper.

I guess the highlight of my fourteen months in India began quietly one day. A huge British Daimler limousine pulled up at headquarters and the word was passed that they were looking for S/Sgt. Tony Martin. I wondered what I'd done now.

My captain ordered me to put on a dress uniform and report at once. I went to headquarters in my best outfit and was introduced to the man in the Daimler, who turned out to be the Maharajah of Cooch Behar. I'd heard of him; he was the head of the state of Bengal, and our base was in Bengal, so he was an important personage there. He was really our landlord.

Baiya, as he quickly asked me to call him, was, as it turned out, an old friend of the beautiful blonde English actress Virginia Field. I'd been at parties and met Virginia a few times and she and Baiya had dated while he was a student at Oxford. In fact, I suspect he was much in love with her. Anyhow, Virginia had written to him, when she'd heard in California that I was in India, and asked him to look me up. So here he was.

"I am a fan of Hollywood," he said to me, as he walked me to his car. "I know you, of course, from your films, and it is a delight to meet you. I want for us to be friends. I have the permission of your superior officers to take you to my palace."

And so began a strange and delightful friendship that continued long after the war and long after I had left India. He took me to his palace that day, and I returned often after that. The only thing he asked in return for his friendship was Benny Goodman records. I asked Nat to send me a batch and, much later, they arrived. (That nearly got me into big trouble—I was questioned for a long time, and suspected of selling twenty pounds of Goodman records for profit.)

Even though he was the Maharajah, he was discriminated against in his own country. The British ruled India then, of course, and they had segregated most of their institutions. Baiya couldn't swim at the Royal Calcutta Swimming Club, although I could. And he couldn't attend the USO dances in Calcutta, which were restricted to GIs. He desperately wanted to go to one of those dances, so one weekend I arranged to have him smuggled in. I loaned him one of my sergeant's uniforms and we made believe he was a black soldier, as he was quite dark. We went in his Daimler, of course, but parked it about a block away and walked to the dance. Captain Laurence Pratt, of the Queen's Rifles, who was the aide-de-camp to Governor General Casey, went with us. He was in on the little deception. It was fun for a while, but Hindus are not good drinkers, and the Maharajah put away a lot of Scotch that night. He began to weave and wobble and I had to get him out of the USO hall. An MP stopped us just outside the door.

"What outfit are you guys with?" the MP asked.

"We're with the ATC, Hastings Mills," I said, propping up the Maharajah as best I could.

"Your buddy sure had a snootful. Let me see his dogtags."

"He lost them."

He must have been in a good mood, that MP, because he bought my story and let us go. Pratt and I half-carried the Maharajah back to his Daimler with the Sikh chauffeur in his elaborate turban. Then Pratt left, and I was stuck with a drunken Maharajah. I didn't know whether to take him back to his palace or what. Finally, I figured if he showed up at his palace, loaded and in a GI's uniform, there would be too many questions to answer. By this time, he'd passed out cold. So I figured if I could get him back to my tent, and let him sleep it off, he'd go home the next day with nobody the wiser.

So we drove back to the base. The big car, with its royal English emblem on the front, was saluted and allowed to pass onto the base. I asked to see the officer of the day, and he finally showed up.

"Sir," I said, "I request a private conversation."

"What's that big car out there?"

"That's what I want to explain, sir. But it must be in private, in the strictest confidence."

He agreed. Then I told him I had a drunken Maharajah in the car. In an Air Force sergeant's uniform, yet. And I was afraid that if he was found like that, in that condition and in that outfit, there might be an international incident. I said that two of the men in my tent were on leave, and there was plenty of room. He agreed that the best thing to do was to dump the maharajah on a cot and let him sober up overnight. So he detailed a couple of men and we laid poor Baiya on a cot next to my own. He groaned royally all night.

The next morning, he sat upright in bed.

"Where are my servants?" he asked.

"Quiet, Baiya."

"Where am I?"

"You're in my tent. Keep your mouth shut."

"Where are the records?"

"They're still in the trunk of the car." That was the night I'd given him the Benny Goodman records Nat had sent. I called in the Sikh driver, who'd waited outside the camp all night long, and he helped me get him to the car. He was still a little wobbly, and I could tell he had a Cooch-Behar-style hangover, the worst kind.

I half-carried, half-dragged him to the car, and he kept mumbling, "I hope they didn't break the fucking records." We became great friends, the Maharajah and me, but I was glad to be rid of him that particular morning.

During my remaining time in India, I was often a guest at the palace, and got to know the whole Bengal royal family—Baiya and his lovely sister, Isha, who was married to another maharajah, the Maharajah of Jaipur. Baiya asked me once if I wanted to go on a tiger hunt. I said no, but I did arrange for some of my officers to go. I just didn't feel like hunting a tiger.

Pratt, Baiya's buddy who was to become a life-long friend, took me once to Darjeeling where there was a rest and recreation camp. I needed a rest at this point and got a pass and it was a great trip. Pratt and Baiya arranged for me to stay at the palace of the English governor-general, a man named Casey. There were no beds in the palace, only benches, but I had known that and brought along a sleeping bag, so I was moderately comfortable. This was a palace in name only—no beds and, in the bathrooms, no thrones, either. All they had were two pieces of metal and if you had to go, you had to squat. Still, it was a change. And Darjeeling is beautiful—around 7,000 feet up, and from there one could see five countries, Sikkim, Nepal, India, Burma and China. I got up early one morning and, with Pratt, we went up to a high point to watch the sun come up. There was an Indian sect called Sun-worshipers there, and they knelt as the first rays of the sun broke over the mountains. They prayed, and I guess I did, too, because I've never seen a sight like that. The sun came up and lit up the whole world and splashed on those glorious mountains, Everest, Kachenjunga and Godwin Austin.

The war was drawing to a close. We heard that the bombs had been dropped on Hiroshima and Nagasaki and everyone knew it was now just a matter of time.

Christmas, 1944. General Tunner asked me to do a favor for him and some boys at an advanced base in a little city called Cian in China, close to Siberia.

"I want you to take my plane," Tunner said, "and fill it with beer and fly up to Cian and do a show for those guys. They've had nothing for years."

So I got Leon Fields, the comic who was still waiting for his shipping orders, and a magician and a drummer. We flew to Kunming and then to Cian and did the show. Coming back, we were supposed to stop at Kunming again, to refuel. But we got the word that while we had been doing our show at Cian, the Japanese had bombed the Kunming airport and the runways were badly damaged. We'd have to try to make it all the way back to Calcutta on what fuel we had. It was touch and go.

Poor Leon. He was moaning and groaning.

"I'm just about to go home," he said. "I'm thirty-eight and my wife is waiting for me. What the hell do those lousy Japs want from me?"

The pilot sent the word back. There was eight minutes of fuel left, and we were ten minutes away from the base. He said he thought he'd have to put down, but it was dark and there wasn't much level ground around.

"You dirty sonofabitch," Leon said to me. "If I get killed, I'll break every bone in your body."

That pilot was a miser with those last few minutes of fuel. He coaxed that plane and babied it and landed with the gauge registering absolute zero.

That was my closest brush with death, or at least with a crash landing. And it was my last mission. From then on, we were left to secure things in the area, as our troops began being shipped home. Naturally, I began to think of home, too, but with somewhat mixed emotions. I had been in contact, by mail, with old friends in Hollywood and I knew that things would be hard for me when I returned. Nobody missed me. The Navy thing was still in people's minds, apparently, and my name was still synonymous with something unsavory. Nobody remembered—or knew—that I had never been court-martialed or even accused of anything. All the public remembered were those dirty black headlines, spelling out my "crime" against the military. Besides, Hollywood is a land of here today, gone tomorrow, a yo-yo culture, and, in the years since I'd been away, new stars had soared into prominence. So I knew there would be no bands playing for me when I came back, no ticker-tape parade.

Then I got to go home. I had the points, because my Navy time counted. General Tunner arranged for me to fly home as part of a project to ship all our planes back to the United States. I went as a crew-member on a C-54, and we flew from Calcutta to Bangkok to Manila to Johnston Island to Honolulu. The pilot knew we were all pooped and could use a rest before we got home, so he told the authorities in Hawaii that something was wrong with a couple of the plane's engines. We stayed in Hawaii for twenty-seven days, getting tan and getting a nice per diem allowance. A couple of us rented an apartment near Waikiki Beach. I lay on the beach and I had a lot to think about.

There was, first, my relationship with Dotty Luft. We had separated in Calcutta. There had been vows of faithfulness, promises to wait for each other, kisses and more. I'd given her a diamond engagement ring I'd bought in China—and a wristwatch, too. She had sailed for home, while I flew, so I'd get there before her. I had told her I wanted her to come to California, to meet my family. She had been hesitant. She said she doubted she could fit into the Hollywood world. We left it up in the air. I might go to Wilkes-Barre to see her or maybe she'd come to Los Angeles. We'd see. As it turned out, this was the end of the affair. So there was that, and there was also the question of my future. Could I regain my place in the movie and nightclub and record world? I'd been away for more than four years and maybe the public had forgotten me—and, if they remembered, maybe all they remembered was the scandal, not the good work I'd done. So I clung to Waikiki, and I was a little frightened about what I'd find when I got home.

Every day, we reported. Every day, our pilot said the parts needed to fix the balky engines hadn't arrived yet. So back we'd go to the beach and the sun and the ocean.

Eventually, of course, that idyll ended. The parts arrived, the engines were "repaired," and we flew back to the United States. I was honorably discharged on December 14, 1945, with the rank of Technical Sergeant. I had the American Campaign Medal, Asiatic-Pacific Campaign Medal, Good Conduct Medal, Bronze Star, World War II Victory Medal, China War Memorial Badge and Ribbon, four Battle Stars, a Meritorious Unit Citation, Distinguished Unit Badge, Meritorious Unit Award and between ten and twenty personal citations. I was separated from the service at Fort MacArthur, the place where I had been issued those ill-fitting clothes. There was just one last brush with military chicken shit.

Our plane was scheduled to be returned to Cincinnati, the ATC's base. I wanted to get off in California. But I had to go on to Cincinnati with the plane—and then they refused us a spot on a westbound plane. Our pilot, however, got huffy about it and everything was ironed out, and I found myself a civilian at last.

I was back in Los Angeles. I had very little money, no clothes, no place to stay. Nat Goldstone had driven up to Fort MacArthur with a suit for me to wear. The Ritz Brothers put me up in their home for a while. Then I stayed for another few weeks with Irving Moss. Lots of my old friends were kind to me—Durante, Cantor, Sophie Tucker, Bob Hope. They got together and hosted a big party for me on Christmas Eve, at Romanoff's. I was so tired of eating from a tray, with all the foods piled on top of each other, that I made them bring everything on separate plates. And I told Mike Romanoff that if he put the ice cream on top of the chicken, I'd dump it on his head.

At last, I started working again. Eddie Cantor had arranged for my first post-war engagement, and it started the day after Christmas. Dotty and I corresponded and called each other for a time, but eventually that stopped. But I will forever hold fond memories of Dotty Luft.

There was a family reunion that Christmas, too. My folks came down from Oakland and they stayed at the Beverly-Wilshire. My brother, Harold, had come back from his wartime service in Utah, too, and we all got together.

Getting back in my profession was as tough as I had anticipated. Maybe it was my imagination, but I had the feeling people were looking at me funny-like. I suppose I might have been hypersensitive. And why not? I wasn't just an ordinary, honorably discharged serviceman, it was more as though I were a convict out on bail. There were fleeting glances into which I read suspicion, dislike, hatred. Many people would approach me and say something like, "Hey, Tony, glad to see you back. Tell me about that fast one you tried to pull." I heard that so often I took to answering, as a defense mechanism, with something like, "Yeah, but it wasn't fast enough—I should have offered them a Cadillac." I was the heavy, and, rather than protesting my innocence, I figured the easiest path was to act the part. I knew, in my soul, that I had vindicated whatever they thought I'd done through my subsequent Army service, and yet everything combined to make me feel uneasy.

And so, even though it began to look like I could pick up the pieces of my career, I wasn't too choked up about my life. I felt as though I'd brought shame on my friends and my parents.

On New Year's Eve, I was invited to a party that Sam Spiegel always hosted in those days. He was not only a great producer, but he was also a first-rate party-thrower, and everybody was there. As the night wore on, and

I had a few drinks, I began to feel better. Maybe 1946 would be a turning point for me. I felt a good year was due me.

It was at that New Year's Eve party that Rita Hayworth came into my life.

10

MOVIES
AND
MEMORIES

The MGM years were one of the high spots of my life. That's only natural. I think those times when MGM was the *crème de la crème* of Hollywood studios, and Hollywood, in turn, was the most glamorous place in the world were high spots of everybody's life. Anybody who was a part of MGM in those days was very fortunate.

Just walking into the commissary at lunch was an experience. The place was regimented, in a way that just sprang up. People sat together in a seating order based on what they did. The producers had their tables, the directors had their tables, the writers and make-up people and publicity men and women—everybody ate lunch with his own group. Except actors. We sat anywhere. Sometimes I'd eat with one group, sometimes with another, most often with one of my particular friends. If I had an interview, of course, I sat apart with the interviewer. I never ate very much at lunch, of course, especially when I had a dance number to do in the afternoon. You can't eat a heavy lunch and then go out and dance. So I'd nibble at some cottage cheese and fruit, that's all. For me, lunch wasn't a time for eating, but for relaxing with friends.

The group, my friends, was varied. Among my very good friends was Helen Rose, the costume designer. I'd gotten to know her, first, during the time when I was doing my practicing at the Fanchon and Marco dance school as a young girl. Another good friend, over the years, was Jeannie Coyne, one of the best assistant dance directors around. At the time, she was assisting Gene Kelly. Carol Haney, a splendid dancer who died so tragically later on, was a friend, too. She was then Kelly's assistant. And

Lillian Burns. And Ann Strauss, of the publicity department, who was always so good to me.

There was never much of a camaraderie among the women stars at MGM. I imagine that was because of envies real or imagined. Whatever it was, the ladies were never very close. In fact, there were often petty little scenes which I could not understand.

I remember when I was in *East Side, West Side,* which Mervyn LeRoy directed. It was only a small part, but it was a good one. I played a model. The star was Barbara Stanwyck. I had only one scene with her, but I'll never forget it. Barbara never even looked at me through the scene. Even when we were off camera, she ignored me. I am convinced her aim was to make things as difficult for me as she could. She succeeded. I was shy and inexperienced, so that was quite a blow.

There was another strange thing about *East Side, West Side.* I was still not at all sure of myself as an actress. I was making progress, I felt, but still acting was not my natural milieu. So I had come to rely heavily on my directors, asking their advice and following it closely. But in that film I ran up against my first non-directing director. LeRoy was then, and remains, one of the dearest men alive, but he just didn't tell his actors what to do.

We would do a scene and he would say, "Cyd, I'd like a little more in the next take."

"A little more what, Mervyn?" I'd ask.

"Oh, you know, a little more."

So we'd do the scene again. And I'd try to give him a little more of something, although I had no idea what. Eventually, we'd do the take in a way that pleased him. He knew what he wanted when he saw it, but he couldn't explain it. Still, his system must have worked, because he directed some of our greatest movies.

I had become fascinated with acting. At first, the acting was just an adjunct to my dancing but, gradually, I became hooked on it and it came to be an end in itself. I asked the studio for some non-dancing roles, and they wanted their people to broaden themselves, and that's how I got to do films like *East Side, West Side* and *The Wild North* with Stewart Granger. But, when I did those non-dancing roles, I came to realize that I missed dancing, so I asked to do musicals again. I learned that dancing and musicals were my true metier. In the long run, I preferred them, even though I did enjoy doing those few roles in straight drama. I still enjoy straight acting.

One thing that took me a long time to grasp was that I had become a star. It hadn't anything to do with me, I decided, it was just that I was there. That was brought home to me when I did that early film, *The Harvey Girls*, with Judy Garland. I went to the premiere. My part was very small, yet I was stopped in the lobby afterward for my autograph. I couldn't understand why they wanted me to sign, and then it came to me—they wanted anybody's autograph, anybody who was in any picture, anybody who had anything to do with Hollywood and the movies.

That realization has stood me in good stead over the years. I learned that being "a star" was important. As far as the public is concerned, anybody and everybody in films is automatically "a star." My definition of a star is much more limited and there are very few performers who merit that description to me. I have never thought of myself as a S*T*A*R, not even after I made my biggest films. Perhaps that's because I am, basically, an introvert. I knew that I loved working, performing. What the public made of it was their business. I hoped that they liked me and admired my work, of course, but that pedestal they stuck me up on was insignificant in my view.

Some of the jobs of stardom were bothersome. As an introvert, I dreaded having to go out on personal appearance tours, and that went with the territory. I have always been very shy with the public. I was never overly fond of interviews, even though the press has been good to me for the most part. But I had to do it all, the P.A.s, the interviews, everything. All those trappings of publicity help sell a film, and I believe that, uncomfortable as it is to me, it's something that has to be done. I did it.

Looking back now on my career, I find certain things stick out in my memory. I am not writing a textbook, so I will not try to be chronological about them.

One of my first location trips was to Mexico for *Fiesta*, another Esther Williams picture, produced by Jack Cummings. She had just married Ben Gage at the time, so, for them, the trip was a combination film and honeymoon. At that time, Esther was a major star, and the studio catered to her. It was also Ricardo Montalban's first film in the United States. Cummings had found him in Mexico and imported him and, as it turned out, Ricardo and I were in many pictures together, and are still dear friends.

We were three months, as it turned out, in a little Mexican village called Puebla. There was one very small hotel in the town and we all—cast and crew—stayed there. In the evening, after shooting, we'd all gather in Esther's suite—really two big rooms, but the best the hotel had. Ben would mix martinis, and Ricardo, Esther, Ben, Akim Tamiroff, the unit publicist, a girl named Malvina Pumphrey, and whoever else was around would have a few drinks before dinner. One evening, the few drinks stretched out to quite a few. When we got down to the dining room, it was closed.

"Very sorry, senor," the man in charge said to Ben, "but it is too late. You have missed dinner. Tomorrow, OK?"

"How dare you do this to us?" Ben Gage said.

"Senor, we have hours here. You know the hours. You are late."

"But we have to eat. Come on, open the place up."

The discussion became louder, and pretty soon Ben and the Mexicans were shouting at the top of their considerable voices. Then I saw one of the Mexicans pull a knife and go for Ben. The man on the desk in the lobby ran outside, yelling for the police.

Tamiroff took me by the arm and ran. He led me around the block, so we would both be out of the way. But pretty soon, we heard the police run up, and we peeked around the corner and they were taking Ben and the make-up man off to jail. Esther went with him. The MGM power was strong, even in Mexico, and they got Ben and Esther out—but somebody had to take the blame, so the poor make-up man, who was barely involved, was sent to jail for a while. And he was replaced on the movie.

The man who had gotten Ben and Esther off was MGM's Mexican attorney, Oscar Obregon. He seemed to like me—this was before I met Tony—and he took me around. When I had a day or so off, he would drive me to see various places in Mexico. We went to Taxco, I remember, and Mexico City. There, we met his uncle, a wealthy banker, and the uncle was a love. I also met, at the time, Neil Vanderbilt, of the Vanderbilts, who was much older than I was, but charming. He would pop up in Puebla from time to time with an invitation to dinner or the bullfights or somewhere.

Fiesta is also memorable to me because of my confrontation with a fighting bull. The studio built a *corrida* just outside of town for the bullfight sequences which were a major element in the story. And they hired the top Mexican matadors and arranged for a steady supply of beautiful but bad-tempered bulls. Esther Williams and I were standing there in a scene, with John Carroll. Suddenly, one of the bulls charged the wall, which was only papier-mâché, and the beast burst through and headed straight for the three of us.

"Cyd, what do you think we should do?" Esther said.

"I don't know, Esther. But we should do something."

Carroll was no help. He just ran as fast as he could, the other way. The bull was getting closer and I think he was angry at us for some reason, or at least that was what it looked like. And I'd never done anything to him.

So we looked around for a place of refuge and, fortunately, there was a car nearby, and we ran for it and got inside. The bull jumped right over

197

the top of the car. If that car hadn't been there, I seriously doubt that I would be here to tell the story at all. I still love to kid John Carroll about that.

I suddenly became very ill down there in Mexico. The doctors said it was amoebic dysentery—extreme *turista*. I lost ten pounds in a few days, and I was pretty skinny to start with. The studio flew me back to Los Angeles, to see my doctor, and then I'd fly right back again for my scenes. That happened several times. But I managed to do all my sequences, including the "La Bomba" number with Ricardo, which was one of the big numbers in *Fiesta*. And the La Bomba dance remains popular to this day.

Those early MGM days were always fascinating. You never knew what you were going to be doing when you reported for work. I had a small part in a film early in my career, a thing called *'Til the Clouds Roll By*. And I found out that I was supposed to be the girl Perry Como sang to when he did his big number, "Blue Room." I had to dance around him while he sang. Also, before he partnered with Marge, Gower Champion and I had one number together in that film, and it was interesting to watch him work. When he was thinking about his choreography, he'd walk around the set in circles, thinking, thinking. I'd get dizzy trying to follow him while he was in that creative, restless mood.

I had a small part, too, in *Three Wise Fools*, in the prologue to the movie. I played a young girl eloping, and the girl turned out to be Margaret O'Brien's grandmother.

And I had a couple of dramatic roles in some other films then, too. In *Tension*, I played a reporter with Richard Basehart, a fine actor, and Audrey Totter. And in *The Wild North*, with Stewart (Jimmy) Granger, I was an Indian girl with braided hair. That was shot in Jackson Hole, Wyoming, which is breathtakingly beautiful. Granger—his real name is James Stewart, which he obviously couldn't use, but everybody still called him Jimmy—was funny. I've never seen a man who could eat so much, yet not gain a pound.

About that time, I had a fascinating experience. It began, one day, when Benny Thau called me in. He had seen that early test Bobby Lewis made and it had impressed him. Thau was a great friend of Spencer Tracy, and Tracy was then about to go back to Broadway to do Robert Sherwood's play, *The Rugged Path*. They were looking for a girl to play Tracy's daughter in the play and Tracy had asked Thau if he knew of anyone and Thau had suggested me. They had shown that test to both Tracy and Sherwood and they had, apparently, liked it and they wanted to meet me. So I was told—in those days at the studio, you were told to do something and you followed orders—to report to Spencer Tracy's house where I would read some scenes from the play with him.

I had, of course, never read for a part in a play in my life. But, for some reason, I wasn't the least bit nervous. I guess I didn't know any better. If it happened today, I'd be shaking like an aspen. But not then. Then, I just drove over, very calmly, and presented myself at the front door of Spencer Tracy's house. Katharine Hepburn was there, naturally, and she was gracious and made me feel at home. She showed me to the patio where Spencer Tracy and Robert Sherwood were waiting for me, and she served us iced tea and then excused herself. Tracy gave me some pages of the play to read and I read them over quickly before we began, while I sipped my iced tea.

Then I began to read. And, out of the corner of my eye, I caught sight of Hepburn, peeking over the hedges and watching me. I imagine she was very interested but felt her presence would distract me. Actually, the sight of her peeking over the hedges was more distracting than if she had just been sitting there. But I tried to ignore her piercing eyes and red hair behind those hedges, and I read as well as I could. When I was finished, she came back and refilled the iced-tea glasses and we chatted a while and then I left.

A few days later, Thau called me in again and told me I had been very impressive and I had the part in the play. I was truly astounded. It was the first time I thought that maybe I could become a real actress, after all. For a while, I was very excited about the coming Broadway debut, but nothing ever came of it. A little while before we were scheduled to begin rehearsals, Sherwood decided the part was extraneous and wrote out the character I was going to play. So it would be many years before I made my stage debut.

Soon after that, I did *On an Island with You*, when I tore all the ligaments in my knee. It took me, as I've said, only two months to recover. They were tough months. From the immobilizing, my leg muscles had virtually atrophied, and I'd have to sit there, swinging my legs with weights attached to them. But Joe Pasternak wanted me in *The Kissing Bandit*, so I swung those weighted legs as hard as I could. I shouldn't have bothered, because that picture was a disaster. It started with a bad script and went downhill fast. Strangely, Tony was supposed to do that film, but he left the studio about then and Frank Sinatra was hired to replace him. I did a number called "Dance of Fire" in that, with Ricardo Montalban and Ann Miller. They inserted it in the film after the shooting was finished, to help save it. As it turned out, it was the only decent thing in it—but it still didn't save it.

The first film I did after I became Mrs. Tony Martin was *East Side, West Side*, for Mervyn LeRoy. It wasn't easy, because of I guess, my post-marital adjustment. Right there on the set, in front of everybody, I began crying. Nothing triggered it specifically, just an accumulation of tensions. I couldn't understand it, but I couldn't stop. I just stood there and bawled, tears streaming down my embarrassed cheeks.

I ran to the dressing room and continued my crying jag. It wasn't rational and I knew it, but even knowing it didn't help. Just more and more tears. Mervyn came in and asked me what the matter was.

"Is it something I did?"

"N-n-no," I said. "I'll be all right in a minute."

But I wasn't all right and they finally sent me home and my doctor, Stanley Immerman, came over and gave me a shot. It was, he said, just fatigue. Despite that day of crying, the picture turned out well and I think my performance was pretty good, too. I was proud of my work in *East Side, West Side*.

During the shooting, or maybe it was soon after, LeRoy gave a party. It was for the crown prince of Belgium and it had been arranged by the State Department. The prince asked me to dance. He couldn't dance. But that didn't stop him. He wouldn't let me sit down. I tried to help him around the floor, but it was a pretty strenuous workout for me and my feet. Even after all the other guests had sat down, he insisted on stumbling around the little dance floor with me. At the end of the evening, my pale blue satin party shoes were black from where the prince had stepped all over them.

I did *Words and Music*, the story of Sigmund Romberg's life, and I had a lovely number with Jim Mitchell, beautifully choreographed by Gene Loring. The most notable feature of that film, as far as I was concerned, was a beautiful outfit Helen Rose designed for me, a fabulous white draped jersey dress with a velvet cape.

If I were ever going to be a real actress, I decided, I would have to study. I needed a coach and I felt that need strongly. I met George Shadanoff, who had coached such stars as Robert Stack and Leslie Caron. He had been a director in Berlin in his younger days, working with Chekhov. I worked with him and I studied very seriously. From then on, whenever I had a new script, I'd work on it with George and he was an enormous help to me.

Then came my first chance to dance with Gene Kelly, in a film called *Singin' in the Rain*, one of MGM's greatest musicals. Arthur Freed wanted one big production number at the end. The picture was all finished, but he felt it needed something else, and he and his fabulous team concocted the "Broadway Melody" finale. At the time, Carol Haney was Gene's assistant and the assumption was that Carol would be Gene's partner for the big number. Freed tested her but, apparently, he was not pleased with her for reasons of his own. Gene wanted her, but Arthur asked me if I'd do it. I was, at the time, completely unaware that Gene wanted Carol and that Freed wanted me. All I knew was that I was being asked if I'd dance with Kelly, and what dancer wouldn't jump at that opportunity? I told Arthur I'd be delighted.

I reported to the studio, not knowing anything about the intrigue that had been going on. This was very soon after I had had Tony, Jr., and I was startled when Arthur said I had to lose some weight. My problem had always been just the reverse—if anything, I was too thin. But he was right; I'd gotten up to 120 pounds which was about eight pounds over my normal weight. Arthur suggested I go to see Louise Long. At the time, she was very popular with those who wanted to lose weight. She was a masseuse who had her own studio in the San Fernando Valley. I went to her and found that her system was, simply, to pound the hell out of you. After my first session, my legs were black and blue. I don't think the public appreciates what some girls do to look beautiful for the audience. But I wasn't about to be tortured. Anyhow, I decided—maybe it was rationalization—that that wasn't healthy, that it was bad for the body to have tissue broken down by incessant pounding. So I stopped and I put my faith in the exercise of dancing to take the pounds off. And it did, without any problem.

Gene and I began rehearsing, and Carol was there, in her capacity of Gene's assistant. It was only then that I heard that she had wanted to do the number. But that didn't stop her from being extremely kind and helpful to me. She was the epitome of unselfishness. Even though she must have been consumed with disappointment, she did everything she could to make things easy for me. There wasn't a trace of bitterness. She and I worked together for days, while Gene was off somewhere, choreographing.

His system in the "Broadway Melody" number was interesting. Kelly put Carol and me on Stage 17, one of MGM's longest, with streamers of China silk about fifty feet long attached to our shoulders. He had them turn on the big wind machines, gigantic fans that blew up a storm. He wanted to see what would happen, what the action of the wind would be on those silk streamers. I could hardly keep on my feet, when the fans were turned way up and the enormous scarves tugged at me. I'd get home at night, with my shoulders sore and aching from the pressure of the wind. He had them try various combinations, and eventually got the effects he wanted, with us dancing and those huge silk streamers undulating in various patterns. The choreography, a combination of music and dancing and flowing silk scarves, was exciting. It had to be timed exactly, to fit the pre-recorded music. The result was a number that many people still remember today.

I'll always remember Carol Haney fondly for the way she helped me, when her heart must have been breaking. If it had been me, I think I might have just walked out. She was truly fond of Gene, so she just stayed and worked with me. I think most girls who knew Gene felt the same fondness for him.

I didn't really have much to do with Gene during that picture. We did the one number together, that's all. During the rest of it, he was busy with his own numbers and with the other dancers in the company. I did have to learn to smoke a cigarette in our number, however. He wanted me to have a long cigarette holder and, as the camera panned up my legs and my body, I was supposed to exhale a drifting plume of smoke. I had never smoked and it took me a long time, plus a lot of coughing, before I got it right.

Smoking never became a problem for me. After that, I did smoke some, but not much. But, years later, when Tony and I were in Las Vegas, rehearsing for my first appearance at a nightclub act, I learned that I needed more stamina. When you're dancing for a movie, you do it in short takes—a few bars of music at a time. For that, you need strength. But for a nightclub act, you need strength plus the stamina to carry you through the thirty minutes or so you're on stage. I found out I didn't have that stamina, so I cut out smoking. I had been smoking only perhaps three or four cigarettes a day, but cutting those out was enough. When I stopped, I quickly developed that all-important stamina, and was able to do the act with Tony easily. Smoking for pleasure may be all right, but certainly not for dancers.

I should mention that when I was doing "Broadway Melody" with Gene Kelly for *Singin' in the Rain* was the first time I met another of his assistants, Jeannie Coyne, who would become a good friend over the years.

I met another great choreographer, Hermes Pan, on my next film, *Sombrero.* Again, I worked with Montalban, plus many others. Pan was the choreographer, and devised a very effective dance number for me. I was playing a superstitious Spanish character and my big number called for me to dance around an idol and then roll down a mountain while the rain poured down. Pan was a joy to work with because of his inventiveness. He was always Fred Astaire's right-hand man and it was Pan who assisted Fred in creating some of Fred's greatest numbers, such as his dancing on the walls and the ceiling. Hermes and Fred are really like brothers—they even look somewhat alike.

We were rehearsing that big number of mine one day when Fred strolled in, and he was always a unique man. He was dressed as only he can dress—a tie for a belt, a straw hat, white and brown shoes. On anybody else, that would look ridiculous, but he has a knack for lending elegance to whatever he wears. I remember Hermes and I were working in Rehearsal Hall C when he came in, nonchalantly, pretending he was just visiting his old friend. But I had heard rumors—MGM was always rife with rumors —that I was being considered for his partner in his next film. And I could see that he was there to size me up—for size. He didn't want to work with girls who were too tall for him which was understandable. So he was just sort of eyeing me, to see how tall I was. Even though we had danced in the same number together—I hadn't been his partner at that time, however —when we did *Ziegfeld Follies*, he wanted to make sure, I guess, that I hadn't grown any. So he was looking me over, glancing at the two of us in the rehearsal hall mirror. He did it very subtly, very tactfully. Then he just smiled and strolled out.

Fifteen minutes later, there was a call from dear Arthur Freed.

"Good news, Cyd," he said. "Fred says he likes the way you look, and he wants you for his next picture."

That picture turned out to be *The Band Wagon*, which was a huge success and a great triumph for me. Vincente Minnelli directed, Pan and Michael Kidd choreographed. Oscar Levant and Nanette Fabray were in it, too. It was difficult, at the beginning, because it took me a while to understand what Minnelli wanted. We have become dear friends but, at first, I found him difficult to work for. I had a scene, soon after we began shooting, with an old friend and wonderful dancer, Jimmy Mitchell, who had worked for a long time with Agnes DeMille. But Jimmy and I couldn't seem to please Minnelli, no matter how hard we tried.

"No, no," he would say, "that's not what I had in mind. That's not it at all. Please try again."

But, gradually, I began to figure out what it was he was looking for. The more I worked with him, the easier it became.

When it came time to work with Astaire, it was hard, too, but in a different way. It has become a cliché to say that Fred Astaire is a perfectionist, but it must be said, because it is his essential quality. I think he came to appreciate my work, too, because I'd work just as hard and long as he did. Long after everybody else had gone home, we'd stay and work with Hermes in anticipation of the next day's shooting. He liked that.

He never said it, of course, because that's not his style. But neither does he say anything critical to your face, I'm sure for fear of hurt feelings. If he had any suggestions to make—about a costume he didn't like or a hairstyle he disapproved of—he would never say it directly to me. His way was to tell somebody else who would tell somebody else who would tell me. It was the long way around, but it freed him from the danger of hurting someone's feelings himself. He was always very considerate that way. Fred is the most perfect gentleman I have ever known.

We danced well together. He has always been the soul of tact, in interviews, and never said which of his many partners was his favorite. I suppose Ginger and Rita and Vera-Ellen and all of them like to think they were, but I like to think the same thing, too. I have nothing to base my claim on, except from what others have told me—that he has said, privately, I was the best dancer he ever worked with. Our first number together, "Dancing in the Dark," has become a classic and was chosen by Fred to be part of *That's Entertainment*. And there was another one we did that I loved but, unfortunately, it was cut out of the finished film. Actually, there were two cut out, and I wish I could get copies of them. Michael Kidd choreographed them and they were excellent.

In the film, I played a ballet dancer, he a jazz dancer. The story had us dancing together, but he didn't want to, because he felt I was too classical for him. So there was one number which emphasized that division between us. It was filmed with a split screen, he on one side, me on the other. He was doing jazz, I was doing ballet, and it was choreographed so the two were in counterpoint. We were dressed in counterpoint, too—I was in a ballet outfit, he was in his jazziest clothes. The other number that didn't make it was similar. He was at a desk in his office, I was in my apartment. And we had a conversation about making a date, using dance as our means of communicating. No words were spoken, only the way we danced conveyed our meanings. I think that was chopped because it was improperly shot.

But there were, of course, many numbers that were retained. One was the "Faust" number, which was a riot to shoot. Jack Buchanan was playing a director, and he was in that, with Fred and me. There were elevators in it and the gimmick was that they weren't supposed to work right. It took hours to rehearse so it would look the way Minnelli wanted it to look. There were explosions and smoke and elevator doors opening and closing, and everything had to be synchronized perfectly—or imperfectly. Because of the magnitude, we could shoot it only once, and we got it done. But with everything going on, everybody was hysterical. If you look at it now, through the smoke, you can see Fred and me laughing hysterically.

And there was the finale, "The Girl Hunt Ballet," which was one of the high spots of the picture. The number is a classic, way ahead of its time, and still looks fresh and inventive today.

The last number, taken from a Mickey Spillane novel, was the hardest to shoot. The picture had taken a long time—it has to take time to be good —and Arthur Freed was getting nervous—budget problems upstairs. He asked Minnelli to hurry up, and Minnelli hates to be hurried. The last thing we shot was in a subway set. I was supposed to slide along the floor, which had been highly waxed to make the slide easier. I had to sit, slide, clasp my arms around Fred's legs. The first two times we did it, my trajectory was off and I missed the target, Fred's legs.

"All right," Minnelli said. "We'll do it one more time, that's all." After shooting for months, suddenly there was no more time.

So I had to do it right. The music began and then it was time. I fell to the floor, slid across it and grabbed. Perfect. I latched on to Fred's legs and when it was over everybody applauded. It was a happy moment.

This might be an appropriate time for me to compare Fred Astaire and Gene Kelly. As one of the handful of girls who worked with both of those dance geniuses, I think I can give an honest comparison.

In my opinion, Kelly is the more inventive choreographer of the two. Astaire, with Hermes Pan's help, creates fabulous numbers—for himself and his partner. But Kelly can create an entire number for somebody else, as he did for me in *Always Fair Weather* later on. I think, however, that Astaire's coordination is better than Kelly's. He can do anything—he is a fantastic drummer. His sense of rhythm is uncanny. Kelly, on the other hand, is the stronger of the two. When he lifts you, he lifts you! Fred could never do the lifts Gene did, and never wanted to. After a session with Gene Kelly, a dancer would go home and be black and blue. When Gene threw you on the floor, you were on the floor. I don't think Tony ever understood why I was so black and blue from simply doing a dance number.

To sum it up, I'd say there were the two greatest dancing personalities who were ever on screen. Each, in his own way, with his own particular charm, was an individual. Each has a distinctive style. Each is a joy to work with (black-and-blue marks notwithstanding). But it's like comparing apples and oranges. They're both delicious.

I made yet another film with Esther Williams and Ricardo Montalban, *On an Island with You.* I might point out, at this stage, that poor Esther's watery numbers were difficult for her to do. Mostly that was because of the special make-up that was required for her, because of working in the water. How fortunate we all were to have people like Sidney Guilaroff and Charles Schram to create hair styles and make-up for us in those days. They were truly artists. Ordinary make-up would wash off or become blotchy and she was supposed to look beautiful, no matter how long she was soaked. So this special make-up was daubed all over her, and a special material—something like glue—was combed into her hair so the water wouldn't disturb her hair-do. She could be working underwater for hours and not a hair would be out of place. That was fine for the camera, but it was a devil of a job to get out at the end of the day. It would take an hour or more for her to wash off her make-up and get that sticky stuff out of her hair. One other thing, and maybe I'm telling tales out of school, but she never did those graceful dives you see in her films. She was quite capable of doing them, but she had ruptured her eardrums, so it was physically impossible for her to dive. There was always a stunt double on hand to do Esther's dives.

I liked working with Esther. She was an easygoing person, without any airs. Off camera, she didn't care how she looked. She was always fun to be around. She did her own cooking in her dressing room, and we would often have lunch together. Her publicity girl, Malvina Pumphrey, was almost always there, too, so it was a pleasant break in the day's work.

I was reunited with Gene Kelly and Vincente Minnelli for one of my favorite films, *Brigadoon,* based on the Alan Jay Lerner Broadway musical play. I was excited about being in it, but it started off badly. That was because Kelly wanted to film it on location, in Scotland, while the studio said no, that was impractical because of the weather there, and insisted it be done in Hollywood. Minnelli preferred shooting inside a soundstage, so tons of earth were moved onto several sound stages and it was all shot inside —even a complete village was built inside, down to the thatched houses and trees and roads and bridges. The sets were unbelievable, but I think Kelly was right. It should have been done in Scotland, where it was set, and it would have been better. I think, from the lavishness of the sets, it would have been cheaper to send the whole company to Scotland, too. But with Scotland's weather, we could have been there a year and a half.

Another problem on that picture was a clash between Van Johnson and Minnelli. Van is one of those who, understandably, likes to work an ordinary nine-to-six day. Minnelli is a slow, painstaking craftsman. He will take hours to set up one shot. The result of that is that often he will work all day and only be ready to do the shot around five-thirty or so in the evening. That makes him nervous, because a director feels he has to get something in the camera or else it's a wasted day. So he would start shooting late in the day, just when Johnson was getting itchy to go home. Van said he would walk off at six, which was when Minnelli needed him. And, often, Van did leave at six. So there was enormous tension on the set between Minnelli and Johnson, and Freed would have to come down to arbitrate the differences.

I think the only time I was ever really angry at Gene Kelly was on *Brigadoon.* For one number, he put Carol Haney and myself on a mound of dirt, said, "You two work something out," and he left us.

So there we were. The mound of dirt, a few sprigs of heather, a tree or two. And we were supposed to devise a dance number. Eventually, the mound of dirt was supposed to be covered with grass, but the studio landscaping department hadn't put the grass in yet, so we were dancing on plain old dirt. And we would get dirtier and dirtier.

For several days, Carol and I worked on that dirt, trying to create something pretty. It wasn't easy. Kelly had, apparently, abandoned us. But then, one day, he showed up, to see what we had done, how far we were along in our creative process.

He was in what I call his Irish mood. Something had gone wrong, and the Irish temper was about to explode. You could see that in his eyes and the way his mouth was drawn tight. I don't think anything Carol and I might have done would have pleased him that day, and, when he saw what we had invented, he said it was no good. He was at the point where anything would set him off—and something came along to give him the excuse. Two secretaries were cutting through the soundstage on their way to lunch. I heard them coming, their heels clicking on the concrete floor. Kelly heard them, too, and the sound of the clicking heels disturbed his concentration. He blew up.

"Hey, you two girls," he yelled. "Come over here."

The girls turned around and, with fear showing in their faces, they came closer.

"Look," Kelly said, "I don't come to your office when you're working, so don't you come here when I'm working." Bravo!

They ran out of that soundstage as fast as they could. Then Kelly, his eyes blazing, turned back to Carol and me, and really told us off. I was tired already, tired and dirty and disgusted. So, naturally, I started to cry. And I walked away. I went back to my dressing room, and began packing my things. Then Kelly came in, all contrite and apologetic. He didn't mean it, he said. He was tired himself and overworked and it was a hard time for all of us, he said. Please excuse me, he said.

When he turned on the charm, nobody could refuse him anything. I realized that his apology had been a genuine one, that we were all tense from the work. So I said that, of course, I accepted his apology and the whole incident was forgotten.

Brigadoon was a beautiful film, but somehow it missed. I've never really understood why that happened, but it did. Motion pictures are funny that way; they can seemingly have all the ingredients, as *Brigadoon* had, and yet when they are all put together, the whole is less than the sum of its parts. Whatever the reason, *Brigadoon* never lived up to our expectations. It made money—I'm proud of the fact that I was never in a financial flop—but it wasn't quite the picture it should have been, despite Lerner's great talents.

I worked with Michael Kidd in *It's Always Fair Weather.* Kidd was another fine choreographer. A few years before Kidd had pleaded with me to go to Broadway with him and do a show he was working on. I couldn't do it, because I was under contract and it was simply impossible. So he had gotten Gwen Verdon as his star in *Can-Can,* and that show made her a star—deservedly so. She had been Jack Cole's assistant dance director for years.

Kidd wasn't choreographing *It's Always Fair Weather,* he was acting. Gene Kelly, again, was the choreographer-director. He created a fantastic number for me. I was playing a reporter, assigned to do a sports story. So he invented this number in a prize-fight ring, me and a bunch of fighters, and the song was "Baby, You Knock Me Out." It was a tough number to do, but fun to be with all those ex-champs in a prize-fight ring. Jeannie Coyne worked with Kelly and me on that number, which had a particularly fast tempo. I think "Baby, You Knock Me Out" showed the Kelly touch at its peak—inventive, daring, totally worked out in his head before we began working together. When he's right, he's very right, but he can have his misses, too. He had one of the latter in *It's Always Fair Weather.* It was a scene in a costume shop and, although it stayed in the picture, it just wasn't very good.

It was almost a disaster for me. I had to do some tap dancing with Gene in it, and tap dancing isn't my forte, although I can do it when I have to. The steady pounding of my feet made my bad knee swell up and it hurt very badly. I remember I was supposed to go to a party that night at Anne and Kirk Douglas' house and I had promised to go, even though Tony was out of town at the time. With my knee swollen and aching I didn't feel much like going out. The studio sent me to Dr. Daniel Leventhal who examined my knee, gave me a shot and said I should go home and rest. But the shot, as I later learned, was cortisone. I went home, as the doctor had suggested, and rested until time to get ready for the party. Then I soaked in a hot tub and got dressed.

Mervyn LeRoy had offered to pick me up and take me to the Douglas party. By now, my knee was throbbing and, by the time we reached the party, the pain was dreadful. It was so bad, in fact, that I couldn't even talk, much less walk. I just sat on a couch, with my leg raised. Mervyn called Dr. Leventhal who, over the phone, prescribed ice packs. Obviously, I couldn't apply ice packs in the midst of a fancy party, so Mervyn thoughtfully took me home. I put ice packs on my knee. When that didn't seem to help, I put hot compresses on it. Back and forth, hot and cold, cold and hot. It was so painful I was climbing the walls. Obviously, I couldn't work the next day. It was, as it happened, the last number to be shot for the film, so they had to shut down production until I was fit again.

The next day, I hobbled over to Dr. Leventhal's office and he looked at my knee again.

"Well, Cyd," he said, "I guess we'll have to open it up, go in and have a look around, see what the matter is."

No way I was going to have knee surgery. I said thank you, put on my slacks and hobbled back home again. I could still hear him saying that if I didn't have the surgery, I might never dance again. That hurt almost as badly as the knee did, and the knee was killing me. With Tony away, I didn't know what to do. I went to bed, but I was so dizzy from the pain and the worry and my nerves that I developed problems of the inner ear. Then I remembered my dear Dr. McKeever, who had been so good to me and for me when I had first torn my knee. I called him, told him what had happened and he said I should come right over. My mother drove me to his office.

"Cyd," he said, when he had finished his examination, "there's no doubt about it. We both know you have a bad knee, a very bad knee. But don't ever have an operation. I tell you what you do. You go home and rest completely for ten days or maybe two weeks. Then go and finish the picture. You'll be fine."

And that's just what I did. The knee has bothered me from time to time since, but I have never had surgery on it and, God willing, I never will.

It's Always Fair Weather was an excellent film, but it didn't do anything special at the box office. The big, lavish musicals were losing their appeal, for whatever reason, and their era was coming to an end. Then, too, the MGM hierarchy was changing and they were shifting their emphasis away from musicals, too. They just didn't push the picture, and no matter what the picture, it needs the push of publicity and promotion before it can score at the box office. However, *It's Always Fair Weather* is in the collection at New York's Museum of Modern Art.

There were still a few more musicals, however, that I did for MGM. One of my favorite MGM films was *Meet Me in Las Vegas*. Joe Pasternak had the story written just for me, by a fine writer, the late Isobel Lennart. I had Dan Dailey, Cara Williams, Jim Backus and Agnes Moorehead in it with me, and Hermes Pan and Gene Loring were my choreographers.

Before it started, we had worries. Dore Schary was now the head man at MGM, and he was not a big fan of musicals. The script had been finished and everything was ready, but the word came down that Schary wasn't sure he wanted to go ahead with the project. First, he said, he wanted a reading of the script in his office, with me and Dailey reading our parts. That didn't sit well with Dailey and he showed up for the reading late. And that, in turn, didn't sit well with Schary. I was there, on time, and Schary was glaring around the room, looking for Dailey. Dan finally showed up and the two men gave each other icy looks.

Dailey was so furious he read his part like a second-grader reading his lesson from his primer. I tried to do my best, but it was hard, with my leading man reading his part like a dictionary. Dore was angry, too, but he was at least objective and I think he recognized that it was a very good script. At the end, he smiled.

"Fine," he said. "It's a good script. We'll go ahead with it."

More problems came along later. The big number in the film was a thirteen-minute ballet based on the classic "Frankie and Johnny" song. We were rehearsing it—me, Johnny Brascia and Liliane Montevecchi—when the word came down from the front office to hold everything. It seems the studio was getting very budget-conscious and they felt that maybe a big ballet like *Frankie and Johnny* was a waste of money. Again, Schary said he'd like to see it himself before giving the OK to proceed. We really weren't ready to show it to anybody yet, because we had just begun rehearsing. I asked Hermes if he thought we could even get through it, and he said there was no choice—we had to do it, and do it that day. Actually, the number was a tremendously difficult one.

So Schary came down to the rehearsal hall, and the three of us did the number. It took all my strength, because it was not designed to be done consecutively. Schary was sitting there, watching, all by himself, and his face showed no emotion. Finally, it was over.

He started applauding. "That was great," he said.

So, at last, the number was officially approved. But the accumulation of tension and the anxiety of the rehearsal took its toll on all of us. I went back to my dressing room and I was absolutely drained. My head ached and I saw lights flashing in front of my eyes. I had to go home and, when I got there, I couldn't see, or just barely. Half my vision was gone. Tony was frightened for me and quickly sent for a doctor. The diagnosis was that it was just exhaustion, coupled with nervous strain, and Dr. Immerman was right. Again, I needed rest. I was fine the next day. I think it was all worth it, because the "Frankie and Johnny" number made the movie and both became big hits. The vocal to that number, special lyrics by Sammy Cahn, was done by Sammy Davis, Jr., whose rendition could never be topped.

I had fun, during the course of the shooting, watching a romance of sorts develop. Jeannie Coyne was helping Loring and Pan with the choreography. She usually worked only with Gene Kelly, but he was in Europe, so she was available. And she became enamored of Dan Dailey and a big romance sprang up. Movie companies are curious sociological units. For the duration of the shooting, they are closer than families and loves and hates sprout like weeds. Then, when the picture is finished, everyone scatters and the loves and hates are forgotten. I've always felt a sociological treatise could and should be written about the motion picture company unit.

One number was done on point. When you are dancing with a ballet company, you spend, at the most, twenty or thirty minutes a night on point. But, in a movie, you work on a number all day long and that means you're in those ballet shoes all day long. You have breaks, of course, but your feet cool off during those breaks, and that's not good, either. By the end of the day, when I did that number, my feet were raw and bleeding. I believe that dancing on point is one of the most torturous things you can do in a film. I'll always recall, with a painful shudder, the director calling out, "OK, we're ready to shoot, Cyd, on your toes."

The location of the picture was the Sands Hotel, in Las Vegas, and so the premiere was held in Las Vegas, too. MGM sent me on a promotional tour with the film.

I actually don't mind interviews, if the reporter turns out to be intelligent and is out to be honest and sincere. Actually, American newspapermen are generally easier to handle than those in Europe or Australia, where the questions tend to be very personal and the reporters seem to have a chip on their typewriters, especially with an American entertainer. So generally interviews were the easiest part of those tours.

I said earlier that one of my toughest decisions was whether to do *An American in Paris* or have my second child. There was another tough decision.

And that was whether to work with Kelly or Astaire. Lucky, lucky girl! Gene wanted me to team up with him, Kay Kendall and Mitzi Gaynor in *Les Girls*. Fred wanted me to be his partner in his next musical, *Silk Stockings*. Because of the timing, I couldn't do both. I had to choose between the two. And, after a week or so of reading the two scripts and mulling over the strengths and weaknesses of each, I knew I had to do *Silk Stockings*. Kelly got Taina Elg to do the part he had wanted me for. *Silk Stockings* had Astaire and a Cole Porter score, it had been based on *Ninotchka*, a successful film, and I was going to play the part Garbo had played, a good acting part. And it was the leading role, whereas in *Les Girls* I would be one of a trio of leading women.

I had many scenes with the three commisars, played by three funny and talented men, Peter Lorre, Jules Munshin and Joseph Buloff. Again, there were Hermes Pan and Gene Loring to choreograph my dances. And Rouben Mamoulian, that very fine director.

Loring devised my big number, "The Red Blues," which was brilliantly choreographed. As usual, Arthur Freed was pressuring us to hurry —that was his style—so we did that entire number in a day and a half. Freed felt there was a let-down near the end of a picture, so he would always give us a boost then.

One thing I'll always remember about *Silk Stockings*. On the day we began shooting, I went to my dressing room and there was a fabulous gift from Fred. He had sent me a cage full of the most beautiful finches, white ones with red beaks, representing the red theme of the movie.

Lorre was already a good friend of ours. He and Tony had worked together in *Casbah* some years before. We had often visited him and his wife, the nurse he married when she helped him lick his drug problem in Europe. But, during the shooting of *Silk Stockings*, he was having troubles again. He was using pills in alarming numbers. It was very sad to watch his decline. We all knew he was very sick even then. He died a few years later. But, despite his problems, he turned in a fantastic performance in the film, and it was, all in all, a smashing artistic success—and for me, personally, too. It opened at the Music Hall in New York.

I feel it was one of the best films I did. It was followed by the absolute worst. MGM loaned me to Universal for a tidbit called *Twilight for the Gods*, based on the Ernest Gann book. It started out as a pleasant enough assignment—most of it was to be shot in Hawaii, and that wasn't hard to take. And my co-star was Rock Hudson, one of the nicest and handsomest men in town. I had a friend, Tense Robinson, with me. Tense had been Laraine Day's stand-in and then had begun working for me, and we were very close. So it began as something of a lark.

We shot on Maui and we stayed at a lovely hotel. Rock was then married to Phyllis Gates and the four of us had a great time for a while. But one day Phyllis told me she was going home and, as it turned out, that was when she and Rock separated. That kind of put a pall on things. But the worst thing that happened, as far as I was concerned, was the director, Joseph Pevney. He took a good book—a best-seller—and did not seem to know what to do with it.

Tense and I had one adventure in Maui. We went for a swim one day, heading out for a reef about one hundred yards or so off shore. When we got there we looked back and everyone on the beach was waving at us and yelling. We were too far away to hear what they were yelling. We assumed it was some friendly greeting, so we waved back and yelled something, too.

We stayed there a few minutes, and then began to swim back. We had only gone a few strokes when a boat arrived and picked us up. It turned out that they had seen something we hadn't seen—two huge manta rays gracefully circling beneath us as we swam. I understand those fish are not dangerous, but I was still happy to be in the boat for the return trip.

From Rock Hudson to Robert Taylor. I worked with two of the handsomest—and nicest—of men, in successive films. *Party Girl*, which I did with Bob, was a good role for me and a good picture. But there were, as always, problems. In this case, it was a strike of musicians which put a tremendous burden on our choreographer, Bob Sidney. Without musicians, he had to be tremendously inventive and creative. For one number, he had me dancing to a prerecorded drum track, that's all. And, for another, I worked with two boys who looked as if they were playing trumpets but, again, the music was all prerecorded. Nick Ray was the director and he was a fine director, but he knew very little about dancing or musicals, and freely admitted it. He had the good sense to leave that up to Bob Sidney and the studio music department, and so it came out fine.

I had known Bob Taylor before, because he was a good friend of Tony's. He was a very pleasant man, but kept himself aloof on the set, just palling around with his own cronies. He drank coffee all day long and chain-smoked—I have a hunch that, around four or five, there was something in the cup besides coffee. It didn't affect him; he was always a gentleman on the set, and a thoroughly professional artist.

It was about this time that I left MGM. I had been called in to see Alfred Hitchcock about starring in *North by Northwest*, but he said I wasn't the type he wanted, and the part went to Eva Marie Saint. Perhaps, if he had used me, I would have stayed on at the studio for a while longer. But it wasn't meant to be.

As in any other business, the studio had undergone another change in administration and the new heads wanted to shake the old place up. They slashed the budget and dropped many of those of us who had been around a while. They were further de-emphasizing musicals, and that was my forte, so I became expendable. My agent at the time, Ed Henry, called me with the bad news. I was, naturally, shocked and disappointed. My films had all been profitable and the public liked me, but there was no point arguing.

MGM felt like home to me, after fourteen years. And, when they said they no longer wanted me, it was as though they had said, "Get out, and never darken my doorstep again," as though a father were booting out his daughter into the snow. Looking back on it now, I only wish it had happened sooner. The studio had over-protected me. They had always treated me well, perhaps too well, and through my association with MGM I had become famous all over the world. Still, it would have been healthier for me and better for my career had I left some years before, and gotten an earlier chance to try my wings on other projects. But, as I say, at the time it happened it was an enormous blow to my ego.

I wasn't at loose ends long. The Ford Motor Company immediately asked me to do a TV special, and I did it. It was one of the early ones and nobody really knew what he was doing, so it soared way over the budget. I rehearsed for days, as I was accustomed to doing at MGM, and you just can't do that for a TV show; they're isn't the money or time for such luxuries. The result was that when all the bills were paid, there wasn't much left for me—although I did save some money by using a singer named Tony Martin as my guest star. It turned out beautifully. It was called *An Evening with Cyd Charisse* and it was nominated for an Emmy. I may not have made much money, but I got some very good reviews—and Mr. Ford gave me a little Thunderbird, navy blue with a white top, which I adored.

My first picture, after MGM, was a labor of love. A producer named Joe Kaufman and a director named Terence Young, both balletomanes, wanted to do a film encompassing four of Roland Petit's ballets. They called it *Black Tights*.

Poor Joe Kaufman. He loved the ballet but he didn't have much money. He made the film on a shoestring, feverishly running around nights to see if he could raise some more money. He finished the picture, but his efforts cost him his life. He died of a heart attack before it was released.

Terence Young loved the ballet, too. You can see it in the pictures he did later. He's the man who directed several James Bond films—*Doctor No, From Russia with Love, Thunderball*—and he did them almost as though they were choreographed. I can see his ballet passion shining through those rip-roaring adventures.

The four Petit ballets chosen were *The Diamond Cruncher* and *Carmen*, both with Zizi Jeanmaire, *Cyrano de Bergerac* with Moira Shearer, and *The Merry Widow*, which I did. As I have said, Joe and Terence were doing everything on the lowest possible budget. I found that out the hard way one terrible day. There was a duel scene, between the husband and the lover, and I showed up in my pink tutu, pink tights, pink shoes. The set was all black, and my pink outfit was supposed to be a colorful contrast. The set had been built overnight, and nobody had had a chance to inspect it before we arrived to film the ballet. It turned out to be layers of gauze, spread across the floor and sprayed with black paint. As soon as I stepped on it, it was as though I had stepped onto a floor covered with charcoal dust.

In seconds, I was covered with black powder—and me in my pink tutu. Terence Young was pale as a ghost.

They finally got some big vacuum cleaners and sucked up as much of the black dust as they could. They had to rectify another problem, too. I had found that the gauze on the floor made it impossible to do even the simplest pirouette; as soon as you began turning, the gauze would wrap around your feet. So, while they were vacuuming, they also put down some pieces of plywood at the places where I was supposed to do my pirouettes. So we managed to do the number, but it was still difficult. Small pockets of the dust had eluded the vacuum cleaners, so after each take, I had to change my shoes and tights completely.

It was, again, a day on point which, as I've explained, is very hard on the feet. Over the years, I'd acquired some expertise in how to handle it. But the poor Roland Petit company had never been through a day like that before. They were in excruciating pain and, as the day wore on, they were dropping like flies. It hurt me just to watch them suffer.

We neared the finale. My part called for me to do sixteen *fouettes*— after a grueling day and still on point, yet. And, after those sixteen *fouettes*, on to a double pirouette after which Petit was supposed to catch me and then we'd go into the coda. OK. Tough, but not impossible. So I do my *fouettes* and my double pirouette—but when it came time for Petit to catch me, he wasn't there.

"Oh, I forgot, I'm sorry," he said.

So I had to do it again. Sixteen more *fouettes*, another double pirouette. And, again, no Petit.

I knew he was an experienced partner. I felt that, for some reason, he was deliberately not catching me. Dancers can be that way. So I went to Terence Young and asked him what to do. He said that I should skip the *fouettes* this time, just do the double pirouette and he could cut in the *fouettes* from one of the earlier takes. And that's what we did. I still don't know why Petit was acting strangely, but, then, I never did get to know him. He is very talented and both he and Zizi could be charming but, even after working with them for a month or so, I didn't get a clue as to what was going on in their minds. Very hard people to know, the French.

Young was an excellent director for a dancing film. Ballet is, I think, one of the hardest things to capture on the screen. So many directors I've worked with, in television as well as movies, just say, "Dance," and turn on their cameras and start shooting and think that they are making a ballet film. You lose seventy-five percent of the dance that way. To do ballet or any form of dance correctly, you have to shoot it using camera angles

215

carefully and painstakingly, and Young was one of the few directors who understood that. I would compare him with Minnelli, Donen and Kelly. They all have a tremendous eye for really knowing how to photograph dancing.

Working in France was pleasant. I found I enjoyed the French work schedule. It's not like Hollywood. In France, I would arrive at the studio at eleven in the morning, have lunch—a roll, some cheese and wine—and dally over that for an hour or so. You shoot, then, straight through from about one until perhaps nine in the evening. Then you quit and have a leisurely dinner, and you can even go out for an evening, because you don't have to get up so horribly early as you do in Hollywood. I remember that Gene Kelly, when he made *Invitation to a Dance* in Paris, came back home and wanted to institute the same sort of schedule in Hollywood. He had no luck. The unions wouldn't allow it. I was told once that Frank Sinatra made the same attempt with the same result. It's too bad, because I think it is a much more civilized schedule, but Hollywood is such a going-home-for-dinner-at-six town that I guess it just will never happen.

The one thing I didn't like about working in France was that they kept the rehearsal hall freezing cold. There was no heat at all. The French dancers were used to it. They would wear tights upon tights—keep pulling them on until they had enough to keep warm. Then, at the end of the day, they'd hang their tights wet with perspiration up on hooks along the wall. It wasn't what I was accustomed to, but it was very French.

I went from France to Italy for my next film, *Five Golden Hours,* in which I played opposite the late Ernie Kovacs. En route, I stopped off in Venice, where *Black Tights,* which they'd rushed through, opened the Venice Film Festival and was warmly received. Tony and Tony, Jr., joined me there, but Tony disliked Venice. For some reason, he developed an intense dislike for gondolas. I love Venice with the beautiful old buildings, the linen shops, the glass factories—but Tony didn't. Maybe it's because he can't swim.

Ernie Kovacs was a lovely man and a funny man, but, like all stars, he had his peculiarities. With him, it was a compulsion to change the script. Every joke that came along he'd stop and rewrite. It slowed things down considerably and, because of it, I found myself often just hanging around while Ernie was fiddling with the script. The result was that the thing I remember most about *Five Golden Hours* was intense boredom.

He had another addiction: practical jokes. That became apparent when we moved from the Italian location, in Bolzano, to London for the interiors. I remember sitting calmly on the set one day and, suddenly, I was in the middle of a barrage of firecrackers. They were bursting all around me. And there was Ernie, laughing his head off, while I jumped like a singed cat. I knew him to be a great wit and I expected examples of his wit and talent. I didn't consider setting fireworks off on a movie set a particularly witty event.

Outsiders, I believe, have a distorted view of Hollywood habits. They assume that every actress is automatically popular, has a date book filled weeks in advance and never has a lonely second. All too often, that is completely untrue. I find actresses are often very lonely people. The public assumes them to be popular and so neglects them. Men will leap to the conclusion that it would be pointless to ask them for dates, because they are sure to be busy, and so don't bother. And I know of many great ladies who spend night after night alone.

I returned to MGM for another Vincente Minnelli film, *Two Weeks in Another Town*. He asked me to make a test for the part and, although I hadn't been required to test in years, I didn't mind. I wanted the part very badly. The test turned out beautifully, thanks to Vincente, and I got the part. Here again, the picture should have been better than it was. After Vincente finished his cut, somebody else took over and chopped it to shreds. When I finally saw it, I couldn't make heads or tails of the story —it was so disconnected—and I'd been in it. It was a shame, yet I had some very good scenes and certainly enjoyed working with the talented Kirk Douglas and getting to know his charming wife Anne.

It was fun to make, whatever the result, primarily because it was shot on location in Rome and Paris, and I had a fabulous Pierre Balmain wardrobe to wear. In Paris, Vincente met his Denise, and she came along to Rome and later they were married. So it was a romantic few months. And Tony was there through much of the shooting, which added to the romance of it all. I remember the fun of night shooting on the Via Veneto, with Tony and Denise scurrying around, trying to find sandwiches because we had had nothing to eat for hours. And dear, brilliant Edward G. Robinson was in the movie, and he was always taking off, when he had even an hour free, rushing to one art gallery after another to add to his fabulous collection of paintings.

While we were in Rome, Elizabeth and Eddie Fisher were there, as *Cleopatra* was finally before the cameras. One evening, they gave a fabulous party in honor of Kirk and Anne Douglas, there for *Two Weeks in Another Town*, and they invited everybody who was in Rome at the time. It was gigantic. Richard and Sybil Burton had just arrived, as he was reporting to work for his role in *Cleopatra*. I think Elizabeth met him for the first time that evening at her party. Burton politely asked Elizabeth to dance, and I remember dancing with Tony and watching them dance by. I wish I could say I sensed the beginning of an earth-shattering romance, but I didn't. All I saw were two stars dancing, and chatting pleasantly as they danced.

One of our oldest friends had a ringside seat as the Taylor-Burton love story began to unfold. His name is Bill Jones and he's an Englishman who always worked for us when we were in London. He was practically one of the family. Tony and Eddie Fisher were friends, so when Eddie said he was going to Europe and needed someone to be his valet, Tony suggested he contact Bill Jones. Elizabeth came to love Bill, who is an old dear and the kind of man everybody loves. He was in show business himself at one time. He came along with the Fishers to Rome for the *Cleopatra* period, so he was in the thick of things as they developed. Bill has told us that he's been offered a fortune to write a book, on just what did happen and how it happened, but he said he would never write it. But he was helpful to Elizabeth and Richard at the height of the furor. The Italian *papparazzi* were dogging their footsteps and they had no privacy at all. One night, when they just had to have some time to themselves, they persuaded Bill to put on one of Elizabeth's wigs and one of her coats. He did, went out the hotel door and dashed into a car. The *papparazzi* followed him, thus leaving the coast clear for Elizabeth and Richard to have some time off together.

As it developed, Bill would keep us abreast of all the excitement, and I guess we knew what was happening before even poor Eddie did.

Something happened during the shooting of *Two Weeks in Another Town* I feel should be written about. There is an old and, I feel, dirty trick that is a custom in Europe. The U.S. customs buys "tips" from shopkeepers and hotel concierges about American tourists who are buying expensive items in European stores. Then customs has some advance notice and gives those tourists a tough time when they return home. I first became aware of that during that trip.

It was Jane Robinson, Eddie's wife, who was the victim. She had bought a gold compact in Rome. The concierge saw it arrive at the hotel, when she had it delivered. When Eddie and Jane flew home, with the Douglases, they took a flight over the pole and went through customs in Los Angeles. The Douglases had problems, too, but when the customs agents got to the Robinsons, they really gave them the once over—twice. They opened everything, searching for that gold compact they had been tipped off about. Jane said she didn't have a gold compact—and she didn't. There was something wrong with it, and she had left it in Rome to be repaired. Then it was supposed to be shipped legitimately to her back home. But the customs agents didn't believe her until they had practically ripped her suitcases apart.

Some years later, the same thing happened to us. That was when we toured the Orient—Manila, Hong Kong, Tokyo, Singapore, Bangkok. Tony had bought a lot of things on our various stops, including some batik paintings in Singapore, and lots of other items in the other cities. I had been fascinated by an enormous star sapphire ring in Bangkok, in a shop in our hotel. I must have looked at it six or seven times. It was relatively cheap, for a star sapphire, and Tony had urged me to buy it. For some reason, I decided not to. When we came home, we did so separately. Tony had to stop off in Tokyo for some military appearances, so he loaded me down with all of our purchases and I flew home directly. The plane stopped in Honolulu, so that's where I went through U.S. customs.

Someone in the Bangkok hotel must have tipped them off and they had wrong information. They had apparently been told I had bought that star sapphire ring, and when I presented myself at the customs desk, that's what they wanted to see. I am a stickler for honesty, and I had declared every single item we had bought, and was prepared to pay the duty on what we owed. I showed him my long list of purchases, and he looked it over, but obviously he wasn't satisfied. There was no star sapphire ring listed.

He began going through everything, opening every suitcase and every box and case inside every suitcase. I remember it was stifling hot in the customs shed, and I stood there while he tore our things apart. All the other passengers left, but I was still there. When he couldn't find what he was looking for—and I still didn't know at this point what it was—he got angry with me. He asked to see my personal jewelry. He'd already seen it, of course, but I showed it to him again. By now, he was rude and I was angry and shaking. He fingered every piece and asked when and where each one had been purchased. He even used a jeweler's loupe to examine every piece minutely. Then he told me he was looking for my star sapphire ring. I said I don't own a star sapphire ring. He looked at me as though I were a liar.

He kept me there, as it turned out, two hours—it seemed like ten—looking for a ring I had never bought.

I am convinced the whole thing is a nasty racket. Customs pays their informers overseas, and these informers, to maintain their informers' pay, will often jump to assumptions—as the one did who said I had bought that star sapphire ring in Bangkok. The result is that some innocent traveler, like me, is forced to stand in a hot shed for two hours while the agent searches for a non-existent item. I'm told the system began years ago when Paris couturiers were the first to tip off U.S. customs about purchasers. I'd like to see a balance sheet on the practice; I bet customs spends more in paying off their informers than they make in collecting duty. Just another example of U.S. taxpayers getting ripped off.

219

When we came back from Europe, I did a small part in *The Silencers* as a favor to Mike Frankovitch. That was a Matt Helm film, and Mike wanted me to do a number at the opening. With Bob Sidney doing the choreography, I did it. The only problem with that was that I really didn't play a role in the film, yet it was advertised as though I did. I later received a great deal of mail about that.

Assassination in Rome was an experience I'll never forget, for many reasons. It was one of those international co-productions which were so popular in the sixties—this one was a joint venture of Spanish and Italian film-makers, with money from those two countries plus France. So the cast had to be from the same countries, too, and they wanted a couple of well-known American actors in it so the picture would appeal to U.S. movie-goers. They signed me and John Gavin. It was going to be shot in Madrid, and I looked forward to that, as I had never been to Spain.

Since Tony was busy with various engagements at home, I asked a dear friend, Bea Korshak, to come with me. And, meanwhile, Tony had asked another of my best friends, Dusty Negulesco, to come with me. So it developed that I had two friends with me, and it turned out to be an absolute ball. We stayed at the Castellano-Hilton and it seemed like an adjunct of Hollywood. So many people I knew were wandering through the lobby every day, it was as though I had never left home. It seemed as though all Hollywood was in Spain.

There were problems from the start, as usual. John Gavin didn't like the script and decided to re-write it. So shooting was held up. Three ladies alone in Madrid are never alone for long; Bea, Dusty and I were invited to parties every night and, while we waited for the filming to begin, it was party time in Madrid. I fell in love with Spain.

The delay lengthened, and the producers decided they could wait no longer. One day, Hugh O'Brian showed up. They'd signed him to replace Gavin. Gavin couldn't believe that he was out, but he was.

I was still partying, and then going to see the flamenco dancers. Madrid doesn't start functioning until nine or ten in the evening. That's when you go to a cocktail party and then to dinner and, around one or two, you go to one of the tiny clubs and watch the flamenco dancers. One night, I came back to the hotel—it must have been around five in the morning —and there was a note in my box at the desk. It was my call to report to make-up at eleven in the morning.

"How dare they?" I said.

Dusty laughed. "Look, Cyd," she said, "if this was California your call would be for six, wouldn't it?"

"Yes, but—."

"But nothing. Your call here is for eleven. Isn't that much more civilized?"

So we finally went to work. As in France we'd shoot from around one in the afternoon until nine or so at night, and then we'd be off and running. With Bea and Dusty, there was always a party to go to. If there wasn't, they'd give one in our suite. The phone rang off the hook with invitations —until one day when Tony showed up. That changed things, and the phone stopped ringing. The Spanish are very proper.

Tony had been working in Puerto Rico and had a very dark suntan. The first morning he was there, the hotel maid came in and saw this dark man in bed with me. I thought she'd faint.

The beautiful Ava Gardner was in Madrid then, and Hugh O'Brian was dying to go out with her. Finally, somehow, he wangled a date. All that day, he was nervous and Tony was kidding him about it. He took her to a great restaurant, The Jockey Club. By coincidence (or maybe, knowing Tony, it wasn't a coincidence) we had dinner at the same restaurant at the same time. Ava, who was being charming, invited us to join them. I had known her at the studio. I don't think Hugh was too happy about it, but we did. And Ava suggested we go on with them to a flamenco place after dinner. Again, despite Hugh's obvious unhappiness, we did.

After a few drinks, Ava became something less than charming. She was infamous in Madrid for having broken up a few clubs. Because of that, we later found out, as soon as she walked in, the price of everything automatically doubled. She began drinking that night, ordering a row of different liquors and downing them. The night wore on, and I was beginning to think about home and bed, but Ava was just getting ready to go. Finally, I said, "Tony, we really must go, because I have to work tomorrow."

Ava glared at me.

The next morning, Hugh was exhausted and looked haggard. I asked him what happened after we left.

"Goddamit!" he said. "I finally got her out of there and took her home. We went upstairs and were just getting comfortable—and in walked the whole goddamn flamenco troupe. She'd invited them all up to her apartment. That really tore it. When I left, the whole bunch of them were still dancing."

Dusty, my friend, is a beauty. And the director noticed her and asked her if she'd play a small part in the film. She said she would, and for no money, if they'd do a small favor for her. There was a trunk she'd left in Rome on a previous visit, and she had forgotten what was in it. If the company would arrange to have that trunk shipped from Rome to Madrid, she would do the part. They agreed, and that trunk became a cause célèbre. There was, apparently, trouble with both Italian and Spanish customs about it. Every day, we would get a progress report on the trunk and its whereabouts. And we all began to wonder what mysterious treasures were inside that fabled trunk. The affair of the trunk lasted for weeks until, one day, it arrived. We all gathered around while Dusty opened it. One by one, she pulled out the treasures she had forgotten she had—first was a sack containing rocks she had gathered on Italian beaches, then a bottle of baby oil, next some old dried-up jars of make-up cream and finally a few old sweaters. Absolutely nothing she ever wanted to see again. But she had to have it—because she couldn't remember what was in it.

I think it was the day after the trunk arrived that the company moved—back to Rome. And so Dusty's trunk turned right around and went back where it started.

The night before the Madrid-to-Rome exodus, we had a party. This was a special one because it was our last night in Madrid. We had shot late that night, to get finished, so it was around twelve-thirty when we finished and we went directly from the studio to a restaurant. I had caviar, which I love, but it was too rich and I was too tired to eat much. We didn't get to bed until the sun was coming up. And we had to get up again in an hour or so to make our Rome flight. Poor Tony had to supervise some twenty-five pieces of luggage, between his and mine and those of Bea and Dusty, plus fight a tequila war in his stomach.

But when we got to Rome, I was sick. I don't know if it was all that caviar or just the usual affliction that strikes tourists, but it was something, and something dreadful. I was so ill that I couldn't move; I just lay in bed feeling sorry for myself. Tony and Dusty and Bea were ready to go out on the town, but there I was, flat on my bed, moaning and groaning. They sat with me the first night and that made me feel worse, the guilt feelings competing with the pains in my body to see which was the more horrible. So, on the second night, I forced myself up and pretended to feel better and I went out with them to a glorious restaurant. I couldn't eat a thing, but I watched them eat and they clucked sympathetically while they downed buckets of delicious Roman pasta.

That trip was great for Tony's ego. He would get up early and Bea, who was also an early riser, would go out with him to see some sights and do some shopping. At noon, he would have lunch with Dusty, who likes to sleep late. Then, at dinnertime, he would escort me, because I'd be working all day. So the denizens of the Grand Hotel lobby would see him with one beautiful girl in the morning, another at noon and then a third at dinner. They concluded he was quite a man.

Tony and Dusty both left after a week or so, Tony for an engagement somewhere, Dusty to rejoin her husband, Jean. Bea and I stayed in Rome until the company moved to Venice for the last week or so of shooting. We stayed at the elegant Royal Danieli Hotel—until one day when the news sifted down to all of us that the company had run out of money. They stopped paying us our per diem, the day-to-day money we lived on.

Hugh O'Brian and I talked the situation over. We were legally free, since they hadn't paid us, to pick up and go home. But, if we did, we would never see the money due us—they couldn't possibly recoup without a finished movie to sell. Hugh said he'd heard that the crew had all agreed to finish the film, on the hope that when it was done the company would sell it to a distributor and they would get paid. So we agreed to go along, figuring that was our only chance to realize anything from the venture.

The last evening of filming, Hugh and I were shooting in a gondola. Then we moved, for the very last scene, to St. Mark's Square, among the famous flock of pigeons. I noticed, on the street behind us, a barrage of floodlights. I didn't think much about it, merely noting it and wondering if there was some opening or premiere or something going on. When that last shot was in the can, the director came to me and asked me if I'd mind stepping over to the next street.

"What for?" I asked.

"Do you see all those floodlights?"

"Yes, I see them."

"They're for you. We're now shooting a TV show—and you are the star!"

He beamed at me, as though conferring on me some great honor. Well, I quickly grasped the situation. They had sold the Italian TV network a Cyd Charisse Show—to raise the money to finish shooting. I refused. He tried to persuade me. He insisted that all I had to do was sit there and talk to the camera for merely one hour, that I didn't have to dance—and I wasn't to be paid for it. When I am pushed too far, I can be very stubborn, especially if I feel justified, and I certainly felt like it that evening.

"Look," I said. "I've worked a week for you for nothing, but I draw the line at doing a TV show without the courtesy of consulting me for nothing on top of it."

I know he wanted to kill me. The Italian was flying—gestures were flying. I just ignored it and went back to the hotel. The next morning, Hugh and Bea and I were leaving. The director was there, too, but he was not speaking. He just stood there and pointedly looked the other way. It took a long time, but I eventually got part of my money for the film. I owe Hugh the thanks for that; he's a very business-minded man and he kept after them until they settled with us.

I was also in Marilyn Monroe's last film, *Let's Make Love,* and it was a harrowing experience watching her, because it was obvious to me that she simply wasn't well. Jerry Wald produced, George Cukor directed and Dean Martin was our co-star. Marilyn had asked for me to play the part, and I was flattered that she wanted me.

My acquaintance with Marilyn began because, at the time, we shared the same publicity gal, Pat Newcomb. And one evening Pat had called me and said that Marilyn had a date with Frank Sinatra and had nothing to wear. She knew that I had seen a Norell showing and she asked if I had happened to see anything that might be right for Marilyn. I recommended a beautiful green sequin Norell gown that I thought would look marvelous on Marilyn. Pat ran out and bought it and I was right; she looked smashing in it. Since then, Marilyn had been grateful to me. She asked for me in the film.

The way the picture was laid out, my part wouldn't begin shooting for some time. The first scenes were with Marilyn and Dean. But I got a frantic phone call from Cukor—Marilyn wasn't well, could I report immediately? Poor George had to rewrite the script as he went along, and use Dean and me until Marilyn felt better and could report for work.

Finally, she began showing up. Her lateness has become legendary, so I won't dwell on it here. But it was true; she might get to the studio on time, but then she and Paula Strasberg, her mentor of the moment, would be closeted in her dressing room, redoing her make-up or reworking the scene. I've always been blessed with patience, so the whole thing didn't trouble me. Besides, my heart went out to Marilyn who was, I realized, battling forces that were simply beyond her capability to battle. Cukor was patient, too, and I respected and admired him for it. But Dean did not have any patience at all.

One day, I was at home when the studio called. They asked if I could report immediately. Then Dean grabbed the phone to urge me to come down.

"Goddamn it," he said, "we haven't been able to shoot an inch of film yet."

So I went down and he and I did a scene together. Dean was pacing up and down, absolutely beside himself. He told me he had another film, a big dramatic film, waiting for him. Cukor kept saying to please be patient and give her time, but Dean was fuming. The next morning I woke up and read the screaming headlines that said, "MARILYN FIRED!"

Now I know that Dean didn't want to finish *Let's Make Love.* It was dragging on too long for him and he had other commitments. I've long felt that he was, somehow, the one who brought the pressure that resulted in her being fired. Later, Fox wanted to replace Marilyn and finish the film, but Dean refused to do that.

The next thing, I had a call from Pat Newcomb asking me if I'd be willing to finish the picture—with Marilyn. I said of course, because I liked Marilyn and thought she was a charming girl and a delightful actress, and I truly felt compassion for her. Marilyn sent me a telegram, thanking me for my support. Cukor wasn't too enthusiastic about going back with Marilyn and I certainly can't blame him because it was a traumatic experience. But he said he was willing to try it again.

Dean Martin, however, wasn't willing because of his commitments. So, without Dean, the whole thing went down the drain. Tragically enough, it was only a short time later that Marilyn was found dead.

Making movies certainly has been a fascinating chapter in my life, but it was only a chapter, not life itself. I was ready to move into other areas.

11

LOVE
AND
LAUGHTER

The war and all my service-connected problems did me one good turn. I went into the Navy a real cocky kid. I think my cockiness was only natural —I was young, successful, making $12,000 a week, and I figured the world was my oyster. They beat that out of me. When I came out, I was pretty humble. I had been chopped down to size.

After the war, I was an entirely different person. I knew what suffering —mental and physical—was like. I'd been there. I'd paid my dues.

I carried with me a letter from Major Terry Hunt, who had been one of my officers in India. He had written it to a Los Angeles columnist who had taken a few swipes at me—that was still the fashionable thing to do —and Hunt's letter said:

"Every serviceman who was a buddy of Tony's in the CBI will say he's a great guy. He was sick with malaria and dengue fever but he gave 400 performances, one when he had a fever of 103. He worked unceasingly to bring a little entertainment, or a happy song, to guys who needed morale bolstering. Ask the boys who know."

I knew, in my heart, that I'd done my part. Maybe I hadn't shot any enemy soldiers, but I'd helped. Still, they were taking pot shots at me all the time. The ghost of that Navy affair was still hanging around. In fact, the scars remain with me to this day, more than thirty years later. I sometimes, even now, wake up in the middle of the night in a cold sweat, from dreaming about it.

The public was slow to forgive and forget. In '46, I was bumped off a radio show—sponsored by Carnation—because they had gotten a lot of letters protesting my appearance. The gist of the complaints was how dare they have a man on the show who was kicked out of the Navy. At first, they just dropped me without any reason. But a dancer, Adam DeGaetino, who was a pal, told me that his brother, a private eye, had been investigating the whole thing. I just shrugged. What else could I do?

About that time, too, there was another blow, a residual effect of that bad publicity. I was recommended for a big part in a big picture at Twentieth Century-Fox. The producer, an ex-general, turned me down. I got the word that he turned me down because of my war record. He didn't even have the courtesy to ask me about it, he just crossed my name off his list.

I knew I had to be patient. That's why I wasn't very anxious, that first New Year's Eve home, to go out and do much socializing. But friends kept hammering at me that I had to start sometime, that I couldn't be a hermit the rest of my life. So I allowed myself to be talked into going to Sam Spiegel's New Year's Eve party.

I had nothing to wear. I'd still not bought anything, mostly because of an intense case of no money. So I borrowed a suit from Nat, and shirt, ties, shoes from some other friends. I looked like I'd been put together from bits and pieces, which was exactly what had happened. So I just sat at the bar, having a few drinks, quietly toasting the new year, and hoping it might be better than the last few. People came over to where I was sitting to say hello, to welcome me home. Most were friendly; a few got in some digs, but I was used to that. Howard Hughes was one of them and then Errol Flynn and Hank Fonda and George Raft all came over to say a few cheering words to me.

And then Rita Hayworth was at my elbow.

"Hi, Tony," she said. "How are you? God, it must be almost five years."

I don't remember what she was wearing. It didn't matter; no matter what she wore she was exquisite. She could have worn a raggedy house dress and still looked better than anybody else.

"Hey, Rita! How's it going?"

We had done a picture together, back in '38, a little nothing called *Music in My Heart.* That was the first picture in which she'd used her new name; before then, she's been Rita Cansino. Irving Starr, the producer, had shown me a list of potential leading ladies and I had picked her. No reason —just I liked her looks. She was grateful then and, at Sam's party, she sat next to me at the bar and reminded me of the day I'd chosen her. She was nice and said that had started everything for her. I think she exaggerated a bit, but it was pleasant to hear. Gratitude isn't the most common emotion in Hollywood. During our conversation, I asked her about her husband, Orson Welles. She said they were separated.

227

Of course I knew. The moment-to-moment romances of Hollywood's reigning sex goddesses were always news, and the fact that Rita and Orson Welles had split was all over town.

"That's too bad," I said.

She shrugged her shoulders, as though to say that it was inevitable.

"You want to dance?" I said, and she got up and took my hand and we danced. As we spun around the floor, Vic Orsatti, then one of the top Hollywood agents and one of the most attractive men in town, tapped her on the shoulder.

"Any time you want to go, Rita," he said, "I'll take you home."

"Thanks but no thanks, Vic," she said. "Tony's taking me home."

That was, to me, the surprise of all time. I had had no designs on her —well, maybe a design but no intention of attempting to implement it— and here, suddenly, I had been commanded to escort her home! She said she had come to the party alone, and that had been hard for her to do. But she felt she should get out and not stay home and brood, so she had come. She didn't want to go home alone.

"Rita, I've got a problem. I came with the Goldstones. I don't have wheels."

"Oh, that's too bad."

"But don't worry. I'll get you home somehow."

I spotted Sid Luft.

"You look happy, Tony," he said. "Something cooking?"

"Yeah. Rita! But I need transportation."

"No problem, old buddy. You can take my car—here are the keys— and I'll drive Lynn's home."

He and his wife, Lynn Bari, had come in separate cars. I went back to Rita.

"It's OK, Rita," I said. "I've got a heap. We're in business."

Of course, the "heap" was a Cadillac, so we were in luxurious business. I drove her home, after we danced and drank and laughed a few hours. I took her to her door, gave her a kiss, wished her a happy new year, and left. My feet never once touched the ground.

I called her the next day. She had a Filipino servant who told me she wasn't there, she was in Palm Springs. I left my name and number. I was staying at the Beverly-Wilshire Hotel until I could find someplace of my own. She called me that evening from Palm Springs and said she'd be home in the morning.

From January 3 on, we were a steady twosome. I was in love again. It was a great feeling. I enjoy being in love; it does something for the ego, for the imagination. It lifts me up, makes me feel on top of the world. And having a doll like Rita Hayworth to squire around town is especially uplifting for the ego. You know that every man is looking at you with galloping envy.

I think I'd cottoned to her back in '38 when we worked together, only then there was nothing I could do about it. She was married then, and so was I. But this time, there were no bars in our way. I was single, she was separated.

Rita Hayworth is one of the nicest people to come down the Hollywood pike. I've yet to hear anyone say a bad thing about her. She worked hard. She was a good mother. She lived a clean and wholesome life. We would have dinner together every night, then go out to a party or a premiere or a screening of just to a nightclub to dance. We both loved dancing and I think we made a dashing couple out on the dance floor.

I was smitten, like I'd only been smitten a few times before in my life —Alice, Lana, Dotty. And now Rita.

For around nine months, we saw each other every day, almost without exception. I proposed to her, and she accepted. I gave her a diamond ring to seal the bargain. By then, I was working again, making good money again, so I could afford to give her the kind of presents gals expect from their boyfriends. I enjoyed giving and she seemed to enjoy receiving. I gave her a beautiful fur coat, other jewelry, knickknacks from time to time. She was planning on divorcing Welles, and then we would get married. I was happy, as I've always been when I'm going with a girl I love. I've always been a one-woman man; I never had a stable. When I'm in love, that's it. My eyes don't roam. Between romances, that's something else again. But when I have found myself a girl to love, I am the most faithful man alive. When I'm captured, I'm nailed.

So I stuck with Rita and was deliriously happy with the way things were going. And she seemed happy, too. Along about September, we were making plans to go to Del Mar, down the coast, to watch the horses run and soak up some of that lovely San Diego atmosphere.

Then she called one morning.

"I can't go to Del Mar with you, Tony," she said. "I've decided to go back to Orson."

She never elaborated; I never asked her to elaborate. Those two short sentences ended that part of my life. It stopped that abruptly.

The next morning I was sitting around the swimming pool at the Bel Air Hotel, where I was then living. Greg Bautzer, one of the most prominent and successful of Hollywood lawyers, seemed surprised to see me there.

"Hey, Tony," he said. "What are you doing here? I thought you were going to Del Mar with Rita."

"No. It's off."

"What's off? The trip or the romance?"

"The whole romance. Over. Finis. Kaput."

I told him about it. I had to talk to someone, and he just happened to be handy. We had breakfast together and I poured out my misery into his sympathtic ears.

"Look, Tony, a man can carry a torch many ways," he said. "You can go out on a toot. You can cry in your beer. You can do a lot of different things. But if I were you, I'd look at it this way—the girl is going back to her husband, and that's her right."

He was absolutely right, of course. After Rita and I broke up, I became one of Hollywood's fun guys for a time. Things were going well for me, again, professionally. I must admit that my publicity, as Rita's boyfriend, hadn't hurt me. Things were breaking my way. I had a big hit record— "To Each His Own"—and I was a regular on a successful radio show, with Victor Young. I was doing very well, as a matter of fact. And my love life kept pace with my professional career. I dated a lot of beautiful and talented girls—Lola Albright, Marguerite (Maggie) Chapman, lots more. Most of my dates were in show business, but there was no way around that. Except for an occasional girl reporter—and I dated a few of those, too— who else would I meet who wasn't a performer? So I played the field. I knew eventually I'd meet another girl I'd fall madly in love with, but I wasn't in a great rush to meet her. It was a time to concentrate on my career. I was getting on—thirty-three, thirty-four—and I'd lost four years out of my life in the war, so I had to get cracking.

Most of that time, I was living at the Bel Air Hotel. It was a fun place, lots of action, lots of pretty girls and handsome bachelors. Whenever the studios would bring in a new girl, she'd be put up at the Bel Air, and we'd all hang around to inspect the new merchandise.

Around about that time I moved my folks down from Oakland to the Los Angeles area. They were getting older and I wanted them closer so I could take care of them. They enjoyed the life in Southern California, and it was nice for me to have them nearby. Whenever I dated, it became procedure for me to take the girl over to my folks' apartment on Friday night for dinner. For a while, I went with a beauty named Iris Bynum— not a romance, just an enjoyable association. Then, for another while, it was Linda Christian, who was a fascinating person. I guess she intrigued me more than anybody I'd met, because of some of her qualities. For one thing, she spoke nine languages. We could go to any restaurant—French, Italian, German, Spanish, whatever—and Linda would speak to the waiters in their native tongue and enter into long discussion in their language as she ordered for both of us. She and I were friends, nothing more. We saw each other now and then, not steadily.

In 1947, Nat Goldstone said that we were going to produce a movie. By "we," he meant he and I. I was stunned. I had absorbed a lot about the movie business by being in it, but I hardly considered myself wise enough to produce a film. But Nat said that between the two of us we could cut it. He had a script, *Casbah*, the third remake of the old *Pepe LeMoko* of Jean Gabin and *Algiers* of Charles Boyer and Hedy Lamarr. It sounded like a good idea to me. A proven property, and a solid story. With music, and that would make it different.

We got a great score by Leo Robin and Harold Arlen, which included such great songs as "Hooray for Love," "It Was Written in the Stars," "For Every Man There's a Woman," and "What's Good About Good-bye?" We got John Barry to direct—the same John Barry who was later black-listed for reasons still unknown to me. And, to star in it with me, we signed two beauties, Yvonne DeCarlo and Marta Toren. Walter Scharf did the arrangements and wrote the score.

I never got to Algiers on that picture, unfortunately. The only people to make that trip were the second unit who shot some background footage. All my scenes were on the good old Universal lot, the soundstages and the back lot.

It wasn't a big picture. Both Nat and I felt that for our first effort, we should take it easy. We had gotten a loan from the Bank of America, and I had naturally agreed to defer my salary. Still, it cost $400,000 when we started, which isn't much for a film but it's a lot of dollar bills when you borrow them. And Barry, the director, was very good but slow. Before he finished it, the $400,000 budget had climbed to over $500,000. Worry set in. When it's somebody else's money, I worry good.

I was out at Hillcrest one day, playing golf, when I was called to the phone. It was Bill Goetz. He and his partner, a man named Spitz, had run a rough cut of *Casbah* and liked it. They offered us a million dollars for it. I figured we should grab it. A quick profit of almost one hundred percent wasn't bad. But Nat and the rest of the people involved turned the offer down. They figured that if Goetz and Spitz were willing to go one million, the picture was probably worth two or three million. So, over my objections, they turned the offer down. As it turned out, I was right.

The picture wasn't bad; in fact, a lot of people remember it very fondly. But, when it was released, we got screwed royally. It was slapped in as the bottom half of a double bill with any dog of a film. So we got nothing from the rentals. Zilch. Eventually, Nat decided to sell the damn thing for five dollars on the steps of the Federal Building in downtown L.A. at some kind of cockamamie auction, so he could get a tax write-off as a result. I think the picture eventually played a couple of hundred times on TV and with that and one thing and another, I bet it grossed five or six million over the long haul. But I never saw a penny. In fact, I didn't even get my deferred salary and I actually lost my retainer.

I have never done anything in the business side of films after that bitter experience. Producing films is for hot-shots, and that's not me. I'm not the worst businessman in the world, but I'm no wheeler-dealer financier. I've stuck to my own thing—singing and acting—since then and I've been happy.

Even though *Casbah* was a financial bath for me, it helped me. I got good reviews for my performance. An RCA-Victor album of the *Casbah* songs was a winner. And I got several offers as a result of it. I remember one that I couldn't do that broke my heart. Michael Curtiz offered me a great part in one of his Warner Brothers films, but there was some hassle over the billing so I didn't do it.

Things were booming for me, even despite the *Casbah* debacle. I became a regular on The Texaco Star Theater on radio and that was one of the biggies then. Each week, we had the biggest names as guests, people like Red Skelton and Jimmy Durante. And my nightclub career was booming, too. I played all the top clubs all over, and made good money. Early in 1947, I was at the Chez Paree in Chicago. And then, the day I got back home, Nat called me and said he wanted me to go with him and his wife, Bernice, to a premiere that night. We were going to see a picture called *Black Narcissus*. He said he was bringing along Cyd Charisse. Was that OK with me? Sure—I didn't know her (Cyd insists we did meet before and I'll take her word for it, although I really don't remember that earlier encounter) but I'd seen her, and she was certainly one of the great beauties of all time in my eyes.

I thought, that night, that she was one of the most fantastic women I'd ever met. I knew I had to see her again. I invited her and her young son, Nicky, to watch the Texaco show from the sponsor's booth, and then we'd go out to dinner afterward. That was our first real date.

Right off the bat, I knew that I'd found a girl who was a precious gem. She was something very special. She was something to be handled with care. If I was to make an impression on her, I would have to proceed very carefully, very gingerly. My old tactics were too crude for this one. I began to have grave doubts, doubts about myself. Was I in the same league as this refined and elegant lady? What the hell could she see in me? All those questions confused me for a while, and then I came to the conclusion that the only thing I could do was to be myself. I wouldn't try to put on any false airs or phony act. I knew that Cyd would be able to see through any gimmickry I used in my pursuit of her. So that's what I did. I was just Tony Martin and I was myself.

Cyd is always dignified. Always the lady. I had to watch myself like a hawk. One night I was driving her home and something happened, something unimportant, but whatever it was it caused me to blurt out, "Oh, shit." She turned a shivering look in my direction.

"I've heard that word before," she said, "but I want you to know that I don't approve of it."

"I'm very sorry, Cyd."

I didn't have to speak in biblical language. An occasional damn was permitted, shucks was fine. But I had to watch myself.

The courtship—for I quickly realized this was no ordinary boy-girl thing, I wanted it to be a genuine, old-fashioned courtship—was going along pretty smoothly. I felt I was making progress. We seemed to get along well, we enjoyed each other's company, she laughed at my jokes—what more can a suitor want? And then I made a mistake. A big mistake. I inadvertently allowed her to be introduced to another fellow. Not just any other fellow, mind you, but another fellow named Howard Hughes.

It happened one night when I had taken Cyd to the Mocambo for an evening of dinner and dancing. When Cyd went to the powder room, I felt a tap on the shoulder. It was Johnny Meyers, at that time Howard's right-hand man.

"Hi, Tony," he said. I greeted him back. "Howard's sitting right over there."

"That's nice." I liked Howard but that's as far as it went.

"Yeah, and he likes that lady you're with." Meyers gestured with his chin toward the ladies' powder room, to show me what he meant by "that lady."

"Oh?"

"Yeah, he likes that. Who is she?"

"Cyd Charisse."

"Do you mind if he calls her?"

"Well, I—."

"Look, Tony. Level with us. Are you in love with the lady?"

"Johnny, it's really none of your goddamn business."

"Is she in love with you?"

"I never asked her."

"OK. But do you mind if he calls her?"

"No, not at all."

I figured that, if I gave Howard Cyd's number, maybe that would be a significant test. That way, I could find out whether she cared for me. With competition like Mr. Hughes, if she still preferred me that would be pretty potent proof that she really did like me. Maybe even love me.

Of course, that sneaky little plot backfired in my face. A long time later, Cyd told me what happened. When Hughes called her, and said that Tony Martin said it was OK for him to call, she immediately got mad at me. She figured the fact that I said it was OK showed that I really didn't care for her. The way she figured it, if I had given a damn about her, I wouldn't have just handed her number out to any Tom, Dick or Howard who asked for it.

People in love do dumb things. I'd hoped that when Hughes called her, she would turn him down. Fat chance! She figured that I shouldn't have given him the OK to call in the first place. So she immediately said yes. The whole thing was a confused mess and for a long time after I kicked myself for being such a dope.

So Cyd began dating Howard. She didn't totally turn me down, but what had been smooth sailing turned into rough water overnight. To compound the problem, I had to go east for a few engagements. And I wasn't about to become a monk, so I was dating and my dates made the columns and she read about my dates. So she figured I wasn't exactly pining away. I read in the columns about her and Howard and figured she wasn't pining away, either.

I am afraid it all might have ended up dismally, except that she injured her knee doing a dance number at MGM. I read about that and I immediately sent her flowers. I think that gesture was the turning point. I know she's a sentimental person and she thought my sending flowers was a sentimental and thoughtful gesture. So I began to creep back in her favor.

Hughes was in Washington, testifying before some Congressional committee. And then I came back, so I had the field to myself. When you're competing against a man like Hughes, you have to take advantage of every edge you get. After all, I couldn't out-money him or out-brain him, so I had to try and out-charm and out-thoughtful him. I called her.

"Did you get my flowers?"

"Yes. Thanks. They're lovely and it was nice of you."

"I heard that you'll be able to dance again."

"Yes, so they tell me."

"Well, that's great. I'm glad to see the injury won't slow you up permanently."

"Probably not. But I see by the columns that you haven't been slowed up at all."

When she said that, I knew I had a fighting chance. That was the first inkling I'd gotten that she even cared. She was showing a touch of jealousy and where there is jealousy there is caring. I knew then that she, at least, had some feeling for me.

But there were still hard times ahead. After Cyd got better, Hughes came back. And he was a dangerous rival for me. There was one particular night—a bad night for me—when he took her out for an evening and never did bring her back home. As it turned out, he took her to San Francisco for dinner and then on to Las Vegas for a little gambling in his private plane. I kept calling. Her mother first said she was out but, as the evening wore on, her mother began to be terribly worried about her. So I went over to her house. The night turned into morning and still no Cyd. She was due on the set at six or seven, and she didn't roll in until five. Her mother kept saying, "Where's my daughter?" as though I had hidden her somewhere, but I hadn't the vaguest idea where she was. It was panic time, and she was very casual and nonchalant when she came in.

Most guys, courting a girl, have a rival. But few have to compete with a man like Howard Hughes. It really made me pull out all the stops. How could I ever do anything like that—I had no private plane, I didn't have the money to pull a stunt like that. I went home that morning, worried that I had lost the game.

I was staying at the Bel Air Hotel then and I went to bed about six, exhausted and depressed. Along about nine-thirty in the morning there was a knock on the door. It was Johnny Meyers.

"Open the door."

"Go away, I'm asleep."

"Come on, Tony, open up. I've got something here for you from Howard."

That piqued my curiosity. What could Howard have for me that was so important he sent Johnny Meyers over with it? Before I could get up, Meyers shoved it under the door. It was an envelope containing two round-trip, first-class tickets on TWA. Anywhere in the world. Just fill in the destination. It was typically Hughes, that gesture. He realized his impetuous evening had hurt me, worried me, so this was his generous gesture to clear the air. And, I think, he had another motive. He figured I'd pick up some dolly and go scooting off around the world—and that would eliminate me from the Charisse chase. He didn't want any unnecessary competition. Even though he was so rich and good-looking, he was very insecure. He felt slightly inferior when it came to courting. So, in this particular case, he was saying, with those two tickets, Tony please get out of town and leave Cyd to me.

(The pay-off: Later, when Cyd and I got married, I used those tickets to take us to London for our honeymoon. I later told Howard about that, and he laughed.)

I wasn't about to get out of town. I called Cyd that day and made another date. She apologized for worrying me, explained it all had started out innocently and mushroomed into an impetuous, fun evening. OK. She was entitled to some fun. She was having a lot of trouble then with her first husband, Nico. She was very worried about him, as a matter of fact. I'd met him a few times around town and it wasn't exactly love at first sight. She had been told that Nico was trying to get custody of their son, Nicky. So she was leading a particularly circumspect life, so he wouldn't get any ammunition. She was always a lady, only now she was trying to be even more so.

We saw each other. She insisted that I get her home at ten-thirty or so, and made it very clear—car doors slamming—that I was leaving in case there were any private detectives watching the house. So we'd go to someplace like the Mocambo and I'd get her home by ten-thirty, give her a decorous peck on the cheek and get out of there. But that was too early for me to call it a night, so I'd go out some more. She asked me why I did that. And I explained that ten-thirty was too early for me to hit the sack. There were no other women—I was back in my one-woman period. Cyd was enough.

Ours was a puritanical courtship. That wasn't like me, but this time I was being very careful. I didn't want to offend her, in the first place, and I knew that she was being especially careful, because of the problems with Nico. So there was never anything with us—although I must admit I was torn apart by desire for this woman. I think Cyd is the most beautiful woman I have ever seen—her face is perfect (she never had a bad side, unlike most stars) and her legs are divine and her body never stops. She always wore clothes beautifully. Her hair was long and black and, at that time, she parted it in the middle. Everything about her was, to me, perfection. In fact, she stepped out of a dream.

But it was obvious I couldn't have her—unless I could get her to marry me. So I proposed.

We were in the car, driving somewhere. I forgot where we were going. And I forget the words I used. But I do remember she said yes. I was stunned. Naturally, I had hoped she would say yes, but when it happened, I really was surprised. I guess I had half expected her to turn me down. When she said she would marry me, it was the greatest moment of my life. Bar none.

I knew, too, that everybody had been advising her to have nothing to do with me. It was like Alice Faye all over again. Arthur Freed had said it would be a big mistake if she married me. Benny Thau had predicted a marriage between us would last a day. People kept telling her that I was nothing but a gadabout, a chaser, a womanizer. They told her I could never settle down. They poured all the scandal they could find—and some they simply invented—into her ears. But she went by what was in her heart, not in her ears. And she accepted my proposal.

There were still problems and obstacles. I arranged for the honeymoon suite at the Del Monte Lodge in Pebble Beach. But then she changed her mind. Four times, the plans were made. Four times, she got cold feet.

I think one of the reasons for her reluctance was that her mother was not too pleased about the impending marriage. I didn't ask my mother. After what had happened with Alice, I knew better than to make that mistake again. So I told her I was going to get married, but didn't even consider asking her for her opinion.

Finally, at my old haunt, Sugie's Tropics, I said to Cyd that this was going to be the time. I said it was now or never. We had a few drinks.

"Let's just go up to Santa Barbara and get married," I said. She looked at me for a long minute, and then nodded. And that's what we did. Nat and Bernice Goldstone came along to be with us on our wedding day.

I had the feeling that Howard Hughes was looking over my shoulder when I said, "I do." It gave me a proud feeling to realize I'd out-courted him for one of the gems of the feminine world. And, down through the next ten years or so, Hughes was to remain a big part in our lives.

In 1957, I made a movie for him, *Two Tickets to Broadway*. I was singing at the Flamingo in Las Vegas when a man came over and said, "Mr. Hughes would like to see you." It was a command appearance. I went. Hughes always used Mormons as his men, because they neither smoked nor drank and he considered them exceptionally trustworthy.

"Hi, Tony," he said. "How's Cyd?"

He spoke in a soft, high-pitched voice. He had ear trouble and so did I, so we both started aiming our conversation at the other guy's good ear.

"Tony, I'm going to make a picture and I'd like you to be in it. But I don't want to mess around with agents or contracts. Just tell me how much you want."

"How long is the picture?"

"About eight weeks, I guess. Maybe a couple of extra weeks."

We talked money but Hughes is sharp. He outwitted me. I got $75,000, but I should have gotten twice that. Eventually, I got more because the film lasted almost six months, not eight or ten weeks. And the reason it lasted so long is because Hughes developed a crush on the girl star, Janet Leigh, and kept it going so he could be around her more.

Hughes knew that Janet and Tony Curtis were in love and wanted to get married. He figured if he kept *Two Tickets to Broadway* going, maybe Janet and Tony would get bored with things and break up. So we shot and reshot. Scenes were added. Scenes were taken out. We'd wait a week for a new costume. Anything to stall the picture.

The Champions, Marge and Gower, were doing the dance numbers. They couldn't stand it, so they left to do *Show Boat.* Hughes hired a new dance director but he made a mistake. The new dance director developed a crush on Janet, too. Hughes had to break that up, and he used me as his means of doing so. Johnny Meyers called me one day in Las Vegas and said that Howard wanted me to rehearse the dance numbers. I said what dance numbers, because at that point I didn't have any.

"I don't know and I don't care," Meyers said. "All you have to do is keep the dance director busy."

I was still doubling at the Flamingo in Las Vegas. But now I had to get into this crazy business between Howard, Janet and the dance director. Actually, there was nothing to break up. Janet was a friendly, gregarious girl and was just being pleasant to this young kid. She had had lunch with the boy, that's all. But Howard had to have it broken up. I played ball with Howard and I went and invented some dance number to work with him. Finally, the kid got disgusted, got loaded and didn't show, and they fired him.

The delays continued. The script was changed every day. I'd learn my lines at night and, in the morning, find a raft of new pages with new dialogue.

It all ended when Janet announced she was going to marry Tony. Instead of more delays, now suddenly they told us we'd have to wrap the picture that midnight. We still had one big eight-minute number, "Big Chief Hole-in-the-Head," to shoot. Ordinarily, it would have lasted a week. We had to finish it that night. We did—at five minutes to midnight.

But that was Howard. When he had a thing for a girl, he didn't let anything stand in his way. His unrequited crush on Janet Leigh must have cost him millions, but that was the way he was.

He had a crush once on Polly Bergen. (You must admit, the man had good taste.) He called me one night and asked me to do him a favor. He said they wanted to photograph a layout for *Look Magazine*, with pictures of me and Polly Bergen. I said sure.

So I went over and posed for this layout with Polly. Howard was there, through the whole session, but never on camera. The pictures were of Polly and me, but Howard was watching every shot. Then I got worried—the pictures made it look as though I was out with Polly.

"Look, Howard," I said, "I'd appreciate it if you'd explain this to Cyd for me."

He called Cyd. She understood.

One night at the Sands, they finally got Howard to the gambling tables. They always wanted him to gamble, figuring that maybe they could get some of his money that way. But he never gambled. That night, though, Polly wanted to give it a whirl. So Howard staked her and she went to the crap table, and I've never seen such a hot streak. She won all the chips. She could do no wrong. That's what happens—money goes to money. Alan King was with us—we just went home.

Howard's admiration for girls was legendary—and probably true. There was the time I was eating lunch in the RKO commissary with Walter Kane. There was a magazine stand in front of the commissary, and Walter was attracted by the cover on one magazine.

"What a beautiful girl!" he said, and he showed me. It was some physical culture magazine and the girl was, indeed, a beauty. Kane figured this was the kind of girl Hughes would appreciate. He bought the magazine and brought it to Howard.

"Find her," Hughes said. "Bring her here."

Kane tracked her down. She was Italian and lived in San Remo with her husband, who was some kind of producer. Kane learned she couldn't speak English, but Howard said he should bring her to Hollywood anyhow. So the girl was imported, and she came with her sister, a child and a nurse. Hughes put her on the payroll at $300 a week, and set her up in a beautiful suite at the Château Marmont.

Then he forgot about her. She was here for six months when Hughes suddenly remembered.

"What happened to that Italian girl?" he asked Kane.

"She's learning English."

"Well, I think she's been here long enough," Hughes said. They sent her home. I don't think he ever saw her.

Once, Alan King and I were at the Flamingo, sunning ourselves at the pool. We noticed an exceptionally gorgeous girl, built like a brick bathroom. She knew that everybody was staring at her, but she was above stares. She ignored the world. Alan and I were trying to guess who she was and we made a few discreet inquiries. We learned that she was living in some private quarters and that there were a couple of men guarding her, night and day. That further aroused our curiosity. I asked Abe Schiller, who was then known as Mr. Las Vegas, and he laughed. He said the girl was Howard Hughes' latest "protégé."

A few days after we had established that, Hughes called me. He said he had "discovered" a girl—I knew he meant his brick-bathroom protégé —and he wanted to make her a star. He asked me about my conductor, Hal Borne. He wondered if Borne might be able to work with the girl. I said Borne was fantastic.

"Good," Hughes said. "He's the man for me. I want him to work with this girl two hours every afternoon."

"OK. Hal's very good."

"What do you think I should pay him?"

"I don't know. He doesn't come cheap. I think $500 a week would be about right."

"All right."

So I arranged the deal. And Hal had to show up every day for four weeks and work with Hughes' girl. Hughes would fly in from wherever he was a couple of times a week. At that time, he flew himself in a converted B-24 bomber. He'd fly in to spend a few hours with that girl.

Hal told me the poor girl was virtually a prisoner. She had told him she wasn't allowed to talk to anybody. Even he couldn't talk to her, except for those two hours a day they worked together. Hal couldn't go to the girl's bungalow alone. He had to be met and escorted there, and two men were watching every moment while he tried to teach her to sing.

Hughes' eccentricities are legendary. But most are true. His passion for privacy, I suppose, was what was at the heart of the matter. Al Parvin was the owner of the Flamingo when I used to appear there. One evening, Al decided to have a card game in his bungalow, and invited a bunch of us to play with him. He called down for some refreshments and, after a while, a waiter shows up, carrying the things on a big tray he balanced on his shoulder.

"You should have brought the things up on a cart." Parvin said to the waiter. "Where's the cart?"

"Well, Mr. Parvin," the waiter said, "we're out of carts."

"Out of carts? Ridiculous. We've got dozens of them."

"I don't know what happened. Call the man in the kitchen. He's the one who told me there were no more carts."

So Parvin checked and it was true. There were no more carts. They'd all gone up, one by one, to Hughes' suite with his meals. And Hughes had not permitted anyone to come and pick them up. So all the hotel's carts were parked in the hall outside Hughes' suite. His suite had its own private elevator; it had originally been built for Bugsy Seigel.

One night, Howard and I were out on the town and we stopped in at a small restaurant for a bite to eat. Came time to pay and he said he didn't have any money.

"I never carry any money, Tony," he said, and it was true.

I think, if I'd asked him for $5,000, he would have written me a check for that amount without hesitation. He was a very generous man. But he never had ten dollars to pay a restaurant check, so I had to treat him to that late supper.

Many times, when I worked in Las Vegas, I'd get a summons from Howard to meet him after my last show. It would be about three in the morning. He'd have his old Chevvy there, and I'd sit next to him. We'd drive around for an hour or so. The thing he liked to do best was to show me how much land he owned.

"I own everything from here to the mountains," he'd say, gesturing with his arm to the mountains which loomed miles away in the moonlight. He wasn't saying it as a braggart would; it was just a statement of simple fact.

He'd often come to hear me sing. He always ate the same thing—a steak and some peas. As far as I saw, he never drank. He'd sleep all day then come to hear me sing and we'd often go out together after my show. He dressed carelessly. He just didn't seem to care about clothes. He was what you might call sartorially inefficient.

He'd always ask about Cyd.

"How is Cyd?"

"She's just wonderful, thanks."

"You're good to her, aren't you?"

"I'm trying, Howard."

"You've got a wonderful girl there."

"Yes, I know."

"Well, at least I did good for somebody some time, when I let you have her."

I never argued with him. But I figured he didn't "let" me have Cyd. I won her, in fair-and-square, *mano-a-mano* competition. Cyd took me over him, for whatever reason makes a woman choose one man over another. I never asked her why. I was only interested in results, not motives, and the result of her decision was my happiness, so I wasn't about to question it.

Our marriage has worked, primarily, because Cyd and I have never

241

been competitive. She's a dancer, I'm a singer. It's like a lawyer marrying a doctor; that can work, they can be happy. But two lawyers? No way. Cyd and I had both achieved success in our respective fields. I never came home and heard her say, "How did you dance today?" and I never asked her how her singing went. Competition can ruin a relationship. We didn't have that problem.

Another reason, I think, why Cyd and I have been happy is that, for both of us, this was the second time around. We'd both had our problems before. Now, this time, we knew what the score was, what the obstacles were, how to compromise, how to give and take. For us, obviously, our divorces led to our ultimate happiness. I don't preach divorce, ordinarily. But, on the other hand, I don't condone the current practice of two kids moving in together. I'm no prude, heaven knows, and I've slept with enough women, but I've always gotten up and gone home.

We started off happy and we've been happy ever since. Our honeymoon trip to London, for example. Nothing but fun. The Maharajah and Maharanee of Jaipur were at a party we attended in Grosvenor Square. Isha, the maharanee, was the sister of my old buddy, the Maharajah of Cooch Behar. We became good friends from that night on.

I sang at the Palladium on that trip. I was booked to follow Danny Kaye, who was one of London's favorite entertainers. I figured it was going to be tough to follow Danny, but I was lucky. I wasn't a comedian, so they didn't try to measure me against him. I sang my heart out and they liked what they heard and it was a pleasant stay. It was a tremendous thrill to find an audience so far from home accepted me. I came to love England and the English people, and English things. I became a fan of English clothes, hats, shoes. I loved the little pubs. We stayed at the Savoy, and we loved that, the absolute elegance of the place.

Then we came back home, and it was back to where we really belonged. Hollywood, for all its faults, and it has many, is our home. I really love Southern California, in general, and the Hollywood scene, in particular. I think what I love about it most is the people. Say what you will, the men and women who make Hollywood movies are probably the most creative group of people on earth. It is stimulating to be around them.

I've been fortunate. I've worked with some of the great ones. Back in 1940, before the war, I was in *The Big Store*, which turned out to be the last of the Marx Brothers movies with the four brothers. Zeppo left then, to try his hand at production. That was the picture in which I sang a great number, "The Tenement Symphony," which Hal Borne wrote with Sid Kuller.

Groucho was always fun to be around. Like most of us, he had to go to a lot of screenings and premieres, and he was always asked his opinion. If what he had seen was lousy, he didn't want to say so and hurt somebody's feelings. Yet he was too honest to praise something when he felt it was bad. So he devised a remark which would enable him to be honest while sparing people's feelings.

"You'll never be better than you were tonight," he'd say.

That position is always a difficult one. Mervyn LeRoy always said, when confronted with that situation, "That was an interesting piece of film." And once, when I was at Fox, I went to a preview with Darryl Zanuck and his contingent of yes-men, including Sol Wurtzel, the king of the "B" pictures. Darryl ran a sneak preview and asked his men what they thought. Wurtzel said, "Darryl, what a picture!" which could be interpreted any way the listener chose. Then he'd wait to see what Darryl said and he was on record as agreeing with him.

Anyhow, when *The Big Store* previewed, it was only so-so. It needed cutting badly. Groucho asked me what I thought of it. I said, "Groucho, you'll never be better than you were tonight." He laughed, getting his own critique thrown back in his teeth.

Of all the brothers, I knew Harpo the best. He was the charmer of the family, a well-read, gentle man. He was fluent in several languages. He loved music, of course, and studied his harp constantly. He was artistic and deep, and a fine bridge player, too. He was also a good golfer and we frequently played golf together. Chico was the loose soul, the one everybody went to if they needed some money. He always had twenty or thirty dollars ready for people with a sad story. Chico was an inveterate gambler and horse player. If he had a few hours off from a scene in the picture, he'd zip off to Santa Anita and bet on a few races. If he didn't have time off, it didn't matter—there were always bookmakers hanging around the set, taking his action. The brothers were nice to me. At the lunch break, we'd all hop in a car, go off to a deli for sandwiches or, if we had the time, drive over to Hillcrest for a good lunch.

Those were the cheerful, nutty days in Hollywood. In '39, I made a film with The Ritz Brothers called *Kentucky Moonshine*. Al, Jim and Harry were always late, and that infuriated Darryl Zanuck, who liked to run a tight ship. So Zanuck gave orders to Dave Butler, the director, to begin shooting promptly at nine A.M., no matter who was there. The next morning, at nine, the only people on the set were Butler and the camera crew. So Butler dutifully rolled the camera. That night, as always, Zanuck saw rushes—or dailies—of the day's work. And there was that scene from *Kentucky Moonshine* which showed the crew wandering around the empty set. Zanuck blew his top, but Butler said he was only following orders.

I guess the best role I ever had was as Chick Bean in *Banjo on My Knee*, another one from '36. Nunnally Johnson produced it and John Cromwell was the director. It starred Barbara Stanwyck, Joel McCrea, Buddy Ebsen, Walter Brennan and me. I really was in over my head in that one, because it was a heavy dramatic part and I had had no dramatic experience to speak of.

Barbara Stanwyck was so nice to me, and she shepherded me through the film. We had one tough scene together, sitting on the edge of a dock, on the Mississippi River. We ran through it and I was so nervous my voice got higher and higher. Somehow, I got through the master scene. But the next day we were going to do the close-ups, and that thought made me even more nervous.

"It's a tough scene," Barbara said. "I tell you what let's do. I'll meet you here at eight o'clock in the morning and I'll help you."

So that's what we did. We met at eight, before anybody else was there, and she showed me how to do the scene. I'll never forget her kindness to me. Everybody liked her. She had the vocabulary of a Marine sergeant and I guess that's what made the crew putty in her hands. She catered to them. And, in return, they couldn't do enough for her.

I worked with a lot of the big stars. Way back when, I was in *Follow the Fleet*, an Astaire-Rogers musical. I had been assigned to sing one of Irving Berlin's best songs, "Let's Face the Music and Dance," but then they changed their minds. They decided that Astaire should sing all the songs, so I never did get to sing that song in the film. At the time, I was doing the Burns and Allen radio show, and I sang it on the show and I was a smash. Then I was chosen, in a poll, as one of the top ten singers, and I received a nice note from Fred.

"Sorry you didn't get to sing 'Let's Face the Music and Dance' in the picture," he wrote, "but I'm glad to see you getting the recognition you deserve. P.S. You're certainly helping the picture."

Even at that youthful point in his life, Fred was losing his hair. In those days, hair pieces were in disfavor, but he had to wear one. And, in one scene, it came off. Poor Fred! He was so embarrassed that, when he did the number again, someone asked to have an entirely new crew, even new extras, so nobody would be there who had witnessed his embarrassment.

I knew Robert Taylor well, too, because Nat was his agent as well as mine. We were both fight fans and we took a trip to New York together to see Joe Louis fight Max Schmeling. Our plane was late, and we just made it. Johnny Broderick, New York's chief of detectives, had saved us a couple of ringside seats. We sat down and everybody was hungry, so I went out to get food for the crowd. By the time I got back to my seat with the hot dogs, the fight was over. Louis had KO'd his man in the first round. I had to go to the Trans-Lux Newsreel Theater on Broadway the next day to see the fight I'd flown all the way from California for and missed.

My work brought me in contact with most of the great names of Hollywood. Many of them had their eccentric sides. One of the strangest days I ever spent happened during the course of the shooting of a film called *Easy to Love,* which was a big musical and had Busby Berkeley doing the musical numbers. We were on location in Cypress Gardens, Florida, for this Esther Williams splashy film. Berkeley didn't say anything to anybody, and took off in a helicopter. We waited. And waited. And waited. No helicopter, no Berkeley, no message, nothing. He was gone four hours while everybody, including me, sat around, twiddling our thumbs or whatever we had to twiddle. When he finally showed up, he casually mentioned he had been scouting locations for Esther's water-skiing number.

When I made *Hit the Deck,* for Joe Pasternak, I worked with Debbie Reynolds, Ann Miller, Vic Damone and Russ Tamblyn. That was the era when the morals clauses in contracts were important; a slight infringement, and they'd invoke that clause and you were out on your ear. Some of the scandal sheets began printing stories about Damone, and he was pretty worried. I told him he ought to get married and that would quiet the gossip and take a load off his mind. One day, he was walking on the lot and saw Pier Angeli, and he was smitten. I arranged for the two of them to meet and they fell in love quickly and decided to get married. They were both Catholics and were, of course, married in a very Catholic ceremony. Only problem was that Vic chose, as his attendants, four men, and none of us was permitted to walk down the aisle. Two of us were Jewish—me and Pasternak; one was a Baptist—Bob Sterling; and the fourth was Dean Martin who, while a Catholic, had been divorced and therefore could not receive communion. So we had to stand in the back of the church, and it was stifling hot.

"If I don't get a drink pretty soon," Martin whispered to me, "there won't be a wedding."

We got Bob Sterling to sneak into the priest's quarters and get the bottle of sacramental wine. He did, and the four of us killed the bottle, sitting there in our full dress suits. And we really needed it—those Catholic weddings last forever.

When I did *Music in My Heart,* the picture in which I first met Rita Hayworth, I had one scene with a monkey—an organ grinder's monkey. His name was Punchinello. We were doing the scene when one of the big lights fell with a tremendous noise. Poor Punchinello got frightened, crapped on my shoulder and ran up into the rafters of the soundstage. He wouldn't come down; even his trainer couldn't coax him down.

We were shooting at Columbia, and the legendary Harry Cohn came into the set on one of his periodic inspections around the studio.

"What the hell's going on here?" he bellowed. "Why the fuck ain't the cameras rolling?"

"We can't get the monkey down from the ceiling," somebody told him.

"Get another monkey."

"It won't match. The monkey has already been established in the scene."

They kept calling—"Here, Punchinello, that's a good monkey"—but he clung to the rafters and wouldn't come down. Finally, we decided to break for lunch. When we came back, the monkey was down with his trainer. I think that cost Harry Cohn a few thousand dollars—and nearly a heart attack.

Mostly, since the war, things have been pretty smooth for me. Mostly —but not entirely. There have been a few bad things. One was ear troubles. I had otosclerosis, as I'd had since before the war. Cyd and I were out driving, one day, and I was listening to a football game on the radio. I kept turning the volume up.

"Must you have it on so loud?" Cyd asked, and that scared me, because, to me, it was barely audible. And I realized that, recently, I'd had to keep asking "Huh?" when people were talking to me. But it was the day in the car that did it. I went to see an ear specialist. He recommended something called a stapes operation. I was hesitant. Nobody likes the idea of surgery. But, as a musician, my hearing was vital. And Cyd urged me to have it done.

"I can't live with a man who doesn't answer me," she said. With increasing frequency, she'd ask me something or say something to me, and I wouldn't answer, simply because I hadn't heard her at all.

So, in '58, I had the operation. It wasn't successful. A year later, it was performed again and, this time, it worked. One ear is "Silent Night," but somehow I can hear. The whole experience made me very sympathetic to people with hearing difficulties. My heart goes out to them. At least, my problems could be remedied.

One physical problem I've never had, knock wood, is a sore throat. I've been singing, as I write this, for almost forty years and I've never had any difficulty with my throat. I attribute that largely to good training I had from a vocal coach named Mark Markov. Fox sent me to him in 1941, and he was a great help. He taught me proper voice placement and, over the years,

I'd often go to see Markov to get a little refresher course. It's paid off.

While I'm on the subject of problems I don't have, I might mention a few biggies, like booze and drugs and gambling. I like to drink but I'm not a drunk, never have been. In common with some others—Dean Martin, Frank Sinatra, Alan King, for example—I like to have a few drinks now and then. But, in thirty-six years in show business, I've never missed a show. I might have toddled on stage once in a while, but I've always made it and always done my act.

Drugs I've never touched. Just once, in Hong Kong, and I'll tell you about that later. I've seen what drugs can do, and I want no part of that. Let me tell you, I believe drinking is better than smoking pot. You can get over liquor the next day.

Gambling can be hell for entertainers. It can tell on your work. Many nights I've lost so heavily at the crap tables in Las Vegas that I've sung my love songs with a genuine broken heart. But something happened in '59 that made me quit. I was at the table in Vegas, and I'd spread out on every number at the table. Five hundred on every number. Bases loaded. As I was rolling the dice, some lady reached over me to put a lousy dollar on hard-eight, and my second die accidentally hit her hand and flipped over. It had been a five. It bounced over to a two—and I lost the whole thing. That was enough for me. I quit that night and haven't played since.

Something of the same sort turned me away from betting on the ponies, too. I was in Florida, this must have been around '47 or so, and I was at Hialeah. I plunged on the daily double, picking a couple of outsiders, and the first horse won and then the second horse came in ahead, too. They figured the payoff would be $1,284—and I had about $40 worth of two-dollar tickets. I was in the process of inviting the whole world to have a drink with me when the inquiry sign flashed on—and, fifteen minutes or so later, that horse of mine was disqualified. Right there and then, I swore off betting on the races.

But there were some problems I did have, real ones. One that caused me a lot of heartache was my involvement in the Friars Club gin rummy exposé. I was not one of those who were fleeced by the so-called cheaters who took a lot of the club members for big money. But they used my name; they wanted to make it sound worse than it was. So the papers included my name when they wrote about how people like Harry Karl and Phil Silvers and Tony Martin were bilked out of thousands. I was never involved in those big games—in the first place, I never played at night, and the big games were all at night, and I never played in the private room upstairs, and the big games were all in that room. But still my name was bandied about as one of the prime victims, and that made the I.R.S. take a tremen-

247

dous interest in me. I hired the finest lawyers, and the I.R.S., who have unlimited expenses, went back ten years into my tax records, and disallowed certain things, and the whole cost for everything was $40,000 to $50,000.

When the accused men went on trial, I was called downtown to testify. And I found I was a witness for the government. I wasn't a defendant, as some of the newspapers indicated. Let me repeat, I'd never been in the really big games. I'd played a few games in the main room with some friends—I'd won some, I'd lost some—but I'd never participated in the games that were rigged. Still, like the Navy mess, the stench of that scandal lingered for some time. It's very hard to live down something like that, even when you're innocent. It's the old guilt-by-association ploy. I was guilty, in the public's mind, of being part of the Friars Club gambling scandal. They never bothered to read beyond the headlines. They didn't know it had cost me $300,000 in cancelled state fair bookings; the fairs all have morals clauses in their contracts, and to them I was a gambler.

There was another scary moment for me. I was in Hawaii, walking on the beach, and I bumped into Morton Downey.

"Jesus Christ, Tony," he said, "you're all over the papers."

"About what?"

"About that gambling thing in Indianapolis."

"What gambling thing in Indianapolis?"

"They're looking for you. The Feds. Better get a paper and read about it."

So I got a paper and, sure enough, Earl Wilson had this big story about how the F.B.I. was looking for me in connection with some gambling scandal in Indianapolis. It was completely news to me. I'd played Indianapolis once, for five days, and there hadn't been any problem.

But I took myself down to the Federal Building in Honolulu and went to the F.B.I. office. I introduced myself.

"Are you fellows looking for me?"

It turned out that nobody was looking for me. I called the Honolulu newspapers regarding the story. They checked it and were sorry they had made a mistake. They rectified it as they always do, on a back page, next to the obituaries. It's tragically funny how papers always do that—they make their mistakes on the front page and correct them on the back page where nobody can see it. It always happens.

I guess the worst thing that happened to me, since the war, came about suddenly. It was a year or so after I was discharged from the Army. I was appearing every week on the Texaco Star Theater, then a big radio program, with Victor Young and his orchestra. In those days, there were a lot of musical programs on Sunday evening, so ASCAP made a rule that the same song could not be repeated within three hours on the same day. That resulted in us having to make changes in our program very often. One Saturday morning, I was playing golf at Hillcrest and I was called to the phone. Our producer told me that ASCAP had struck again, meaning I had to come down to the studio and pick out two new songs for the Sunday evening's show. OK, I had to go. I didn't like it, but I knew the problem so I went. I hopped in my car, still wearing my golf shoes, and drove to the studio with my buddy, Mickey Houston, a friend from Chicago.

I was doing fifty in a twenty-five m.p.h. zone when the cop pulled me over. I signed my citation, went down to the studio, picked out the two new songs and went back to Hillcrest. I was playing bridge with Jack Benny, George Burns and Harpo Marx when I received a call to appear in court —immediately. I thought that was curious. I'd never had any problems with the police. It had been years since I had had a ticket. And, actually, I'd done many shows for the motorcycle and regular police every year both before and since the war at L.A.'s Shrine Auditorium. Still, they seemed insistent that I go with them. I borrowed two hundred dollars from Harry Karl and went. I told Benny Rubin to take my bridge hand and I'd be back as soon as I could.

When I got to court, I found the presiding judge was a man who had a reputation for hating entertainers. For some reason, he had it in for anybody who made his or her living in the field of show business. He had once given Linda Christian five days in jail for a simple traffic ticket.

"How do you plead?"

"Guilty, your honor. I'm ready to pay my fine."

"Three days. No bail. Next case."

I had called Greg Bautzer, my lawyer friend. But there was nothing he could do. He advised me to do my three days and consider it a vacation. They led me away. The press was there in force. I have a feeling the judge, or somebody, prearranged it. Otherwise, why would there be a dozen reporters and photographers at a traffic court in West Los Angeles. But there they were, snapping pictures and firing questions at me. I tried to make a joke of it.

"Tell my friends at Hillcrest that I can't finish the bridge game," I said.

They put me in a tank. Most of my tankmates were drunks. The only thing they wanted to know was whether I had any cigarettes. I did. I handed them out to the drunks.

The three days weren't too bad. They let me have visitors, and the Ritz Brothers came by. They thought it would be funny if they smuggled in a file and a couple of bottles of beer. Of course, those items were discovered before they got to my cell—they weren't making any effort to hide them—and those men on duty didn't have much of a sense of humor. So for an hour or so I was in deeper trouble, until they realized it was meant as a gag.

When my time was up, I knew the press would be waiting. And I didn't want them to see me like that, unshaven with my clothes messed and wrinkled. The night guard was a decent sort of fellow. He happened to be a fellow Mason I'd met at lodge meetings. He said he could sneak me out a back way, through solitary confinement in the basement. But first I'd have to be put in a solitary cell. I said OK. So, the night before my release, I was transferred to solitary confinement. All night, I worried. Suppose that night guard died during the night? I'd be stuck in solitary for God knows how long. I didn't sleep all night, worrying about that possibility. And then, sometime around three or four in the morning, they threw another prisoner into the cell next to mine. He was a Filipino who'd killed his girlfriend in what must have been a brutal fight, because he was cut to ribbons himself. He asked me for a smoke and I threw the whole pack into his cell. I wasn't about to get close to that rascal.

"What you in for?" he asked me.

I wasn't about to tell him that I'd been doing fifty in a twenty-five-mile zone. He'd have laughed.

"I robbed a bank," I said. "In broad daylight."

"Hey, you are a solid man."

He tried to talk to me some more, but I feigned sleep. At that point, I wasn't looking for a lifelong friend. So I lay there, every minute dragging out to an hour, while I waited to see if I was going to be rescued. Around five, as promised, the night guard did come along, opened my cell, and led me out the back way. Not a reporter to be seen. Bautzer was waiting for me, and drove me home.

Gregson Bautzer is a great lawyer, and a great friend. I think, if he had decided to pursue criminal law, he would have given F. Lee Bailey a run for his money.

After I was out of jail a few days, I was once again asked to do a benefit for the police at the Shrine Auditorium. Even though I was still upset at that miscarriage of justice, I agreed—it hadn't been the fault of the police. They sent a motorcycle troop to escort me downtown. What a difference a few days makes!

In general, however, my life has been definitely pleasant since Cyd and I were married. We have had no real problems between us. We're human, of course, and we have our disagreements and conflicts, but, knock wood, nothing major so far.

At the beginning, one of my main concerns was making friends with her son, Nicky. At first, he had questions in his little mind, putting me in the proper category. Who was I? I could see him trying to puzzle it out. I wasn't his Daddy, because he knew his Daddy and that was another guy. And yet now I was living with his Mommy and kissing her and hugging her. He'd come running in to our bedroom soon after we were married. He'd want to say hello to his mother, and there she'd be and there I'd be, too. He couldn't quite straighten that situation out in his mind. But that didn't stop him. He jumped in bed between us.

"Nicky," I said, "I'm your Pop. You still have your Daddy, but now you have a Pop, too. Isn't that great?"

A few pieces of candy, a few presents, and a slow, unforceful approach and I won him over. We've been friends ever since. I think of him as my son. Maybe it was the way my own stepfather, Mike Myers, treated me that made me especially careful of little Nicky's feelings. After all, I'd been through it.

When I had the Nicky-Tony relationship straightened out, everything was clear sailing. The disagreements Cyd and I had were ordinary husband-wife things, and they were settled in ordinary husband-wife ways. The first big one, I remember, came soon after we were married. Cyd had a pair of yellow shoes, and I didn't like them. I let the dog play with them which didn't do them much good. I guess she had a right to be angry with me over that. We established certain ground rules as a result of *l'affair* yellow shoes. Years later, Cyd had a big production number in *Meet Me in Las Vegas* called "The Girl with the Yellow Shoes." Sammy Cahn had written it, and I knew Sammy well and I'd told him about our little yellow shoes spat. So I figured he wrote the number with that in mind. He said, no, he'd forgotten about it—but I had a hunch he subconsciously remembered it. Every year, since then, I send him one yellow rose.

When our son, Tony, Jr., was born on August 28, 1950, I guess it was one of the great moments of my life. Nicky had become a son to me, and still is, but I wasn't there when he was born. And I didn't go through his infancy and his toddlery and his learning to speak and walk. So it was a whole new experience and I must say I revelled in every new triumph for Tony, Jr.

His arrival was somewhat hectic. Cyd had had a few days of false labor and I'd spent two nights in a row at St. Johns Hospital. Then the doctor, Joe Harris, finally said, "Well, tonight's the night," and I looked at him, bleary-eyed from lack of sleep and I said something witty like, "I sure hope so." Then it was back to the waiting room for a few more hours of pacing and worrying. I had company while I waited. There was another expectant father sharing my vigil. But, where I was pacing, fingernail-biting, unshaven, he was neat and tidy and calm and cool. Turned out he was waiting for his eighth child. He didn't have to be told that this was my first.

When the doctor finally arrived with the cliché news—"It's a boy! Mother and child are doing fine!"—this cool character pulled a bottle of Scotch out of his attaché case and we killed it. He might have been cool on the outside, but by the way he guzzled that Scotch I had the feeling he was pretty nervous despite all his past experience.

Tony, Jr., and Nicky. My two sons. I honestly don't differentiate between the two. I love them equally, respect them equally and sometimes they've exasperated me equally. I guess that's normal with a couple of healthy, normal boys.

Over the years, they've given me something to come home to, something solid and permanent. Between Cyd and my sons, I've had that Gibraltar to cling to when the going got tough. They have provided me with a haven of normalcy amid the nonsense in which I have existed. And a lot of what I've gone through—what every person in show business goes through—has been fairy-tale-land.

Some of the people I've had to deal with you wouldn't believe. I've worked for a few of the giants and they are pretty quirky.

There was Louis B. Mayer. When he wanted me for a certain part in a certain picture, he'd call me down to his office. And he'd act out the part. I'd sit there, trying to keep a straight face, while this rugged man acted out all the parts in the picture—and he may have been the world's worst actor.

There was Darryl Zanuck. He issued orders like a colonel. I think they were whims that came to him and then he barked out orders and his whims became our facts. One day, for example, he came to the conclusion that none of his actors should have widow's peaks. And, as it turned out, three of his top stars—Ty Power, Don Ameche and me—all had widow's peaks. Down came the command: widow's peaks must go. So Ty, Don and I had to report every day to an electrolysist and get those hairs burned off our foreheads. It was painful and, what was worse, foolish. (At this point in my life, I'd give anything to have my widow's peak back.)

I met the great politicians, too—presidents from F.D.R. through Nixon. When Lyndon Johnson was president, our paths crossed in Miami, when he was campaigning and Cyd and I were appearing at the Fontainebleu. We were staying on the same floor—we were in Suite 14H and the Johnson party was in Suite 14G. He was scheduled to deliver a speech one night and, in the afternoon, he and his wife, Lady Bird, had gone to dedicate an airport and it had started to rain, as it often does in Florida, and they were caught in it. Lady Bird's hair was ruined.

We got a call from a Secret Service man.

"Mr. Martin," he said, "we know your wife has a hairdresser with her, and Mrs. Johnson wonders if she might borrow him this evening to fix her hair."

So Julius Bengtsson, Cyd's hairdresser, was drafted to do Lady Bird Johnson's hair. He reported back that she was very nice, but that her daughters were not traditionally beautiful. He wouldn't accept any money for his artistry, and I thought that was a nice gesture on his part.

That evening, we were doing our show when suddenly the audience burst into a tremendous round of applause. We thought we were good, but not that good. So we looked around and there were L.B.J. and one of his daughters being shown to a table. The entire audience was on their feet applauding. They had wanted to see our show. It was unusual for a president to go to a nightclub, and he was surrounded by Secret Service men.

I once flew from Memphis to Chicago and my seat-mate was Wendell Willkie, in the days when he was running for the presidency. He didn't know me but, of course, I knew who he was. He was working on a speech. We were talking, and he mentioned that all his speaking had given him a chronic sore throat. I suggested a gargle of baking soda and salt.

"How would you know what's good for a sore throat?" he asked.

"My brother is Tony Martin, the singer," I said.

As I've said, I've been fortunate and never did have a sore throat in all my career, but I'd picked up that remedy from other singers who had problems.

I knew Estes Kefauver well, in his glory days when he ran the investigation into organized crime. He was a bourbon drinker—he called it "Tennessee rotgut"—and I performed for him at a charity affair in Chattanooga, for his biggest fund-raiser. I sang, again, for John F. Kennedy; I sang the National Anthem twice in one night, because his affair was so big it spread into two ballrooms.

One of my greatest honors was meeting Winston Churchill, and I called on him at 10 Downing Street, when he was still prime minister. I was nervous, because I didn't quite know what to say to him. When I finally was ushered into his presence, I said, "You're looking well, Mr. Churchill." He offered me brandy and a cigar and laughed.

"Thank you for saying I look well, Mr. Martin," he said. "But I find it curious. You know, I've caroused a lot in my life. In my twenties I drank a lot of gin and tonic and people said I looked tired. In my thirties, more gin and tonic and people still said I looked tired. But now that I'm in my seventies, I may drink as much, but people always say I look well. That's the problem with getting old—people say you look well when you feel bad."

I've known most of the great performers, too. Al Jolson. I think he was the loneliest man I knew. I'd sit with him and play cards and we'd talk about singers and singing, one of the few topics we had in common to talk about. Mostly, he'd talk about what a great singer Buddy Clarke was. I liked Clarke, but I thought there were some other pretty good singers around.

"What about Bing?" I asked him one day.

"Bing is great. He's above the world. The greatest that ever came along."

"What about Frank Sinatra?"

"Him? Let me tell you, Tony—Frank Sinatra couldn't shine Buddy Clarke's shoes."

I disagree. If I were to rate all the greatest pop singers, I'd say that Bing was tops for flexibility, Russ Columbo outshone them all when it came to tenderness, and Frank was the greatest who ever came along for his phrasing. He sang like Tommy Dorsey played the trombone.

He is not one of my all-time favorite people, however. But I never let my personal likes and/or dislikes interfere with my assessment of a person's professionalism. Years ago, when I was probably the top nightclub attraction in America, Bill Miller asked me about Sinatra. It was during the time Frank had had a slump. Miller was offered a chance to book him and asked me what I thought.

"Grab him," I told Miller. "He's still great and he'll pack this joint."

So he grabbed him and he did pack the joint, and I think that was helpful to Frank as he made his comeback. I've always admired the man as a singer. I remember once, when he was opening at the Fontainebleu in Miami Beach, I took six people to see him and the bill was a whopper. But I wanted to see a great artist and cheer him on, so I did.

As I've said, I try to dissassociate my personal feelings from my judgment. I think Frank and I approve of each other, but we don't need each other. He leads his kind of life, I lead mine. We've never tangled, romantically or any other way. We've never had words, never come to blows. But I think he once did me a dastardly deed, and I doubt I'll ever forgive him.

One holiday season, Cyd and I were staying at our home in Palm Springs. You have to understand about Palm Springs. It's a little town. Everybody knows everybody, everybody knows what everybody is doing. OK. Along comes the word that Frank Sinatra is going to host a New Year's Eve party. And we aren't invited. Everybody else in town is invited. But not Tony and Cyd Martin. Now I'm hot. You get left out of a major event like that, everybody knows it and suddenly you feel ridiculous. Cyd felt hurt. I felt hurt. And I couldn't figure out why. A lot of my friends—

Sammy Cahn, Dean Martin, Jimmy McHugh, Mervyn LeRoy, Jack Benny —all went to Sinatra and asked why he had left the Martins off his invitation list. I knew his beef must be with me, because nobody dislikes Cyd. She's everybody's favorite. I knew it must be me, but, for the life of me, I couldn't figure it out.

So we didn't go to his New Year's Eve party. We spent a quiet New Year's Eve at home, the two of us, and it was a pleasure. Champagne, toasts, some TV and we both collapsed about one.

Actually, Frank and I go back a long time. It was before the war, in 1939 as I remember it, when I was playing the Paramount in New York. Artie Shaw had just cut his fantastic record of "Begin the Beguine." I was with Decca then and Jack Kapp, the president of Decca, called me at the theater and asked me if I could come over to Nola Studios on West 57th Street after my last show—that would make it about three in the morning —to cover "Beguine." In those days, when anybody had a hit record, all the other companies rushed to cover the hit—get their own artist to record it—so they'd get part of the gravy. Ray Sinatra, a great arranger and conductor, came over and, between shows, we worked on the arrangement. Ray said his young cousin, Frank, was around and would it be OK if he sat in the booth and watched while I cut the record? I said it was OK with me, as long as he kept quiet. So Frank watched that night while I cut the record—"Begin the Beguine," backed with "September Song"—which turned out to be a blockbuster for me.

I mentioned Bill Miller's Riviera. That was my home away from home for a long time. I was king of the hill at that nightclub—it was in Fort Lee, New Jersey, just over the George Washington Bridge from Manhattan— for a long time. And that was when the Riviera was the top night spot of the world. Everybody came to the Riviera in those days. Society came and sports figures came and show biz people came and, naturally, the racketeers came. Joey A (as Joey Adonis was known) and Frank Costello and Leo Durocher and Casey Stengel and Joe DiMaggio rubbed elbows with the greats in other fields. And for weeks, year after year, I was the attraction they came to see. Some nights, the place was so crowded and the demand so feverish that I'd have to do four shows.

I have a wristwatch which cost more than $2,000 which the Riviera's maitre d' gave me. He could afford it. He did so well on tips when I was playing there that he became a rich man. He eventually bought a home in Florida and retired. I wouldn't be surprised if he made more money than I did—and I wasn't exactly working at slave labor wages.

In my career, I've played almost everywhere. In the early fifties, Maury Aroff called me. After he'd gotten that raw deal in the Navy, he'd returned to the plumbing contracting business and did well. He said he had a friend named Teddy Lewin, a hero in the Philippines, who wanted us to come over there. The reason was to attend a Boy Scout Jamboree, which Lewin was promoting. It sounded like a fun trip, so we agreed to go. In those days, long distance airplanes had berths for sleeping, so we flew off from Los Angeles, via Hawaii, and slept most of the way. When the word had gotten out about our trip, the Navy had asked me if we'd schedule a stop in Guam to do a show for Navy personnel stationed there. I was still angry at the Navy, but I had no personal grudge against the enlisted men and if they wanted to see us, I had no objection.

The only problem was one of time, as it turned out. Our plane was late taking off from Hawaii. Cyd was exhausted so she took a light tranquilizer and climbed into the berth. It was around four in the morning, Guam time, when we landed there. I figured nobody would be up at that time, and assumed that the show had been canceled because of our late arrival. So I turned over and decided to go back to sleep.

"Tony, Tony!" It was Cyd, pulling at my arm. "Look out the window. You have to get up."

I looked out the porthole and there were thousands of people, Navy men and civilians, lined up alongside the runway. And a formal Navy band. So I quickly jumped up and went out and they let out a big cheer. They kept calling for Cyd, so I finally went back in the plane and told her she'd have to get dressed and come out, too. She was so drowsy from the pill that she could barely make it. I gave her a brandy and that helped, and she put on a dress and combed her hair and wearily came outside. It turned out that they had a lot of festivities planned and they weren't going to let a little fact like our four A.M. arrival stop them. They escorted us to a car and drove us to a place where there was a reception with a lavish buffet and we were introduced to a receiving line of one hundred and fifty. They had stayed up all night to wait for us, so we did our best. It wasn't bad for me —in fact I enjoyed it—but poor Cyd could barely keep her eyes open.

We went on from there to Manila, where Teddy Lewin introduced us to a wonderful guy named Arinetta. We met the president and our ambassador, Chip Bohlen, and a lot of other dignitaries, but it was Arinetta who stole the show. He was a beer and rubber baron, but his big love was cock fights. He raised fighting cocks and would bet up to a half-million on the outcome of one cock fight. He took us to see one and we were quickly turned off—the miserable, bloody things lasted barely ten seconds, but that was more than enough for us.

Lewin took us on a tour of Corregidor. He had been in the death march on that rocky little island. At the time, just before World War II broke out, Lewin had run a gambling casino in Manila. For some reason, he knew a secret tunnel on Corregidor. And, when the Japanese closed in, he led some 25,000 people to safety through that tunnel.

We were royally entertained, mostly by Arinetta. We dined at his home one evening, and then he proudly led me to his garage where he had eight expensive sports cars. He pointed to one, a Ferrari he had bought at an auto show in Paris.

"You've been so nice to come here, Tony," he said, "that I want you to have this car. It's yours. In six weeks, it will be in your garage in California."

When I got back to California, I got a call from the U.S. customs office in Long Beach, who said there was a car there for me. I went down with Aroff—I must admit that I was surprised that Arinetta had actually sent the car—and appeared at the customs shed to claim my new beauty. But they wanted $8,072.16 in duty. I wouldn't accept it.

On another trip to the Orient, I was in Hong Kong and ran into a cloak-and-suiter from New York I'd first met years before in Florida. I was just checking into our hotel with Cyd and this character was dashing around the lobby like a madman.

"Tony! Great to see you! Better hurry—the stores are still open."

"What stores?"

"Clothing stores. Shoe stores. Hat stores. All kinds of stores. Greatest bargains in the world, right here in Hong Kong. If you don't spend $2,000 a day, you're losing $1,000. Hurry up!"

I caught the buying fever, I must confess. I got so many suits and shirts and shoes and hats that I didn't have to buy any more clothes for a year. Just suitcases.

We went to Run Run Shaw's home for dinner. He is the big movie mogul of the far east—he owned some 2,200 theaters from Hong Kong to Malaysia. He had all his little starlets there, but we were the guests of honor. After dinner, the women were escorted to another room and the men were alone, and one of the servants approached me and said, "Mr. Martin, do you drink or smoke?"

It took me a few seconds to realize he was offering me my choice of brandy or opium. The Chinese people, I learned, take a few puffs of opium and it serves as a sort of tranquilizer. They never overdo it. I figured when in Hong Kong, do as the Hong Kongese do, so I took a puff of opium. It made me yawn. I said it was time to go home.

I played in South Africa, too. That was somewhere around '67, and I had to be very fast on my feet to avoid becoming an international incident. When we landed at Johannesburg, the reporters and photographers were out in force. And they kept asking me for my opinions on *apartheid*.

"I don't know anything about it," I said. "I've just landed. I have no information on which to base an opinion. And, besides, where's the john?"

I had to go to the bathroom. I looked around and found six of them. There were these signs on the six doors:

WHITE—MEN; WHITE—WOMAN; COLOURED—MEN; COLOURED—WOMEN; BLACK—MEN; BLACK—WOMEN.

I thought maybe I'd strike a blow for tolerance by going to a coloured or black john. The airplane pilot, who was with us, probably read my mind, because he took me firmly by the elbow and led me over to the door marked WHITE—MEN.

"Mr. Martin," he said, "go to the bathroom where you belong."

I disapproved of *apartheid*, when I learned about it. But I felt it wasn't my business to make an issue of it. I do not believe in interfering with another government's ways, with another country's culture. I'm supposed to be an entertainer, not a politician.

I did form one independent conclusion about South Africa. And that is that the best-looking women in the world are there. I've studied good-looking women everywhere, and I can make that statement without fear of contradiction.

While we were in Africa, we were taken one day out into the bush country to visit a Zulu tribe. They put on a show for us and we looked in their tents—the smell was overpowering—and bought some trinkets. Hal Borne, my conductor, was with us that day. He had to go to the bathroom and was led to a privy in the jungle and he gratefully sat down. A moment later he came screaming out of that place, with his pants down around his ankles. While he was sitting there, a six-foot snake had come slithering up from the commode and scared him to death. From then on, all of us stood up in bathrooms in Africa.

I knew Hal Borne as a hypochondriac. I used to kid him about it— perhaps I am one myself—and, that day we visited the Zulus, I had fun. We knew we were expected to tip the Zulus for their show.

"Just be careful you don't touch them, Hal," I said. "I hear they all carry a highly contagious fungus."

So when it came time for him to tip them, he threw the money at them. He wasn't about to get any closer than throwing distance, not with all that fungus.

We hit Australia, too. Fair dinkum! That was when Cyd was appearing in a musical there and I missed her so I snapped up an offer to appear in a Melbourne hotel. I didn't give a damn what I was making, as long as

I had a chance to be with her. After Melbourne, I took an engagement at a nightclub in Adelaide. I was working there when I got a call from home that my mother was in bad shape.

Naturally, I took the first plane home. The people running the Adelaide nightclub threatened to sue me. OK, I said, keep my money. I wasn't about to sing in a club in Australia when my mother needed me in Los Angeles. When I got home, I found my mother was no longer in intensive care. She seemed to be over the worst of it, so I flew right back to Australia. But no sooner had I landed than I got word she'd had a relapse.

I made three Australia–Los Angeles round trips in a little more than two weeks. The last time, I was too late.

I'd been in Australia before. Years ago, I forget when but it was when Tony, Jr., was just a punk, I played a club called Checkers in Sydney. We stopped off, en route, in Hawaii for a brief vacation. The only thing I remember about that trip is my stupidity. When we flew from Hawaii to Australia, I wore a white suit, partly to show off the suntan I'd gotten on the Waikiki beach, partly to enhance the reputation I had then as being one of the best-dressed men in Hollywood. So I stepped off the plane in Sydney, resplendent in my snazzy white suit. But I'd forgotten that the seasons are reversed in the southern hemisphere, and I stepped off the plane into winter—in my ridiculous white suit, my white shoes, my straw hat. Everybody laughed. I laughed, too, and we became friends.

I learned to like the Aussies a lot. Great people. They can convert a Scotch drinker into a beer drinker in nothing flat. I've tried beer all over the world, and I think Australian beer is the best there is. Whenever an Australian friend of mine comes to L.A. to visit, I ask him to bring a case of Foster's or Swann's Lager for me. It's like drinking silk. You pour a glass of lager, and the head fizzles forever.

We played on the island of Aruba, too, long before it was discovered and became the big resort it is today. Cyd and I feel that we discovered Aruba. When we first went there, it was nothing much—just heavenly beautiful. A friend, Jake Kozloff, invited us down to do a show and have some fun at the hotel where he operated the casino. You could walk for five miles on the sand, in those days, and see nothing and nobody. Just an endless expanse of beautiful sand. We began talking Aruba up and it has since become a mecca for sun-worshipers. Much later, I was made an honorary governor of Aruba for my services to tourism for the island.

We were in Aruba at the time when I got word that my father was dying of a heart attack. We caught the first plane, but it was at the height of the tourist season, so we had to work our way back to California in stages. We flew from Aruba to Puerto Rico, then to Miami, Atlanta, New Orleans,

259

Houston, Phoenix and finally Los Angeles. It was so frustrating, because I was anxious to see my father once more. It took twenty-seven hours, with all our stops, and I arrived at the hospital an hour too late. He was gone.

My mother said his last words were, "Hattie, I must see that boy."

His last years had been happy ones, I think, and I'll always be proud that I had a hand in that happiness. Often, I'd go over to their apartment and he'd take me aside and say, "Maybe, if you're going to the Friars, you could take me and I'd have an afternoon off?" We'd have lunch—my mother would make two hundred potato pancakes—and then I'd say, "Mom, why don't I take Dad to the Friars Club with me today?" and she'd say that would be nice. Dad and I would wink at each other. And he'd be happy there, playing pinochle with some friends.

Now he was gone. I think my mother started to die, herself, when Dad left her.

Joe Castro was my conductor for a few years, and he conducted for me in Aruba a couple of times. Joe was going with Doris Duke and she came with him to Aruba. Joe was a fine musician and a fine man, but his relationship with Doris was chaotic. Whenever they'd have a fight, he'd go off on a tangent and it took some doing to get him back again. He told me that he and Doris had gotten married, and I have no reason to doubt his word. She wound up giving him a house in Honolulu, so I guess they were married.

I played Havana often in the pre-Castro days, too. It was a wonderful city, exciting and alive. We were there once, around '55 or '56, when Tony, Jr., was very young. Cyd took him that day—she called me from Los Angeles to tell me—to the park where he rode the roller coaster. I did my show in Havana and, between shows, two very respectable Cubans asked to see me in my suite. George Raft, who was there then, said they were OK, so I invited them up. They were dressed very decently, looked fine, spoke perfect English. We chatted a while and they refused my offer of a drink.

Then one of them took a $100 Cuban banknote from his breast pocket. It was carefully folded and he unfolded it, and out came a white powder. The two of them sniffed it. Cocaine. I'd never seen it before. Seems they were hooked on it, but their wives didn't know, so they had to find somewhere where they could get their fix. That's why they had "borrowed" my room. When they unfolded the $100 bill, I thought some of the powder spilled into my drink, which was on the table. But I drank it anyhow and learned a lesson about the power of suggestion. I went to bed that night and dreamed about Tony, Jr., and that roller coaster—I saw it crash, saw Tony, Jr., falling out and getting killed. I woke up, petrified, and quickly called home. Cyd said Tony was fine. But just the thought that I might have drunk some of the cocaine had brought on that strange dream.

I worked in Havana for five years, for people like Raft and people who had names like Fat and Butch and Meyer Lansky and Charley White. I even worked for Battista, the dictator who preceded Castro. I spoke pretty fair Spanish and I was working there one day in '59 when a kid who worked for me in the dressing room rushed in.

"Señor," he said. *"Lunes Castro. Vamos."*

In other (English) words, he was telling me that Castro was coming Monday, and I'd better get out. This was on a Friday night. Marty Krofft was there, with the Liberace show, and I told Marty and we all made plans and we got out Sunday. Sure enough, Castro marched in on Monday, right on schedule.

I even played Viet Nam. When it looked like my son, Nick, was headed for the war, I paid my own way over there to entertain, to tell the brass to watch out for my son. One night, the owner of the hotel where I was staying said, "Do you want to see the war?" and he took me up on the roof of the hotel and we watched a bombing raid some twelve miles away. I always thought that was something, to watch a war from a hotel roof. Entertaining the troops gave me a nice feeling, but my mission was unnecessary, as it turned out. The only one in my family who ever got to Viet Nam was me.

Of course, I've worked all over the United States, too. From the beginning of my career, I've played them all—the big cities, the tank towns, the fanciest clubs and a few crummy joints along the way. Mostly, though, I've been fortunate and played the best.

In '74, I was on the bill with Jack Benny at the Mill Run Theater near Chicago. Jack's manager, Irving Fein, asked me how long I did. I said usually forty-five minutes or so. Fein nodded. The first night, that's what I did.

"Tony, you're on too long," Fein said. And I had to agree, because between Jack and me the show was running very long, perhaps twenty-five minutes too long. Obviously, they didn't want to cut Jack's time on stage. Fein asked me if I could cut fifteen minutes from my act. I said, sure. I'd just do my songs and eliminate the patter. And that's what I did.

Jack wasn't feeling too well during that engagement. He had a touch of diabetes for a long time and it was bothering him. The doctors had advised him not to drink at all. But Jack liked a nip of Scotch, so he'd go to Tom Turner, my pal-aide-secretary, who has been working for me for almost twenty-five years, and he'd hold up his fingers in the shape of the letter C and say, "Tom—fix." Tom would pour him a couple of shots of straight Scotch. I don't think it hurt Jack any.

We'd been playing a while, with the shortened version of my act, when Jack came up to me and said, "Hey, Tony, why did you cut out the medley you did in the first show? It was great—put it back."

I'd first met Tom Turner at the Riviera in '48. He was working as a busboy. A couple of years later, I was appearing with Lena Horne at the Clover Club in Miami, and there he was again. He'd come up from busboy to being the assistant to Jack Goldman, who ran the club. Tom's job was to help the acts, and he was fantastic. I'd come to my dressing room and everything would be laid out perfectly, even to a fresh, opened pack of cigarettes. So I asked him if he'd like to work for me, and he's been with Cyd and me ever since.

He was very good to my mother and used to take care of her. She'd confide in him, tell him things she wouldn't even tell me. He did all her shopping, and took care of her money. When she died, she left some money for him in her will. I was the administrator of the will and I knew Tom, knew he'd just give that money away. So I had the will changed and deposited that money. Tom will always be taken care of.

Cyd and I began working together after she left MGM. They'd taken care of her for fourteen years and then she'd done some free-lance acting for a while. I worked on her for a long time to join me but she was hesitant. For me, it was a way of being with her more, which is what I wanted. She wanted that, too, but the idea of working in clubs was totally alien to her, and it took a lot of persuading to get her to do it.

Finally, she agreed. Bob Sidney put the act together and we went to the Riviera in Las Vegas. We played five weeks the first time, in 1964, and then, three months later, we did another six weeks. They loved her and, after a touch of cold feet, she found she liked doing the act, too.

It wasn't easy, of course. I've always ad libbed a lot during my act, playing with and to the audience. But Cyd preferred to stick to the rehearsed material. We had a few fights about that, but it all worked out. It always does if you give it time.

One thing we didn't fight about was the billing. It's traditional in show business that the man's name always comes first.

So it's been Tony Martin and Cyd Charisse. I hope it continues forever. Of course, if this Women's Lib thing gets any bigger, I may have to change that to Cyd Charisse and Tony Martin. It won't matter, as long as we're together.

12

TRIPS
AND
TROUPING

I had begun life as a dancer and had become a motion picture actress almost by accident, or perhaps it was fate. Over the years, as I've said, I had flirted with the stage, but had never really attempted to do anything else. I was content; my movie career was enough for me, because actually it was my husband, my children and my home that were of greatest concern to me. But when my boys grew up and Tony was away so much, and the bottom dropped out of the Hollywood movie industry, I found myself with increasing amounts of spare time on my hands. Since I had been busy and active since I was a child, this excess time was a problem. There are just so many hours you can spend taking care of an empty house and getting your hair done.

Tony and our dear friend, Sidney Korshak, talked me into appearing with Tony in Las Vegas. That was the first step. I must admit that it took a lot of persuading before I agreed. I was, frankly, frightened by the prospect of appearing in public. Since I'd left the Ballet Russe, I had never done it. In films, you have the protection of another take if the first one is bad. But, when you are working on a nightclub floor, there is no such protection. You're out there, all alone, and if you fall on your face, you fall on your face for a thousand people to see. So the whole idea of working in nightclubs seemed a high hurdle for me.

Tony pooh-poohed my fears. He's spent his life in front of the public and couldn't understand what I was worried about. He kept saying that they would love me. But he didn't understand. To him, walking out on a nightclub floor is as simple and natural as going to the kitchen for a glass of water. He had no sympathy for my trepidations. But, gradually, he and

Sid Korshak wore down my objections and, finally, I agreed. I must say it was pleasant to learn that the Riviera, in Las Vegas, was so excited about the prospect of having a Tony Martin and Cyd Charisse attraction that they gave us a lucrative contract, sight unseen. That helped wear down my resistance, too.

We got Bob Sidney to put our act together. I had known Bob at MGM, of course, and he was also the man who staged Mitzi Gaynor's act, which has long been one of the finest in the field. So we began working, and I quickly found that all those years of making movies had cost me my stamina. I just was not physically up to doing thirty minutes of virtually uninterrupted dancing, not after so many years of doing my dancing leisurely as you do in movies. It took a while—and I quit smoking—before I was up to it.

The idea of opening at the Riviera cold scared me out of my wits. I asked if we couldn't possibly break the act in somewhere else first. Bob Sidney suggested Dallas and that was fine with me, because I felt that in front of my fellow Texans I'd be more at home. But Tony was working, so he vetoed the idea of a Dallas break-in before Vegas. All that we had, as it turned out, was a dress rehearsal before an invited audience at the Television Academy in Los Angeles, a Beverly Hills rehearsal hall, and one performance for servicemen in Las Vegas. They went all right, but I was still very nervous. I felt that the invited audience for a dress rehearsal and the appearance before the servicemen really didn't mean a thing, not compared to what I might confront when I finally went on at the Riviera.

Helen Rose, who did my wardrobe, and George Masters, my hairdresser, flew up to Las Vegas with us. I was very jittery. Tony couldn't understand my nerves.

"It's nothing," he kept saying. "You'll be fine."

As it turned out, he was right. Once I was out there, and felt the warmth of the audience, I was fine. At first, working before an audience was strange. It took me a few weeks until I could stop my knees from knocking before I went on. But, gradually, I built up my confidence and the overwhelming audience response helped. They did seem to like me and they liked the act. Now, after ten years of working with a live audience, I find I love it. I can judge their response by some instinct, as all live performers can, and it is a great feeling to be surrounded by their applause and appreciation. I only wish I'd done it a long time before.

Now, too, I am physically stronger than I ever was. I like to draw a comparison between track events and the two forms of entertainment. When you make a movie, it's like sprinting—you have to be able to go very fast for a very short span of time. But nightclub work, or the theater, is like the long distance events; you must pace yourself and be able to continue for a long period. They are two separate and distinct skills and I had to build myself up so I was capable of sustaining a performance on a nightclub floor, twice a night, night after night.

That first Las Vegas appearance was, I believe, in 1965 or thereabouts. Once I had gotten into the swing of it, I enjoyed the six weeks there. I enjoyed the people I met, and Las Vegas can attract some strange and wonderful people.

One of those who was around during that first engagement at the Riviera was the playboy Francisco "Baby" Pignatari. He was waiting for a divorce to come through, so he had lots of time—and, of course, money —on his hands. He had just had his face lifted, but was absolutely without self-consciousness about his condition. Where most people in that position hide in their bedroom until the evidence disappears, Baby would mingle freely—and you could plainly see all the stitches and signs of the recent surgery on his face. He developed a fondness for Tony, Jr., which was reciprocated, and one day Baby had a gift for my son—an electric guitar. It was the first one he had ever owned, and I think it had a lot to do with his deciding on music as his career.

Even though he was fabulously wealthy, Baby would not gamble. Maybe that was why he was fabulously wealthy. But Las Vegas is a culture built around the wager, and they look with disfavor on non-bettors. The casino bosses saw the way he spread his money around, the lavish gifts he gave people, his excessive tipping, yet none of that money came their way and they began to be a little disgruntled about it.

So Tony approached him one evening and said, "Baby, please do me one favor. Place one bet around at the tables one night. All the guys have seen your generosity and they wonder why you never patronize them. It would be a good thing to do once."

Baby was agreeable about it. He went around from table to table placing one bet on each, and the croupiers were happy. Their happiness didn't last long. Baby had a fantastic streak of luck and wound up the evening some $40,000 ahead. They never asked him to bet again. He turned around and gave the money back in tips all around the hotel.

He wasn't supposed to leave the state, of course, since he was in residence pending his divorce. But he got very itchy and restless and, one evening, he told us he was going to Hawaii the next morning.

"But, Baby," I said, "you can't go. That will ruin your divorce action."

"It's OK, Cyd," he said. "I'm using Tony's name. They'll never know I was gone."

That first experience working in front of a real, living, breathing audience was a revelation to me. There is nothing as exciting as a standing ovation. Even a sitting ovation is pretty good. I found the whole experience turned me on, and I became excited by it. I could have kicked myself for waiting so long. Since then, Tony and I have worked together many times, in many places, and I love it.

I usually work with two or three boy dancers in my act. Recently, before another Las Vegas engagement, I needed a replacement badly. It was only a few days before I was scheduled to open, and one boy dancer had been injured. So I called Ron Field, the man who had directed *Applause,* and our act, who said he had someone for me. Ron's assistant said Nicholas Dante and he would love the job. So I contacted him and he agreed to fly out from New York the next day.

And he did.

"Oh, I'm so excited!" he said. He was full of excitement. "Do you know, all my life I've wanted to be Cyd Charisse!"

Well, I was taken aback at that. I happened to be with Tony, Jr., at the time, and we both laughed. But he was so sweet and so eager that we didn't mind. Nicholas turned out to be a fine dancer, but he was very emotional. He didn't get along well with my other dancers, but he stayed with it. We were talking one day and he said he had to go back to New York soon, because he and a friend were putting together a show for off-Broadway. The friend's name, he said, was Michael Bennett, a well-known choreographer, and he did go back and the show did get put on and turned out to be that colossal hit, *A Chorus Line.* When I finally saw it, I was astounded by it. I think it is the most honest and moving portrait of dancers I've seen. A great show.

To my mind, dancers are given a tough break in the theater. They work the hardest and get paid the least. They sweat and struggle for weeks, with very little pay, and it is generally the singers and the other principals who get the attention and plaudits.

Nicholas Dante tells his own story in *A Chorus Line*—the show has a group of dancers telling their stories in response to a choreographer's questions—and sure enough he used the line about how he has always wanted to be Cyd Charisse an example of the complete honesty of the show. I enjoyed that line, as I enjoyed the entire show.

It is true that many homosexuals become dancers here in America. I imagine that's because they are so deeply attracted to artistic things. I have generally found them to be likeable people, soft and sympathetic and enjoyable and invariably very talented. They have their problems in their own way, but don't we all.

I think, and I am very serious about it, that there is a problem with

266

American parents over boys dancing. If a boy here, when he's growing up, shows the slightest inclination toward the dance, he is generally chastised.

"Oh, I don't want my son to be a sissy," the mother or father will say. "Here, kid, here's a football, go outside and play like a real boy."

That's a shame, because there is no reason why dancing cannot be a very masculine and rewarding career for a man. It is in Russia, for example; there, dancers of both sexes are admired and respected. And a dancer can have a long and noteworthy career. That's another reason I admire men like Astaire, Kelly, Johnny Brascia and Edward Villella—all very male men, all had to battle the prejudices of this prejudiced country, all managed to scramble to the top despite many slurs on their masculinity.

Over the years since I began, I've known hundreds of male dancers. They had a tough row to hoe here, because as soon as they mentioned the fact that they were dancers, the average response was a lifted eyebrow and a step back. I hope someday that attitude changes.

I think dancing is a noble career. And, I might add, I think choreography is a tremendously creative and most underrated art form. I cannot emphasize too strongly how important the choreographer is to the dancer, or the whole of any musical production. I've worked with many of the greatest—from Fokine in the classical ballet to men like Loring, Pan, Sidney, Kidd, Kelly, Ron Field and Tony Charmoli in the realm of popular dance. Each was a brilliant and inventive creator. Everyone knows that actors are only as good as the words they are given to say, but most people forget the same relationship is true in the field of dance, too. A dancer is only as good as what the choreographer gives him or her to work with.

My pleasant experience on a nightclub floor made me receptive when I had an offer to do a play. I guess, in the back of my mind, I had long wanted to try it, but the right vehicle at the right time in the right place had never come along. It did, in 1968.

I was offered the chance to play one of the leads in a production of *Once More, With Feeling* at the Drury Lane Theater in Chicago. Actually, it was a wonderful woman at the William Morris Agency here who persuaded me to do it, and I'll always be grateful to her, because it turned out to be a delightful experience. To begin with, it's a lovely play, a light and frothy comedy about sex and marriage. I played the part in Chicago for six weeks, and loved it. I imagine, if I'd done that before I tried my wings on a nightclub floor, I would have been nervous, but that club work was great experience for me. It had taught me that the public is generally nice and receptive and that has given me confidence.

The Drury Lane Theater is a theater-in-the-round, a relatively small one, seating around eight hundred people. At first, the thought of the audience being so close to me made me a bit apprehensive, but I quickly learned that the only way to handle that is to concentrate. My movie camera training was a big help. When you're shooting a film, the camera can be right on top of you, staring into your pores, but you have to ignore it. The same thing applies, I found out, to the audience in a theater-in-the-round. Concentrate on the role. The rest of it works. The round-style theater gives you a freedom of movement that is lovely. So I found the whole six weeks a pleasure.

One of the nicest things about that Drury Lane Theater experience was the continuing presence of Jack Benny. He and Tony were old friends —they had worked together many years earlier—and we had become close, too. At the time I was doing *Once More, With Feeling,* he was appearing at the Palmer House in downtown Chicago. We were both staying at the Ambassador Hotel. And, very often, he would call me.

"Tula?"

"Yes, Jack." It had to be Jack; nobody else ever called me Tula.

"Will you be my date tonight?"

If Mary was away and we were both free, or we were going to the same party, we'd go together. And, frequently, we'd meet at the Pump Room late at night, after his performance and my play, and we'd have a late supper together. One of the nicest things about Jack was that he never lost his enthusiasm. To him, everything was the greatest, the best, the funniest. He said, after he'd come to see me in my play, that it was the best little-theater production he'd ever seen. And the supper later was also the best he had ever eaten.

The only time I've ever seen Jack angry was once years ago—and the objects of his anger were Mary and me. It happened one year when Tony was making a movie in England with Vera Ellen. We all went along, the whole family. And it was pleasant, because Ty Power was in London for another film, and he rented a house two doors from the one we were renting, and Ty's daughters and Tony, Jr., would go to the park together and play.

The Bennys came through London and said they were bound for Italy, to do a TV show in Venice, and would I like to come alone. It sounded lovely, so I went with them. Besides, it had turned cold in London and my bones ached for some of that Italian sunshine. It was a pleasant trip and Jack and Mary and I had a lot of laughs. Then, on a whim, Mary said she'd like to drive to Rome. I was game and Jack is always ready to move on, so he rented two Cadillacs with drivers for the trip from Venice to Rome. In our car, which led the caravan, was me, Mary, my son Nicky and our driver. Jack followed in the second car with Mary's brother, Hickey, and his wife.

"Now, girls," Jack said to us, as we started out, "you be sure and look back once in a while to make sure we're still behind you. You know, these rented Italian cars break down a lot."

We said that we would look back to make sure Jack's car was following. And, for a while, we did. But we were having such fun—Mary Benny is a very witty woman—that pretty soon we completely forgot our instructions. Finally, I remembered.

"Mary," I said, "have you looked back lately to see if Jack's car is still there?"

"No. I thought you were doing it."

"Well, I thought you were."

We both looked back—and there wasn't another car in sight. The road was frighteningly empty. We had the driver stop. We pulled over and waited fifteen minutes. The other car didn't show up. So we turned the car around—the driver didn't want to, but we persuaded him—and went back to see what had happened. And, of course, we came to the place where Jack's car had broken down. He was furious, positively livid. He was pacing up and down and gave us a very black look as we arrived on the scene.

But he didn't say a word. For five or ten minutes, he just gave us the silent treatment, looking over at us with that furious expression and shaking his head in exasperation. Then, finally, he could contain himself no longer.

"Didn't I tell you to look back?"

There was nothing we could say. He had told us to look back and we'd just forgotten. To make matters worse, Mary and I started to laugh. The car turned out to be beyond fixing that day, so we wound up with seven people and all our luggage piled in that one car. All the way to Rome, we were jammed in and Jack didn't say another word until we got there. Our gondola hats were piled on top of the car. We looked like gypsies as we pulled up to the Grand Hotel in Rome.

But back to my stage career. Once my feet were wet and my confidence shipshape, I decided I liked it out there on stage. So I accepted other offers. One summer, I toured up and down the East Coast in *Illya, Darling*. That musical had just closed on Broadway, with Melina Mercuori as the star, and that was a break for our company. We absorbed many of the original Broadway cast. They reworked the show a little to take advantage of my dancing; Melina was never a dancer. Onna White's assistant built up the dance numbers that existed and added new ones. The only problems I had were trying to learn those Greek songs—I even had to sing "Never on Sunday" in Greek. But the production worked and was a big hit in stock.

I was approached with a nice offer to star in the Australian production of *No, No, Nanette*, but at first I turned it down. I certainly thought I was not right for the part. So they signed Betty Grable but then, as luck would have it, Betty became ill. The producer, Michael Edgley, a brilliant and forceful young Aussie, flew to Los Angeles and begged me to take over. They were already in rehearsal in Melbourne, he said, and if I didn't say yes he didn't know what he would do. He made me an offer I could have refused, but I didn't.

The engagement was for thirteen weeks, which didn't sound too long. There was an option clause in my contract, but my agent said it was nothing to worry about, so I didn't worry about it. I would later live to regret my trustfulness.

It was an all-Australian cast, save for me and Paul Wallace. I brought my old friend, Tense Robinson, with me so I would have some company, since Tony couldn't come for a while. When we arrived in Melbourne, the Australian press was there in force. I had heard about them, how they were rougher than even the English press, and so I was prepared. I guess I handled them all right, because the stories were uniformly good to me— but poor Paul hadn't been similarly briefed. For some reason, they developed an instant dislike for him, and the stories reflected that dislike. They crucified him. Our American reporters and columnists are milquetoasts next to those in Australia and some of the other places I've been. But, as I say, I must have done something right, because they were kind in their reports on my arrival. But, later, when we opened, the reviewers' chauvinism triumphed. All the Aussies got great reviews, while Paul and I were received in a lukewarm manner. It didn't seem to bother the box office; we were a solid smash.

Again, they had taken advantage of my particular skills. The choreographer, an Australian woman named Betty Pounder, added a tango for Paul and me, which was not in the Broadway production. But, of course, we had to keep the big smash number, when Sue Smith (the character I played, and the character Ruby Keeler played on Broadway) tap-danced on stage with the entire chorus line. I believe I've mentioned that tap-dancing is not my forte, but I had to learn it, and I did. I still prefer other forms of dance, but one does what one has to do.

The opening night was a blast. The Aussies do things in a big way— klieg lights, old cars, the whole works. I enjoyed being part of it, and I enjoyed the Australian people—there's never a dull moment around that crew.

Somewhere around the sixth week of the run, Tony flew in. He had, happily, accepted an engagement at a hotel in Melbourne, so we had a grand reunion. Our living quarters were ideal. They had found me a penthouse apartment only a block away from the theater. Carol Channing was in Melbourne at the time, and that was fun, because she's a great character. She traveled all the way from home with her own supply of bottled water; she doesn't trust anybody else's water. She also brought along enough of her special food—somebody told me it was goat meat, but I'm not sure about that—to last as long as her Australian stay.

It was good having Tony there, of course, and it made the stay pleasant. But Tony missed home, particularly the sports events. He is, I suspect, the world's number one sports fan. There was one game he desperately wanted to hear, while we were in Australia. So he called a friend in Los Angeles and listened to the game over the telephone. As I remember it, the bill for him to hear that game came to somewhere around nine hundred dollars. He felt it was worth it.

The weeks wore on. My big regret was that here I was in another country, another continent, and I saw nothing but the apartment, the theater and the block in between. Playing eight shows a week, with only one day off, doesn't give you any time for sightseeing excursions. Besides, Australia is so vast that you need a few days to get from one city to another. So I've been to Australia, but I can only say I've seen one block in Melbourne. I was asked to do a commercial for some brand of panty hose and was offered a nice chunk of money, so I agreed. It was the $12,000 fee that did it—but, as of this moment, I haven't seen a penny or a farthing of that money. Every time I inquire about it, they tell me it all went to pay Australian taxes.

By the time I was into my thirteenth week, I was ready to go home. Galloping homesickness had overcome my natural penchant for traveling. Tony had done his two weeks and flown home because his mother was desperately ill. Before he left, he bought me an Australian dog. Tense and I had complained of coming into an empty apartment with not a living soul to greet us. So now I had something alive to be there when I got back from the theater. It was some comfort. I began counting off the days until my final performance, and was down to four or five when the blow came. The producers announced that they had exercised their option and were going to play an additional thirteen weeks. At first, they said another year, for a tour all over Australia, but I found they didn't have the right to demand that, so I turned that down quickly. But, as it developed, there was no way I could back out of the thirteen-week extension.

Thirteen more weeks! I don't mean to imply that I didn't like Australia or the Australians, because I did. It was simply a case of wanting to go home, to see my sons and my friends and be in familiar surroundings. But I had to stick it out. Every day dragged like a year, and I thought that last month would never, never end. When Yvonne DeCarlo flew out, to take over my role, it was as if she were the warden come to tell me I had been paroled. I fell into her arms and gleefully took her down to Her Majesty's Theater to begin rehearsing my part.

Closing night was a great thrill. Not only did it mean the end of my six-month stay—I was booked on the first flight out the next morning— but I was treated to a display of typical Australian friendliness. It was really a very touching evening, and I'll never forget it. First, as was the custom, I introduced Yvonne to the audience after the final curtain had fallen. And then, spontaneously, the audience stood up and serenaded me with "For She's a Jolly Good Fellow," with the whole cast joining in behind me. Talk about goose pimples! I must confess that I was crying as I stood there, basking in the warmth of that lovely farewell. I really melted. Then, when I got back to my dressing room, everyone was there and bottles of champagne were being opened right and left. We drank and toasted each other for an hour or so, and, when I left, the cast joined hands and formed a human arbor and I walked beneath their clasped hands to the stage door. I truly have never been more touched.

At the airport the next morning, the company was all there again, and my last sight of Australia was those wonderful people waving as my plane disappeared.

It was a long time, but, looking back on it, a lovely time. I find the Australians a delightful people, although they have their quirks. For one thing, they'll bet on anything and everything. I remember the housekeeper in my apartment, Mrs. Lee, was forever dashing out to get groceries. Once, on my day off, I kept seeing her go in and out and she always said she was going for groceries, but she never came back with any. Finally, out of curiosity, I followed her—she was going to a betting parlor to wager on a horse race.

One of the great things about the life of someone in my business— actress, entertainer—is the chance to travel. And it is travel unlike that of the average tourist. Wherever you go, when you're working, you automatically meet the most interesting people. Over the years, Tony and I have been virtually everywhere. It gives me a glorious chance to country-drop during idle conversations, and it's really led to a very wonderful life, with wonderful friends all over the world.

We've been so many places and so often that there's no point in trying to give you a chronological rundown of our travels. Then, too, it would be pretty boring. But let me tell you of a few of our adventures, here and there, over the years.

We were in Florida once—Tony was appearing at The Beachcomber Club—and Harry Richman, the great entertainer, was our host. We stayed with Harry and Yvonne and it was a pleasant time. Harry, who projected such worldly sophistication, was the kind of man who was happiest in his garden, picking his tomatoes. He had a small fishing boat and Tony kept urging him to take us out for a little expedition.

"I'd like to," Harry would say, "but it's much too rough out there. Maybe tomorrow."

That kept up for several days until after work one night when Tony took a look out toward the ocean and decided that this was the time.

"Come on, Harry," Tony said. "Let's go. Look—it's smooth as glass out there."

"It's too rough," Harry said.

"Nonsense. It's like silk. Let's go."

"OK, you asked for it," Harry said.

So we went out, Harry and Yvonne, Tony and me. As soon as we cleared the breakwater and were out in the ocean proper, we found out what Harry meant. It was rough! Yvonne was down in the cabin, being sick. I stayed on top, praying that a wave would come and wash me overboard and then I'd forget all my misery. Tony had a bottle of whiskey and that seemed to help him a little. And Harry just watched us all, and seemed to take delight in seeing how dreadful we all felt.

Somehow we made it to one of the keys. Once we landed, I said to Tony there was absolutely no way they were going to get me back on that boat for the return trip. And Tony and Yvonne, and even Harry, agreed. We hired a car and drove back and I think Harry got somebody to bring the boat back. And, all the way back in the car, Harry kept chuckling and saying, "From now on, when I say it's rough you'll believe me!"

Those were the days when Miami was a fun place, something like Las Vegas is today. Those days, unfortunately, are gone forever for Miami and Miami Beach.

Incidentally, the story of Harry Richman had a sad ending. Some time later, he came out to visit us in Los Angeles. He was having trouble with his voice. Tony tried to help him, but there wasn't much he could do. Richman ultimately became a recluse, Yvonne divorced him, and he ended his days sadly alone and virtually forgotten.

I remember with joy one evening that started in London. Tony had been playing at the Palladium, where he was a tremendous smash. John Mills (the restaurateur, not the actor) had given us a great party in his place, Les Ambassadeurs, which lasted from eleven-thirty until somewhere around five in the morning. Our friends Jai and Isha, the Maharajah and Maharanee of Jaipur, were there, together with some members of Parliament and, I believe, the man who was then chancellor of the exchequer. It was a glorious evening. And then, on the spur of the moment, Tony said let's go to Paris, and we did. John Mills came with us and introduced us to a magnificent restaurant there, the Scheherezade. Mills is the kind of man who will send champagne back if it doesn't come up to his exacting standards. We drank champagne—he finally accepted some—and ate caviar and were serenaded by strolling violinists. It's not a bad way to live. And then the bill came and I peeked over Tony's shoulder and I almost died. It was for $900.

In England, we went to Epsom Downs, the racetrack. When I go to the track, I don't worry about past performances or the condition of the track or how good the jockey is. I bet solely on a name that strikes my peculiar fancy. And, that day, there was a horse running named My Love which, to my romantic nature, sounded like a winner. Tony gave me $500 worth of five-pound notes, but I got confused and thought that each five-pound note was worth $5, instead of $25. I bet what I thought was $50, but it was really $250, on My Love. The horse galloped in, an easy winner, and paid 11–2, so I wound up with a profit of more than $1,000. Tony said I shouldn't be allowed out alone, but he helped me spend my winnings anyhow.

We flew, one year a long time ago, to London for one of Tony's Palladium appearances. That was in the era when there were berths on planes, and you slept your way across the Atlantic. One of our fellow passengers, a man we had met, was a high official from the little oil-rich country of Kuwait. His name was Izzak Gaffar, and he came aboard the plane in his ordinary costume, a long white robe. Before we took off, the stewardess came through the plane, greeting all the passengers with her pretty smile, and she noticed Gaffar in his white robe.

"Oh, sir," she said, "I see you're ready for bed. As soon as we take off, I'll make up your berth."

Gaffar wore a very distinctive and very strong cologne. And, later, after London, we went to the south of France and we walked into the hotel lobby and I sniffed and it was Gaffar's cologne.

"Tony," I said, "Izzak Gaffar is here."

Sure enough, five minutes later we spotted him. I have a very sensitive nose for things like that.

Gaffar was with us when, a few nights later, we were invited to a cocktail party aboard a yacht. We were enjoying ourselves, cocktails in hand, when the anchor was lifted and the yacht began moving. So that cocktail party turned into an all-night trip. We cruised to an island off Cannes, and they served supper on the island. Everyone was polite and well-behaved on the way over and while we were having supper, but on the trip back to Cannes, it turned into quite a wild party. They were dancing on the tables and really ripping things up. Then the yacht stopped and the group began a session of nude bathing. Somebody manned the ship's searchlight; the game was to try and zero in on the bathers with the searchlight.

I must tell you that there were only three people aboard the yacht who didn't participate in that mini-orgy. The three were the only representatives of Hollywood there—Tony, myself and another actor who happened to be with us. Hollywood has a reputation for wild parties, but I've seen more wild parties outside Hollywood than in it.

On another trip to England, we were invited to the home of a printing magnate named Derek Hallcaine for dinner. We didn't realize at the time that the British were still under their austerity program and that the Hallcaines had saved up their ration stamps for months to buy a roast beef for our dinner party. This beautiful roast was carried to the table by the butler, and everyone oohed and aahed over its perfection.

"All right," said Derek. "Now, who would like to carve?"

Tony quickly jumped up and said, "I'll carve." I was astounded; he had never carved a thing in his life. But I guess he felt it was the polite thing to do, or perhaps it was the pre-dinner sherry talking. Anyhow, the roast beef was brought to him and he was handed the carving knife and fork. He stabbed it with the fork—and the damn thing skidded off the plate and landed on the floor. The butler rushed in, picked it up and took it back to the kitchen. I'm sure they just washed it off, because pretty soon it was back again. This time, somebody else carved. And Tony has never volunteered for carving duty again.

On one trip to Paris, we ran into our good friends, Jean and Dusty Negulesco. Before her marriage, she was Dusty Anderson, a top New York model who had come to California and had become one of the famous Goldwyn Girls. It was on that trip, under the tutelage of Jean, that I became interested in painting. Jean took me around to quite a few galleries. My first purchases were a group of Jean Paul watercolors of horses. I bought eight for $50 each, as gifts. I kept only two of them. Today, each is valued at between $1,700 and $2,000. I bought a Utrillo on that trip, too, but my big disappointment was that I didn't buy a Renoir I saw. Actually, what happened was that Sidney Sheldon was there at the same time, and we both discovered the Renoir simultaneously. He wanted it very much, so I let him have it. As I remember it, he paid less than $2,000 for the painting. Later, he sold it for $6,000 and today, I'm told, it's valued at around $30,000.

On another Paris trip, when I was pregnant, I wasn't feeling too well. That, in itself, was curious, because I had been fine before—swimming every day, fixing up the house. And yet, when we got to Paris, I began feeling miserable. Tony bought me a Vlaminck to cheer me up, and it helped my mental state but not my physical. I went to the American Hospital in Paris to see what was wrong. The baby was due in six weeks and I was naturally concerned. Tony had to go back for an engagement at Bill Miller's Riviera in New York and he came to see me in the hospital just before he was due to leave. Many doctors had been in and out, examining me, and they said they thought I should stay another three weeks for testing and to rest up.

"Tony, pack my bags," I said. "I'm going home with you."

I was not about to stay in that hospital for three weeks, with my baby due in six weeks. So Tony packed my things and we tiptoed out of the hospital and I flew to New York with him. I rested up for a few days at the Waldorf-Astoria in New York, where we stayed with a dear friend, Abe Shushan, until I went back home to have Tony, Jr.

Tony and I travelled once to Hawaii on a ship and among our fellow passengers were Harry Karl and his wife Marie McDonald. It was a delightful crossing. As we arrived in Honolulu, one lady came over to where the four of us were standing and said, "I just want to tell you all that, for show business people, you have really conducted yourselves like complete ladies and gentlemen."

Marie looked at her for one shocked moment and then said, "Go fuck yourself."

One of our greatest trips was to the Orient—Hong Kong, the Philippines, Singapore and some other places. My husband went mad in Hong Kong with the tailors and shirtmakers and shoemakers. He'd be out in the shops all day, ordering things. And then, when we would get back to our hotel late in the evening, all those little men would be lined up in the hallway, waiting to fit him with the suits, shirts and shoes he had ordered. I had heard of a woman who had good jewelry to sell and contacted her and she came to our hotel room, with a shawl full of the most exquisite things—emeralds, pearls, rubies—at very inexpensive prices. She dumped them on the bed and I marveled at them. It was a fantastic collection. I tried to get Tony to look, but he was too busy with his fittings, and I wouldn't buy anything without his approval. So I didn't buy a thing, and I've always regretted it, but maybe it was all for the best. I've been robbed a few times and probably none of it would still be here had I bought the things. Still, I rue the day I passed up those bargains.

When we arrived in Hong Kong, we were met by a man named K.Y. Pan, who was then the head of MGM's office in Hong Kong. That was another delightful feature of being with a big studio in those days. Wherever we went, we were met by a local man who knew the ropes and he would help us through customs and see that we arrived safely at our hotel. Mr. Pan was a charming man and was very good to us. He introduced us to the fabulous Run Run Shaw, the very wealthy and successful movie impressario of the Orient, and Run Run entertained us lavishly. We had dinner at his home. After the meal, the opium pipe was passed as a matter of course. I declined, with thanks.

One evening, Mrs. Shaw took us out to dinner, to a famous floating restaurant, the Aberdeen. I remember there was a fish tank aboard, with a three-hundred-pound bald-headed man presiding. You picked out the fish you wanted for dinner and the big man would spear it and take it to the kitchen. Everything was fine until the waiters came with an enormous fish head which they ceremoniously placed in the center of the table. Apparently, that was the *pièce de résistance* of the meal—the Chinese ate the eyes and the brain of the fish, digging right into the head for those treats. I got through the evening, but barely.

There was one luncheon where I was served a delicious soup. I ate every spoonful. It was called bird's nest soup. I thought that was a picturesque name—but then I found out it was really made from a bird's nest. I went back to the hotel and lost my lunch.

I didn't like Japan as much as Hong Kong. I found the Chinese people open and friendly, while I was depressed and oppressed by the crowded Ginza in Tokyo. I got a stiff neck from bowing. Besides, I didn't like the Japanese raw fish, although Tony did.

We had a wonderful trip, one year, to South Africa, where Tony and I made a smash personal appearance in concert. We flew from Nice to Johannesburg, with a stopover I'll never forget. That was in Kinshasa in Zaire, which had formerly been Leopoldville in the Belgian Congo. Because of South Africa's *apartheid* policy, the rest of Africa doesn't like the South Africans and, by association, doesn't like anybody who is en route to South Africa. We learned that quickly in Kinshasa. When we got off the plane there, we were escorted by a group of soldiers, both men and women, to a small room. "Escorted" may not be quite the right word. They had guns and herded us to that room as though we were prisoners. I wanted to go to the ladies' room and I started out. I speak a little French and tried to explain my mission. But a girl prodded me with her gun and said, *"No! Back. Back."* So I went back and waited for my trip to the ladies' room until we were once again airborne.

We found the South Africans most pleasant and the theater we played was one of the best, from the standpoint of sound and the warmth of the audience reception, we had ever seen. But life in South Africa is a bit scary.

Tony, Jr., was with us on that trip and, when we were in Durban, he needed some new guitar strings, as he was appearing with us on stage. He went out with a driver, who was a native African. They were gone for some time and I began to notice that everybody seemed to be worried, and they began whispering and looking at me worriedly. Tony, Jr., and the driver eventually returned and only then did the others tell me that they had been very concerned for my son's safety. They explained that some parts of the city aren't healthy for a white person and, even though he was with a black, they had been upset over what might happen to him.

Some of the blacks working there, such as those in the hotels, are only a few weeks removed from the jungle. We were staying in a very nice, modern and comfortable hotel. We unpacked on our first night and then, the next morning, the housekeeper arrived with five other men, to clean our room. It was just a small suite, so I couldn't understand why it took such a large troop to do the job. I found out it was because of their total inexperience with things like hotel rooms. They simply were not equipped to deal with the situation. I learned that if you asked them to bring you, for example, some soap and a towel, that was too much for one native boy to remember. He could get the soap, but he would forget the towel. Or vice versa. So they needed all those bodies to do the job that one maid could handle easily in the United States. Curiously, when we visited Nairobi, in Kenya, which has a black government, we found very sophisticated accommodations.

Much of our traveling has been for fun, not business. Take our Acapulco experiences. It began when I met Miguel Aleman, who had been Mexico's president. We met in Los Angeles, then he later came to see Tony and me perform in Las Vegas. We became friendly, and he invited us to visit him in Acapulco, where he has a magnificent old home. He even sent his private plane to Mexico City to pick us up.

Aleman's home, as befits a man of his stature, is superb. He had round-the-clock guards, carrying machine guns. He loaned us—Sid and Bea Korshak were with us—his yacht and we were cruising that awesomely beautiful Acapulco Bay one day when we spotted the fin of a huge shark slicing through the azure water. The captain said we owed it to the swimmers—this wasn't far off the Las Brisas Hotel swimming club—to catch the dangerous fish. They put about and threw lines over and eventually did catch the shark, which turned out to be an immense hammerhead. I still have some teeth from that shark.

The Mexicans are strange. One day, while we were there, Sid Korshak discovered his toilet wasn't working. In his halting Spanish, he tried to explain to the staff that the toilet was out of order. He came back to his room later to find they had removed the entire commode.

Another Mexican excursion was entirely different. Tony got some of his pals—Leo and Laraine Durocher, Helen and Spike Jones, Bob Stack with a girlfriend, some others—and planned a weekend in Tijuana. The excuse was to catch a famous bullfighter named Aruza in action. Tony conned Howard Hughes out of a plane, and we flew down—twenty or so of us in a plane designed to seat a hundred or more—and it was a fun weekend. Leo Durocher and I had long had a running gag. He loved to tease me with pseudo-risqué remarks, like, "Hey, baby, you can have me whenever you want me!" I'd make believe I was shocked by his forwardness, and we both enjoyed the exchange. Well, on that flight down to Tijuana, Tony suggested I turn the tables on Leo and, when he made his inevitable pitch, I should call his bluff.

So, sure enough, we were on the plane and he said, "OK, Babe, how about it? You and me—tonight—OK?"

And I turned to him, cool as an iced cucumber, and said, "OK, Leo. Tonight's the night."

You should have seen him. He turned all shades of red, and slunk back to his seat. And I heard Laraine whisper to him, laughing, "What's the matter, Leo, lose your guts?"

There was another great time, this one in Monte Carlo. Tony had gone over to do the fabled Gala there, and we met all the jet setters, including Aristotle Onassis. He was married to Christina then, and he was so powerful and so important that he practically ran Monte Carlo. Prince Rainier was unimportant compared to him at that time. We got to know Ari and Christina and she told me they lived on their yacht, and didn't have a home ashore. I felt sorry for her, not having at least a small villa.

Ari gave a cocktail party for us and Mary and Jack Benny, who were in the south of France then, so at last we had a chance to be on the yacht, the *Christina*. It was almost like an ocean liner—a crew of thirty-two, a seaplane attached to it, a swimming pool that converted to a dance floor, a display of all his ships, miniaturized, so he'd know where each one was at all times, doorknobs of semi-precious stones, a winding staircase, El Greco paintings. After one look around, I didn't feel sorry for Christina Onassis any more. Ari invited Tony into his private quarters, after dinner, for some brandy and a cigar. And Tony told me later he had complimented Ari on the softness of the leather on the chairs. Ari told him they should be soft—they were made from the scrotums of elephants.

One of the great features of travel is that you always bring things back, and our homes have always had items around that remind us of our various trips. We've accumulated a lot, and whenever I look around our house now,

I'll see something that will bring back memories of the places we've been. And we have had several homes, down through our many years together.

Our first house, the Beverly Glen house, remains close to my heart. It was the first house we'd owned, and I enjoyed dabbling and decorating. I remember Dusty and me pasting antique sheets of music on the walls of the breakfast room. I had never done anything like that before—I had never had either the time nor the inclination to do any interior decorating —but I found that I got a big kick out of it. For a while, I went domestic in a big way. We had some great parties in that house. I remember one where the feature was a big popcorn machine. Nancy Davis was there and she said she had to get one of those popcorn gizmos for Ronnie Reagan, whom she was then seeing. I still tease her about that.

We had an elderly couple working for us at the Beverly Glen house. One morning, sometime around seven, I was awakened by the sound of fire-engines pulling into our driveway.

"My God, Tony, wake up," I said, shaking the body next to me. "There must be a fire."

"It's OK," he said. "The fire-engines are here."

And he turned over and went back to sleep.

I ran downstairs and found that the couple had been burning trash in an incinerator and the fire had spread to some leaves and then to the back of our garage. The firemen quickly put it out. When I went back upstairs, Tony was still sleeping.

We entertained Jai and Isha, the Maharajah and Maharanee of Jaipur, in that house one summer. Jai spent most of his time going to shops for Western clothes, which he brought back with him to India. Then, you couldn't get anything like our jeans anywhere but here. This was the pre-jeans era.

As I have said, we entertained often, but that was only when we knew we would be at home for any length of time. If we were here only for a week or so between out-of-town engagements, we wouldn't let anyone know we were back. We craved some privacy during those brief times home.

Recently, the pattern of Hollywood entertaining has changed drastically. This used to be a town for big, lavish parties. No more, except for business or professional affairs. I remember, in the old days, going to Gary Cooper's parties. We were very close to Coop and his wife Rocky, and they loved entertaining, but, strangely, he was very insecure about being the host. He would usually invite people over at eight, but he would ask us to get there early.

"I need to have some friends come ahead of time," he would say.

"Then I'll be relaxed enough to be a genial host by the time the rest of the guests arrive."

In some ways, Coop was a funny man. He was very wealthy but he would drive only a Bentley. He refused to buy a Rolls-Royce, because he said it was ostentatious. The only difference between the two cars is the front radiator—and the difference in cost was only $512.

One of the reasons we built our next house was to give us room to entertain on a larger scale. But the main reason we decided to give up the Beverly Glen house was because it was in a zone of heavy traffic. With my sons growing up, I wanted to be in an area where there weren't as many cars whizzing past my front door.

We've always been lucky and sold our old houses fast. Maybe too fast. When we decided to build on Shadow Hill Way, we put the Beverly Glen house on the market—and it sold in a few days. So we were stuck without a place to live. We rented Macdonald Carey's house, and that was a strange experience. It was a big old house with a winding staircase. Downstairs was furnished nicely, but the upstairs bedrooms were sparsely furnished. Maybe a bed in one, a cot in another. It was very curious. They just kept adding rooms every time a new Carey was born.

At the time we were living in Mac Carey's house, we had a Swedish couple working for us. One evening, Tony was out doing a TV show and I was somewhere. My mother walked in and found the man, drunk as a coot, trying to put a coffeepot on the stove and totally unable to make it. And, in the couple's room, she found the wife unconscious on the bed. The wife, too, was drunk. She called an ambulance. It turned out that they were alcoholics and had been AA members who had fallen off the wagon. They had gotten into our liquor cabinet and had drunk themselves into oblivion. If they had only told us they were AAs, we would have kept that liquor cabinet locked.

The Shadow Hill Way house was my pride and joy. I worked on the plans and design for it with an architect, Bill Stevenson. Together, we managed to avoid making many mistakes, although no house is totally free of them.

It was a lovely home. It was large and modern, and there was a flow to it. We did Edward R. Murrow's *Person to Person* program from that house. And we spent many happy years there. Many lovely experiences were part of those years. There was the Sunday morning when the front doorbell rang; it must have been around seven. The maid answered and reported that David Niven was there. At that point in his life, David was living in Switzerland and was only allowed a day or so a year in the United

States. So, on those few days, he had to make the most of his time. He wanted to see all his "chums," as he called his friends, and would go around, visiting people unannounced. We happened to be first on his list that morning. So he came in, said he just wanted to see us and say hello, stayed for a fast cup of coffee, and then bounded off to his next stop.

Our home on Shadow Hill Way was large and comfortable and I'll always have a soft spot in my memory for it. We'd still be there, I suppose, except that what happens to most American families happened to us. Our boys grew up and moved out, and we were left with a house that was much too big for just the two of us.

There's a sort of follow-the-leader syndrome in and around Hollywood, as there is in so many other places. In the late sixties, Mary Benny rented an apartment and, suddenly, everyone was renting apartments. It became a craze, like canasta and pizza. The Los Angeles area had always been a place of houses and house living, but now the apartment thing became popular. Many of our friends sold their homes and moved into apartments or condominiums. Tony suggested that sort of move made sense for us, too. So we put our home up for sale and went into a condominium.

It was beautifully decorated, by Helen Franklin, and was the most elegant. Yet, from the beginning, I never liked it. We were very high up, the thirtieth floor, and I'd get up in the morning and hear the wind whistling by the window and assume, naturally, that it was chilly outside. By the time I got downstairs, I found out that the wind was just an illusion and it was boiling hot down there on the street. I didn't cherish having to wait for an elevator before I could go out. The whole thing made me feel confined and I was unhappy there. But, for a while, Tony liked it and I assumed I would adjust eventually. Then, one morning, Tony got a glass of water in the kitchen and exploded—the glass was filthy. It seems, we discovered, that the air conditioning system was drawing soot and dirt in from the outside.

"Cyd," he said, "let's get the hell out of here. Why don't you look for a house?"

Those were the magic words I had been waiting to hear. That same day, I contacted real estate agents and began looking around the area for a house. Tony had certain things he wanted—a Beverly Hills home, and one with a view—so that limited me. I found two or three I thought were possibles, including one that was interesting, although it had its drawbacks. The worst feature was that it needed a lot of work, but it did have the view Tony wanted. So one day I took him around to see all the houses I had selected. We drove up to the one that needed work. He got out of the car, and looked at it a moment and said, "I'll buy it." He never went inside. That's Tony, ever impulsive.

"But, Tony," I said, "you should look inside. It needs a lot of work. The closets—."

"I don't care about the work and the closets. I like it. Buy it."

And we bought it. With a little work, it became a charming home and we're still living in it today. I don't ever want to move again.

It seems to be a lucky house, too. One thing we've been plagued by, in the past, has been robberies. So far, knock wood, we've had no trouble in our present home. If it hadn't been for those robberies, I'd have quite a nice collection of jewelry now, but so much of what I had is gone.

I mentioned earlier the kite-shaped diamond stickpin that my father wore, which came to me after his death. That was stolen, along with many other lovely things, in Florida. That was my first experience with robbery.

I became very careful. When I went to do *Once More, with Feeling*, in Chicago, I was extra careful. I guess I still had the old cliché in mind, about Chicago and gangsters, and I took great care that my jewels were always in the hotel vault when I wasn't wearing them. And I had no problems at all there. But that all changed the same night I came back to Los Angeles from Chicago. Tony and I were doing the *Hollywood Palace* on TV and right after that we went to Denise Minnelli's birthday party. I was very tired so I asked someone to drive me home. I wanted to be there by midnight, because Tony, Jr., had just started driving and I had told him to be home by midnight and I wanted to be there to be sure he checked in on time. As it happened, he and I arrived simultaneously. We went in the house together, and everything seemed normal. My bed was turned down, my watch was on the night table next to the bed. Nothing was out of place.

But when I woke up the next morning, I happened to open my jewelry drawer—and it was bare. I couldn't believe it; it was one of those moments when you can't grasp for a few seconds what has happened. Your eyes tell you one thing, but your brain cannot comprehend it. I called my maid, Velma, and asked her to look in the drawer.

"Mrs. Martin," she said, "those drawers are empty."

I woke Tony and he called the police. One of the first questions they asked was whether I had any furs. My God! I hadn't thought to look in the closet. I ran and looked—gone. My chinchilla, my leopard, one of my minks. I was lucky, at that. Velma, our long-time houselady, had fortunately put my good mink in another closet and they hadn't found that. But all the other furs and the jewels were gone. And Tony discovered they had found a drawer where he kept a lot of gold mementos, and that had been cleaned out, too.

Nothing was insured. And nothing was ever recovered. Insurance is too high these days; show people are considered maximum risks. If I were to insure my jewelry, it would cost more than what it is worth. So I keep it all in a vault. When I go on a trip, I take out a short-term policy to cover just the pieces I take. Curiously, insurance in England is cheap but here, I suppose because of our high crime rate, it's prohibitive.

A few days after the robbery, a couple of F.B.I. men came to the house.

"We'd like to talk to you about the robbery," they said. I thought that was curious, because robbery isn't a federal offense, but I let them in and they started talking about the case with me. But then they showed me some pictures of men and asked me if I'd met any of them at parties. Then they said, almost in passing, could they speak to my husband? When Tony came in, they began asking him about his experiences playing cards at the Friars Club. That, as it turned out, was the start of the whole investigation into cheating at the club. They had merely used the robbery as an excuse to talk to Tony about the Friars Club gambling scandal.

It became a big thing, and I'm sure Tony has told his version of the story himself. As far as I'm concerned, though, it was the nerve of the F.B.I. that annoyed me. They had insinuated themselves into my home, on a pretext, and were only concerned with their problems, not mine. Even afterward, when the probe and the grand jury investigation made Tony very nervous, their harassment continued. One day, Velma called me to say that two more F.B.I. agents were at the door.

"Have you come to talk about my jewelry?" I asked them.

These were the same two agents who had come the first time.

"No, Mrs. Martin," one of them said. "We want to talk to you about the Friars Club thing."

I said you'd better see my husband's attorney, and I closed the door in their faces. Those were two stunned F.B.I. gentlemen.

My most frightening experience with criminals took place in New York, when I was staying at the Plaza Hotel. Tony was playing at the Copa and one evening we'd gone downstairs for a bite to eat before he went to the club. I returned to our suite and was in my nightgown, washing out some stockings, waiting for the night maid to come in before I went to bed. I heard a key in the door. I thought it was Tony, who had forgotten something. I went into the living room and saw the silhouette of a man. He was large and black and menacing.

"Don't be afraid," he said. "I'm from security."

For a moment, I believed him. But then I noticed he was wearing white gloves and I realized a hotel security man wouldn't have white gloves on. I knew he was up to no good. I raced to the door, ran outside and slammed the door. There was a man in the hall, and I ran up to him, even though I was wearing only a nightgown, and I said, "I'm being robbed!" His room was across the hall, and he let me in and I called the front desk. Within two minutes, a couple of hotel detectives were there, guns drawn. The man was gone.

I was fortunate at that. Only a minute or two before he came into the suite, I had put my diamond ring in the toe of my shoe, and he hadn't found it. All he took was my purse. He had left by the window because, on that floor, there was a balcony running around the building. They found my purse on the balcony later, with the money gone, of course, but all my credit cards intact.

The hotel people told me later that they had had trouble with that cat burglar before. He apparently knew the hotel routine, knew that on certain nights there were only two security men on duty, and knew which floor had the balcony for a quick and easy exit. So, on those nights, he worked those floors. I had them move me immediately to a room on a floor without a balcony. When Tony came back, hours later, he found I was in a different room. He knocked on the door, because I had said I didn't want anybody to have a key to that room, not that night.

"Who's there?" I said.

"It's me."

"How do I know it's you?"

"Come on, Cyd, open up."

"Sing a few bars of 'Begin the Beguine.'"

He did, and only then would I open the door and let him in.

Looking back, I've often wondered what might have happened to me had I turned down that first movie offer and stuck with ballet. I guess that was the most significant decision I ever made. It changed my entire life.

Being in a ballet is like being in a fairy tale. I loved ballet, loved it with all my heart. And there have been times when I've said to myself that I made the wrong choice when I went into motion pictures.

And, yet, there have been times when I'm glad I did what I did. It's a different world, certainly, and my life has obviously developed in an entirely different way than it would have had I stuck to ballet. But my life, since I turned to films, has been a lovely one. I achieved fame and, I think, brought some moments of happiness to millions of people all over the world. That's not something to be taken lightly.

14

NOW
AND
FOREVER*

To the best of our recollection, it has all happened as we have told it here. Our lives have been exciting, we believe, and, God willing, will continue to be so. Show business is a profession of yo-yos—you have your ups and downs, and we have had our share of both.

All of us are put on earth to accomplish certain things. We will continue trying to fulfill our own particular missions.

We have two fine sons and we have survived twenty-eight years of marriage, of giving and taking. For us, every day is an adventure. We look forward to each new day, for it brings us golden opportunities to do new and exciting things, to make new friends and to enjoy the comfort and sincerity of the old ones.

It's all been wonderful—every step, every note, every inch of the way—and we wouldn't have changed a thing.

We have a lot of hard breathing and *pliés* left, a helluva lot of high notes yet to sing and high steps yet to kick.

If you happen to see us anywhere—a theater, a nightclub, on a plane or aboard ship—please come up and say hello. If you see us in a movie, on a commercial, in a play or a TV show, wave at us.

We hope we can consider you our friends, especially now that you know just about everything there is to know about us. The world is our oyster:

CYD: I love oysters!
TONY: Personally, I prefer lox and bagels.

* We're not superstitious, but we can always use chapter thirteen if an emergency arises.